D0214966

MORRELL HEALD AND
LAWRENCE S. KAPLAN

Culture and Diplomacy

THE AMERICAN EXPERIENCE

Contributions in American History, Number 63

 GREENWOOD PRESS
Westport, Connecticut · London, England

Library of Congress Cataloging in Publication Data

Heald, Morrell.
    Culture and diplomacy.

    (Contributions in American history ; no. 63)
    Includes index.
    1. United States—Relations (general) with foreign
countries. I. Kaplan, Lawrence S., joint author. II. Title.
E183.7.H36   301.29'73   77-71863
ISBN 0-8371-9541-1

Library of Congress Catalog Card Number: 77-71863
ISBN: 0-8371-9541-1
ISSN: 0084-9219

First published in 1977

Greenwood Press, Inc.
51 Riverside Avenue, Westport, Connecticut 06880

Printed in the United States of America

To Barbara and Janice

Contents

Preface

The primary intention of this volume is to offer a view of American diplomacy that will range beyond the familiar textbook treatment of intergovernmental relations and the generalizations in most current texts about the domestic sources of foreign policy. To accomplish our aims, we agreed to explore the circumstances behind events or decisions in foreign relations. If there is a distinctive pattern in the American diplomatic experience, it emerges from the fact that the cultural setting is less a backdrop than a vital cog in the workings of foreign affairs. We decided to employ the essay form, emphasizing major problems on the assumption that explorations in depth of selected issues would be more useful than an attempt to cover every phase of history at the price of superficial treatment. A chronological pattern is followed, with five of the essays dealing with nineteenth-century affairs and seven with twentieth-century. There is a geographical distribution in the essays reflecting American concerns since World War II outside western Europe and eastern Asia.

The decision to probe into the cultural context more deeply than most texts have done made desirable the contribution of two authors with different specializations. Morrell Heald, chairman of American Studies at Case Western Reserve University, is an intellectual historian with interest and experience in Asia.

Lawrence Kaplan, a diplomatic historian at Kent State University, has specialized in European-American relations. We felt that our complementary backgrounds would be useful in writing a book in which each chapter required not only such expertise as each contributor could offer but also a blend of intellectual and diplomatic history that neither individually could supply. While each chapter has been subjected to careful evaluation by both authors, Heald has been the primary writer of Chapters 5, 6, 8, 11, 12, and 13; Kaplan is largely responsible for Chapters 2, 3, 4, 7, 9, and 10.

Acknowledgments

Assistance came to us from many quarters as we developed our ideas for this book. Robin W. Winks of Yale University ignited the project with suggestions he offered during his service as cultural attaché in London in 1970. Colleagues at Case Western Reserve and Kent State have read chapters and made useful criticisms at every stage. Maury D. Baker, John W. Culver, James W. Gilreath, and Morris Rossabi were particularly helpful with Chapters 4, 12, 6, and 5 and 8, respectively. Albert H. Bowman of the University of Tennessee at Chattanooga gave valuable advice on Chapter 2, as did Douglas W. Ensminger on Chapter 11. Sears, Roebuck and Company assisted with materials not available elsewhere for Chapter 12. The libraries of the two universities deserve special recognition for the resources they provided and the patience with which their librarians endured the authors' frequent calls for aid. Jenifer Chapko, Sarah Heald, Betty Suber, and Ruth Kohn typed successive drafts of the manuscript. Jen Chapko had the chore of coping with the unreasonable handwriting problems of one of the authors. Without attempting to unload responsibility for the results on anyone but ourselves, we wish to identify two teachers, the late Samuel Flagg Bemis and Ralph H. Gabriel, for their inspiration and examples over the years.

Morrell Heald
CASE WESTERN REVERSE UNIVERSITY

Lawrence S. Kaplan
KENT STATE UNIVERSITY

Culture and
Diplomacy

CHAPTER ONE

Introduction

When Caroline Ware and her colleagues examined the cultural approach to history over a generation ago, they criticized historians for dealing exclusively with articulate groups, or rulers of an elite class, rather than with the masses that made up the nation. They urged that a concept of culture devised by anthropologists be applied to the writing of history. "The pattern of culture," Ware observed, "conditions individuals, providing their basic assumptions and their tools of observation and thought, and setting the frame for their living. It determines the forms of institutions, the types of personality which will be developed, and the types of conduct which will be sanctioned."[1]

The advice to historians to address new questions to the periods they studied has been heeded in good measure, although more by social and economic historians and psychohistorians than by diplomatic historians. Yet the question of American culture applies with special force to the American experience with foreign relations. Foreign policy for much of the history of the United States was the instrument of groups with special interests abroad to protect or to advance. The nation itself seemed to lack a national interest in most affairs of the outside world except briefly in its earliest years and in the years following World War II. The result was that those elements of American society with their own concerns—commercial, religious, humanitarian—

exercised an influence frequently disproportionate to their numbers. Reactions of the nation at large to their activities were a measure of how Americans looked at the world and at themselves.

A point of departure for an examination of American foreign affairs is the belief that the United States enjoyed a special destiny in its relationship with the outside world that no other nation could share. The differences lay both in the conception and in the conduct of foreign policy. It was not that all American objectives were distinct in themselves from those of other nations; such fundaments as survival of the state, security of boundaries, protection of commerce abroad, and even propagation of national virtues among less favored peoples were common to all. What truly separated the American experience was the conspicuous rejection of Old World models and the concomitant establishment of an approach to foreign relations as distinct from that of Europe as presumably American societal values were from European values. As Nathan Glazer noted in the bicentennial year, American national values do not arise from "race, blood, and soil." In light of the disparate origins, it is fitting that the very name of the nation has no ethnic content and that its people call themselves " 'Americans', a term with so little ethnic specificity that it can refer to any of the peoples of the New World."[2] What was considered most American was also considered universal; self-government, equality of all citizens, and individual opportunity were to be models for all men.

The term *isolationism* expressed an ideological as well as a geographical distinction between the two worlds. For America to be of service to humanity, it must be freed from any political connection that would contaminate or corrupt the new order of society fashioned in the seventeenth and eighteenth centuries. Experience with Britain as an imperial master in the colonial years and with France as an exploitive ally in the first generation of nationhood confirmed perceptions of the danger that European politics held for Americans.

America rejected the type of diplomacy practiced by European dynasts who used war as a method of advancing selfish personal or class interests at the expense of the needs and wishes of the unrepresented masses of their peoples. Europe was identified with shifting political alliances, frequent and unnecessary wars, an uneasy and immoral balance of power, and restrictive economic relations among nations. America by contrast represented unrestricted international economic intercourse, the abolition of war, abstention from alliances which produce war, and the promotion of international law to promote peace everywhere. At the same time, the new nation recognized in the expansion of commerce a means to prosperity as well as a deterrent to war. It accepted as reasonable the evaluation of those European *philosophes* who looked upon America as the ideal society, free from class divisions and irrational conflicts. Americans may have felt some discomfort with the European classification of America as a primitive Eden in the New World, but they had no doubts about their location in a new Zion where they were commissioned to set an example to an inferior world.

The example they were to set contained a basic ambivalence that was to disturb Americans in the future. On the one hand, the superior way of life demanded isolation, a "city on the hill" removed from the temptations and ills of the Old World. On the other, the mission involved a positive exercise of American influence to make the world a better place for the sake of American ideals and interests as well as for the welfare of other peoples. The unstated compromise between activity and passivity manifested itself in the relatively passive role of government pursuing a national interest abroad as opposed to the relatively active role of private groups and individuals pursuing their own interests in the name of the nation. American business enterprise abroad would help to break down economic barriers which had encouraged war at the same time that it was producing profits for its entrepreneurs.

If this was America's self-image, the techniques of statecraft to manage international relations would have to be divorced from their European precedents. In a land with minimal interest in foreign politics, diplomacy itself was a marginal occupation. It is significant that no foreign ministry was established in the cabinet system and that a secretary of state was to perform functions of a foreign ministry whenever they should arise. The result was a consciously underdeveloped foreign office; its primary concern was with the consular aspects of relations abroad, the protection of American business interests in foreign ports. This derogation of diplomatic functions was ideologically understandable, and after the perils of the first generation's problems had been surmounted, it was also politically reasonable. American relations with the world at large from 1815 to the twentieth century were sufficiently slight to permit both the atrophying of conventional instruments of diplomacy and the enlargement of the direct role of public opinion where foreign policy did intrude upon the domestic life of the nation. While the conduct of foreign affairs was in the hands of the president, it was shared by his constitutional partners in the Congress and hence subjected to the vagaries of public opinion.

Consequences of divided authority were minimal in the nineteenth century. Since foreign affairs assumed a small place among national priorities during most of America's history, the making of policy was accomplished by the political activity of those elements of society which had private objectives in mind. Understanding of American foreign policy, therefore, follows less from the study of diplomatic correspondence in government archives than from an examination of extragovernmental forces—economic, political, religious, ethnic, or humanitarian—which rose out of American society to make themselves heard in foreign affairs. American foreign affairs, from the beginning, were an expression of a variegated culture.

The initial reaction of the new nation to foreign affairs underscored the revulsion against European ways of diplomacy. Although the creation of the United States may be attributed in large measure to the intervention of one European nation and its subsequent survival may be credited to the balance of power in Europe, recognition of these factors did not produce converts to the European arts of diplomacy no matter how much these skills were utilized in the early national years of the republic. One of the most noteworthy elements in the Franco-American alliance was the ambivalence of America toward its patron. As Chapter 2 illustrates, the tone was patronizing rather than grateful on the part of a government which built its new world on French arms and money but believed that it would have triumphed whether or not France had assisted. The French Revolution later confirmed the American sense of superiority as well as the soundness of their model. The betrayal of that revolution by Napoleonic imperialism then underscored the essential untrustworthiness of any European nation as well as the hopelessness of Europe's attempts to equal America's success.

There was an opacity in America's vision of the outside world which might have been catastrophic. Despite its wish for nonentanglement, after 1793 the nation was caught up in the European balance of power. A final Napoleonic victory over Britain might have yielded a very different outlook on foreign affairs. Certainly, the Federalists and their mercantile allies, involved in a world economy dependent upon British independence of Napoleon, had few illusions about isolationism. To them, French republicanism and the French empire would destroy American commerce as well as American freedom. As shown in Chapter 3, there was a neocolonial reaction among Federalists which induced Great Britain to misread American intentions during the Napoleonic Wars, to the disadvantage of both countries. British miscalculations, combined with unrealistic Federalist assumptions about American policy, helped to push the United States back into the maelstrom of European wars in 1812.

Yet the results of the War of 1812 did not change America's conception of itself as apart from and superior to the Old World. The trials of this period simply deepened the national resolve to isolate America from a world that could not be reformed and to obviate potential future conflicts both by making territorial readjustments and gaining acquisitions from European colonial powers and by ending dependence upon European markets and European supplies. The peculiar historical circumstances of the nineteenth century, in which a vast continental empire lived with weak neighbors to the north and south and oceans to the east and west, permitted America a freedom from the outside world which had not been available before 1815. The Chinese wall of separation which Jefferson had wistfully sought for his country when he was in France in 1785 arose symbolically a generation later. The United States was free to present to an erring Old World a new order of values in statecraft which should be emulated by every nation.

Opposing this conception of America as a beacon to humanity

was the European perception of an opportunist state initially battling for survival in a hostile environment and then exploiting the divisions among the great powers to prosper and expand. In this light, Americans appeared to the French, who had given them so much aid during their war for independence, as an ungrateful people, demanding continued support while refusing to reciprocate in France's time of need. The British, on the other hand, felt they had always understood Americans for what they were: ruthlessly competitive in trade and manufacture, jealous of British predominance in the world, and hypocritically masking their aspirations in the language of international law and natural rights.

It was probably Spain, the weakest of European nations in America, which had the most legitimate concerns about a malevolent United States. Their fear of an aggressive menace to their empire was fed by American traders and farmers pushing to Spanish borderlands and beyond. Even Spain's colonies in the midst of revolution against the mother country had cause for doubts about America's intentions. Despite fraternal encouragement from American friends and occasional military aid delivered surreptitiously, American political missionaries to Latin America lost the support of American businessmen, whose zeal for the liberation of Mexico and South America was checked by a recognition that Great Britain would be the primary economic beneficiary of the political change. As Chapter 4 suggests, the United States was less than wholehearted in its zeal for revolution in Spain's American colonies. But the government's ambivalence was rooted as much in suspicions about republican stability among Latin peoples as it was in the projection of an unfavorable economic balance sheet. Whatever the reasons, the idealism of North America's pan-American mission was compromised.

It is possible to reconcile conflicting ideas about American foreign policy by observing that national aggrandizement and altruistic motives may complement each other. Strengthening international law to benefit the rights of neutrals in wartime served all weak maritime nations; it served particularly an American neutral seeking to profit from belligerent respect for neutral rights. Similarly, a missionary church seeking government protection of special privileges in Asia or Africa may be correct in believing that its importunities are in the service of unselfish ends. As Chapter 5 points out, American missionaries consciously transported American civilization into China in the nineteenth century to advance China's welfare. At the same time, the land they patronized and hoped to redeem from European exploitation was inextricably linked to the promotion of American commerce. The open door admitted missionaries and businessmen in a partnership in which the idea of profit occasionally conflicted with the idea of mission. The line between altruism and selfishness, like that between reality and illusion in the Far East, was frequently very thin.

The potential strains between American benevolence, exhibited in the sharing of its technology or its distinctive ideas about international law and the self-determination of peoples, on the one hand, and the pursuit of private or national profit, on the other, became evident when the United States competed for empire with other nations at the turn of the twentieth century. The experience in the Philippine Islands, considered in Chapter 6, showed the temptations which overtook the nation when it annexed those islands. The exploitation of the economy, the hope for a stepping-stone to the China market, and the wish to celebrate a new imperial glory seemed to overwhelm the altruistic impulses behind America's presence in the Philippines. But if annexation took place and an American colonialism followed, it was the product of external pressures upon the McKinley administration rather than a fulfillment either of a plan to plunder Filipino resources or a grand design to join the European powers in the division of China.

The events of the Spanish-American War did presage a time when American state interests, whether or not propelled by a military-industrial complex in control of the society, would abandon isolationism and use their power to effect the mission of America more directly than in the past. The twentieth century was to witness the United States promising the world, through the Truman Doctrine, to "assist free peoples to work out their own destinies in their own way." It was a magnificent vision, but it was also flawed by the condescension displayed in its translation, by the military cast of its methods, which inevitably distorted the ends, and by the concomitant pursuit of economic advantage which was implicit in its promise.

But the weight of a traditional outlook on the world was too powerful to yield until mid-century. While America was, in size and strength, a great power, the major questions on foreign relations in the 1920s and 1930s devolved on the wisdom of extended engagement in foreign affairs. Suspicions of presidential involvement in European politics summoned bitter memories of America's experience in the Great War. The reasons for Wilson's League of Nations entanglement in 1919, one of the major expressions of America's mission, appeared ingenuous or spurious. The Allies had been faithless, American leaders guileless, and the outside world ungrateful for the services the United States had rendered to it. The long circuitous route toward recognition of the Soviet Union, described in Chapter 7, becomes comprehensible in light of the xenophobia generated by the failures of the Versailles Conference of 1919. Delay in recognition was not simply the result of religious revulsion against Bolshevik atheism, or shock over communist massacres, or even the ideological challenge of communism to capitalism and democracy; it was the revival of knowledge that Americans had always nursed about the innate evil of an Old World ever ready to corrupt the New.

Until the mid-twentieth century, American foreign policy was the end product of the conflicting cultural influences which compose American society. Given the absence of a clearly perceived national interest in external relations over a long period of time, it was natural that policy would be shaped by those segments of public opinion most concerned at any given moment with matters diplomatic. The dynamics of American foreign policy turned on forces within the society strong enough to push the government along channels of their choosing. Without suggesting that the Department of State was only a tabula rasa exposed solely to external impressions, one may reasonably suggest that it was an inefficient and frequently inchoate organization without a conception of a national foreign policy and without the means of handling one if it had been identified.

The question of precisely when the United States first became a world power will always be open to debate. A new status may be claimed after the Spanish-American War or upon entry into

World War I, but no commitment to permanent political involvement with Europe—in defiance of the precepts of the Farewell Address—was made before the North Atlantic Treaty of 1949. Until then, the distinction between interests in Latin America or Asia and those in Europe remained an inhibiting factor in American foreign relations. No matter how far-ranging American economic interests may have been in Europe or elsewhere, they were not accompanied by political or military obligations to the Western world. Despite America's links to the world economy which resulted from its new creditor status in the 1920s, the impotence of American foreign policy during the rise of Hitler reflected the continuing grip of isolationism upon American conduct. Only with American involvement in World War II did the State Department, supported by new agencies, assume a prominence in foreign affairs equal to the roles played in the past by powerful economic interests. The state, in the name of the national interest, superseded private interests in the shaping of foreign policy. This judgment has been challenged, however, by a point of view that finds the private sector just as powerful as it had been in the past. The joining of industrial with new military forces created a new complex in which the public interest was inextricably bound with special private interests, to the disadvantage of the former.

Whichever is the more accurate conclusion, there is little doubt that changes which followed the war can fairly be characterized as revolutionary and pervasive. They were most visible in two of the facets of the American experience which had appeared different from the European precedent: the institutions of foreign policy making and the attitude toward political entanglement with other nations. With respect to the former, the leisurely pace of the State Department was accelerated both by increased personnel and by the addition of new specialized bureaus. At the same time, it was threatened by eclipse from the rise of ancillary units in the government with specific interests in foreign affairs. Among them were quasi-autonomous agencies such as the Office of War Information and the Office of Strategic Services, products of World War II. Traditional departments, such as War and Commerce, expanded their functions to include matters of foreign affairs. The establishment of the National

Security Council in 1947 was a natural expression of a new foreign policy establishment that embraced foreign economic relations, intelligence operations, and propaganda as well as the more familiar duties of the State and Defense departments. The machinery of foreign relations burgeoned in new and unaccustomed directions.

Traditional attitudes toward the Old World changed just as radically. Abstention from entangling alliances, the very substance of isolationism, was transformed into intervention in the name of national security and world peace. The break with the past was sharp as one measure followed another in the decade from 1945 to 1955—from American membership in the United Nations to the spectacular alliance with eleven other nations of the Atlantic alliance in 1949 to the establishment of an elaborate Southeast Asia Treaty Organization in 1954. Within that decade bilateral and multilateral treaties stretched around the world.

But at the time of their making, especially in the beginning of the Cold War with the Soviet Union, the pattern was not clear to most Americans, not even to the figures involved in the change. Many of the agencies emerging in the war or immediately afterwards were products of crisis, with functions rarely well defined and even more rarely coordinated with cognate agencies. Nor was the road to alliance free of obstacles or even visible in the distance. The development of a leadership of the "free world" posited the existence of an unfree world, and this was not the expectation of the founding fathers of the United Nations in 1945. The immediate postwar hope was for a world of international comity free of war forever.

The stereotyped older images of the world did not disappear completely; they were too deeply imbedded in the American psyche. A major stereotype that would plague planners over the next generation was the vision of China as an American client. In the 1930s Chiang Kai-shek, the hero who led embattled China against imperialist Japan, personified the virtues of a transplanted American civilization. He stood for modernization, democracy, and Christianity in the Far East. Given these values, Americans were unable to assimilate the record of corruption, military ineptitude, and dictatorship which characterized Nationalist China during and after the war. As shown in Chapter 8,

American newspaper correspondents in China in 1944 divulged this information to the American public. Nor could the public or its leaders accept the startling reports of journalists and diplomats of the efficiency, humanity, and success of Chinese Communists during the war. It was not that the journalists themselves were wholly liberated from illusions; many of them indulged in the romantic notion of Chinese Communists as simply agrarian radicals in an American mold. But they were beginning to penetrate the dynamics of a changing China and offered advice which, had it been taken, might have made the burden of foreign relations in Asia lighter over the next thirty-five years.

Isolationism manifested itself in the American approach to Europe. The Roosevelt administration had invited a faith in the United Nations as a surrogate for alliances and involvement, as if membership in this organization would fulfill the old goals of the "new diplomacy" of the Founding Fathers. As pointed out in Chapter 9, the United Nations was sold to the American public as a substitute for future balance-of-power politics. Unfortunately, when the gulf between the United States and the Soviet Union widened in the next few years, the Truman administration was forced to justify Old World techniques of statecraft by claiming that they were in the service of the United Nations and in conformity with American traditions. The Marshall Plan and the Atlantic alliance were indeed new departures, but they had to be introduced as a part of the older tradition, not as a deviation from it.

There were limits to the pretense of continuity. As a consequence of the institutionalization of new instruments of foreign relations and the articulation of new plans of leadership, Truman's America identified a comprehensive national interest which subsequent administrations bent every effort to continue and fulfill. Opposition to communism demanded coherence in every phase of policy making. This meant either resisting traditional public pressures or at least diverting them. The debate over the North Atlantic Treaty in 1949 revealed a manipulation of public opinion in a manner different from that in the past. Previously, it was the private sector of the nation which produced policies and worked on a relatively neutral administration and public. After World War II, it was frequently the executive branch itself which lobbied in the Congress and among the public, with a forcefulness and consistency never found in the past, to win support for policies it perceived to be vital to the national interest.

The reversal in the roles of the public and private sectors sometimes produced an apparent schizophrenia within an administration, particularly when its judgment was divided between its political and bureaucratic sections. This problem is well illustrated in Chapter 10 where conflict between the Congress and much of the leadership of the Truman administration over Palestine between 1945 and 1948 confused the United Nations as well as the American public. Unlike earlier encounters with ethnic and religious pressure groups, the executive branch for the most part resisted popular sympathy for a Jewish commonwealth in Palestine, and to a surprising degree those elements in the administration hostile to Zionism succeeded in frustrating both public opinion and the wishes of the White House counselors. Their opposition was made in the name of the nation's interest, indeed of its security, as fear of Soviet penetration of the Middle East along with a Soviet threat to Europe's survival dominated the thinking of the military and state departments.

Since peace keeping became equated with the containment of communism, the American presence abroad increasingly took on a military cast. American intervention around the world appeared to assure more than an opportunity for maintenance of freedom among beleaguered peoples; it would also sustain institutions and ideologies, liberal or otherwise, considered favorable to propagation of American values. The world was required to choose between the United States and the Soviet Union in the 1940s and 1950s, and the reward for enlistment on the side of the "free world" was economic assistance and military guarantees. Failure to choose sides in this contest, especially in the period of John Foster Dulles's service as secretary of state, often meant loss of economic as well as military aid by the offending nation. The contest extended to South Asia where American concern for winning allies in the ideological war against communism had brought Pakistan into a Southeast Asia Treaty Organization in partnership with the United States.

India, with its democratic institutions and important ties of friendship with Americans, including mutual hostility to past British imperialism, stood outside the circle of American allies. Although some of India's leaders did express sympathy with communist objectives, the majority did not; but most Indians shared a contempt of the simplicity of American anti-communism, which permitted the United States to build the power of India's rival, Pakistan, on the unsound basis of common anti-communism. There was a suspicion that America's ideological war concealed a drive for domination behind a facade of economic and cultural benevolence. But while Nehru and his government resented crude American attempts to manipulate India's foreign policy, Indians at many levels of society appreciated the American mission at work. In some ways, its promise was never better realized than in the remarkably effective labors of American agronomists, economists, and diplomats who helped to inaugurate the "Green Revolution" in food supply. Chapter 11 demonstrates how public and private collaboration in expressing American altruism can mitigate unfavorable reactions to America's importunities as a superpower. The Indian experience of the United States brought together sharply two familiar elements on the American mission abroad which were intended to be complementary: the export of American technology for the welfare of its beneficiaries and the export of its crusade against evil. Unlike the experience in nineteenth-century China, the United States government was much more actively involved in both areas.

It was in Latin America, however, that the past and present mixed even more explosively. The Western Hemisphere had always been exempted from the strictures of isolationism as long as it was implicitly understood that America's borders extended to South America. This was the view from North America. To Latin American nations, the United States either consciously neglected their interests most of the time or unconsciously exploited their resources whenever it did pay attention to them. America's assumption of world leadership exacerbated both the sense of neglect and of exploitation, despite the ostentatious conversion of the Monroe Doctrine from a unilateral declaration into the multilateral alliance of the Organization of American States

in the 1940s. American intervention in Guatemala and its out-
lawry of Cuba in the 1950s and 1960s reinforced Latin American
memories of the "banana republics" and the "dollar diplomacy"
of the early twentieth century. Under a new guise, that of anti-
communism, the United States either ignored Latin America in
favor of largesse to Europe or exercised imperial powers in the
name of protection against Soviet influence.

Whatever the American purposes, its professions of cooperation lacked acceptance. The uneven distribution of power in the
hemisphere made even the most benign operations appear malevolent. Chapter 12 explores the activities of Sears, Roebuck
in Latin America and its apparent success in generating profits
for the American parent company and for its branches in South
America. North American business techniques could serve both
the parent company and its foreign branches. But the political
limitations of these enterprises always lurked in the background.
The label of colonialism was affixed to Sears, even when it served
the host country well; the company shares the reputation of the
United Fruit Company of one generation and the ITT of another.

Perhaps the most striking phenomenon of foreign affairs in the
past decade has been the rise of the Third World, struggling to
identify itself in the United Nations and in relation to the super-
powers. The United States has played a role in the growth of solidarity in the emerging nations of Asia, Africa, and Latin
America, and most of it has had a negative cast. Fairly or not,
America has succeeded Europe as the major symbol of colonialism through its excessive wealth, superior technology, and racial
arrogance. Attempts to contrast democratic freedom with
communist enslavement never held much meaning for the underdeveloped world, and the apparently changing face of communism in the 1960s and 1970s has reduced such force as this argument may have had in these areas. Rather than being a war for
freedom from external control, the Vietnam conflict was depicted
as a struggle of white racists against peoples of color, of repressive government against genuine nationalism, and of economic
exploitation against egalitarian reform. The events of the past
decade have eroded much of America's claim to moral leadership.

But the African experience, particularly the Pan-African
movement, as identified in Chapter 13, implied that the more

positive aspects of American foreign policy were still relevant, that the anticolonial tradition still had potency. While evidence of the anti-communist impulse in America's attitude toward Africa was certainly present in the Congo problems of 1960 to 1964, there was an equally, perhaps even more fundamental American motive behind its support of African economic and political development. Part of it stemmed from a traditional American anticolonialism, and part from the growing voice of American blacks on behalf of an ancestral homeland in Africa. This segment of public opinion has been increasingly audible in America's African policies and will compete for national attention with the voice of white business interests in such places as South Africa even more vigorously in the future.

In most respects, the contemporary position of policy making in foreign affairs is as parlous as it has ever been in the past generation. One can sympathize with George Kennan or Walter Lippmann, who deplored the intrusion of ignorant, biased, and selfish private interests into the realm of foreign affairs at the time that the survival of the nation hung on the success of its policies. It would be preferable, they seemed to say, for experts outside the political arena to determine the welfare for all. Ethnic pressures might be controlled, business drive moderated, and humanistic impulses diverted if a closet diplomacy could be restored. But such an option was never available to Americans; it resembled too closely the dynastic statecraft rejected in the eighteenth century. It is unlikely that it would be acceptable now, or even workable.

Despite all the changes the achievement of power has wrought in foreign relations, the United States remains an open society in which private interests continue to affect the public. If their influence is less than in the past, it may be that new public units, notably the diplomatic bureaucracy itself with its ideas of national interests, have arisen to make their own imprint on foreign policy. Although revisionists may be correct in claiming that a new military-industrial complex has subjected politics to a domination never possible in the past, competing forces have not disappeared from the scene. They have strong voices in the press and the Congress, and they remain an important resource for the study of American diplomacy in action. The powerful presidential role in foreign affairs which grew out of the Cold War will not give way, as it had in the past, to a congressional initiative or to the control of any single pressure group. But the role of the public or the legislative branch of government remains both a check on the freedom of action of the executive and a continuing expression of the cultural influence on foreign relations.

NOTES

1. Caroline Ware, *The Cultural Approach to History* (New York: Columbia University Press, 1940), p. 11.

2. Nathan Glazer, "American Values and American Foreign Policy," *Commentary* 62 (July 1976): 32.

CHAPTER TWO

Republicanism in a Monarchical World: The United States and France, 1775-1815

That Americans from the beginnings of colonization were conscious of the differences between their society and those of the Old World is no matter of wonder. Everything pointed to the New World as a laboratory for the perfection of the peoples of the Old. One major catalyst was the Commercial Revolution of Europe, which attracted men's attention to the secular opportunities inherent in an empty land rich in resources and open to exploitation by those fit enough to profit from it. Another was the Protestant Reformation, which sparked the religious conviction that America was the New Zion made visible and available in the New World to those elected for salvation in the next world. The rapid secularization of Calvinism in the optimistic environment of America ultimately made the conception of Zion broad enough and liberal enough to include all who wished for salvation. God would embrace anyone—or almost anyone—willing to be reborn in His Chosen Land. Given these perceptions, it is scarcely surprising that the Americans who separated themselves from Great Britain during the American Revolution should have regarded both their foreign policy and their statecraft as involving goals and methods distinct from those of Europeans.

Robert R. Palmer has made the point that the Founding Fathers collaborated in the propagation of these differences by telling the world that their system was a *Novus Ordo Seclorum* ("New Order of the Ages"). Lest this notion be overlooked, they inscribed the phrase on the Great Seal of the United States and had it "conveniently printed on the back of the dollar bill."[1] If their experiment was to succeed, they needed to gather support from every source, and they wisely counted on the interest this concept aroused among the influential men of Europe's Enlightenment in the eighteenth century. The men who made the American Revolution and built a republic knew exactly what they were doing with the image they projected to the outside world. They were not innocent colonials emerging suddenly into nationhood and groping for ideas and institutions that would permit them to survive. These had been acquired and refined over the century preceding the revolutionary ferment of the 1760s and 1770s.

British mercantilism, emphasizing economic controls in the form of navigation laws, allowed colonial assemblies power over the governor and command of their own affairs. The executive as well as the legislative experiences of assemblies in royal colonies produced as sophisticated a cadre of legislators and diplomats as any European nation could boast, perhaps even more than England itself. The limitations of colonial status required more skill and more guile from American statesmen than were necessary for their counterparts in Parliament to demonstrate. Colonial agents, assigned initially to serve in London as creatures of the royal government, became valuable instruments of colonial lobbies in Parliament. Their clients were the colonial elites which controlled the legislatures, and diplomacy in their hands was an advanced art. When the break with Britain finally came, it was no coincidence that the London agents who followed the colonial cause—Benjamin Franklin and Arthur Lee—became the first formal diplomats of the new nation. Michael Kammen may have strained his comparison between the colonial agents of American interest groups and later diplomatic representatives of the United States, but his analogy is worth considering: "Just as Samuel was simultaneously the last of the biblical judges and the first of the prophets, so Arthur Lee was the last of the colonial agents and the first national diplomat."[2]

Expertise in the arts of diplomacy, while vital to the success of the republic, could not of itself solve the problems inherent in revolution and independence. The violent separation of the colonies from the mother country inevitably had its traumatic aspects. Much of the unhappiness between the two was of recent origin, and the steps finally taken to resolve it had frightening implications. Not the least of them was the fear of chaos, of destroying a venerable fabric of society without replacing it with something equally solid. The men who managed the Revolution had no wish for the complete overthrow of the social order; most were pillars of colonial society who felt that British policies after 1763 undermined the foundations of their system. How to make a revolution without sacrificing the benefits of the past would be a feat almost as difficult as fashioning a nation out of thirteen separate entities.

The answer to both problems lay in good measure in the acquisition of a legitimacy which would satisfy the revolutionaries' consciences while quieting the fears of Europeans. Seymour Lipset has referred to the idea of "charismatic authority" embodied in George Washington as a source of instant legitimacy, since the President was a man above criticism at home and abroad whose reputation would shield a nation.[3] But before Washington could be accorded such distinction, legitimacy had to be found in the collective behavior of Americans and in the world's understanding that their actions met the test of the philosophy of the Enlightenment. The Declaration of Independence was designed to inform a "candid world" that evils of British government had forced Americans to form new governments to secure their rights. The support of European philosophers, and of princes influenced by them, would bolster the republican experiment of a nation that lived by the rules of nature according to the dictates of reason. To secure this support—in England as well as on the Continent—the leaders of the Revolution cultivated the art of diplomacy at its highest levels to win expected assistance for America both from the monarchical establishment and from antimonarchical liberals.

From the outset of revolutionary activity, France was the major object of American attention, just as America was becoming increasingly of interest to Frenchmen. Ever since the Treaty of Paris in 1763, the ministries of Choiseul and later of Vergennes had perceived opportunities in the troubles between the colonies and the mother country from which France could derive advantage. Informal observers traveled throughout the colonies to report on the possibilities of rebellion. The results of French agent Jean De Kalb's tour did not encourage intervention in the internal quarrel, but they suggested continuing French vigilance in American affairs. The Foreign Minister's concern was paralleled by a swelling curiosity about America among intellectuals that had first been aroused by Voltaire's *Lettres Philosophiques*, in which the virtues of the simple Pennsylvania Quaker were celebrated. For physiocrats, members of a school of economists supporting free trade and seeking models of the good society where man, uncorrupted by the sins of civilization, might achieve a better life, America appeared to be a perfect vehicle to contrast with Europe. The influence of the intelligentsia in court circles might sway the government's judgment about the United States. Or so American statesmen thought.

Benjamin Franklin, colonial agent in England, certainly had French opinion in mind when he made his first visit to France in 1768. There he enjoyed the acclaim of a philosopher-prince and rural philosopher who tamed electricity and who had lessons of many kinds to teach Europeans. Fresh from his struggles with Parliament over the Stamp and Townshend acts, he saw value in the friendship of the physiocrats, who sought free trade for France and found in agriculture the primary source of social as well as economic virtues. He was particularly aware of their vision of an international order in which trade, unencumbered by government regulations, would move freely from one country to another. He not only professed his admiration for their ideas but linked them with colonial resistance to the Stamp Act and Townshend laws. America, as Franklin portrayed it, was the exemplar of physiocratic ideas.

Despite the pleasure he took in the responses of his French friends to the image of the noble American and his works, Franklin was disturbed about some anti-American currents circulating among French intellectuals. The Rousseauian conception of the noble savage, if extended to its logical limits, could leave Americans exposed to unfavorable and unflattering opinions. Savages lived in a society in which arts and culture generally could not flower—and should not—if the view that civilization corrupts had merit. The danger in this view was that French observers would be inclined to attribute the relative absence of art, music, and science in America to a natural degeneration of organisms in the New World, reflecting a natural inferiority of its inhabitants. Such were the observations of the Dutch scholar, Cornelius de Pauw, the French naturalist Buffon, and the French cleric Raynal. If they were correct, there would be no case for the dream of the philosophes that the perfectibility of mankind could be found in the American example.

Franklin labored hard to refute the canard that the American climate accounted for the inferiority of species, animal and vegetable. He was, as Durand Echeverria noted, "a veritable Johnny Appleseed, planting seeds of the American Dream back and forth across the fields of Europe."[4] But the blow to American pride went deep even though he largely succeeded in his efforts; the condescension of Frenchmen toward Americans was never fully dissipated. A generation later, Jefferson still felt it necessary to insist upon the equality of American life, and proved it by shipping quantities of flora and fauna to exhibit in Europe.

Such sensitivity, however, was to be found more among Americans abroad than at home. The founding fathers of the Continental Congress were confident enough in the power of their position vis-à-vis the outside world to expect foreign help in their war with Great Britain. Not only should European intellectuals apply their considerable influence on the courts of the Continent to rally aid for the American Eden, but the self-interest of such nations as France would complement their exhortations. To the practitioners of old-style diplomacy, the United States offered in 1776 the destruction of Britain's monopoly of trade and power and the consequent opportunity for France to step into the resultant vacuum. Even British friends were expected to aid in this adventure. The Committee of Secret Correspondence, of which Benjamin Franklin was a member, was appointed "for the sole purpose of corresponding with our friends in Great Britain, Ireland, and other parts of the world."[5] The time was November 1775 and the break with Britain was not yet complete. There was still some hope that a combination of British dependence upon the American economy and their respect for the rights of Americans as Englishmen would resolve the problems between the two societies. Should these forces fail, the role of "the other parts of the world" would assume greater importance.

When Great Britain pursued its obstinate course, French arms, munitions, supplies, and funds became vital for the survival of independence. No matter how difficult a time American military forces might be having in the New World at the time of the Declaration of Independence, the congressmen in Philadelphia were convinced that the forces of the Old would redress the balance if only out of self-interest. To reduce British power, to extract a measure of revenge for the humiliation of past defeats, and to win glory at a small cost were profits possible to France, if it promoted the fortunes of the new nation. Franklin was dispatched to France to join Arthur Lee and commercial agent Silas Deane in reminding France of its appropriate course of action. He was equal to the task, probably far more than his more impetuous and business-minded colleagues. He made the point to them of avoiding the stigma of a business deal in negotiation with the French court. As he put it late in the war: "Trade is not the admiration of their noblesse, who always govern here. Telling them their *commerce* will be advantaged by our success, and that it is in their interest to help us, seems as much as to say, help us, and we shall not be obliged to you. Such indiscreet and improper language has been sometimes held here by some of our people, and produced no good effects."[6]

But in the early stages of the Revolution, Franklin shared with other Americans the expectation that with proper management, France would play her role at little cost to the United States. France would welcome the opportunity to cut Britain down to size and win revenge for its humiliation in the Seven Years War. Helping the United States achieve independence would serve both those objectives. That strings might be attached to French assistance, thus exchanging French for British controls, was unthinkable. The American plan in the model treaty of 1776, drawn up by John Adams, was wholly unilateral, with no corresponding commitment for Americans to join an alliance or in any customary European way perform the duties of an ally. Only a commercial treaty would be permissible, and this primarily to facilitate France's presents of "Arms, Cannon, Salt Petre, Powder,

Buck, Steel." Or so Adams assumed. Any political entanglement would make Americans, according to Adams, "little better than puppets, danced on the Wires of the Cabinetts of Europe."[7] Acceptance of commitments furthering the interests of any European dynasty would offend the sensibilities of those liberal friends abroad whose appreciation of America was based specifically upon its resistance to corrupting links to the Old World. Indeed, a major incentive for supporting a liberal construction of international law was its harmony with the ideas of the philosophes. The treaty, of course, would have the additional virtue of benefiting small maritime powers wishing to profit from the wars of the Old World.

Reality intruded upon this American plan. France's foreign ministry, under the shrewd guidance of the Comte de Vergennes, had its own purposes in developing relations with the new republic, and they did not always coincide with those of the Congress's Committee of Secret Correspondence or of its successor, the Committee on Foreign Affairs. An alliance of any kind, with or without mutual obligations, was a serious matter for a country in as chaotic a financial state as France was in 1776. To risk war with Britain would require a guarantee of successful military activity that the United States was unable to make. It is worth noting that Turgot, the chief financial officer of France, was a distinguished physiocrat whose American sympathies were pronounced enough for him to state that America was the "hope of the human race," but whose sense of duty forced him to recognize the folly of French intervention. Moreover, Vergennes was equally mindful of the political dangers fraternizing with a republic could have for the Bourbon monarchy. The journalist Simon Linguet claimed that the United States, if successful as a republic, would be a cancer which would spread across the Atlantic and destroy the monarchies of Europe.[8] In this context, the most that America could extract early in the Revolution was the sympathy of the majority of the intelligentsia for its cause and surreptitious fiscal assistance from the French and Spanish courts through a dummy business company, Rodrigue Hortalez et Cie, designed to funnel supplies to the American armies.

Given French reluctance to make firm commitments, a premium was placed on the art of statecraft. Not all of the American practitioners were equal to the occasion. Arthur Lee proved to be a stubborn, insensitive negotiator unable to conquer his prejudice against the French or even to conceal it. Silas Deane lacked acquaintance both with the French language and with the techniques of diplomacy. He did manage to keep the illicit pipeline of goods in movement, albeit not without incurring the charges of speculation in the process.

It was the return of Franklin late in 1776 that advanced American interests in Paris. From the moment he stepped ashore in Brittany wearing a fur cap to keep his head warm, he kept his cap on to play a game that made him the rage of Paris. He knew its uses: "Figure me in your mind as jolly as formerly, and as strong and hearty," he wrote in February 1777, "only a few years older; very plainly dressed, wearing my thin grey hair that peeps out under my only *coiffure*, a fine fur cap, which comes down to my forehead almost at my spectacles. Think how this must appear to the powdered heads of Paris."[9]

Franklin impressed heads, powdered and unpowdered. He left no group to chance in his zeal for converts to the American cause. If the fashionable court circles fancied the American as a simple Quaker, the American commissioner obliged in costume and manner. For the more philosophically minded, he wrote articles for the pro-American journal, *Affaires de l'Angleterre et de l'Amérique*, celebrating American virtues, and saw to it that the new American state constitutions were translated into French. For the middle class, his *Poor Richard's Almanac* offered assurance of his profound personal respect for the true values of society. And for the titillation of all Frenchmen, he planted tales of atrocities committed by Indians and Hessians against innocent Americans. Few diplomats anywhere have been his match in capturing the imagination and devotion of a country's public opinion. Certainly, none can claim the success symbolized by his portrait in lockets on the necks of Parisiennes.

Whether his tireless activity helped in securing the treaties of 1778 is open to questions. But his function in fostering a climate of friendliness to an American republic in monarchical France is indisputable. Franklin understood the French psyche; he also understood the hard realpolitik which underlay Vergennes's position. France's offer of an alliance followed the major American victory at Saratoga in 1777, and its timing was intended to undercut a British mission of conciliation. Each man exploited the opportunities the other presented. In manipulating French opinion, Franklin knew well that there could be no alliance until the United States was in a position of strength, but once in that position, he appreciated Vergennes's appetite for involvement. The French Foreign Minister, for his part, saw through Franklin's posturings and made use of them. They helped him to persuade reluctant colleagues that a republic capable of producing a Franklin was worth the risks war with England would bring. The two men complemented each other's purposes in this period.

The treaties themselves may not have realized fully the model fashioned in 1776, but they were a model themselves of accommodation of ideals to realities. The commercial treaty contained the liberal provisions supporting freedom of the seas which many Americans—and Frenchmen, too—thought would lead the way to a better system of international relations. The treaty of alliance, on the other hand, was just the kind of entanglement that Adams and Paine had warned against two years earlier. There was no alternative.

Once the alliance had been concluded, the attraction of a republican Eden diminished among the liberal partisans of America in France. For one thing, increasing exposure of Frenchmen to American society produced disillusionment with the ideal. The trouble basically was that French officers and political advisers found the American personality and character less than engaging. They observed the crudities of American life, the rude manners at meals, and the badly prepared meals themselves, and they experienced the greed of the farmer and merchant battening on the foreigner's cash, not his culture. In short, the arrival of French troops in Boston and elsewhere meant confrontation between soldiers and civilians, with the usual mutual resentments. For too many French gentlemen of philosophic bent, the encounter with a culture preoccupied with material success cooled much of the excitement that the image of America had raised abroad.

Still, the influence of a republican ideal survived such experiences and perhaps increased among those less sensitive to individual lapses among the natives or more readily persuaded by the positive aspects of American life. Between the lines of Crèvecoeur's *Letters from an American Farmer*, by a Frenchman who had lived among Americans until the Revolution, one can read a negative message from his comments on the merchant as the prince of American communities, on an equality that ends with "an unlettered magistrate," and on a material goal reflected in "*ubi panis ibi patria*." But such American shortcomings pale before the emergence of "a new man, who acts upon new principles."[10] And occasionally this new man was a Thomas Jefferson, whom the Marquis de Chastellux discovered to be the perfect blend of frontier virtue and civilized art. Even when materialism offended, Frenchmen felt a respect for the freedom and contentment among Americans everywhere. This was especially true of the 8,000 enlisted men, peasants from every part of France who witnessed free and prosperous farmers owning their own land. "That these men could return to France," claimed Forrest McDonald, "without bubbling enthusiasm and new ideas is as inconceivable as if a twentieth-century American were to go to the moon and return without comment."[11]

No such romantic notions affected the labors of French diplomats in Philadelphia, who exploited the dependence of the American Confederation upon French money and manpower during the Revolution. The two ministers, Gérard and La Luzerne, regarded themselves as proconsuls over a client state with the natural right to direct the course of American foreign policy. La Luzerne boasted that he influenced the selection of Robert Livingston as secretary for foreign affairs.[12] The latter in turn placed the American peace commissioners in Paris under French control for the forthcoming peace negotiations with Great Britain. The initial consular treaty that followed from the alliance allowed French consuls in America to enjoy extraterritorial privileges similar to those imposed by Europeans in nineteenth-century China. The republican virtues of America appeared to have little impact upon French policy makers and their agents. What impresses the observer most about Revolutionary statecraft is not the authority France was prepared to exert over Americans. This was a fitting return for the country that paid the bills for both members of the alliance. Nor was French willingness to sacrifice American territorial interests in the Transappalachian West an appropriate subject for complaint. France's financial plight, its obligations to Spain, and its inability to cope with the British navy in 1782 rendered perfectly comprehensible the notorious Rayneval memorandum, in which the French secretly expressed their consent to dividing the West between Britain and Spain. Commitments to a weak America were low on France's scale of imperatives. It should have been sufficient for Americans that a gracious ally continued to assure independence to the United States at considerable cost to itself.

Such attitudes may offend American sensibilities but should not provoke surprise. French statecraft belonged to the classical school of the Old World, with which Americans were very familiar. The genuine surprise in the peace proceedings was the ability of America's envoys to shake loose from French instructions and win their own terms from Great Britain. The congenitally suspicious John Adams and the Francophobic John Jay, fresh from Madrid, were quicker than Franklin to resent Vergennes's intrigue in the West. If the United States was able to succeed in these maneuvers, it was a tribute to the peculiar qualities of the New World as well as to the shrewdness of its negotiators. Rules which ordinarily governed weak client states did not apply to the United States. Franklin's veiled threat to return to British suzerainty was only part of the reason for France's compliance. The idea of a special destiny for the new nation fitted into the image of America Frenchmen had been making for almost a generation. Small wonder, then, that the republican model continued to exert a meaning in France after 1783.

In the United States, the euphoria of the Peace of Paris wore off quickly as the republic faced almost insuperable problems of governance. To manage and coordinate thirteen separate sovereignties appeared beyond the powers of the Articles of Confederation and the government it created. Of the numerous mortal weaknesses, at least two required the services of diplomacy. One was the problem of finance. Unable to raise monies through direct taxation, the Confederation had to look abroad again for loans to repay old debts and avert bankruptcy. Another urgent need was foreign assistance in counteracting the active hostility of Great Britain and the passive hostility of Spain, each using its neighboring territories as weapons in campaigns against the United States.

The United States found it difficult to respond in kind to these provocations. The British used American inability to restore Loyalist properties or to repay British creditors as an excuse to stay in the Northwest posts. They could refuse American ships admission to the West Indies, knowing that retaliation through a national navigation law was impossible while the states individually regulated their own commerce with foreign powers. The Spanish operated more surreptitiously but no less effectively as they organized the Indians of the southwest against Americans or plotted with Kentuckians and Tenneseeans to detach those territories from a Confederation that might never give them equality with the original states. The zenith of their activity was reached in 1786 when Diego de Gardoqui, the Spanish minister to the United States, and John Jay, secretary for foreign affairs, agreed to close the Mississippi to American trade for twenty-five to thirty years in exchange for opening Spanish ports to eastern shipping. This abortive treaty would have pitted section against section, as Westerners dependent upon the right of deposit at New Orleans for their prosperity saw the special favors granted the eastern mercantile centers.

There were few places in Europe where diplomats might find help. True, Franklin had made a treaty with Sweden in 1783 and Jefferson with Prussia in 1785 for most-favored-nation agreements, but political and economic relations were slight in both cases. Substantial economic assistance could only come from Holland and France. In both countries, the projection of republican virtue might serve once again, provided that it was joined with specific pecuniary advantages for the French.

John Adams in Holland had made the most of his opportunities in 1782 under adverse circumstances. That country was split into factions. But even those who were republican and pro-American in sympathies were hobbled by the close relationship between the ruling stadtholder of the House of Orange and the British Crown. Adams's hopes of gaining financial assistance lay in a combined appeal to republican sentiments and to the business sense of the burghers of Amsterdam. His message had been that support of America would be a prudent investment for the future. But it was something more. Adams was in Holland in a time of ferment when a patriot movement, angered with Britain for declaring war on the Netherlands in 1780, looked to the republican example of the United States for inspiration.

Adams made friends of such figures as the nobleman J. D. vander Capellen tot de Pol, the merchant Peter Vreede, and John Luzac, the influential editor of the liberal *Gazette de Leide*, supporting their movement against the Anglophile Prince of Orange. It was no coincidence that in the year 1782, when the Patriots won a majority in the Estates-General, Amsterdam bankers, previously inhibited by the Orangemen, provided a loan of five million guilders to the United States. Much as Franklin had done in France, although without his deft touch, Adams prepared the way for closer ties by encouraging the publication of Massachusetts's constitution of 1780 and the translation of his own account written in 1774 of the dispute with Great Britain. Adams exulted over the signing of the treaty of commerce with the Netherlands. "When I go to heaven I shall look down over the battlements with pleasure upon the Stripes and Stars wantoning in the wind at The Hague. There is another triumph in the case, sweeter than that over our enemies. You know my meaning; it is the triumph of stubborn independence." [13]

Dutch willingness to rally in support of the stumbling Confederation was a vital factor in the survival of the republic in the first years of independence. But to Thomas Jefferson, and even to Adams when he moved on to the ministry in London in 1783, France was much more important to America's future. As in the case of Holland, Americans in Paris had hoped for the continuing flow of monies and credits after the war had ended. Jefferson, succeeding Franklin in 1784, looked to France also for new markets and the generation of new commercial exchanges. Among his many roles in Paris was that of business agent for American producers, New England whale-oil fishermen as well as Virginia tobacco farmers. For both, he relentlessly pursued a course to whet France's appetite for consumption. At one time he would impress his audience with the potential profits possible from expanded trade; to another group he would expatiate on the financial losses their British rival would suffer from the transfer of commerce; and to still another body of supporters he could use oil or tobacco as prelude to the free trade of a new world order. And he won some victories. As a result of the intervention of Lafayette, whale-oil duties were lifted, and the restrictive contract of Philadelphia entrepreneur Robert Morris with the French tobacco monopolists, the Farmers General, was abridged for a time.

Jefferson's concern was less with the ideal of free trade which underlay the commercial treaty of 1778 than with his hopes of exploiting the Franco-American relationship as a counterforce to the pervasive and dangerous British influence over America. His obsessive fear—to be with him for a generation—was that Great Britain would never accept the reality of America's independence and would plot to keep it in economic if not political subservience. France, in this circumstance, was to be more than a source of financial or military support; it would be the guarantor of America's survival.

Like Franklin before him, Jefferson was sensitive to the various kinds of resistance he encountered in France, including the folly of the economic system. No matter how much good will or self-interest Vergennes or Montmorin might display in the Foreign Office with respect to the loosening of trade restrictions, there were limits beyond which no foreign minister could go. The economy could not withstand the effects of the changes Jefferson had projected. Such advances as he made came through the cooperation of the same allies Franklin had used to win a treaty. The best organized were the influential physiocrats, who joined in the battle against the tobacco monopolists. His relations with Quesnay, Turgot, and their company of economists, however, were essentially pragmatic, not ideological. Jefferson lacked an attachment to the principles of the school; for him, physiocracy was an instrument to break the British stronghold on American commerce, not the panacea for all the world's ills that it was for much of the French intelligentsia.

Even with their connections at court, the physiocrats had to retreat in the face of the rigidity of France's bureaucracy and the hostility of merchants unable to accommodate themselves either to Jefferson's or to Quesnay's version of a new France. The American minister early recognized the elements of revolution in France's problems of the 1780s, and he recognized also the useful model set by the United States for his friends among potential revolutionaries. Not that he advocated a republic for the French in 1787; he doubted their ability to absorb one. He advocated instead a gradual liberation of France's polity and economy that might do for Americans what the old regime had failed so signally to do, namely, to rescue the United States from the bonds of Great Britain.

To effect this end required care in guiding the thinking of French reformers, molding their views toward the United States in such a way that their attitudes would continue to be benign and their behavior, once in power, would be reflected in new policies toward his country. Part of his efforts went into the kind of propaganda used to win friends a decade earlier—articles for Brissot's *Société Gallo-Americaine*, contributions to the *Encyclopédie Méthodique*, and continuing refutations of the persistent slanders about the degeneracy in the American environment. Additionally, he had to cope with problems emerging from the French experience in America over the past few years. Too many of his French connections still held impressions about America which firsthand experience would have dispelled. He worried over the unsophisticated reactions of some of his friends and tried to prepare them for the realities of American life. The mirage of America had to be tempered without destroying the usefulness such visions could have for the United States. The idealization of America in Brissot's writings particularly agitated Jefferson. He knew that no reality could satisfy a Frenchman nurtured on utopian myth. When another wandering intellectual, Chastellux, returned from his tour with some unflattering views about the Quakers of Pennsylvania, leaving the impression that America itself was something less than perfect, Brissot attacked him for his slanders. Jefferson, unable to confess that Chastellux's account was probably too mild rather than too harsh, did his best to dampen Brissot's enthusiasm and those of other Americanophiles who asked too much of the New World.[14]

At the same time, Jefferson urged friends at home to modify policies and institutions which exposed America's shortcomings because of their disillusioning effects upon susceptible Frenchmen. He was dismayed over the prominence given to the Society

of the Cincinnati. This organization of former Revolutionary officers, with George Washington as president-general, had been
founded in 1783. Given its visibility—its membership included
Lafayette and Rochambeau and there was even a branch in
Paris—the society was a natural target of those who scoffed at
republicanism and saw this elite body as an incipient American
hereditary aristocracy. Similarly, Shays's rebellion in 1786
stimulated mixed emotions among Frenchmen, and Jefferson
was concerned with the notion that its suppression was the consequence of repressive government in Massachusetts. Indeed,
his early reservations about the Constitution itself were influenced by French suggestions that the new government might be
a retreat from the liberal system of the Confederation. On all of
these issues the minister sought to calm doubts in Paris. And
when Americans such as Judge Aedanus Burke of South Carolina led an attack on the Cincinnati, or when Madison celebrated
the virtues of the Constitution, he quickly communicated these
evidences of republican virtue to the appropriate audiences,
sophisticated or otherwise. Jefferson was anxious to avoid any
possibility of misunderstanding among people of influence at
court.[15]

Few diplomats have ever enjoyed the sense of success, illusory
as some of it may have been, that Jefferson experienced when he
left France in 1789, a success that derived from the transfer of
ideas he himself was instrumental in transmitting. It was a
heady experience. The French Revolution had begun, and its
leaders were not only sympathetic toward the transatlantic republic but even considered themselves its disciples. They came
to the minister for advice and guidance, and were apparently
ready to adopt the American example. It is not surprising, then,
that Jefferson's early doubts about French capabilities of making their own American revolution gave way to wonder about his
own powers of persuasion and appreciation for the remarkable
learning abilities of his French students.

As France moved toward the American example, Jefferson
was all the more anxious to conceal the blemishes of American
society. The benefits that would accrue to the new nation from
the discipleship of a great ally were tangible. A liberal, if not a republican, France would rally to the causes the Americans had

been attempting in vain to promote since the Revolution. Free trade would permit a Franco-American economic relationship with political undertones that would have incalculable value for both parties. The United States would be liberated from a dependence on Britain, and France would have struck a blow against British economic power. True, mercantilism was an integral part of France's society. True, also, French policy makers still preferred in 1787 to see the United States in continuing weakness. They worried over the strength the new constitution would give it, and they supported concession in the West Indies only as a means of ensuring American membership in France's sphere of influence. None of these factors, even if fully perceived, could have penetrated Jefferson's optimism in 1789.

Once the Estates-General had met in 1789, Jefferson abandoned his earlier advice to the French that they should not aim at more than a limited monarchy, "lest they should shock the dispositions of the court, and even alarm the public mind, which must be left to open itself by degrees to successive improvements."[16] Since that time, the men who made the changes establishing limited government had gathered at his house, which was a meeting ground for dissenting factions. The Archbishop of Bordeaux openly asked Jefferson to serve as adviser for the Declaration of Rights of Man and the Citizen being framed in 1789.[17] Diplomatic proprieties were set aside since Jefferson felt he could personally influence French reformers. Such excesses as occurred in the fall of the Bastille were merely "the rags in which religion robes the true God."[18] His mature judgment in his last days in France was one of unbridled confidence in the future. "It is impossible to desire better dispositions towards us than prevail in this assembly. Our proceedings have been viewed as a model for them on every occasion; and tho in the heat of debate men are generally disposed to contradict every authority urged by their opponents, ours has been treated like that of the bible, open to the explanation but not to question."[19]

Even before Jefferson returned to the United States to assume his duties as secretary of state, the analogue between the American experience and the fundamentalist Bible had lost what validity it may have had. This is not to minimize the influence of the American example among the French literati or among the people. As observed earlier, the veterans of the American Revolution had their impact on French public opinion. Those sectors of France where large numbers of veterans lived were the most radical in the attack on feudal privilege. But how long could America — a new, weak, and uncivilized people — retain the position of teacher? France was too proud, too powerful, and ultimately too important in the world of the eighteenth century to maintain a disciple's role. As Robert Palmer put it, if America first proclaimed a new religion with her revolution, "within two decades the United States was in the worthy position of a kind of Israel, and the ecumenical church, as embodied in the New Republican Order, had its center — complete with power, doctrines, and abuses — in Paris." [20]

This was apparent, as well as inevitable, almost immediately. Early carpings over the purity of America's republican institutions were preludes to other doubts. For example, the Declaration of Independence and the various bills of rights of the individual states written since 1776 were known to Frenchmen and had their influence upon the various declarations of rights that were issued by successive French revolutionary governments. The French declarations restated the ideology of the American Revolution, and France's constitution of 1791 borrowed specifically from the practices of the American state constitutions. Admitting all of these influences, Frenchmen involved in constitution making, as well as historians looking back on the events, have displayed impatience over the shortcomings of the American model, particularly the bicameral legislature. The international climate of the Enlightenment, refined by the French environment, was, to them, the real revolution. American bills of rights were for specific juridical purposes; France broadened them by making them universal truths. So went the argument. [21]

But it was more than the amour propre of Frenchmen that was involved. Substantive differences between American and French republicans appeared in the debate over the virtues of a unicameral versus a bicameral legislature and over the supremacy of the legislature. In these regards, American practice met with suspicion among most Frenchmen. The American Constitution, with its elevation of a strong president and creation of a powerful and less democratic upper house, appeared to open the way to autocracy and aristocracy. The fears of John Adams of excessive power in a single house as expressed in his "Defense of Constitutions" contradicted the French revolutionary obsession with a single house speaking the voice of the people. Ultimately, a national assembly snuffed out the life of the dangerous first two estates as well as the monarch himself. The pro-American Mounier may have been receptive to the division of governmental powers, but in 1791 Mounier was identified as a counterrevolutionary. In the light of the direction the Revolution took in France, the putative fraternity between the United States and France weakened as America appeared the deviationist, as much a threat to truth as any member of the old regime.

American diplomats recognized dangers in this relationship with the French and played their roles accordingly. Franklin had earlier allowed the unicameral government of Pennsylvania to be elevated into a model, not because he valued it particularly, but because his French friends admired it. Since it pleased them, he would not spoil their pleasure. Even Adams himself felt that a unicameral system might indeed be temporarily better for France than his "balanced government" because the senate could be composed of only those nobles and clerics who "would have obstructed the progress of the reformation in religion and Government, and procured an abortion to the regeneration of France." [22] Jefferson had done his part by blurring as much as he could those lines of historical difference separating the two countries. What he and the others wanted was not the specific credit for creating one or another institution, but rather the building of an ambience that would bolster America's reputation, credit, and strength in a hostile world.

The fact of American survival until 1789 owed something to a friendly France, helpful often despite itself. Jefferson always understood that monarchical France had had grave reservations about the American experiment and would have had no compunction about keeping the new nation weak even if it had had the power to do otherwise. But America's stock in the world rose after the French Revolution in 1789. A great nation following the lead of a smaller was a wonderful tonic for confidence.

The question, however, was how long the good feelings could last. France's reservations about America had their counterpart across the Atlantic. As secretary of state, Jefferson felt rebuffed when the reformed monarchy of Lafayette and Mirabeau, in 1790 and 1791, and later the liberal republic of the Girondists failed to respond to American inquiries about opening France's colonies to American trade. Jefferson had expectations that an enlightened government would appreciate the mutual advantage in a free trade that linked the two economies more closely. Instead, he encountered a new mercantilism among the middle-class spokesmen of the National Assembly. Revolutionary France was actually becoming more efficient in imposing duties on foreigners than the monarchy had been, and such friends as Lafayette now had less influence on commercial policy than they had had under the ancien régime. To Jefferson, extra duties on American shipping were "such an act of hostility against our navigation, as were not to have been expected from the friendship of that nation."[23] Yet even those French merchants not hostile to American interests recognized the futility of weaning American businessmen away from their accustomed British ties and gave up their attempts.

While merchants may have written off serious possibilities of competing with British rivals for the American market, French politicians and ideologists still had room in their plans for America, but not in a manner Jefferson or other American friends of France could accept. The conviction of many French intellectuals in the heady days of French military successes in the 1790s was that France had moved ahead of the United States in the advancement of liberty. Having coped successfully with the first coalition of reactionary monarchs, the governments of both the Girondists and the Director, briefly interrupted by the more parochial Jacobins, projected a world liberated by French arms, in which allies everywhere would further the French cause. Americans should not only help France by resisting British policies but help improve their own imperfect system, which was threatened by aristocratic elements in the form of Anglophile Federalism. From 1793 to the advent of Bonaparte's Consulate, a seeming legion of scholars and philosophes visited America with the ulterior motives of spying out the western lands for future French armies or recruiting American supporters, troops, and supplies for the invasion of Spanish territory. France had its eye on the return of Louisiana and expected America to applaud this liberation from monarchical Spain.

In the heat of political rivalry between Federalists and Republicans, there were Americans who rallied to the French banner. Democratic societies in town after town confused republicanism in France with republicanism in the United States. Even Jefferson as secretary of state was carried away in 1793 by the vision of an embattled France fighting England for the liberties of the world. For a time, he suppressed his earlier irritations in view of the new threat from England, which he felt intended to reconquer America or impose on it an Anglophile monarch or dictator. He committed an indiscretion in aiding Genet's designs on Louisiana, claiming that he "did not care what insurrections should be excited in Louisiana" so long as America was not blamed for them; he grandiosely spoke of dining with the French general Pichegru in London in 1795 to "hail the dawn of liberty & republicanism in that island."24 No wonder French statesmen could talk of a French party in the United States that would serve their interests much as their friends in Italy, Holland, and Switzerland.

One of the remarkable by-products of the French Revolution was the service unwittingly and unhappily rendered by Frenchmen of intellectual distinction and liberal sympathies to the imperialism of the mother country. Even a Lafayette and a DuPont, who suffered exile from the Revolution and hostility from Bonaparte, could never suppress the emotion that no matter how a Napoleon perverted the goals of the Revolution, France's society was still superior to that of any other European country. Their advice to their friends in America reflected this sentiment. 25

For the tough-minded military politicans who governed France after 1795, America was simply another pawn in their board, and the tender-minded intellectuals—American or French—were to be servitors in their North American game. France's abuse of its American ally after Jay's Treaty and the Anglo-American economic rapprochement was not the consequence of shock and disappointment over American betrayal of the spirit of 1778; it was a calculated attempt to break Anglophile power in Philadelphia and replace it with a friendly Republican. When Talleyrand, the foreign minister, realized that he had overplayed his hand in attempting to extract bribes and loans from American negotiators in return for normal relations in 1797, he was willing to turn to the American community in Paris for help. And they were glad to serve. Thomas Paine, for one, had been a mediator between the United States and France, urging the French not to lose faith in the essential republicanism of Americans. When the XYZ affair threatened to erupt into full war between the two countries, John Adams was able to turn to the letters of such businessmen as Richard Codman and to his son, John Quincy Adams, as well as to his diplomatic agent, Elbridge Gerry, to assure himself that France repented of its misdeeds and desired peace. Joel Barlow, poet and businessman, won over Washington himself on this issue and gave Adams the blessing of the former president by sending out a new peace commission to France in 1799. Napoleon Bonaparte agreed to end hostilities and terminate the alliance of 1778 to serve the larger purposes of French policy. He no longer needed or counted upon any American support beyond quiescence while he plotted the reoccupation of Louisiana. It was a tribute to his shrewdness that he knew the potential hostility of the United States toward a French Louisiana, even though the United States government was in Jefferson's hands. But he was able to play upon the old chords of friendship to soften American feelings.

Thus, it appeared that the tables were turned. In the American Revolution, Frenchmen had been exploited as agents of American policy while the mature French Revolution now appeared to use Americans in turn to win its objectives. Bonaparte intended to use the occasion of Washington's death in 1799 to identify himself with the American leader and to remind Americans of the unity between France and the United States. In a wonderfully cynical gesture in 1800, the Convention of Mortefontaine, which ended the Franco-American alliance of 1778, was the scene of a magnificent fete in which the liberal maritime principles that both nations had violated were toasted by both parties. The First Consul attempted to use these apostrophes to neutral rights as proof to the hesitant northern maritime powers that the United

States was on the point of joining the projected new League of Armed Neutrals against Great Britain. [26]

For some of the practitioners, the play upon cultural and ideological ties was not simply exercise in cynicism. Those Frenchmen who served the plans of the Directory or the ambitions of Napoleon usually carried a genuine affection for America throughout their careers. And for their part, Francophile Americans of the order of Franklin and Jefferson never overcame their weakness for French society, even as they hoped to bend French sentiments to their national purposes. But the "mirage in the West," as Echeverria labeled it, had ended with the conversion of the French Revolution into Napoleonic imperialism. Frenchmen perceived both the frailties of real Americans and the limited fraternity inherent in the policies of the United States, while Americans had learned even before the advent of Napoleon that French republicanism was as different from the American as the Old World was from the New.

Jefferson's applause for the success of France's arms in the mid-1790s may have symbolized his succumbing for the moment to the charms of the French Revolution, but more likely it was a reflection of deep domestic problems of American politics of the time. By 1801 President Jefferson held no illusions about First Consul Bonaparte, whom he bracketed unflatteringly with Alexander Hamilton as a man-on-horseback who would destroy freedom in the pursuit of his own fame. [27] Napoleon never rose higher in his estimation. The President's acceptance of the termination of the French alliance in the Convention of Mortefontaine, his articulation of isolationist ideals in his First Inaugural Address, and his hostility toward French ambitions in Louisiana and to their depredations upon American commerce on the high seas all confirmed the fears of those French diplomats, such as Pierre Adet, who recognized that the American was the "born enemy of all European peoples." [28]

Just as Talleyrand or Napoleon was ready to seize upon an American poet or businessman in Paris for occasional diplomatic services, so Jefferson made use of his French philosophical friends to influence the Emperor. The Louisiana crisis was notable among other reasons for his shrewd dispatch of Pierre Samuel Du Pont, Jefferson's philosopher friend, with a message not only for the American minister in Paris, but indirectly for the leaders of France themselves. Jefferson could count upon the American sympathies of men of influence in Napoleonic circles. He emphasized to Du Pont the vital interest of America in having France cede all of Louisiana, not merely New Orleans, for the sake of good relations in the future. To underline the urgency of his appeal, he asked the physiocrat, then embarking for France, to carry a note to Minister Livingston in Paris, which dramatically included a warning that "the day that France takes possession of New Orleans . . . we must marry ourselves to the British fleet and nation."[29] The Frenchman was happy to do what he could to avert this fate.

The President, of course, had been aware of the importance informal relations with like-minded men could have in diplomacy ever since his days as minister to France. As he pointed out to Monroe in 1804, he had followed a practice for over a generation of making "private friendships instrumental to the public good by inspiring a confidence which is denied to the public, and official communications."[30] Napoleon had made sure that Jefferson was elected to his prestigious National Institute, and the American was pleased to join this select group, convinced as he was that this was the shortest route to power in France. For similar reasons, Jefferson arranged for Destutt de Tracy and Du Pont to become members of the American Philosophical Society during his tenure as president of that organization. Jefferson thus continued in the tradition of Franklin.

Who outwitted whom in this game? On one level, Napoleon emerged the victor by virtue of America's service to France in the embargo of 1807 and in the War of 1812. Such was the view of Henry Adams in his magisterial judgments of the times. Yet Jefferson and Madison were subject to no illusions in forming their judgments about either the weight of "republicanism" in the Empire or about the conformity of France to America's outlook upon the world. Fraternity had disappeared from the American side. Jefferson's and Madison's behavior, wise or not, was based on the thesis that France was less dangerous to America than Britain. If affection remained, it was largely on the other side, from the incurable Americanophiles among the

French ideologues who maintained deep feelings of loyalty for their conception of America. The land may not have been the Arcadia of Rousseau, but it was still the place where man could enjoy greater freedom than anywhere else on earth. In the face of Napoleon's onslaught, the American counterparts of the philosophes and ideologues had abandoned their dreams about the French Revolution. But French dreams endured—and served the United States.

The republican image as seen by Frenchmen helped the new nation at birth and in its critical weaning years. By 1800 the special relationship had formally terminated, and by 1815 subsequent American experiences with Napoleonic France deepened the growing American isolationism. While it may be claimed that realpolitik had always governed Franco-American relations, the bonds created by a common encounter with revolution played as large a role in their relationship as did the common enmity to Great Britain. As late as 1812, the French minister to the United States, Louis Sérurier, could claim without irony that America's pursuit of a liberal construction of neutral rights was not just a sensible posture for a small maritime country, but a special attribute of American idealism, expressed in a decision for war on behalf of universal principles insufficiently appreciated by France and other naval powers.[31] Napoleon may have won an embargo by exploiting American illusions about French interest in America, but the United States won independence and status as a nation by raising among the French even greater illusions and profiting from them. The latter victory was the more significant.

NOTES

1. R. R. Palmer, *The Age of the Democratic Revolution: A Political History of Europe and America, 1760-1800: The Challenge,* 2 vols. (Princeton: Princeton University Press, 1959), vol. 1, p. 240.

2. Michael G. Kammen, *A Rope of Sand: The Colonial Agents, British Politics, and the American Revolution* (Ithaca, N.Y.: Cornell University Press, 1968), p. 318.

3. Seymour Martin Lipset, *The First Nation: The United States in Histori-*

cal and Comparative Perspective (Garden City, N.Y.: Anchor Books, 1967), p. 19ff.

4. Durand Echeverria, *Mirage in the West: A History of the French Image of American Society to 1815* (Princeton: Princeton University Press, 1957), p. 29.

5. *Journals of the Continental Congress*, 34 vols. (Washington, D.C.: Government Printing Office, 1905), vol 3, p. 392.

6. Franklin to Livingston, March 4, 1782, in Francis Wharton, ed., *The Revolutionary Diplomatic Correspondence of the United States*, 6 vols. (Washington, D.C.: Government Printing Office, 1889), vol. 5, p. 215.

7. Notes on relations with France, March-April 1776, in L. H. Butterfield, ed., *Diary and Autobiography of John Adams*, 4 vols. (Cambridge: The Belknap Press of the Harvard University Press, 1961), vol. 3, p. 329.

8. See Echeverria, *Mirage in the West*, pp. 64, 69.

9. Franklin to Mrs. Thompson, February 8, 1777, in Albert H. Smyth, *Writings of Benjamin Franklin*, 10 vols. (New York: Macmillan Co., 1905), vol. 7, p. 26.

10. J. Hector St. John de Crèvecoeur, *Letters from an American Farmer* (New York: E. P. Dutton & Co., 1957), p. 40.

11. Forrest McDonald, "The Relation of the French Peasant Veterans of the American Revolution to the Fall of Feudalism in France, 1789-1790," *Agricultural History* 25 (October 1951): 159.

12. Luzerne to Vergennes, August 11, 1781, Archives du Ministere des affaires strangeres, correspondance politique, Etats-Unis, XVIII, quoted in William C. Stinchcombe, *The American Revolution and the French Alliance* (Syracuse: Syracuse University Press, 1969), p. 87.

13. Adams to Francis Dana, September 17, 1782, in Wharton, *Revolutionary Diplomatic Correspondence*, vol. 5, p. 732. Claude Fenlen disputes McDonald's thesis in "The Impact of the American Revolution on France," Library of Congress Symposium on the American Revolution, *The Impact of the American Revolution Abroad* (Washington: Library of Congress, 1975).

14. Jefferson to Brissot de Warville, February 11, 1788, in Julian Boyd and others, eds., *The Papers of Thomas Jefferson* (Princeton: Princeton University Press, 1950-), vol 12, pp. 577-588.

15. Lawrence S. Kaplan, *Jefferson and France: An Essay on Politics and Political Ideas* (New Haven: Yale University Press, 1967), pp. 26-27.

16. Jefferson to Washington, December 4, 1788, in J. P. Boyd, ed., *The Papers of Thomas Jefferson* (Princeton: Princeton University Press, 1958), vol. 14, p. 330.

17. Archbishop of Bordeaux to Jefferson, July 20, 1789, ibid., vol. 15, p. 291.

18. Jefferson to Paine, October 14, 1789, ibid., vol. 15, p. 522.

19. Jefferson to Madison, August 28, 1789, ibid., vol. 15, p. 366.

20. Palmer, *Age of the Democratic Revolution: The Struggle*, vol. 2, p. 509.

21. See a recent statement of this view in Albert Soboul, "La Revolution francaise dans l'histoire du Monde Contemporain," in Mathé Allain and Glenn R. Conrad, eds., *France and North America: The Revolutionary Experience* (Lafayette, La.: University of Southwestern Louisiana Press, 1974), pp. 59-75.

22. Discourses on Davila, in Charles F. Adams, ed., *The Works of John Adams*, 10 vols. (Boston: Charles C. Little and James Brown, 1850-1856), vol. 6, p. 274.

23. Jefferson to William Short, July 28, 1791, in Andrew A. Lipscomb and Albert E. Bergh, eds., *The Writings of Thomas Jefferson*, 20 vols. (Washington, D.C.: Thomas Jefferson Memorial Association, 1904), vol. 8, p. 217.

24. Jefferson's Anas, in Lipscomb and Bergh, *The Writings of Thomas Jefferson*, vol. 1, p. 362; Jefferson to W. B. Giles, April 27, 1795, in Paul L. Ford, ed., *The Works of Thomas Jefferson*, 12 vols. (New York: G. P. Putnam's Sons, 1905), vol. 8, p. 172.

25. Lafayette to Jefferson, March 31, 1803, in Gilbert Chinard, ed., *The Letters of Lafayette and Jefferson* (Baltimore: Johns Hopkins University Press, 1929), p. 218; Du Pont to Jefferson, March 10, 1806, in Gilbert Chinard, ed., *The Correspondence of Jefferson and Du Pont de Nemours* (Baltimore: Johns Hopkins University Press, 1931), p. 108.

26. Arthur A. Richmond, "Napoleon and the Armed Neutrality of 1800: A Diplomatic Challenge to British Sea Power," *Royal Service Institution Journal* 104 (1959): 1-9.

27. Jefferson to T. M. Randolph, February 2, 1800, in Lipscomb and Bergh, *The Writings of Thomas Jefferson*, vol. 10, p. 151.

28. Adet to Minister of Foreign Affairs, December 31, 1796, in Frederick Jackson Turner, "Correspondence of the French Ministers to the United States," in *American Historical Association Annual Report, 1903* (Washington, D.C.: Government Printing Office, 1904), pp. 982-983.

29. Jefferson to Livingston, April 18, 1802, in Lipscomb and Bergh, *The Writings of Thomas Jefferson*, vol. 10, p. 313.

30. Jefferson to Monroe, January 8, 1804, in Ford, *Works of Thomas Jefferson*, vol. 10, p. 61.

31. Introduction, Louis Sérurier Papers, Centre de microfilm des archives de Seine at Oise.

CHAPTER THREE

The Neocolonial Impulse: The United States and Great Britain, 1783-1823

Of all the nations confronting the new republic in 1783, none was more important or more threatening to its survival than Great Britain. The reasons for a continuing intimate relationship were obvious. The American language, literature, and economy maintained ties with the old country that no political separation could rend. The reasons for hostility were equally obvious. By the terms of the peace treaty of 1783, the United States was obligated to repay debts to British creditors without the power to redeem this promise, and to "earnestly recommend" that the states restore properties confiscated from Loyalists without power to enforce its recommendations, no matter how earnestly they might be made. Within American borders, British troops still remained at seven posts, giving rise to temptations for the stronger power to test the weaker's strength within the next generation. Similar temptations affected the economic connection. British markets and British credit continued to dominate American commerce after the war. These temptations were not to be resisted until the British were prepared to accept the United States as a permanent member of the society of nations, beyond the patronizing acknowledgment of its existence in Article I of the Treaty of Paris. This acceptance would not take place until another war had been fought.

While the pattern in the first generation of independence is complicated, one may discern in it a classical Creole* relationship on the part of both Americans and Englishmen. Envy and resentment coexisted with admiration and affection. Americans both imitated and rejected the parental model, while Englishmen both patronized and despised their American clients. In this context, the conventional distinctions between Hamiltonian and Jeffersonian attitudes toward Britain are often blurred. For example, Jefferson's Anglophobia, though genuine and deeply felt, became virulent only when events fed his periodic fears of British reconquest of America by their arms or by their followers. Nevertheless, he always recognized British virtues, particularly their superiority in the arts of governance over the rest of Europe, which belonged to a heritage he claimed for Americans. After the War of 1812, he was willing to contemplate an informal entente with Britain against French or Spanish designs on Latin America. Even at the height of his Anglophobia, he had the prudence to keep Federalist Rufus King as minister in London and to exploit French concern about the British navy to extort concessions in Louisiana.

What united all Americans of this time in their views of Great Britain was the recognition that the relationship was important, for better or worse. For the United States, a foreign policy toward Britain was shaped by the political and economic insecurity of the new nation, a condition aggravated by British power. British posts in the Northwest threatened American control of the frontier; Britain's rule of the seas affected the fundaments of American international commerce; British credits determined the extent of America's economic expansion. Here is sufficient justification for the national schizophrenia over the British, which would have existed even if the special psychological scars from the recent war had fully healed. Anglophobes would have one method of dealing with the British challenge, Anglophiles quite another.

For Britain, the American issue was of far less importance. America was only one part in the British imperial scheme. It is true that the American market and resources were of increasing

---

*A Creole was originally a person of French or Spanish descent who was born and raised in a colonial region (*Webster's New International Dictionary*).

significance to the British economy. Even in the 1780s, in the midst of the disarray of the Confederation, Great Britain exported 10 percent of its products to the United States, and this figure was to rise to one-third of its total exports by 1801. Nevertheless, the British could afford to indulge their prejudices and resentments against Americans, reasonably secure in the knowledge that the United States was unable to strike back effectively. It could be punished for its revolution and restricted in its role as a competitor without damaging either Britain's market in America or Britain's position as a belligerent in wartime. Successive British ministries acted on these assumptions until the War of 1812.

Diplomatic, commercial, and cultural agents were busy on both sides of the Atlantic to promote partisan views of the proper Anglo-American posture. British mercantilists, fearful of American movement into the fur country of the West, and manufacturers worried over American rivalry did their best to keep the ministry to a hostile American line with the assurance that the republican experiment was bound to fail. To counter these pressures, Americanophiles, ranging from banking partners of American firms to West Indian nabobs dependent upon Carolina provisions, and from free traders following the advice of Adam Smith to libertarians of the order of Richard Price and Joseph Priestley — scientists and divines of rationalism — urged a policy of accommodation with America, noting the benefits a reconstituted Anglo-America would yield.

The different governments of the United States in the postwar period were similarly importuned with advice either to support a Britain under attack from the French Revolution or to strike out at the country which still held posts in America and discriminated against American commerce. Given the greater relative importance of the relationship to Americans, lobbying was understandably more intense in New York, Philadelphia, and Washington than in London. Anglophile propagandists not only made their arguments heard from official positions but occasionally precipitated crises which a softer stance might have averted. Indeed, they fostered misjudgments in England which laid the groundwork for the resumption of war in 1812, long after they had lost all influence with the government.

A reasonable point of departure in any examination of the Federalist relationship with Britain is the Creole complex, which affected the behavior of both parties. For the British, this took the form of a "supercilious assumption of superiority," as H. C. Allen has phrased it. [1] Even when the British court finally accepted an American minister, the latter observed that American concerns "would not be answered with high language, but with what would be more disagreeable and perplexing—with a contemptuous silence." [2] The minister was John Adams, whose sensibilities were easily ruffled. But his perceptions are echoed repeatedly in the diplomatic relationship, including an offhand notation of his son, John Quincy, that two of his British counterparts at Ghent "had the English prejudice of disliking everything that was not English." [3]

American irritation over manners and deportment was reciprocated in full by Englishmen of every generation. In fact, there was a remarkable consistency about the views of Englishmen in America, particularly in the diplomatic community. The hostility of Harriet Martineau and Charles Dickens, so celebrated in the nineteenth century, may be found in almost every envoy to Philadelphia or Washington. Since most British official visitors in the first two generations after independence were influenced by the most disaffected segments of the Federalist party, their distaste was understandable. Still, it often appeared vehemently rather than as just a reflection of the views of American Tories. Even when George Hammond, the first British minister to the United States, married an American, his dislike of the people as well as the climate was such that he never returned to the United States after his service ended. Those British representatives who did enjoy some popularity outside the circle of Anglophiles did so at the cost of repressing their genuine feelings. In the case of Augustus Foster, the result of this exercise in restraint was to offer Americans a "bland exterior," which turned out to be an offense in itself. [4] The energy Foster expended in controlling his amusement of repugnance over the uncouth behavior of the natives may have been one of the blocks that made him unresponsive to the threat of war during his ministry in 1811 and 1812. Even the most popular of ministers in the early national period, Sir Charles Bagot, could not stand the environment of Washington. He managed to confine his distress over life in America to confidential communications. As his successor, Stratford Canning put it: "I consider my residence in America as a second and rougher period of education; one's passage through it is not unattended with the privations and annoyances of school, but I do not quite despair of being able . . . to look back upon it as I now do with thankfulness on the restraints and disciplines of Eton."[5]

Those who sought to give meaning to a new Anglo-American community either failed to win approval for their recommendations of conciliation from official policy makers or succeeded unwittingly in distorting the position of their own country in their communications with leaders abroad. The British friends of America belonged to the first category, while the American friends of Great Britain fitted the second category. Of the two, the American Anglophiles had more power and influence in their government, but they ultimately committed more mischief than service to their cause by fostering illusions in London about American attitudes and plans at critical moments during the French Revolution and Napoleonic wars.

No comparable illusions about British positions were raised by Americanophiles in Britain, although they were as earnest and as zealous in promoting the American cause as were their Federalist counterparts. British friends of America were numerous and steadfast, if not as influential. The Whig tradition had a pro-American stamp. Such prominent figures as Charles James Fox, Edmund Burke, and even Lord Shelburne vied with one another in their criticism of their government's American policy during the Revolutionary War. Regrettably for the Americans, these sentiments may have been widespread, but they were rarely translated into permanent service to their friends.

From the Treaty of Paris to the Treaty of Ghent, British ministers treated Americans with condescension, contempt, or malevolence. They would concede nothing except under duress, they forced American commerce to conform to their regulations with few gestures of reciprocity, and they injured American pride even when the exigencies of war with France made American trade more important than it had ever been. Great Britain never opened the West Indian ports legally to American shipping, refused to send a minister until 1791, and did not evacuate the Northwest posts until after Jay's Treaty had been signed, and then only after that treaty had yielded the same advantages that France had received in the alliance of 1778. Moreover, the French wars were the occasion for greater restrictions on American trade as the British navy enforced an illegal blockade and put forth unilateral interpretations of maritime law. Throughout this period, Great Britain practiced a policy of impressing into the British navy sailors who were charged with desertion to the American merchant marine or navy.

Relations between the two countries were not uniformly hostile. Bradford Perkins has marshaled impressive evidence to show a genuine rapprochement between the two nations between 1795 and 1805.[6] Foreign ministers Grenville and Hawksbury displayed some appreciation of American sensibilities and participated in propelling the United States for a time into a period of prosperity as neutral America serviced belligerent Europe. During the quasi-war with France, Great Britain winked at American trade with its own West Indies and permitted fraudulent trade between the French and Spanish West Indies and Europe, through its *Polly* decision in 1800, wherein shipments from West Indian colonies were supposedly Americanized by being reshipped from an American port. At the height of fraternization, weapons were even supplied to the Americans, while both parties talked of collaborating in an attack on Latin America. Nor did the election of a Republican president necessitate an abrupt change. In 1803 Jefferson wrote of "marrying ourselves to the British fleet and nation" unless France made the necessary concessions in Louisiana, and Rufus King, the Anglophilic minister to Great Britain under the Federalists, retained his post for two years because the Jefferson administration valued his access to the Court of St. James.[7]

Nevertheless, the price for accommodation with Britain was ultimately too high — subordination to its economy, and acquiescence in its war of attrition with France and, especially, in the role of the inferior in the Anglo-American relationship. If there were periods of remission between 1783 and 1814, they were expediential and short-lived. As the normal British mood of condescension and contempt was intensified by wartime resentment of American profiteering from Europe's troubles, the dominant Jeffersonians mirrored these feelings. To Jefferson and Madison, Britain's discrimination and hostility were a species of the same attitudes that had determined the Revolution itself. The Republican solution, going back to 1789, was to liberate the nation from British economic control even if the French substitute was not suitable. Until long after his presidency, Jefferson felt that England had reconquest in mind and believed that the Federalists, or at least a substantial number of them, participated in schemes for the reestablishment of the British Empire in America.

The ultimate breakdown of relations in war was unwittingly fostered by those Americans who had tied their fortunes to Great Britain. It was their view of America that made the British behavior toward the nation more than a matter of revenge for the Revolution or protection of special economic interests. If British governments disparaged republicanism as an ineffectual system or if they saw themselves as the saviors of the West and guarantors of America's economy, they did so in response to the intelligence that streamed across the ocean for more than a generation from public and private correspondents, on paper and in person, from figures as influential as Alexander Hamilton, secretary of the treasury and adviser to Washington, and Timothy Pickering, secretary of state under Washington and Adams. Representing the wealth and power of New England and the seaboard cities, the Anglophile party controlled American politics in the 1790s and dominated British thinking about America long after it had lost political control.

The Jeffersonian charge that the Federalist elite attempted to create a society modeled on the mother country and in subservience to its interests has considerable merit when one observes the impressions received in Great Britain. For two generations, British ministries operated on the assumption that America would yield in a crisis and that the opposition to Federalism was unable to manage power properly if it ever acquired it. But the charge requires refinement to account for motives. Only a small minority would defer automatically to British wishes. For such Federalists as Hamilton, Morris, and particularly John Adams, the support of Britain was to serve American objectives.

In Hamilton's mind, only Britain could provide both the instruments of economic advancement and territorial expansion. Hence, his advice to Washington in 1790 to permit British passage through United States territory in the event of a war with Spain over Nootka Sound in the Pacific Northwest was cool and calculating in origin. If he would accommodate Great Britain, it was because he feared that a denial would be ignored and British forces would then move into Florida and Louisiana without American approval, thereby enhancing British influence along the borders to a dangerous degree. Moreover, by "rendering New Orleans the emporium of the products of the western country, Britain would, at a period not *very* distant, have little occasion for supplies of provisions for their islands from the Atlantic States; and for their European market they would derive from the same source copious supplies of tobacco and other articles now furnished by the Southern States; whence a great diminution of the motives to establish liberal terms of commercial intercourse with the United States collectively."[8] If this was Anglophilism, it lacked both an emotional and ideological base.

Yet Hamilton's behavior went beyond this advice to the President. In his anxiety to counter the Secretary of State's recommendation to use the Nootka Sound controversy to extort concessions from Great Britain, he sought out George Beckwith, a British agent in Philadelphia, and with the authority of his rank assured the Englishman that the expeditionary force dispatched against the Indians was not intended for use against British posts. Such information undercut the attempts of Jefferson and Gouverneur Morris, Washington's special emissary in London, to exploit the crisis to remove the British from the Northwest and to win commercial concessions in the West Indies. Knowing that the United States would not side with Spain and would not impose a punitive tariff stiffened the British at a moment the ministry might have yielded. By his secret communications to Beckwith, Hamilton gave the British confidence to postpone the very benefits his demonstrations of friendship were supposed to achieve. The most that the Cabinet would concede was the dispatch of an official minister, George Hammond, whose instructions specifically precluded a commercial treaty or any serious changes in the Anglo-American relationship. So, no matter how cold-blooded Hamilton's motives may have been, the results of his actions at this moment fitted the role of agent or dupe implied in the title of Julian P. Boyd's book, "Number 7," the code term applied to Hamilton in Beckwith's dispatches. [9]

With the beginning of the French Revolutionary wars in 1792, the emotional dimension of Anglophilia dominated the Federalist outlook on the world even as Great Britain's treatment of American commerce took a turn for the worse. If ever retaliatory action was in order, it was early in 1794 in the aftermath of repressive British orders in council which illegally blockaded France and unjustly seized American ships carrying goods to or from the French West Indies. Chief Justice John Jay was sent to London to protest not only British violations of American neutral rights but also the continuing problem of British troops in the Northwest, now aggravated by British anti-American propaganda among the Indians on the frontiers. Only the Jay mission saved the British from Madison's strict Navigation Laws, which would have imposed retaliatory duties on British imports. But rather than modify the Federalists' Anglophilism, the party under Hamilton was fastened more firmly than before to the belief that Great Britain was protecting civilization from assaults from atheism and anarchy originating in the French Revolution and extending to France's Republican friends in America.

Such considerations moved Hamilton to intervene once again to affect British policy toward the United States. Given the depth of American anger, the British feared an American membership in a new League of Armed Neutrals as much as they did a duty against British shipping. While Jay was deep in negotiations in London, George Hammond, the British minister in Philadelphia, was able to report Hamilton's judgment that "it was the settled policy of the Government in every contingency, even in that of an open contest with Great Britain, to avoid entangling itself with European connexions, which could only tend to involve this country in disputes wherein it might have no possible interest, and commit it to a common cause with allies, from whom, in the moment of danger, it could derive no possible succour." [10] Secure in the knowledge that the United States would not join a revived league with or without Hammond's information Foreign Minister George Grenville was free to ignore Jay's implied threats and to fashion a treaty that yielded little of substance to the American position on neutral rights.

How much the spirit of abhorrence of France animated this private communication and how much, in the case of Hamilton, the service to Britain rested on continued expectations of British commercial advantages or on a common purpose against Spanish America will always be open to speculation. Certainly, other Federalists made no bones about their identification with the British cause, particularly after the French Revolution became identified with French imperialism in the quasi-war between France and the United States from 1798 to 1800. The independent Gouverneur Morris, who had displayed conspicuous annoyance with Englishmen during his mission in 1790, was sufficiently affected by the threat of the French Directory to serve voluntarily as an observer and propagandist for Great Britain during visits to Prussia and Austria in 1796 and 1797. He urged Grenville to identify the war with the idea Federalists had always associated with the conflict, namely, a crusade against anarchy: "This kind of crusade will not indeed be so wonderful as that which was produced by the preaching of Peter the Hermit, but may answer better purposes." [11]

Anxiety over the possibility of a French victory moved Ministers William Vans Murray in Holland and Rufus King in London to serve the British cause in undiplomatic ways. Neither statesman was as hopelessly infatuated with the British as some of their more rabid colleagues who had never experienced Englishmen firsthand; King and Murray were of the moderate strain, closer to President John Adams in mood and seeing with Adams the dangers of a full-scale American war with France, which Hamilton and Pickering did not choose to see. Yet King was willing to turn over to his friend Grenville the private correspondence of Murray on the matter of the counterrevolution which Dutch patriots hoped to make against their French-controlled regime with British help. With King as his intermediary, Murray became Grenville's agent in arrangements with the Dutch underground. Although hopes of Anglo-Dutch cooperation foundered on Britain's insistence upon the restoration of the stadtholderate, the clandestine involvement of American diplomats and the easy acceptance of these activities by Whitehall suggest the role assigned to Americans of whatever rank in the British official mind. The nuances of difference between an independent Adams Federalist and a devoted Hamiltonian went unexamined. For Great Britain, American behavior, even when occasionally indecorous as in King's protests against impressment or obstreperous as in his stand on prerevolutionary debts to British creditors, was still that of the Creole: useful, slightly contemptible, and taken for granted. There was little in Federalist service to the Empire to dispute this judgment.

Regrettably for both countries, the advent of Jefferson to power did little to modify Britain's policy toward the United States. French power under Napoleon was more formidable than under the Directory, and the British governments understandably had less appreciation for the sensibilities of Americans under conditions of greater stress. If anything, resentment over America's profiting from her trials helped to produce new frictions and gave Britain justification for its measures. George Canning, foreign minister and leading British antagonist of Jefferson's second administration, asserted in 1808 that "the Strength and Power of Great Britain are not for herself alone, but for the world," and America should be properly appreciative. [12] Augustus Foster was more candid: America should beware. "The two greatest Commercial Nations in the Globe cannot move in the same Spheres without jostling one another a little; where we were aiming blows at the French Marine, we want Elbow room and these good Neutrals wont give it to us, & therefore they get a few side Pushes which makes them grumble." [13]

This mood of truculence toward the United States was translated into a series of offensive actions dating from the Essex Decision in 1805, which denied Americans indirect trade from the West Indies to the Continent, to the Orders in Council of 1807 which denied Americans any trade with Napoleonic Europe unless American ships yielded a middleman's profit paid to Britain through special license fees. All of these decrees were accompanied by the rise in impressment and the expansion of the definition of contraband. Great Britain appeared to be determined to use the crisis with France to destroy rival American shipping in-

terests. In the face of Britain's challenge and Napoleon's counteraction in the Berlin Decree of 1806, which placed the British
Isles under blockade, and the Milan Decree of 1807, which
ordered any American ships licensed by the British to be seized,
the Jefferson administration instituted an embargo on trade
with Europe that was specifically aimed at Great Britain.

Great Britain had purposely provoked the Anglophobia of the
Jeffersonians to a degree that exceeded the tensions of 1793. The
difference in 1807 was that the Jeffersonians were in power and,
unlike the earlier years, were in a position to put into effect an
anti-British policy. But the British ignored the hostility and expected the same conformity with their interests they had received from the Federalists. It was not that they were unaware of
Jefferson's attitudes, particularly after the Louisiana Purchase
had ended the skittish détente with Britain which the administration had been apparently moving toward in 1803. They
claimed to have exposed clearly the service of Jefferson to
France, and they rationalized the punitive elements in their
decrees to Jefferson's Francophilism. The President, in their
view, was either an unreconstructed servant of French revolutionary ideology or in such fear of Napoleon that he subordinated
his independence to the Emperor's wishes.

The result of such information, freely and extensively offered
by Federalist newspapers, correspondence, and visits, was not
the modification of British behavior in deference to American
Francophilia or American anger. The message that Canning and
his associates received was that Jefferson was an enemy but an
impotent and inefficient enemy. They could share with the Federalists contempt for the resolution of the Jeffersonians and for
their ability to execute an Anglophobic policy successfully.
Rather than look upon the embargo as a shrewd and potentially
destructive mode of warfare against Britain's wartime economy,
they chose to listen to the Federalist diatribes and concluded
that the embargo was a last desperate action of a coward unable
to strike out in conventional warfare. Moreover, the weapon Jefferson selected would, if pursued, destroy America by ruining its
economy and dividing it as a nation. So New Englanders assured
the ministry as they volubly opposed measures to close their
ports and conspired to separate their section from the Union.

England could take comfort in the knowledge that true Americans supported the mother country's fight to defend civilization, American and English. The minority of French sympathizers would eventually be turned out of office. In the meantime, their gestures were too feeble to be taken seriously. Such was the view of America from Parliament, a view formed a generation earlier and unchanged in the Napoleonic period.

Against the massive British confidence built on Federalist prejudice the British voices of opposition could scarcely be heard. As in 1783, distaste for Americans and their revolution prevailed, as well as a continuing unwillingness to have them profit from their new position at British expense. Just as economic advantage had joined with a sense of national interest to give victory to Lord Sheffield's arguments in 1783, so the arguments of Admiralty lawyer James Stephen in his pamphlet, *War in Disguise: Or, the Frauds of Neutral Flags*, found a ready audience in 1805, the year of Trafalgar. Neutrality, he claimed, really never existed; the American neutral trade served France, since most of the cargoes transported to the Continent carried French goods under the fraudulent reexport trade from American ports. Let British seapower stop this trade. If raw materials or manufactured products reached the Continent, there should be a British profit from such trade. Such was the rationalization for the revocation of the permission to "break" a voyage. Stephen's philosophy was justifiable as a vital measure that prevented the enemy from receiving contraband goods as well as a means of forcing British products onto the Continent. Whether or not officially inspired by the Pitt ministry, this pamphlet had Pitt's blessing. The Prime Minister had seen it before publication and advised a private printing.

The hypocrisy, as much as the hostility, of British policy aroused Americans. Conceivably, the emergency would have elicited many concessions even from Jeffersonians. The abortive Monroe-Pinkney treaties, drawn up by two diplomats with impeccable Republican credentials, repeated the formulas of the Jay treaty on neutral rights and even remained silent on impressment in exchange for some relaxation of the issue of broken voyages. Jeffersonians on the scene had some understanding of Britain's problems. Despite his long Anglophobic record, Monroe recognized that there were limits beyond which Great Britain could not go, "when the very existence of the country depended on an adherence to its maritime pretensions." [14] But the insolence of Stephen's approach to Anglo-American relations undid the steps toward reconciliation implicit in Monroe's treaty as it confirmed the malevolence which Jefferson had always believed was the main characteristic of British feeling toward America.

The few Englishmen who tried to stem the tide of economic war and expose the sophistry of the arguments in its favor were isolated and ignored in Parliament. Lord Grenville was unable to work with the followers of Fox to moderate, if not reverse, the Orders in Council. New men appeared in the Commons to serve as spokesmen for America, and some of them, such as Samuel Whitbread and Alexander Baring, were forceful and articulate. But they lacked prestige and power. Whitbread, a former brewer, also lacked familial connections, and his rigorous criticism could be written off as the posturing of a self-made man. Baring, the most persuasive and resourceful of the critics, was a member of an influential banking family with close American connections; his wife was the daughter of Senator William Bingham of Pennsylvania, and he had financial ties with the Philadelphia house of Willing, Morris & Company. Indeed, he was too closely linked to the United States and vulnerable to charges that his devotion to American causes was more a matter of private than public welfare.

The fears of Whitbread and Baring were realized in 1812. War did result from the divisions between the two countries. The Jeffersonians generated none of the moderating forces that led to accommodation under the Federalists. President Madison's war message referred specifically to Britain's "carrying on a war against the lawful commerce of a friend that she may better carry on a commerce with the enemy." The predictions of economic disaster also seemed verified. Instead of profiting from America's discomfiture, British planters and merchants encountered the beginnings of an American manufacturing base created by the nationalism British enmity had fostered. Even if the British depression of 1810 could not be blamed wholly on the American problem, the decline in commerce with the United States certainly worsened it. The friends of America, Cassandras to the end, at least had the satisfaction of crediting the qualified removal of the offensive Orders in Council on June 17, 1812, to the distresses they had foreseen.

At the same time that the Americanophiles seemed to find vindication for their stand in London, there was a change in the tone and even the substance of the advice given by friendly Federalists from Washington and Boston. Federalists of an earlier day, such as John and John Quincy Adams, reflected the growing nationalism in America. While many of them abhorred the idea of war with England, their fears were less for the fate of England than for the suffering an unprepared America would endure, as Rufus King saw it, or for the special advantages France would gain from an intimacy inspired by a common enemy, as Theodore Sedgwick recognized. 15 While deploring the behavior of Jefferson's successor, Madison, they were willing to express their disagreement and even distress with British rigidity toward the United States.

The activity of Harrison Gray Otis, a Massachusetts congressman and firm supporter of England, represented the new direction of the more moderate Federalists. In 1811 he tried to persuade the ministry to make partial concessions which could be made with minimal sacrifice of British security. "The American Cabinet is doubtless weak and perhaps not very well affected towards your Country," he wrote. "But you must allow in return that John Bull, though a good sailor, soldier, and in fact on the whole a good fellow, is a bad negotiator and politician." While many Americans were intimidated by France and prejudiced against England, the more intelligent "tremble for the prosperity and fate of Great Britain, and consider her justly as the Bulwark of the liberties of this country and mankind." 16 A year later he urged Parliament to repeal the Orders in Council even if the Berlin and Milan decrees had not been genuinely revoked. Otis was convinced that the French would repeat their provocations in the future and awaken Americans to the real enemy of their country. If the ministry did not respond on the grounds that Napoleon's conciliatory gestures toward America were a sham, "the scrupulous adherence of your Cabinet to an empty punctilio, will probably unite the whole country in opposition to your nation, and sever for generations, perhaps forever, interests that have the most natural ties of affinity, and men who ought to feel and love like brethren."[17]

These good pieces of advice were communicated directly to Prime Minister Spencer Perceval by Harrison Gray, Otis's Loyalist uncle in London. They were also published by an opposition paper, the London *Morning Chronicle*, and republished on April 28, 1812, by the Boston *Centinel*. The London *Evening Star* on July 13th of that year, before news of Madison's declaration had reached England, suggested that the Otis letter had hastened the repeal of the Orders in Council, although the validity of this claim was somewhat weakened by the revelation that the editorial was written by Gray himself. He had paid a pound for the privilege. It was further vitiated by the caustic reply Perceval had made to Gray in February 1812, in which the Prime Minister made it perfectly clear that British policy was based on motives far more complex than the "punctilio" noted by Otis.[18]

A brusque rejection of Otis's offices probably would have followed from more discreet approaches to the ministry. The moderate Federalists did not fit into the pattern of American reaction the British had been accustomed to find. Friendly warnings that hinted at unity in America or fault in Britain were more than counterbalanced by the familiar information supplied to Minister Augustus Foster in Washington or to London correspondents of such High Federalists as Timothy Pickering. As the Boston *Independent Chronicle* pointed out, "In every measure of government, the federal faction have rallied in opposition and urged the Ministry to persist in their Orders."[19] Many of this group welcomed rather than deplored the prospect of war in the expectation that the crisis would destroy the Madison administration. Foster's dispatches disclose conversations with Federalists who wanted Britain to push the government into war to expose its weaknesses. If Madison fought he would collapse, if he retreated he would be disgraced. Alexander Hanson, influential editor of the Baltimore *Federal Republican*, informed former Minister Francis J. Jackson in March 1812 that "the only way to dislodge the prevailing party from the post of power is by saddling them with a war which they have neither the means [nor] the ability to conduct."[20] Given these goads to war, Britons in Washington or in London could be excused for believing that either Americans would not fight, no matter what they said, or could not, no matter what they did.

With the coming of war, a case can be made that the Federalist information and British contempt for American behavior were both confirmed. With some success, Federalists of New England made strenuous efforts to prevent recruiting of troops, to refuse financial service, or to resist British incursions into their territory. Some of the more rabid enemies of Madison attempted to use the war as the occasion for separating from the Union and making a separate peace. The conduct of the war from Washington offered few reasons to expect victory from the Republicans. While the peace commissioners were at Ghent in the difficult days of the fall of 1814, New England Federalists were openly preparing for a meeting at Hartford to promote "a radical reform in the national compact," in the words of the Massachusetts General Court. At the same time, the governor of that state, Caleb Strong, was secretly employing an agent to visit General Sir John Sherbrooke in Halifax with oral instructions to find out in what ways Britain would help Massachusetts in the event of a clash between the state and the federal government. Sherbrooke promptly asked Lord Bathurst, secretary for war, about the course of action he should take in response to Strong's queries. Had peace not followed almost immediately, the British general would have been authorized to give logistical support to Massachusetts but no specific promise of troops. [21]

What was noteworthy about this exchange was the eagerness of Bathurst to have Sherbrooke sign an armistice with Massachusetts at that particular point. Only two weeks before the conclusion of the Treaty of Ghent, the Secretary for War sent four dispatches to Sherbrooke concerning the options open to the general in the event the treaty aborted. Given this information, it is hardly surprising that the British had some reasons for confidence about the future of their war in America no matter what happened at Ghent. As Liverpool observed to the foreign secretary, Lord Castlereagh, one day before the treaty was signed: "The disposition to separate on the part of the Eastern states may likewise frighten Madison; for if he should refuse to ratify the treaty, we must immediately purpose to make a separate peace with them, and we have good reason to believe that they would not be indisposed to listen to such a proposal." [22]

There is no doubt that the divisive actions of a Federalist minority played a role in the contingency planning of the British government in 1814. Secretive though their behavior was, there is also no doubt that some of the zealots were building hopes for a new government from the defeat of American armies in America. Should the Hartford Convention not meet their wishes—and it did not—they were prepared to continue treasonable negotiations with the British, which were made acceptable by their consistency with preachments they had been making for a generation. Such luminaries as Pickering, Gouverneur Morris, and Charles Carroll counted on British General Sir Edward Pakenham's anticipated victory in Louisiana to serve their purposes. As Pickering put it, "From the moment that the British possess New Orleans the Union is severed." [23]

The trouble with the scenario the High Federalists visualized was that events did not break as they envisioned; New Orleans did not fall, and the Union was not severed. Furthermore, the invasion of Louisiana was undertaken a month after the British and Americans had concluded their treaty at Ghent. With all its opacity, the Cabinet was ultimately more perceptive than its American advisers. Although the failures of American arms early in the war appeared to confirm British contempt for the intelligence and strength of the Republicans, they began to perceive before it ended the reservoirs of strength American nationalism could tap. They had the sense to realize that the enormous effort that would still be needed to defeat Americans was not commensurate with the results to be gained. In making peace in 1814, British diplomats exhibited a grasp of reality that their Anglophile friends overseas never acquired.

The realism Great Britain displayed in bringing the war to a close characterized both sides of the Anglo-American relationship in the next generation. The experience of war and the even more impressive recognition of American economic power sobered many of Britain's emotions about Americans. In Foreign Minister Castlereagh, Charles Webster found "the first British statesman to recognize that the friendship of the United States was a major asset to Britain, and to use in his relations with her a language that was neither superior nor intimidating."[24] The new rapprochement developed partly from the disappearance of both the Federalists and neutral rights from the scene, and partly from a fresh appreciation of a community of interests vis-á-vis Europe. If America had not come fully of age, it had emerged from a colonial status in the official mind of Great Britain.

NOTES

1. H. C. Allen, *Great Britain and the United States: A History of Anglo-American Relations (1783-1952)* (New York: St. Martin's Press, 1955), p. 23.

2. Adams to John Jay, December 3, 1785, in Charles Francis Adams, ed., *The Works of John Adams*, vol. 8, p. 355.

3. John Quincy Adams to Louisa Adams, October 28, 1814, in W. C. Ford, ed., *Writings of John Quincy Adams*, 7 vols. (New York: The Macmillan Co., 1915), vol. 5, p. 175.

4. Bradford Perkins, *Prologue to War: England and the United States, 1805-1812* (Berkeley and Los Angeles: University of California Press, 1961), p. 275.

5. Quoted in Bradford Perkins, *Castlereagh and Adams: England and the United States, 1812-1823* (Berkeley and Los Angeles: University of California Press, 1964), p. 209.

6. Bradford Perkins, *The First Rapprochement: England and the United States* (Berkeley and Los Angeles: University of California Press, 1967).

7. Jefferson to Du Pont de Nemours, April 18, 1802, in Andrew A. Lipscomb and Albert E. Bergh, eds., *The Writings of Thomas Jefferson*, vol. 10, p. 313.

8. Hamilton to Washington, September 15, 1790, in Harold C. Syrett and Jacob E. Cooke, eds., *The Papers of Alexander Hamilton* (New York: Columbia University Press, 1963), vol. 7, pp. 46-47.

9. Julian P. Boyd, *Number 7: Alexander Hamilton's Secret Attempts to Control American Foreign Policy* (Princeton: Princeton University Press, 1964).

10. Quoted in Samuel Flagg Bemis, *Jay's Treaty: A Study in Commerce and Diplomacy* (New Haven: Yale University Press, 1962), p. 337.

11. Quoted in Perkins, *First Rapprochement*, p. 104.

12. Quoted in Perkins, *Prologue to War*, p. 176.

13. Ibid., p. 73.

14. Ibid., p. 138.

15. See Robert Ernst, *Rufus King: American Federalist* (Chapel Hill: University of North Carolina Press, 1968), p. 314; Theodore Welch, *Theodore*

Sedgwick, Federalist: A Political Portrait (Middletown, Ct.: Wesleyan University Press, 1965), p. 247.

16. Quoted in Samuel Eliot Morison, *Harrison Gray Otis, 1765-1848: The Urbane Federalist* (Boston, Mass.: Houghton-Mifflin, 1969), pp. 321-322.

17. Ibid., p. 323.

18. Ibid., pp. 323-324.

19. Quoted in Perkins, *Prologue to War*, p. 436.

20. Quoted in Roger H. Brown, *The Republic in Peril: 1812* (New York and London: Columbia University Press, 1964), p. 96.

21. Samuel E. Morison, *et al.*, *Dissent in Three American Wars* (Cambridge: Harvard University Press, 1970), p. 18.

22. Quoted in J. S. Martell, "A Sidelight on Federalist Strategy During the War of 1812," *American Historical Review* 43 (April 1938): 558.

23. Quoted in Morison, *Dissent in Three American Wars*, p. 24.

24. Charles K. Webster, ed., *Britain and the Independence of Latin America*, 2 vols. (London: Oxford University Press, 1938), vol. 1, p. 42.

CHAPTER FOUR

The Independence of Latin America: North American Ambivalence, 1800–1820

It is hardly surprising that the romantic qualities in the American war for independence should have inspired responses from libertarians everywhere. That Kosciusko the Pole or Lafayette the Frenchman would have Spanish-American counterparts was a natural consequence of a vision of a new society in which liberty triumphed over tyranny and in which the New World triumphed over the Old. While Latin American revolutions were deferred until the Napoleonic conquest of Spain and were not won until British sea power asserted itself, the American model was always present in the minds of revolutionary leaders. Such dynamic figures as the Venezuelan Francisco de Miranda and the Chilean José Miguel Carrera were deeply affected by the example of the United States. The former's service with the Spanish forces in Florida during the American Revolution inspired his efforts to reproduce the experience for his own country. Carrera dramatically chose July 4, 1812, to dedicate the symbols of Chilean independence. The American Bill of Rights, the state constitutions, and even Washington's Farewell Address were translated into Spanish and acclaimed in Latin America as goals of the liberation movements against the mother country.

The spectacle of the ferment among the Spanish colonies understandably stirred Americans. Even without expectations of material advantages from revolution, the imitation of the American example was a powerful form of flattery. It evoked sentiments as high flown as those expressed by Latin admirers. Among leaders succumbing to the attractions of revolution were Speaker of the House Henry Clay, whose presidential ambitions were linked to his embrace of the revolutionary cause. Although he was not unwilling to exploit a popular issue for his own advancement, his response to Latin American calls for assistance rings true: "We were their great example. Of us they constantly spoke as of brothers, having a similar origin. They adopted our principles, copied our institutions, and in some instances, employed the very language and sentiments of our revolutionary papers."[1] His rhetoric suggested that it would have been unnatural for Americans, of all people, not to offer full support to this fraternal revolution.

Given the enthusiasm of the American public, the recognition of five new Latin American nations in 1822, when no other power would grant recognition, could be interpreted as a logical corollary of hemispheric solidarity. Such is a traditional reading of the Monroe Doctrine, which not only supports Latin American independence but also speaks out in defense of the hemisphere's rejection of monarchical Europe. A new chapter in American history seemed ready to open in 1823.

To advance this relationship in the United States, a score of ship captains, commercial agents, and adventurers, such as William Shaler of Connecticut and Joel Poinsett of South Carolina, carried copies of the Constitution with them on mercantile ventures and saw in Latin American fraternity an opportunity of striking down the British as well as the Spanish enemy. At any event, a well-placed Anglophobe like Poinsett and an enterprising shipmaster like Shaler shared the excitement of participating in the building of a free world in the southern hemisphere. Their counterparts from Latin America, who moved in large numbers to Washington and Philadelphia after 1810 to enlist American aid and recognition, exulted over the response they encountered at the grass-roots level in the United States. The *Gazeta de Caracas* in August 1810 told its readers about the treatment accorded Venezuelan agents Juan Vicente Bolivar and Telefforo de Orea: "Although we have not received any official statement, we have the satisfaction of announcing to the public that English America is very much in agreement with the sentiments of the Venezuelans. Our memorable resolution has filled the sons of Washington and Franklin with enthusiasm, and the subjects of Ferdinand the VIIth in Caracas, have succeeded in having the illustrious and liberal people pray to heaven for a fortunate conclusion to their patriotic efforts."[2]

This ideological kinship was promoted among Americans for reasons other than a fraternal or even self-protective interest in striking a blow at the Old World. Economic advantages in the Caribbean and Latin America beckoned to American traders. The trade which had been fueled by Spain's periodic opening of its West Indian ports under the stress of war in Europe at the end of the century could be expanded indefinitely if independence was achieved. The facts seemed to support such expectations. American entrepreneurs such as Stephen Girard had already built a trade, licit and illicit, in the Caribbean, had moved as far as the west coast of Latin America before the revolution, and saw possibilities in Chile as an entrepôt for the China market. Between 1795 and 1810 commerce with the Spanish empire quadrupled. By 1808 it was one-fifth of the nation's total foreign trade.

With so many incentives for assistance linking the United States to the new republics, a hemispheric system, economic and political, of the order envisaged from time to time by Henry Clay, seemed realizable. Even if the official reaction to importunities of provisional governments was cautious, it did not preclude support along the lines of France's in the American Revolution. When Joel Poinsett was appointed consul general at Buenos Aires in 1811, Secretary of State Monroe observed: "The disposition shown by most of the Spanish provinces to separate from Europe and to erect themselves into independent States excites great interest here. As Inhabitants of the same Hemisphere, as Neighbors, the United States cannot be unfeeling Spectators of so important a moment. The destiny of those provinces must depend on themselves. Should such a revolution however take place, it cannot be doubted that our relation with them will be more intimate, and our friendship stronger than it can be while they are colonies of any European power."[3] While the tone of this communication hardly places the government in the role of an enthusiast, it might have opened the way for an active role in the liberation of the American continent.

If the United States did not emerge as the liberator of Latin America or even as the assistant of revolution in the manner of France a generation before, much of the credit—or blame—fell upon Secretary of State John Quincy Adams, whose influence governed American policy for a decade after 1817. His doubts and suspicions about Latin America extended from dislike of the Anglophilia of many of the new states to scorn for Clay's extravagant idea of a pan-American counterpoise to Europe. They were well summed up in his harsh judgment of the Latin revolutionaries: "As to an American system, we have it; we constitute the whole of it; there is no community of interests or of principles between North and South America. Mr. Torres and Bolivar and O'Higgins talk about an American system as much as the Abbé Corea, but there is no basis for such a system."[4] His recognition of Latin America would be forthcoming only when the governments of the area had proved their vitality, and his defense of their territories would only follow a genuine danger of invasion of the American continent.

Adams's views prevailed. Official assistance to the Latin American cause never materialized; recognition came over a dozen years after the revolution had begun; and a division between the Americas developed in the nineteenth century that ranged from mutual indifference to mutual hostility. How much of this record can be attributed to the power of Adams? How was he able to stem the tide of American sentiment, which appeared ready to extend a fraternal embrace to the new nations to the south?

The answers lie not in the personality of Adams, formidable though it was, but in the men and circumstances which governed Latin American relations from the stirrings of independence to formal recognition. Among them was the coincidence of the Latin American uprising of 1810 with the increasing entanglement of the United States in the same Napoleonic conflict which had bred revolution in the Spanish colonies. Such temptations as there were to give official blessings to the revolutionary cause were counteracted by the exigencies of war with England. And when that war ended in 1814, the reduced fortunes of the Latin rebels and the necessity of maintaining a minimal level of amicability with Spain combined to divert the Monroe administration until the acquisition of the Floridas had been secured in 1821. These practical deterrents to recognition were reinforced by doubts of many kinds which assailed even the best disposed of Americans. Some were disturbed about the reality of a revolution limited to wealthy aristocratic Creoles, others were concerned by the special favors consistently granted to Great Britain by the revolutionary governments, and still others questioned whether either commercial or ideological ties would result from new republican governments in Latin America.

To resolve these doubts and to quicken the pace of American support, American and Latin American agents of all sorts used their considerable energies and influence. Despite American vulnerability to the claims of revolutionary fraternity displayed by Clay and Monroe, the lobbyists failed to budge the government into overt support of the new states. Despite interest in Latin American economic opportunities, entrepreneurs such as Stephen Girard and John Jacob Astor failed to pursue them. What emerges from the propaganda and pressure are fundamental flaws in the arguments and the personalities of the lobbyists. Long before Adams presented his blocks against major aid, disillusionment had set in among Americans in Latin America and Latin Americans in the United States. If the Secretary of State succeeded in frustrating demands for recognition or alliance, he was able to exploit the underlying weaknesses among the agents on both sides, of which the most noticeable was the absence of a permanent community of interest.

The romance of the Latin revolution notwithstanding, its impact on the administrations of the United States was shaped from the beginning by advantage, not sentiment. Opportunity to be derived from Spain's troubles took two forms. One was the expansion of trade with the new republics willing to free American commerce from the restrictions of Spain's mercantilism. During its troubles in the 1790s, Spain had temporarily opened Caribbean ports to the United States, and the consuls it had permitted to reside at Santiago in Cuba and at La Guaira in Venezuela continued to operate illegally but successfully even after Spain had rescinded privileges to American shipping. Freed from Spain, the former colonies could open a new era in commercial relations. The second consideration inspiring American action was the ambiguous prospect of a revolution that might bring European monarchism down upon all the Americas or might alternatively leave areas of the Spanish Empire open to American acquisition. The former would have to be resisted with military force; the latter should be accepted as a happy fortune. As long as Louisiana or Florida or Cuba was the object of Spanish territorial expansion, the United States would not fail to display a lively concern for the fate of the Spanish Empire in America.

The case of the Venezuelan adventurer, Francisco de Miranda, is instructive not only because he was the first of many revolutionary figures to come before the American public but because his experiences — enormous initial private support from the highest public figures degenerating into failure and disavowal — were to be shared in the future by other hopeful supplicants in the United States. As early as the 1790s Miranda appeared in London and Philadelphia to intrigue Federalist leaders with his ambitions. The prospect of a free Latin America was all the more attractive to such men as Alexander Hamilton and Rufus King because the realization of this project would invoke a close military collaboration with Great Britain on the basis of Anglo-American equality. Hamilton dreamed of the personal glory and power to be gained from a war against Spain in the Americas. The wonder of Miranda's long campaign for American help is not that he failed for so long, but that his visions could appeal to a Paine and a Jefferson as well as to the Federalist Anglophiles.

The climax of Miranda's activities in the United States occurred under Republican auspices. Having failed for the moment with his British connections, he was in New York in 1805 at a time when Spain's relations with the United States were at a low ebb. Benjamin Rush, the Philadelphia physician and a leading Jeffersonian, gained an interview for him with Madison and a dinner engagement with Jefferson himself. The latter, in his customarily gracious way, extended his blessings to the cause of Spanish American freedom, regretting that he was born too soon to see the New World achieve its full measure of splendor. Madison was less elliptical in his comments, coupling permission for American citizens to assist the revolution with a barrier against direct governmental support that might compromise the position of the United States. American relations with Spain required, according to Madison, that "nothing would be done in the least inconsistent with that of a sincere and honorable regard to the rule imposed by their situation." Whether this conversation should be interpreted as the administration's "tacit approval" for Miranda's ventures, as the Venezuelan represented it to his British friends, is doubtful, but his reception helped him to secure vessels from New York merchant Samuel Ogden as well as an advance of 20,000 dollars for arming and provisioning three troopships.[5]

Despite the American ships and supplies and some clandestine help from the British navy, Miranda's Venezuela expedition ended in a fiasco in 1806. The American role did not go unnoticed by the angry Spanish minister to the United States. Spurred on by Spain's protests, the United States indicted Ogden for arming Miranda's ships, along with Colonel W. S. Smith, a customs official in New York and son-in-law of John Adams, on the charge of collusion. The administration's position was that Ogden and Smith had acted illegally without its knowledge in assisting the Miranda expedition. Madison disavowed Miranda's letter in which the Secretary of State was thanked for his good offices, which would be kept secret until the "delicate affair" was accomplished.[6] But Smith and Ogden protested that they had acted with the consent of the President and Secretary of State. In a strong memorial to the Congress, they claimed that federal officials not only knew of the plan but did nothing to stop the departure of the expeditionary force. Both men were acquitted, to the acclaim of most of the public and to the satisfaction of most newspapers. As for the administration's reaction, the President explained its role as delicately as he could: "To know as much of it as we could was our duty, but not to encourage it."[7]

As more successful revolutions unfolded after 1806, the official positons of Jefferson, and later of Madison, remained unchanged. They recognized popular interest in the insurrections, they saw opportunities for expanded trade, and they explored possibilities of territorial acquisitions in Cuba and Mexico; but they weighed these potential assets against the lack of preparation for self-government among the new juntas, the losses in antagonizing Spain, and the gains Britain or France, rather than the United States, might win from autonomous governments in Latin America. It was the latter concern that governed Jefferson's dispatch of General James Wilkinson to New Orleans in 1808 to talk with Cubans and Mexicans about America's unwillingness to have those territories fall into the hands of the two great European belligerents. Wilkinson urged American intervention to steal a march on Britain. While Jefferson was not prepared to extend recognition immediately, his Cabinet agreed in October 1808 to "sentiments which should be unauthoritatively expressed by our agents to influential persons in Cuba and Mexico, to wit, 'if you remain under the dominion of the kingdom and family of Spain, we are contented; but we should be extremely unwilling to see you pass under the dominion or ascendency of France or England. In the latter cases should you choose to declare independence, we cannot now commit ourselves by saying we would make common cause with you but must reserve ourselves to act according to the then existing circumstances.' "[8]

The ambivalence felt by Americans is obvious, as is their regret that Latin America was unable to sweep it away by succeeding in a clean break with all of Europe. But rather than a muddled or aborted revolution that would invite British or French intervention, the United States preferred to keep the status quo. If insurrection did come, the government would have no choice but to encourage it and seek profit from it discreetly. In all the deliberations of the cabinets of Jefferson and Madison, there was recognition that a formidable combination of merchants looking for new commercial outlets and libertarians envisaging republican fraternity would demand a strong anticolonial policy from the government. It is against this background that the United States in 1810, following the first major upheavals in Buenos Aires, Mexico, and Venezuela, appointed "agents for seamen and commerce" to those centers to serve as political observers and, even less officially, as adventurers and entrepreneurs in the thickets of Latin American revolutionary politics.

The line between official and unofficial American agents was always thin and sometimes invisible. Since the United States recognized neither Ferdinand's government in exile nor Bonaparte's monarchy, agents had considerable leeway in their handling of provisional governments which professed nominal allegiance to Ferdinand but in practice governed themselves. Their vague title, "agents for seamen and commerce," enhanced the informal character of the missions, since no Senate confirmation was necessary. Their functions included the gathering of intelligence.

It required no leap of imagination for a libertarian of Poinsett's disposition in Buenos Aires and Chile or a merchant navigator of William Shaler's interests in Cuba to place the broadest of interpretations upon their instructions. Most of the agents were republican zealots, like Poinsett, whose revolutionary passions had been stoked by residence in Europe, or merchants and ship captains, like Shaler, with a buccaneer's temperament and an eye to the advantages independence in Latin America might have for the shrewd investor. Poinsett had learned from experience to regard the United States as a "country which Liberty, leaving the nations of Europe to mourn her light in the gloom of despotism and corruption, has chosen as her favorite asylum."[9] Having found in Great Britain the enemy of America as well as the enemy of liberty, Poinsett's concern was less with the spread of American commerce than with the blocking of British imperialism in Latin America. He never lost his obsession with the issue. When he left Buenos Aires for Chile in 1811, he departed with the conviction that the concerted opposition of British merchants had frustrated the intentions of the governing junta to liberalize commercial arrangements for American shippers. His subsequent experiences in Chile reinforced his disillusionment with Latin revolutionaries.

But he never failed for lack of personal initiative. Indeed, Chile at first seemed to be an ideal place for American influence to work to mutual advantage. Poinsett took up the cause of the Carrera family and became a close friend of youthful José Miguel

Carrera, who rose to power under the spell of the American and French revolutions. As president of the junta in Valparaiso, Carrera turned to Poinsett for advice, drawing both on his knowledge of constitutions and on his official connections with sources of arms and munitions. The American consul, enjoying his intimacy with the new government's leader, went far beyond his instructions. He urged full independence, advised on suitable tariff legislation, offered a draft of a bill of rights, and finally joined the Chilean revolutionary forces as a participant in the battle against the royalist government in Peru. What better augury for close continental relations than in these acts of revolutionary cameraderie?

In the end, the excitement of combat and political involvement subsided into bitterness on all sides, raising doubts about the wisdom of Poinsett's particular militia diplomacy. His influence inevitably declined when his friend and client Carrera first split with his family and then was ousted from power and from the country in 1814. The triumphant factions of O'Higgins and San Martin as well as Spanish royalists identified Poinsett with the discredited Carreras and blamed the United States for the troubles of Chile. The winner in the confused struggle for power in Chile was Poinsett's bête noir, Great Britain.

In the future, Poinsett was not to keep his back turned fully against independence, but his guard was up; he remained suspicious of Latin ties with Britain, the Latins' lack of democratic experience, and their domination by an authoritarian Church. In one form or another, Americans encountering opposition or failure in their enterprise in South America would invoke memories of the "Black Legend," the brutal behavior of Spanish conquistadors of the sixteenth century, to explain the unfitness of their descendants in the nineteenth century.

Latin American agents who went north in search of money, men, and arms as well as official American recognition of their governments experienced equal disillusionment before they returned home. Most of them initially received such warm welcomes on triumphal marches to Washington that they were encouraged to expect much more than Madison or Monroe was prepared to give. Even a figure like José Bernardo Gutierrez de Lara, a Mexican bourgeois with very questionable credentials—

his junta chiefs were captured and executed within a week of his departure — was enchanted with the people he met as he traveled toward the capital in 1811. He appreciated, as did Miranda before him, the freedoms the people enjoyed, although he would not advocate them for the average man in his country. He was so touched by the public rejoicing in the insurgents' victory at Vera Cruz that he reported his impressions with hyperbolic effect:

> . . . I am delighted with the desire of everyone to see the insurgents win. They say that these are defending the most righteous (*justa*) cause that has ever been defended in all the ages. I have noted also the great desire which many of them have to go to Mexico, and many of them have put themselves to school to a teacher whom they have paid to teach them the Spanish language. I am of the opinion that if a free passage were given to these people, there would be more than a million inhabitants who would go in a short time. [10]

Inevitably, this euphoria dissipated when Gutierrez finally met officials and placed his requests. Monroe expressed a cool and tentative interest, which was hardly unreasonable in light of the envoy's vanishing constituency. Gutierrez at least had the consolation of having his travel expenses paid by the United States government. According to the Mexican agent, however, he was promised 10,000 muskets if a provisional government was formed, a generous offer if it was actually made. Lending the color of truth to the claim, however, are conditions attached to this generosity which all Mexicans would have found offensive.

Offers of American assistance to Mexico were clearly linked to an American annexation of Texas, or at least to an extensive revision of the Louisiana border. The most that Gutierrez would concede with respect to the Texas issue was creation of a neutral territory, presumably to be carved out of the Mexican claim, that would separate the two countries and obviate "the many discords which commonly result from the close contact of two powers." [11] A further clash between Mexican nationalism and American expansionism was averted by the unwillingness of the

United States in wartime to do more than talk about its interest in the territory.

Because of its absorption in other affairs, the Madison administration refused to give any assistance to Gutierrez's venture. The agent did better with the American private sector. In 1812 he was able to return to Mexico with 400 volunteers whom he had recruited openly and easily in New Orleans. Emboldened by this success, he made a proclamation of rebellion from American territory and set up a provisional government in Texas. Plots and counterplots, including those of American conspirators, soon pushed him out of his own "government" and doomed the whole revolutionary enterprise for a time. Before Gutierrez terminated his operations, he alienated most of his American friends and collaborators, including such influential men as William Shaler, the United States agent to Vera Cruz.

Most Latin American visitors had similar experiences to relate, and many of them indeed did relate them in books and pamphlets. The pattern usually entailed enormous initial optimism stemming from a warm American reception, then a cooling of relations as the caution of government officials became evident, and then suspicion and resentment if they left empty-handed or felt, as in the case of Mexico, that assistance from the administration would be only a prelude to American occupation. From private citizens, particularly businessmen and soldiers, responses were more positive. Guns, ammunition, volunteers, and money did find their way out of American ports to the various insurrectionary forces. But even here the aid was never massive, the strings frequently oppressive, and the prudence of the entrepreneur annoying or demeaning to the revolutionary cause. Such were the impressions brought back to Latin America by agents as diverse as Gutierrez, Aguirre of Buenos Aires, and Telefore de Orea of Colombia, each of whom between 1810 and 1822 spoke for governments in being or in the process of formation.

Of all the agents from Latin America, the most successful and persuasive as Manuel Torres, the first accredited minister from Latin America when recognition was granted. Torres had lived in the United States since 1796 and knew the ways of the country.

Like many other revolutionaries, he looked upon the American Revolution as his inspiration. Like other agents, he found friends in influential places. Where he differed was in his patience, persistence, and ability to flatter his adversaries, which won him a wide range of admirers. He even won the grudging respect of John Quincy Adams, who thought it fitting that this representative of Gran Colombia be granted the honor of inaugurating a new era in international relations in the Americas in 1822.

Torres was the exception. If his sensibilities were ruffled by American presumptions, indifference, or hostility, he managed to conceal his anger or recognized that assets outweighed debts in the American connection with revolution. Despite the official reserve reflected in two Neutrality Acts in 1817 and 1819, the United States government never placed any serious obstacles in the way of mounting filibusters or the shipment of men, munitions, and supplies. Even during the most delicate periods of Spanish-American relations, the South American delegates lobbied openly in Philadelphia and Washington. They had friends in high places who patronized and reproduced their arguments in the newspapers of a William Duane or the speeches of a Henry Clay.

When José Miguel Carrera arrived in the United States in 1816, an exile from Chile and an opponent of the insurrectionary regimes on both sides of the Andes, his cause was neither friendless nor hopeless. A close companion of both Poinsett and navy captain David Porter, he anticipated the recouping of his fortunes and his country's independence. Carrera's American connections paid almost immediate returns. Porter presented him to Madison and Monroe. He was patronized by the owner of the ship that took him to the United States, Henry Didier, a leading Baltimore merchant with a stake in the outfitting of privateers. Through Didier he met John Skinner, postmaster of Baltimore and dabbler in Latin American ventures, who made a personal loan of $4,000. When he returned to Latin America in November 1816, it was with two ships, paid for by Baltimore businessmen, which were scheduled for an invasion of Chile and filled with American recruits.

But Carrera was dissatisfied with American assistance. It could have been much greater. He accused Poinsett of timidity and implied disloyalty when no official recognition was given to his cause. Perhaps this petulance was a consequence of failure. By the time his expedition had reached Buenos Aires, he learned that San Martín had liberated Chile without him, and his enemy O'Higgins was in command of the country. Carrera's army joined the victors, and Carrera himself was left with frustration and imprisonment at the hands of the Argentines. He went to his death by execution in 1821 convinced that America could have done more.

But how much more for him, or for others? The unofficial aid offered Carrera by Baltimore entrepreneurs was made possible by official America's looking the other way. For a time Carrera attracted great merchants, such as John Jacob Astor and Stephen Girard, as well as men on the make. Astor's interest was a natural byproduct of his involvement in the fur trade of the Pacific Northwest and in the China market. Carrera carried with him to the United States letters to Astor from the merchant's commercial agent in Buenos Aires, David DeForest, aide of the revolution in that area. And Astor himself was indirectly involved in insurrections, whether or not he wished it. The mariner Richard Cleveland, a close friend and former partner of Shaler, had Astor's goods on board his ship when he stopped in Valparaiso in 1818, ostensibly to facilitate a shipment of wheat to Lima, but primarily to negotiate for an armed ship of the East India Company on behalf of the patriot government. This activity was fully known to the New York merchant prince through Cleveland's detailed correspondence. [12] If Astor did not pursue the channels, political and economic, which were afforded him in Latin America, it was largely because the debits of enterprise there appeared greater than the assets. His correspondents made it clear to him that the factional quarrels among revolutionaries, the excessive duties imposed by their regimes, and the omnipresent rivalry of Great Britain would combine to limit success of any venture.

Girard was even more explicit in his evaluation of opportunities in Latin America. The Philadelphia merchant was looking for new trading outlets after the Napoleonic conflict blocked his European markets. His commission house sent its super cargoes to Valparaiso and Canton instead of more familiar ports. Noting the meaning of this change, Venezuelan agents in 1810 approached him to serve as broker in obtaining help for their revolution. But he was cautious, requiring first that his service as a private citizen not be "unlawful or disagreeable to the President" and secondly that "the Government will facilitate me the means of obtaining said muskets &c, either by selling or lending them to me under such terms and conditions as will be judged reasonable."[13] Legality and propriety aside, Girard wanted guarantees from the State Department before making any commitment. When Monroe failed to respond to his questions, Girard dropped the matter completely. Since his republican sympathies were deeper than those of most of his peers, his unwillingness to continue negotiations with the Latin Americans may have derived from the advice of his own agents, such as the captain of the *Rousseau* who observed from Valparaiso that the revolution had caused "stagnation of business very prejudicial to your affairs for in such times as these it is dangerous giving credit and the scarcity of money is such that few sales can be effected without it."[14]

The evidence all suggests that the reluctance of merchants to invest seriously in South American revolutions was not the product of fear of Madison's or Monroe's disapproval. They shared many of the misgivings which disturbed the government and acted accordingly. But they wished the revolutions well and, like the government, did nothing to injure their prospects. There were other entrepreneurs, too, who expected profit from the revolution and entered into the game with zeal. Many of them were shipbuilders and privateers with headquarters in Baltimore who made fortunes out of the troubles of Spanish America. If they were ultimately curbed, it was only when their operations became too blatant and their privateering took a toll of American shipping as well as Spanish.

Unlike Astor and Girard, the Baltimore shipping magnates whose rise coincided with the fast "Baltimore Clipper" in the War of 1812 had no compunctions about using their influence in the Congress or in the administration to help their friends and partners in Latin America. Foremost among individual leaders was Skinner, the postmaster, his father-in-law Theodorick Bland, and Gen. William Winder. Their intimacy with Carrera and DeForest brought Baltimore close to Buenos Aires and Valparaiso after 1815. DeForest and Manuel Aguirre, both agents of La Plata, were as much the spokesmen of the "American Concern," Didier and Darcy, the most active privateering operation in Latin America, as they were of their provisional government for which they sought recognition in Washington.

The wrath of the Baltimoreans and the unhappiness of Latin Americans were particularly keen in 1817 and 1818 when the election of James Monroe, reputed to be sympathetic to revolution, led instead to neutrality laws and to the appointment of the unsympathetic John Quincy Adams as secretary of state. Under Adams's sponsorship, privateering was an object of government hostility, which moved lobbyists for business interests to mobilize sympathizers in the country and in Congress.

The opposition to Adams was formidable and by no means from Baltimore or privateering interests alone. Libertarians and Anglophobes could now find a more active response from a Congress freed from the burdens of war, as America's own increased pride in nationalism found a natural expression in the call for the independence of Latin America. The most sensitive note played, and one which could win attention from Adams as well as Monroe, was always the British threat.

One of the first blasts came from the pen of William D. Robinson in *A Cursory View of Spanish America*, published one month after the Battle of New Orleans had been won in 1815. Robinson was a veteran of filibusters along the Texas border who had been in as many scrapes with Mexican leaders as he had been with Spanish authorities. But his primary passions were directed against Great Britain. While recognition of independence was necessary to keep the mines of Mexico out of Spanish control, it was only because Britain controlled Spain. Robinson was convinced that Britain intended to use Mexico as a stepping-stone in the detachment of Louisiana from the United States. What it had failed to achieve by force of arms in open combat it would gain by temptations offered from its Mexican base. Robinson's proposed counteraction was simply American recognition of the new governments. "The *independence of this new world will alone arrest the ambition and influence of Great Britain.*—This event would give birth to a new and auspicious order of things not only over the Western Hemisphere, but throughout the whole world."[15]

The appeal of the Latin American revolution was not confined to paranoids or romantics. William Duane, the powerful editor of the Philadelphia *Aurora*, repeatedly underscored the economic benefits recognition would bring. In 1817 his journal publicized the important speech of Isaac Briggs, chairman of the House Committee of Commerce and Manufactures, on the necessity of a country embarking on a protective tariff to find markets in the Americas for cotton and woollen manufactures. In their emphasis upon the economy, both Duane and Henry Clay borrowed heavily from Manuel Torres's pamphlet, *An Exposition of the Commerce of Spanish America*, published in 1816, which employed circumspect flattery and an invitation to American self-interest to make its point. Observing that Spanish America annually consumed "the value of one hundred millions of dollars in articles of foreign manufacturing industry," Torres proposed that the United States be the country to sell these articles. Once Latin America has won freedom, "we cannot doubt that the spirit of enterprize, which has hitherto distinguished the American merchant in so remarkable a manner will be conspicuous in that part of the new world, under the aid and protection of the best of governments."[16] Torres's case, called by Clay a "valuable little work," gave the Kentuckian the facts and figures he needed to win over his audiences.[17]

Under the impact of emotions arising from so many sources during his first year in office, President Monroe felt the need to take some positive measure on behalf of the revolutionaries. "An instinctive apostle of the rights of man," as Samuel Flagg Bemis has called him, Monroe inclined toward recognition when he appointed a commission to report whether conditions in Latin America were suitable for recognizing any of the provisional governments.[18] Such a step might have been a prelude to a new relationship with Latin America that reflected the wishes of the Latin American agents, the Baltimore businessmen, and the congressional friends of the revolution. The fact that one of the three commissioners was Theodorick Bland gave substance to expectations of a major change in official policy.

Despite all the favorable portents, no change developed out of the commission's activity. It is tempting to ascribe its failure to the return of John Quincy Adams from London to take up his duties as secretary of state. Adams was not in Washington when the commission was conceived or when the commissioners were chosen, and his opposition to recognizing the United Provinces of La Plata or any other aspiring government was widely known. But if he checked the belligerent Clay and the complaisant Monroe, he did it with considerable assistance from men who ordinarily would have been the leaders in the revolutionary cause. In 1817 Joel Poinsett, who had been asked to join the mission, refused to accept the assignment out of disillusionment over his experiences in Chile and disappointment with the leadership of the revolutions. Bland, whose interest in going to Latin America, according to Adams, was solely to collect the 100 percent interest on his son-in-law's loan, divided the commission with a negative judgment on the question of recognition.[19] His friends were on the losing side of the factional strife in La Plata and Chile, and hence the change was unworthy of assistance.

Commissioner Bland's attack diluted the very favorable reports of Buenos Aires's revolution which Commissioner Caesar Rodney offered and which were fervently reiterated in the observations of Secretary Henry M. Brackenridge. While Bland foresaw no prospect for reconquest by Spain, he was certain that "unless present civil dissensions are healed, and the warring provinces are pacified and reconciled with each other, a very great proportion, if not all, the benefits and advantages of the revolution which would accrue immediately as well to themselves as to foreign nations, will be totally destroyed, or at least, very much diminished and delayed."[20] Rodney's distinction as former congressman from Delaware and attorney general under Jefferson and Madison did not counterbalance the strictures of Bland. In fact, Rodney's praise was so overblown that the third commissioner, John Graham, chief clerk of the Department of State, was moved to submit a separate report since he felt that Rodney had exaggerated his account of the stability of the Latin American regimes.

The disarray of the divided commission in the fall of 1818

further dampened American enthusiasm for the Latin American cause. The Latin American lobbyists were not content to wait for the results of the investigating commission. Spurred on by the Neutrality Act of 1817, which was aimed against arming privateers in American ports, they used the arrival of Manuel de Aguirre from Buenos Aires as the official representative of the United Provinces as an occasion for a test of Adams's power. Under the benevolent eyes of Clay, Aguirre rebuked the Secretary of State for the unfairness of the Neutrality Act and the hardship it created for the young states seeking freedom from the Old World. Secondly, he accused the United States of violating the territory of Latin America when it seized Amelia Island, a haven for smugglers and privateers between Georgia and Florida. And finally, he warned that if the government did not act to recognize the regime at Buenos Aires, and if it did not provide arms and ships for San Martin's campaign in Peru, the United Provinces would cut off trade with the United States. Perhaps Aguirre's stridency was the result of special frustrations over Acting Secretary of State Rush's disavowal of unauthorized agreements between American agents in Buenos Aires and the provisional government whereby loans had been assured to Aguirre for the purchase of arms and ships. Whether his temper was contrived or genuine, it was orchestrated in early 1818 with a congressional campaign to force the President to send to the House all correspondence with the revolutionary governments.

Aguirre went beyond the bounds of common sense as well as of propriety, and Adams cut him down to size. When the Secretary asked if his request for recognition developed from a new set of instructions, since his original instructions made no mention of it, Aguirre confessed that he was influenced by congressional suggestions to him on this subject. On Aguirre's threat to revoke the temporary privileges given to American commerce on the La Plata, Adams threatened to close the ports of the United States to his government. But it was over Amelia Island that Aguirre lost the sympathy of much of his American audience. Even when he admitted that Buenos Aires was not assuming a "superintendency" over all Spanish territories in the Americas, his protest invoked a question about the sovereignty of Florida, an issue which united all factions against Latin Americans as well as against Spaniards. [21]

Aguirre's retreat in the face of Adams's counterattack did not stop the momentum for recognition of the new republics developed by his friends in the Congress. Although Clay succeeded in having the documents connected with the occupation of Amelia Island opened to the inspection of the House, he failed in his major test of strength with Adams. He had expected that the administration's unpopular repression of privateering activities, combined with the Secretary of State's surliness toward Aguirre, would arouse Congress to force recognition upon Monroe, thus winning new prestige for himself. Clay's device to tap these sentiments was to attach an amendment to a bill defraying expenses for the Rodney commission which would appropriate 18,000 dollars as annual salary for a ministry and legation in the United Provinces of the Rio de la Plata. The Speaker employed all his great oratorical skills to force the administration into a backdoor acceptance of at least one of the revolutionary governments. He failed by a margin of 115 to 45 on March 28, 1818, and had to settle for an amendment to the Neutrality Act that deleted mention of vessels armed outside the limits of United States sovereignty. This concession was undone the next year in a new Neutrality Act that permitted American naval vessels to retake ships unlawfully seized on the high seas.

Even the charming Manuel Torres found his way blocked by the stubborn resistance of the United States government to pressures for official assistance to the provisional regimes. Despite his impressive connections, Torres was unable in 1819 to win the massive private aid he had counted upon from American investors. Bolivar's triumphs over Spain on behalf of the new Gran Colombia, as Venezuela and New Granada were now called, had to be weighed against the effects of the Panic of 1819 upon the American economy. In desperation, the agent turned again to the administration for surplus arms for Bolivar's army and won the votes of Secretary of War John C. Calhoun and Secretary of the Navy Smith Thompson. But once again Adams's negative prevailed. The Secretary of State had the last word: "To supply the arms professedly for the purpose set forth in the memorial of Torres would be a direct departure from neutrality, an act of absolute hostility to Spain."[22]

What stayed America's hand from 1817 to 1822? Concern for Spanish reaction was certainly one factor, as suggested above. The Spanish Minister Louis de Onis was convinced that the Latin American agents were in close collaboration with the Monroe administration, and he looked upon the Neutrality Act of 1817 as prejudicial to Spain's attempts to curb rebel spoliations of its commerce. In fact, Aguirre was jailed for four days for illegally outfitting ships, and the action which exposed his lack of diplomatic immunity was done in deference to the anger of Onis. As long as Florida was a subject of negotiations, the Secretary of State was unprepared to allow either pressure for recognition or blatant violations of neutrality to block the acquisition of the Floridas.

But it was not fear of Spanish power that moved Adams. He was not above using Spain's own fears to nudge negotiations along. The occupation of Amelia Island was not only an affront to Latin Americans; it was a warning to Spain that Florida itself could be as easily taken if the Spanish position remained obdurate. And after the treaties had been concluded, Adams successfully resisted the potential blackmail in Spain's attempts to link the matter of recognition of Buenos Aires with ratification of the cession of Florida. The United States refused to comply. The most that would be conceded was a statement that the United States "probably would not precipitately recognize the independence of the South Americans."[23] Before the end of 1820 Spain ratified the treaty, well aware of the success of Clay's relatively mild resolution of May 10th of that year in which the House had agreed to the outfitting of ministers for service in Latin America when the President, "by and with the advice and consent of the Senate," saw fit to send them.[24]

The possibility that the Old World might mobilize its power to force the rebellious states back into subordination to Spain represented another inhibition against recognition. In 1818, the same year in which Clay attempted to force the President's hand, the European powers met at Aix-la-Chapelle where the French delegate, the Duke de Richelieu, recommended a general plan of pacification to thwart American recognition of La Plata. The idea had originally been circulated by Pozzo di Borgia, the Russian ambassador to France, and was no secret from the United States. But it inspired no special caution in the Secretary of State, who advised Albert Gallatin, the American minister in Paris, to "take occasion, not by formal official communication, but verbally as the opportunity may present itself, to let the Duke de Richelieu understand that . . . we can neither accede to nor approve of any interference to restore any part of the Spanish supremacy of any of the South American provinces."[25] The threat of military counteraction notwithstanding, Adams was well aware that British coolness toward a European invasion had rendered the conference a failure before it had adjourned.

It was the British position that created the major distress for Adams. Not that its position was unclear or even hostile toward the ultimate aims of American foreign policy. The British gambit in this period went back to the Napoleonic period for its source. Castlereagh wanted preservation of a nominal Spanish sovereignty in the interest of monarchical legitimacy, and at the same time he intended to keep the fruits of a profitable trading relationship which had grown out of the revolution in Spanish America. Popular opinion and a ministerial sense of reality informed Britain of the impossibility of restoration. Richard Rush, the American minister in London, perceived the heart of British policy to lie in the aborted mediation proposal whereby Great Britain would assist in the return of the colonies if their ports would remain open to British ships. The nuances of the Cabinet position were clear enough for Adams to exploit Castlereagh's dilemma and deflate Clay's demands in 1819 by having Rush suggest Anglo-American cooperation in completing the emancipation of the Americas. Castlereagh politely declined the invitation, and Adams continued his resistance to the Congress.

Adams's concern about Britain, then, was not over a potential clash with the old enemy. It rested in the special relationship between the rebellious governments and Great Britain, and it took the forms of both ideology and commerce. The new republics seemed to Adams to lack the political framework, the popular infrastructure, or the historical traditions to make a democracy

that would have a political or philosophical kinship with the
United States. The provisional governments represented a
Creole elite, an aristocracy whose sympathies would incline them
to ties with France and Great Britain, even if they remained republics. The likelihood of their returning to monarchy seemed
reasonable when ideas of a Bourbon princeling's assumption of
control over La Plata were not dismissed as absurd by the
juntas. A genuine libertarian like Simon Bolivar, the liberator of
much of Latin America, was far more in tune with the society of
Great Britain than he was with that of the United States,
although he spoke with reverence of George Washington and
with appreciation of the American freedoms. Bolivar knew that
his people would not become North Americans and that they
needed a dictatorship to maintain the republic. While those
Latin American leaders and agents who looked to American
state constitutions, the Bill of Rights, or the Declaration of Independence for inspiration were men of talent and integrity, they
were not the men who completed the revolution. Furthermore,
their North American visits left them disaffected with the
United States—fearful of American imperialist ambitions,
doubtful of future trade relations, and resentful over the self-
interest which governed American attitudes. Adams recognized
all these symptoms in his analysis of relations with Latin
America.

As for commerce as a binding tie for the future, the subtle
propaganda of Torres or the blunt assertion of Duane that vast
fortunes were to be made in Guatamalan trade in indigo had to be
countered by the facts that trade with Latin America had been
declining over the years and the beneficiary replacing the United
States was Great Britain. The record of trade with the United
Provinces of Rio de la Plata tells the story: in 1825 United States
commerce there was valued at a little over one million dollars,
while Great Britain's approached 6 million dollars. For all of
Latin America, from 1808 to 1830 American commerce declined
from 30 million dollars to 20 million at a time when the British
trade climbed from 25 to 30 million. The United States appeared
as a competitor in the production of raw materials in many areas
of Latin America, Great Britain as a supplier of finished goods.
As Adams expressed it in 1822, "Do what we can, the commerce

of South America will be much more important to Great Britain than to us, . . . for the simple reason that she has the power of supplying their wants by her manufactures."[26]

In light of these realities, Adams intended to defer recognition of revolutionary governments until the time was ripe. When that time came in 1822, the United States was the first nation to recognize their independence, and both Adams and Poinsett gave the act their blessings. What made the time appropriate was that the Floridas had been secured and the revolution, after new victories by Bolivar and San Martin, seemed irreversible. With reasonable grace, although with continued wariness, the Secretary of State appeared to acquiesce in the triumph of Henry Clay. The latter had never accepted defeat in 1818. Each succeeding year, congressional resolutions were offered to no effect, until Monroe finally responded. In March 1822 a willing President called for recognition from the Congress and received it in the form of an appropriation of 100,000 dollars to defray the cost of diplomatic missions to Mexico, Gran Colombia, and the United Provinces of La Plata, Peru, and Chile. It was especially fitting that Manuel Torres was received as the first minister of the Latin American republics shortly before his death.

What should have resulted was the realization of Clay's dream of an American-led continental association as a counterpoise to European influence or, at least, a series of separate alliances with the United States along the lines of Torres's recommendations. The Monroe Doctrine which followed closely upon these acts a year and a half later symbolized the linking of the western hemisphere. Instead, the common destiny, whether political, economic, or ideological, turned out to be the illusion Adams always feared it was.

The record of American involvement with the revolution of Spanish America reveals that America contributed eager partisans, intrepid adventurers, speculating businessmen, and considerable quantities of arms and ammunition. Yet, the interests that divided the Americas were deeper than those that linked them. It may have been unfair for Great Britain to receive the credit for and benefits of revolution, but given the differences between Anglo-Americans and Latin Americans, their ultimate mutual indifference, if not hostility, should not have been surprising to leaders on both sides. It was not to John Quincy Adams or to Simon Bolivar.

The vital differences were also apparent to those who had most at stake in the future collaboration of the Americas: the propagandists and lobbyists, the agents and missionaries—both North and South American—who wanted to exploit the common revolution against the Old World to the advantage of their country or their faction or their private enterprises. The biases on both sides that emerged from the experiences each had in the other's society laid the groundwork for the mistrust that was to characterize future relations. For a brief time in the first quarter of the nineteenth century, circumstances permitted a commingling of the destinies of the Americas based on common sentiments. Although this harmony turned out to be fleeting and insubstantial, it remained the source of the rhetoric of a pan-Americanism that was to revive in the next century.

NOTES

1. James H. Hopkins *et al.*, eds., *The Papers of Henry Clay*, 2 vols. (Lexington, Kentucky: University of Kentucky Press, 1961), vol. 2, p. 520.

2. Quoted in José de Onis, *The United States as Seen by Spanish Writers* (New York: Hispanic Institute of the U.S., 1952), p. 24.

3. James Monroe to Joel R. Poinsett, April 30, 1811, in William R. Manning, ed., *Diplomatic Correspondence of the United States Concerning the Independence of the Latin-American Nations*, 3 vols. (New York: Oxford University Press, 1925), I, p. ii.

4. Charles Francis Adams, ed., *The Memoirs of John Quincy Adams*, 12 vols. (Philadelphia, Pa.: J. P. Lippincott and Co., 1874-1877), vol. 5, p. 176.

5. *Miranda's Diary*, in W. S. Robertson, *The Life of Miranda*, 2 vols. (Chapel Hill: University of North Carolina Press, 1929), vol. 1, p. 296.

6. Ibid., p. 300.

7. Ibid., p. 301.

8. Cabinet meeting, October 22, 1807, in *The Anas*, in Andrew A. Lipscomb and Albert E. Bergh, eds., *The Writings of Thomas Jefferson*, 20 vols. (Washington, D.C.: Thomas Jefferson Memorial Association, 1904), vol. 1, pp. 484-485.

9. Quoted in J. Fred Rippy, *Joel R. Poinsett, Versatile American* (Durham: Duke University Press, 1935), pp. 18-19.

10. "Diary of José Bernardo Gutierrez de Lara, 1811-1812," *American Historical Review* 34 (January 1929): 283.

11. Ibid., p. 72.

12. H.W.S. Cleveland, ed., *Voyages of a Merchant Mariner, Compiled from the Journals and Letters of Richard J. Cleveland* (New York: Harper and Bros., 1886), pp. 187-193.

13. Quoted in John B. McMaster, *The Life and Times of Stephen Girard, Mariner and Merchant*, 2 vols. (Philadelphia, Pa.: J. B. Lippincott and Co., 1918), vol. 2, p. 171.

14. Ibid., vol. 2, pp. 162-163.

15. William D. Robinson, *A Cursory View of Spanish America* (Georgetown, D.C.: Richards and Mallory, 1815), p. 20.

16. Manuel Torres, *An Exposition of the Commerce of Spanish America with Some Observations on Its Importance to the United States* (Philadelphia, Pa.: G. Palmer, 1816), pp. 11, 14.

17. Hopkins, *The Papers of Henry Clay*, vol. 2, p. 522.

18. Samuel Flagg Bemis, "Early Diplomatic Missions from Buenos Aires to the United States, 1811-24," in Bemis, ed., *American Foreign Policy and the Blessings of Liberty and Other Essays* (New Haven: Yale University Press, 1962), p. 344.

19. Samuel Flagg Bemis, *John Quincy Adams and the Foundations of American Foreign Policy* (New York: Alfred A. Knopf, 1949), p. 344.

20. Manning, *Diplomatic Correspondence of the United States*, vol. 1, pp. 433-434.

21. Adams, *Memoirs*, vol. 4, p. 45.

22. Ibid., vol. 5, p. 46.

23. Ibid., vol. 5, pp. 86, 94-95, 104 (May 1, 4, 1820). See Bemis, *John Quincy Adams*, p. 352.

24. *Annals of Congress*, 16 Cong., 1 Sess., 2228 (May 10, 1820).

25. Quoted in Samuel Flagg Bemis, "John Quincy Adams," in S. F. Bemis, ed., *American Secretaries of State and Their Diplomacy*, 10 vols. (New York: Pageant Book Company, 1958), vol. 4, p. 45.

26. Adams, *Memoirs*, vol. 6, pp. 24-25. See Bradford Perkins, *Castlereagh and Adams: England and the United States, 1812-1823* (Berkeley: University of California Press, 1964), p. 299.

CHAPTER FIVE

Missionaries, Merchants, and Diplomats in Mid-Nineteenth-Century China

The official relations of the United States with the Chinese Empire were defined in the middle years of the nineteenth century by three treaties, those of Wang-hsia in 1844 and Tientsin in 1858, and the Burlingame Treaty of 1868. The treaties, however, emerged from a welter of interests, attitudes, and conditions, both in China and America, which their terms barely suggest. In the shifting relationships between these cultural influences and interests and the men whose behavior they governed can be found the roots of America's century-old China policy and of much contemporary misunderstanding between two powerful nations.

Mixed motives characterized American involvement in China from the beginning. Samuel Shaw, the first American consul at Canton, was a merchant who held the office until his death in 1794 without compensation and, it must be added, with very few responsibilities. Shaw transmitted information on the state of trade in Chinese waters both to Secretary of the Treasury Alexander Hamilton and to his fellow merchants and business partners without apparent concern on any one's part that, at such a distance and in the early stages of their development, American public and private interests in Asia might not fully coincide. For more than half a century, until 1854, Shaw's successors in the consular office were usually merchants whose compensation consisted chiefly of incidental fees, the prestige of office, and, as Tyler Dennett has pointed out, "such information as to the business transactions of . . . competitors as would become available . . . because of access to official reports."[1]

The small American community in China was enlarged and diversified with the arrival of a number of Protestant missionaries in the 1830s. These clergymen, a zealous group some of whose members, in their eagerness to convert the Chinese, took the trouble, unlike the merchants, to study the language and culture of their would-be converts, were to play important roles in Chinese-American relations as translators and as officials for both governments. They also compiled Chinese dictionaries, translated religious literature, founded hospitals, and published and wrote for the *Chinese Repository*—for twenty years the most accurate source of information on Chinese affairs—and eventually founded schools and colleges which contributed importantly to the modernization of China. Although small in numbers in the 1830s, the missionary community was also influential in the United States where evangelical Christianity had swept into the American West and was already beginning to conceive of its mission of salvation in global terms. Missionary ideas about China and the Chinese were largely shaped by the religious commitment that sent them halfway around the globe to seek converts within the oldest and richest society of the East. This evangelical vanguard was to play an important part in shaping American ideas about Asia. Most of what Americans learned of China in the nineteenth century they learned through the writings and preaching of the missionaries.[2]

In time the American community in China came to exercise a significant influence, but at first it was outnumbered and outshone by the representatives of other Western nations. Europe, with the Napoleonic wars behind her, had launched into a new era of economic expansionism and imperial rivalry, driven by the powerful forces of industrialism. Having consolidated their position in India, the British in particular were pursuing new markets and territories on Asia's eastern rim. France and other European states were less aggressive, but the French had historic religious ties established and maintained by the Jesuits in China since the sixteenth century, while the Portuguese held

Macao as a legacy of earlier glories and a meeting place for ships and traders from all over the globe. From the North, the Russians pressed down to maintain and extend their influence. Amid these European ambitions and rivalries, the Americans' role was modest, but their hopes and expectations were nevertheless great.

As late as the 1850s the British supplied about half the foreign concerns engaged in the China trade, while Indian traders under British domination added another 25 percent to the total. The number of American mercantile houses was much smaller, roughly equal to that contributed by all of the other Europeans together. Yet American ships were carrying almost a third of the foreign trade, and the proportion rose to half at Shanghai, which was by then becoming the most important Chinese port. American trade with China, relatively static in the 1840s, more than doubled in the following decade.[3]

American merchants had acquired a stake in China which they did not hesitate to advance in Washington when they felt the need. Cotton and cotton goods provided a growing source of legal commerce, and there was a flourishing trade in opium both before and after the Chinese government attempted to ban it in the late 1830s. Missionaries might have qualms about the opium trade, but Chinese profiteers cooperated in it actively or passively with the Western merchants. The American government deplored the trade officially but was powerless to block it. American mercantile interests were content with the status quo; they were accustomed to accepting Chinese regulation—generally ineffectual, if occasionally irksome—as a condition of doing business. Briefly uneasy that the British might gain an advantage by military force during the Opium Wars of 1830 to 1842, they asked Washington in 1839 to negotiate a treaty on their behalf, but when it became clear that the concessions granted in the Anglo-Chinese Treaty of Nanking would be extended by the Chinese government to all Western nations, the Americans were content to leave well enough alone.[4]

Merchant complacency, however, was matched by missionary restiveness. The Chinese could understand and tolerate Western commercial objectives, but no concessions had been made for foreign missionaries, especially evangelical Protestant mission-

aries blind to Chinese traditions and seeking converts to an up-
start religion. To enter China at all, British and American missionaries had often to disguise themselves as clerks or translators in mercantile houses. While their numbers remained small,
this arrangement was tolerable. Some American merchants,
faithful Christians themselves, had welcomed and supported
missionary endeavors. D.W.C. Olyphant of New York, in particular, had subsidized the work of the American Board of Commissioners for Foreign Missions and its printing office in Macao.
Most merchants were perhaps not so pious as Olyphant, but relations between the two groups had been necessarily intimate, if
not always cordial, at the outset. The abilities and ambitions of
the missionaries had outstripped this dependent relationship by
the late 1830s. Businessmen might prosper under mild Chinese
restrictions, but the word of God could not be preached nor converts won without official recognition and sanction. Freedom to
hold religious services in their own churches rather than in the
merchants' drawing rooms or warehouses, the right to operate
freely in the Chinese cities and countryside, guarantees of
security for the persons and property of Christians—all these
seemed essential conditions to those who were staking their lives
and careers on the drive to win China for Christ. The missionaries did not hesitate to let their needs and wishes be known in
Washington.[5]

Akira Iriye makes an important point, however, in arguing
that American policy toward China, as well as American images
of China and its future, were not primarily the result of such
pressures, influential though their sources might be. Rather,
they reflected a self-image of America and its destiny widely
shared by political leaders, intellectuals, and the American public at large, including the clergy, few of whom had seen Asia and
whose primary concerns lay elsewhere. If America, as was widely
believed, was young, dynamic, democratic—in the vanguard of a
new era of historical progress—China was the opposite in all respects. And if America's mission was to symbolize and carry the
benefits of the new civilization around the world, then its role and
responsibilities in China were already defined. American resources, ingenuity, and virtue would eventually combine,
despite present disadvantages, to overcome all obstacles.[6] Such

cultural assumptions and preconceptions were an invisible but nonetheless important item in the intellectual luggage carried to China by merchants, missionaries, and diplomats alike. They held an implicit blueprint for China's future which was shared with Americans at home and which guided and sustained them abroad more firmly than official directives, policy statements, or pressure-group influences could ever have done. The British brought to China an imperial practice which placed political-military power firmly behind their mercantile interests. But although the Americans expected and received little direct help from their government in similar circumstances, their aims were at least equally ambitious. Neither European nor American designs, whether material or religious in nature, held much hope for the peaceful survival of the old order in China.

The arrival early in 1844 of Caleb Cushing, the first commissioner of the United States to the Chinese Empire, marked the beginning of continuous formal relations between the two countries. Cushing's mercantile and political connections equipped him well for the task. His instructions from Secretary of State Daniel Webster charged him to secure for American merchants benefits comparable to those recently won by the British in the Treaty of Nanking, especially equal access for American ships and traders to the five ports now open to western trade. Ironically, as historians have pointed out, this objective had already been granted by the Chinese themselves under the principle of equal treatment for all foreign nations. The Tyler administration had its own political reasons, however, for wishing to match any apparent British initiative, so the treaty negotiations went forward.[7] With the merchants satisfied, Cushing was especially sensitive to the wishes of the missionaries. Dr. Peter Parker, a clergyman whose Opthalmic Hospital in Canton had won him the respect of Chinese officials, had pressed for the Cushing mission on a recent visit to the United States. Together with another influential clergyman, Reverend E. C. Bridgeman, Parker joined Cushing's staff and served as chief negotiator. Still another missionary, S. Wells Williams, a scholar and publisher of the *Chinese Repository*, served as a translator for Cushing in the preparatory phase of his mission.

Of all the Americans who lived in nineteenth-century China,

Williams's career was the longest and, at least in some respects, the most intriguing and revealing. In addition to his services to Cushing, he acted as chief negotiator of the subsequent Treaty of Tientsin in 1858; ten years later, when the Burlingame Treaty was signed, Williams was secretary of the American Legation in Peking. His service thus spanned the major negotiations defining Chinese-American relations during a crucial period. In his missionary capacity Williams was also unusual. A scholar, rather than a clergyman, he brought an intellectual curiosity and a breadth of interest to his work which was rare among his colleagues. Many Protestant missionaries in mid-nineteenth-century China were men of limited education and imagination. Zeal, rather than sympathy, colored their approach to the Chinese. Dedicated evangelists, their appeal was to the emotions over the mind; with few exceptions they understood little and cared less for Chinese culture. Relying more on energy than sensitivity to attain their goal, they alienated the educated Chinese without winning the masses. Only slowly, in the course of more than half a century, did Protestantism begin to establish a limited base among the Chinese people. And the views of China that missionaries carried homeward did much to reinforce assumptions and prejudices already prevailing in the United States. While S. Wells Williams shared the zealous sense of superiority which motivated his fellow missionaries, he was too curious and sensitive to be entirely dominated by it. His continuous, if restricted, struggle to move beyond his own religious and cultural horizons offers revealing evidence of their power to hamper understanding between peoples. A closer look at Williams's career and ideas, therefore, may help to clarify the issues underlying a formative period in Chinese-American relations and the cultural chasm that made understanding between two proud peoples extremely difficult to achieve.[8]

The insensitivity displayed by most Westerners toward the Chinese people and civilization was matched by the ignorance and pride with which Chinese officialdom faced the intruders and their seemingly incessant demands. Traditional Chinese assumptions of cultural superiority, as well as past experience in dealing with foreign "barbarians," proved less than helpful in guiding relations with a new wave of invaders who came from

distant lands, spoke of unfamiliar gods, were devoted to the advancement of lowly mercantile pursuits, and held military-tech-
nological advantages enabling them to exact their demands at
every key point. Confused as to the scope of Western intentions
and ignorant of the forms of Western diplomacy, the Chinese
mandarins and courtiers charged with "barbarian management"
were still intelligent men. They understood Western objectives
initially as focussing almost exclusively on trade, but they soon
discerned differences between the foreign nationals with whom
they had to contend, even if their explanations for the differences
were sometimes inadequate. The dispatches which the Chinese
commissioners at Canton sent back to the Imperial court at Peking bristled with references to the "inscrutability" of the barbarians, but, as with similar references by Western writers then
and since, what this really meant was that the Westerners did
not conform to Chinese cultural patterns or expectations and
that the Chinese had not managed — or, perhaps, even tried — to
penetrate the core of values and assumptions which inspired the
unfamiliar behavior. Cultural confrontation and misunderstanding, indeed, underlay the entire range of economic, religious, and
political issues over which Chinese and American representatives debated. If this fundamental fact of Chinese-American relations is more obvious today than it was earlier, it was no less true
then than now.

From the outset, the Chinese saw a distinction between the
British and the Americans which they interpreted, however, in
different ways at different times. The former, advance agents of
a self-confident empire, treated Asians as colonials and backed
their demands with military force. The latter, perhaps decep-
tively easygoing and informal, relied on private initiative and
persuasion. If fear heightened Chinese hostility toward the
British, the Americans' relative weakness made them appear
less dangerous, possibly more friendly, and often more contemptible. Chi-ying, the Imperial commissioner who received
Caleb Cushing at Wang-hsia, thought of the United States as the
"most uncivilized and remote" of the Western nations. Later,
another Chinese official noted that the Americans usually followed in Great Britain's wake and exploited the advantages first
won by others, concluding that they were therefore "not in the

least worthy of our concern." On occasion, however, the Chinese were tempted to try to exploit American pliability to promote moderation or division within Western councils. Such efforts had little success, however, and the more cynical or realistic Chinese leaders came to see little hope in this tactic. American power and influence were too feeble to weigh effectively with the British, while the Americans' zeal in pursuit of their own interests was such as to offer little hope for restraint.[9] By 1844, although they might continue to speak in the language of superiority, Chinese diplomats—if not necessarily the court circle at Peking—were beginning to recognize the ability of the West to enforce its will in a test of power. They were prepared to use any tactics to avoid or postpone such a test—appeasement, delay, and concessions. Caleb Cushing, the trade concessions which constituted the initial objective of his mission already won before negotiations began, was received with courtesy and further concessions when he reached Wang-hsia.

The Treaty of Wang-hsia, in addition to formalizing the right of access by Americans to the five treaty ports, eased requirements governing the landing and reshipping of cargoes as well as the payment of duties. These gains were quickly extended to the other Western merchants under the Chinese equal treatment, or "most favored nation," policy. A more fundamental issue, perhaps the most basic raised by the treaty, involved the principle of extraterritoriality, which permitted foreigners to be tried and punished for crimes by their own rather than by Chinese authorities. Around this issue swirled many of the underlying assumptions of Western superiority that have long dogged Chinese-American relations. American merchants had willingly acknowledged Chinese authority even though they had suffered periodically from harsh or inequitable treatment; the benefits of trade, in their view, outweighed the occasional inconveniences. Yet the British and the Portuguese had won an exemption from the vagaries of Chinese justice, in part by securing exclusive jurisdiction over the colonies at Hongkong and Macao. American ideology and weakness together blocked the acquisition of such colonial enclaves, but as a politician, Cushing recognized that a treaty which did not accord the Americans equal status with that enjoyed by European nations would hardly be acceptable at

home. Extraterritoriality offered a neat resolution of this problem. Cushing justified it further by appeal to traditional practice
in Western relations with Muslim and other non-Christian states
whose level of "civilization" and responsibility were deemed
inferior.

The full implications of extraterritoriality as a cultural issue
become even clearer when considered from the viewpoint of Chinese sovereignty. The Chinese granted extraterritoriality reluctantly in response to Cushing's appeal for equal treatment. Both
they and the Americans emphasized that the United States had
pressed no territorial claims and had, indeed, acknowledged Chinese sovereignty and integrity. Yet extraterritoriality, in effect,
negated such statements. As China gradually opened not only
its ports and rivers but its inland cities and countryside to foreign penetration, extraterritoriality meant that wherever Americans or other foreigners went, they carried with them immunity
from Chinese authority and justice. Few arrangements could
have been more expressive of contempt for China. [10]

The modest claims and gains of the American mercantile community at Wang-hsia contrast sharply with those which reflected
American religious and ideological concerns. It is clear that the
missionaries saw in extraterritoriality a guarantee of protection
against interference with their efforts to spread the Gospel. The
assumption of cultural superiority behind the demand for extraterritoriality was deeply rooted, as Cushing himself made clear,
in the Christian world view. The influence of the missionary community, which had staffed Cushing's mission, was further reflected in other treaty provisions. These included permission to
employ Chinese teachers and to buy Chinese books, resources
essential to their Christianizing purpose. The right to acquire
property for churches, cemeteries, and hospitals was also
granted, laying the foundations for the establishment of permanent Christian communities. To the missionaries' chagrin,
religious toleration was not itself formally granted but it was
clearly implied. The principle of toleration was accepted in the
Chinese-French treaty signed soon after Cushing's negotiations
and was extended to other nationalities on the equal treatment
basis. Thus, the way was cleared for an expanded effort by

American Protestantism in the five treaty ports now open to the West. [11]

On one issue, the right to be received at the Imperial court in Peking and to maintain an American minister there, the Chinese held firm. Their custom prescribed that foreign barbarians might, under special circumstances, approach the Celestial Throne bearing tribute or petitioning for favors, but permanent residence by the representative of another nation implied an unthinkable equality. Of all the Western powers only Russia had, since 1728, been permitted such representation. The pretensions of Chinese superiority and exclusivity implicit in this ban rankled Westerners, smugly confident of their own preeminence. They also concealed from Chinese ruling circles the full measure of the disadvantages under which they labored. Peking served as both a symbol and a tool to the West. To preserve its isolation, the Chinese would concede much in the way of trade and other benefits valued by Westerners. Yet until Peking was opened, the West could not gain the recognition or scope its ambitions and power demanded. Given their differing perspectives, what the Chinese held dearest the Americans found most expendable, at least temporarily. Caleb Cushing readily waived his claim to be received at the imperial capital in exchange for more immediate advantages, but his successors would renew the claim and press it until it was granted.

The Treaty of Wang-hsia established regular diplomatic relations between the United States and China and a framework within which Americans could pursue their several interests with greater freedom. Cushing and succeeding U.S. commissioners to China tended to sympathize with the Chinese government in its struggle for self-preservation. Hostility to British pride and power was, after all, deeply ingrained in American attitudes, and China's position as the most recent victim of British aggression touched this sensitive nerve. Yet American anxiety not to be bested by Britain outweighed more generous sentiments, leaving little but hollow gestures of support for Chinese self-determination. American diplomats struggled to find a basis for reconciling the preservation of China's government and territory with the insistent demands and pressures from their own and other Western interest groups. Chinese incapacity, British power, and their own lack of experience and influence rendered this an essentially hopeless task. Cushing's treaty symbolized and embodied American ambivalence in its combination of professed respect to Chinese sovereignty with provisions which actually opened the doors for steady erosion of that sovereignty.[12]

In the decade after Wang-hsia, American interests in China expanded unevenly. Trade flourished in the heyday of the clipper ships, with cotton and opium as the chief sources of mercantile prosperity. Meanwhile, problems closer to home preempted the attention of the American government, leaving wide scope for private initiative overseas. Consular offices continued to be filled by untrained, ill-paid merchants or missionaries who were incapable of pursuing a consistent policy. When Congress failed to adopt President Tyler's proposal to establish consular courts, Americans protected by extraterritoriality in China were assured until 1848 of virtual immunity from prosecution for wrongdoing. Tyler Dennett's comparison of conditions in the treaty ports with those of an undeveloped frontier settlement is an apt reminder that American expansionism in China was grounded in many of the same impulses that propelled the restless transcontinental movement at home.[13]

For the moment, American merchants and officials might be contented or indifferent under these conditions, but the missionary community could not share their complacency. Recognition at Wang-hsia had encouraged a growth in missionary numbers, and their influence was greatly enhanced by their services to the American government, especially those of the Rev. Peter Parker, who was appointed secretary of the American legation in 1844. Missionary objectives were considerably more ambitious than those of their business or governmental colleagues. They aspired to nothing less than the total conversion of the largest and most ancient of nations to the Christian Gospel. Each gain, however significant, could therefore only heighten awareness of how much remained undone. In point of fact, the gains were remarkably slight in proportion to the energies expended. Actual conversions were few and the motives behind them sometimes questionable; the term *rice Christians* suggested that bodily as much as spiritual hunger was often involved in the winning of converts.

As one missionary noted, Christianity posed a fundamental threat to many of the strongest traditions of Chinese culture. It demands "so complete a surrender to all that belonged to his education, his theory of government, and society, his views of nature, his ancestral worship, his domestic relations, and his modes of life, that it is a wonder that a convert is made." Few were so perceptive, however; what weighed overwhelmingly on missionaries' minds and spirits was the obligation to bring backward heathen to Christ. Insensitivity was reinforced by reaction to the antiforeignism that swept Chinese cities in the wake of the defeats and losses of territory imposed by Western power. As part and parcel of the expansionist thrust, missionaries could not have divorced themselves from the antagonisms it aroused even if it had occurred to them to make the attempt.[14] The missionary community, of course, contained many types. Although Dr. Peter Parker's medical skills had initially won favor with Chinese leaders, his increasingly hostile, aggressive policies as a diplomat aroused their suspicions. Even worse was the notorious evangelist, I. J. Roberts, described by one of his contemporaries as "intolerant and bigoted to the Baptist dogmas, irritable, peevish, inconsistent, and vacillating—a man singularly illiterate, without stability of character or pleasantness of manner." Roberts conducted his mission in a flagrantly insulting manner, bribing the poor to attend his services. When his actions provoked Chinese retaliation, Roberts filed excessive claims for compensation. Contrary examples can be cited, however, of missionaries whose genuine interest in the Chinese inspired constructive efforts on their behalf. Men such as W.A.P Martin and D. B. McCartee eventually won the respect of the Chinese and were invited to serve as teachers and advisors. Moved by a broader sense of Christian brotherhood and touched, perhaps, by a Calvinist awareness of their own limitations as agents of the God in whom they devoutly believed, they achieved a sense of common humanity with the Chinese people which enabled them to make lasting, if limited, contributions.[15]

Among this small group of dedicated missionaries was S. Wells Williams, whose ties with the religious, governmental, and mercantile communities in China were bringing him into a more prominent, if still unofficial, position by the early 1850s. In addition to his language studies, Williams had long gathered data on trade and shipping conditions which he published for the benefit of the merchants. His curiosity and interest in Chinese geography, history, and culture led him to collect a wide range of materials to be used as the basis for lectures on the Chinese and their civilization during a visit to the United States in 1844-1845. The lectures were published in book form as *The Middle Kingdom: A Survey of the Geography, Government, Literature, Social Life, Arts and History of the Chinese Empire* in 1847. Williams recognized the need for fuller understanding and appreciation of China by his fellow Americans. He wanted to counteract "that peculiar and almost indefinable impression of ridicule" which he found many Americans applied to the Chinese "as if they were the apes of Europe and their social state, arts and government the burlesque of the same things in Christendom." Although Williams's initial responses to China had followed the stock patterns of assumed Western superiority to a backward, pagan society, his intellectual curiosity had been aroused by the achievements and culture of the Chinese. Frequently exasperated or depressed by Chinese failures to cope with the challenges facing them, Williams never entirely gave up hope in their ultimate capacity to attain, with God's help, a position of equality with the West.[16]

For all his insight and sympathy, Williams remained at heart a Westerner and a militant Christian. He could deplore on occasion the rude and grasping outlook of other Americans, especially the merchants. His honesty forced him to fear that China might learn "an even worse style of depravity" from the example of the West; he was convinced, however inconsistently, that only Christianity could save the Chinese "from the destruction . . . this [Western] pseudo-civilization . . . is bringing upon them." Toward the end of his long career, Williams offered perhaps his most balanced evaluation of the society in which he had spent his life. China, he wrote, had "risen as high as it is possible in the two great objects of human government—security of life and property to the governed, and freedom of action under the individual restraints of law." Yet the Chinese lacked, in his view, the essential capacity for "truthfulness," honesty, and responsibility in their dealings with others, Without these virtues, which only Christianity could instill, they could not "organize and cooperate effectively for improvement"; only missionary work could furnish "sufficient stimulus to improve a man's social conditions, by giving him adequate reasons for changing his life and religion." [17]

Conditions in China in the 1850s were such as to try the patience and understanding of the most sympathetic Westerners. For more than a decade, the already shaky authority of the imperial government was dangerously threatened by the Taiping Rebellion. Its leader, Hung Hsiu-ch'uan, was a self-baptized Christian who had associated briefly with the notorious Rev. I. J. Roberts in Canton. By 1850 Hung's movement had reached threatening proportions. Ineffectively opposed by the Peking government, Hung's forces had, by 1853, seized Nanking where Hung established his capital and announced a new dynasty with himself as emperor. At the outset, the Taiping movement had appeared promising to many Westerners, the Protestant missionaries most of all. It was strongly hostile to the traditional Chinese religions and it had a marked Christian orientation. More than this, the breakdown of the old regime which had so staunchly resisted Christian encroachments offered hope that at last the basis for a full-scale missionary endeavor might be in the making.

But there were uncertainties that restrained and, in the end, prevented the West from wholeheartedly supporting the Taipings or even taking full advantage of the confusion and weakness the rebellion exposed. Catholics found the movement too Protestant. Protestant missionaries, on the other hand, were themselves uncertain about the depth of its commitment to Christianity since the new religion retained many traditional Chinese features and customs. Since few missionaries were prepared to compromise on matters they held essential to the practice of the true religion, there was ample room for doubt as to the genuineness of the Taipings' conversion. Only total acceptance of Christian doctrine and practice in every detail could satisfy the eager evangelists; indeed, controversy has continued to flicker over the question of whether the Taiping Rebellion represented a missed opportunity for the West to ally itself with an indigenous yet potentially sympathetic movement for the reform and reconstruction of Chinese society. [18]

The disruption of China by the Taiping Rebellion posed touchy problems for America's diplomats. Fearing that further dismemberment of Chinese territory and authority might benefit the European powers more than the relatively weak United States, in the 1850s a succession of American commissioners ended by officially supporting the imperial government. In the course of the decade, however, they had wavered between several alternative positions. Some missionaries had urged support for the Taipings, hoping to secure from them concessions denied by the Emperor. Yet neutrality between the contending factions had offered the possibility of winning concessions from each. Finally, however, disillusionment with the Taipings' religious eclecticism and political ineptitude pointed to the desirability of upholding the old regime. Such a policy would minimize the danger of European intervention and assure Americans of a reasonably equal position in the international competition; it could command some degree of gratitude and recognition by the Peking government while at the same time it would not seriously block Americans from taking advantage of the general confusion.

As Dennett and Tong have argued, the policy evolved by American diplomats in China during this period contained the essential elements of the Open Door policy enunciated by Secretary of State John Hay half a century later. It upheld the territorial integrity of China against foreign encroachment while securing equal commercial privileges for all Westerners. It coupled gestures of sympathy for the plight of the Chinese with official support for the private interests and objectives of Americans in China. It balanced an officially noninterventionist stance on the part of a weak and distracted American government with the aggressively expansionist aims of American merchants and missionaries. [19]

These interests and aims, by the 1850s, were ranging beyond the coasts of China alone across the entire Pacific region. The annexation and settlement of California by the United States had extended the horizons and ambitions of many groups. The advent of steam navigation brought Asia closer to the Americas at the same time that it heightened the importance of assured access to harbors and coaling stations. On the map of the far Pacific, the islands of Japan attracted particular attention by reason of their strategic proximity to the mainland as well as the mysterious isolation from contact with the West which their government had for centuries jealously preserved. The Japanese had avoided the infiltration and disruption of their empire that so complicated the problems of China, but they had simultaneously whetted Western interest and curiosity. Sooner or later Japan, too, was bound to confront a determined approach by the Western nations. Geography, and their relative lack of other overseas commitments, largely determined that it would be the Americans who undertook the opening thrust. Commodore Matthew Perry's mission to Japan in 1853 and 1854 was ostensibly intended to secure protection for American sailors who from time to time were stranded along the Japanese coast and to negotiate the right of American ships to purchase coal at Japanese ports. In fact, however, it opened the second major phase of American penetration into the rim of Asia. [20]

S. Wells Williams, who had first visited Japan on a merchant vessel in 1837, was in many ways a logical choice to accompany Perry in the capacity of interpreter. Williams's interest had been aroused by the strength and self-confidence of the Japanese, in sharp contrast to China's feebleness and pretentions. He had immediately set to work to learn the Japanese language, anticipating the day when another promising missionary field would be opened. Thus, Williams was one of very few Americans with Japanese as well as Chinese experience. Accounts of his role in the Perry expedition vary considerably. Samuel Eliot Morison, Perry's biographer, believes Williams was more useful as an amateur botanist collecting interesting items of the Japanese flora than as an interpreter. Williams's religious scruples were evidently somewhat ruffled by the bluff, tough ways of the navy; he was unhappy at the absence of religious services aboard Perry's flagship, the *Powhatan*, and he questioned the Commodore's forceful, domineering approach. Yet evidently a degree of respect did develop between the two men. Williams is credited by Dennett with responsibility for the absence of an extraterritoriality clause in the Japanese treaty, although he himself made no such specific claim. Williams did believe, however, that he had moderated Perry's treatment of the Japanese. He was obviously impressed by Japanese society and by the opportunity to bring this hitherto isolated people into the community of Christian nations. At the same time, sensitive to what nominal Christians were doing to China's ancient civilization, he had qualms about Japan's future in this regard. Behind Perry's official objectives, Williams feared, the real reasons for the mission included the "glorification of the Yankee nation, and food for praising our-selves." Despite these selfish aims, however, Williams believed "that the seclusion policy . . . is not according to God's plan of mercy for these peoples, and their governments must change them through fear or force, that all people may be free. Korea, China, Lewchew (the Ryukyus) and Japan must admit the only living and true God, and their walls of seclusion must be removed by us." Yet he was less confident of short-run developments, for on the day that Perry's treaty was signed, he wrote a rather doubtful prayer that "they may never have occasion to repent of the privileges ceded on this day."[21]

Williams's assignment with Perry marked the beginning of his career as a public servant; soon after his return to China he ac-cepted an appointment as secretary of the American legation, succeeding Peter Parker, now promoted to the commissioner's post. After twenty-one years of life and study in China, Williams was well prepared for his new responsibilities, although he ac-cepted them only after having been assured by Perry that they were not inconsistent with his continuing missionary interests. As with the earlier merchant-consuls, the appearance of a new group of missionary-diplomats was indicative of the degree to which American policy in China remained under the influence of private interests and objectives.

Peter Parker's career as secretary of the legation and its chargé d'affaires had displayed an increasingly harsh, unsym-pathetic impatience with Chinese incompetence and resistance to Western demands. Now, reversing the policy of his predeces-sors, Parker entered into close cooperation with the British and French to force further concessions from reluctant China. He proposed a joint military expedition to Peking to demand the re-negotiation of treaty rights, and he further suggested that if

Western terms were not accepted, the French should seize Korea, the British, Chusan, and the Americans, Formosa, as hostages for Chinese acquiescence. Parker, in association with some ambitious merchants, was evidently prepared to go even further in the direction of a project for permanent American occupation of Formosa. His aggressiveness was curbed, however, by the Buchanan administration, which recognized the military commitments involved and which was, in any case, too deeply embroiled at home to consider a more active policy in China.[22]

How S. Wells Williams felt about Parker's approach to the Chinese we do not know, although we can surmise that he would have favored a more cautious policy. Yet the growth of his sympathy and respect for China had not been without its setbacks. Returning to Canton in 1848 after a trip to the United States, Williams had acknowledged, "It is much easier loving the souls of the heathen in the abstract in America than it is here in the concrete, encompassed as they are with such dirty bodies, speaking forth their foul language and vile natures, and exhibiting every evidence of their depravity." China, he found, was a "valley of dry bones" where everything was needed—hospitals and schools, as well as missions. Yet his bitterness was moderated by his editorial and scholarly interests, which regularly reminded him of the glories as well as the shortcomings of Chinese civilization. Like other Americans, Williams reacted with impatience to the combination of snobbery and ignorance with which China confronted the forces of modernization. He shared the frustration of equally dedicated, if less sympathetic, missionaries whose confidence in their mission was matched, only by the reluctance of the Chinese masses to respond to it. Briefly, in the early 1850s, Williams agreed with those who thought the Taipings would soon bring the downfall of the Manchu regime and open China to the West, but he was not näive enough to believe that they would remake China as a Christian nation. If Williams's discouragement with the Chinese was moderated to a degree by his respect for their past achievements, his visits to Japan evidently suggested to him another model for East-West relations, one which combined respect for Asian culture and national integrity with a still-staunch conviction that Christianity had a role to play in bridging the gap between peoples. To the end of his life, Williams remained a dedicated, mission-minded Christian. But his sensitivity and scholarship had shown him a dimension of the encounter of America with China which few of his fellow countrymen recognized. He was aware that Western intentions and actions were far from universally benign, and he came to see, too, that the Chinese might themselves offer constructive contributions to the encounter of cultures across the Pacific. [23]

With the recall in 1857 of Peter Parker, whose ambitions had far overreached American interests and capabilities, Williams found himself involved in a train of events which led directly to the signing of a new treaty between China and the United States. The new commissioner, William B. Reed, was a lawyer and public servant who had taught American history at the University of Pennsylvania and as a young man had served as private secretary to Joel Poinsett in Mexico. Reed brought explicit instructions from the Buchanan administration to secure from the Chinese government redress of claims and grievances and revision of the terms of the Treaty of Wang-hsia. He was to cooperate peacefully with the English and French but to avoid joint military actions or any projects threatening Chinese territorial integrity. Reed found the Chinese, under heavy pressure from the British and French, who had seized Canton, resisting proposals for negotiations. When the allied ministers proposed a combined expedition to Shanghai, Reed and the Russian minister, Poutiatin, with whom he had been instructed to cooperate, agreed to accompany them in the hope of finding a better climate for negotiations. It soon became apparent, however, that the British and French intended to force their way to Tientsin, on the road to Peking, and dictate terms to the Chinese. While the allied force was gathering at Taku, near the mouth of the Pei-ho River leading to Tientsin, Reed and Poutiatin approached the Chinese again. Now anxious to split the foreigners' apparently united front, the Chinese met with Reed in early May 1858. Since the American commissioner spoke no Chinese, the burden of subsequent negotiations fell on Williams and another missionary, Rev. W.A.P. Martin, who understood the Mandarin dialect. [24] American-Chinese discussions were interrupted by the Anglo-French seizure of the Chinese fortifications and by their subsequent movement inland to capture Tientsin. Since the terms demanded by Reed were moderate in comparison to those of the British, agreement was quickly reached and the Treaty of Tientsin was signed on June 18, 1858.

The treaty provided for the opening of additional ports, the easing of restrictions on the leasing of property, yearly visits by the American minister to the Peking court, and a series of conferences to settle American claims and secure tariff reductions. At the request of the British minister, Lord Elgin, Reed dropped the clause banning trade in opium which had been in effect since Wang-hsia. Reed's withdrawal of the American ban paved the way for legalization of the trade in the subsequent Sino-British Treaty. This action violated the spirit, if not the letter, of Reed's instructions and it distressed the missionary community, but since legalization reduced the pressure for smuggling, it could at least be rationalized as reducing the temptation to evade the law.

British and American merchants had been pressing for the opening of the Chinese interior to trade and navigation. Reed did not insist upon this point, however, and Williams had by this time become convinced that such a concession would be a serious infringement upon Chinese sovereignty, a loss of "the integrity of their own territory to the lust of gain and power." Williams, on the other hand, saw no such danger in urging the inclusion of an article which specifically secured religious toleration for Protestant Christians and their Chinese converts. Williams pressed hard for this point and won it, although Reed himself was indifferent to the matter and it clearly exceeded Washington's instructions "not to interfere in China's domestic affairs." The initiative and responsibility for securing religious toleration was clearly Williams's; Reed accepted it out of gratitude for the missionaries' assistance and perhaps, in Martin's view, because he thought it would be popular with Christians at home. [25]

The negotiations at Taku and Tientsin constituted Williams's most important diplomatic contribution, and they consolidated another major breach in the wall of Chinese sovereignty. The process was virtually completed when access to the Chinese interior and the right of permanent residence at Peking were granted in the treaties signed with the British and the French; under the most favored nation principle, these advantages were extended to others as well. Although the Chinese negotiators considered the Russians and Americans less warlike and more "affable" than the English or French, they found little difference in their determination to win concessions. They found that, rather than moderating allied hostility, the Russians and Americans were taking advantage of it at little cost to themselves; "if we probe their hearts they are just like the English and French." All foreign nations were equally greedy, it seemed, although they might vary in strength. The Chinese diplomats refused until the last moment to accept the article on religious toleration, recognizing it as a threat to their traditions. And, although at the time he was unyielding, Williams later conceded that there was a point to their fears. 26

The frustrations of negotiating with the Chinese stirred Williams's anger and impatience. "Since I've seen that crowd of conceited and helpless officials," he wrote, "my pity is more excited at their ignorant confidence than my indignation at their refusal of our demands. I am afraid that nothing short of the Society for the Diffusion of Cannonballs will give them the useful knowledge they require to realize their own helplessness." Only fear could win concessions from the Chinese, he concluded, "for they are the most craven of people, cruel and selfish as heathenism can make men." In this frame of mind, Williams looked upon the allied fleet assembled at the mouth of the Pei-ho "as a part of the great course of missionary work" which would open China to the forces of Truth. In the end, however, his feeling for the Chinese people and their problems reasserted itself. Finding no evidence of ill-will toward foreigners among the people of northern China, he concluded that it would be "a sad thing to make them enemies just as we are forming their acquaintance." He found nothing to be gained by destroying the "whole structure of government" in the process of bringing China to terms with reality. Despite temptations to rely on forceful means of persuasion, Williams seems to have sensed a Chinese potential for passive resistance against which the Western powers might fight in vain. In any event, he preferred another approach, "to try to teach them, patiently, kindly and with hope." Perhaps, he mused, "God has it in his scheme to join these opposite modes and carry out his plans of improvement by judgment and mercy joined." 27

Williams was well aware of the arrogance of the English and French and the relentless pressure they were applying. He recognized the divergent self-centered interests of each of the contending nations. Although he seldom, if ever, criticized his missionary brothers, he was appalled at the example set by traders and other "so-called Christians plying the rivers of China for their own purposes." Only his unquestioning faith reassured Williams that, in the end, God would care for the needs of Chinese and Westerners alike. It was this conviction alone which enabled him to reconcile an expansive Christianity with a genuine concern for China and its people.[28]

In 1859 Williams accompanied the new American minister, John E. Ward, to Peking for the exchange of ratifications of the Treaty of Tientsin. Their experiences again revealed the curious combination of attitudes and policies which marked the relations of the Western nations with one another and with China. Although Ward agreed to travel to the Chinese capital along a route prescribed by the imperial authorities, the English and French were determined to force their way to Peking on their own terms. When their forces attacked the Chinese forts at Taku once again, they were surprisingly and ignominiously defeated. In the confusion of the unanticipated setback, Commissioner Ward and the American mission departed from the posture of peaceful neutrality stipulated by American policy to help the wounded and retreating British. Surprise, chagrin and anger provoked the American commander, Commodore Josiah Tattnall, to a memorable expression of the underlying racism which had colored many Western attitudes and policies toward the Chinese from Wang-hsia to the present. "Blood is thicker than water," the Commodore exclaimed, and he'd "be damned if he'd stand by and see white men butchered before his eyes."[29] Commodore Tattnall, bluff sailor that he may have been, certainly was not alone in the high value he placed on "blood." S. Wells Williams had, in effect, acknowledged and attempted to counteract racist influences among those Americans who scorned the Chinese and blinded themselves to the virtues and values of an ancient culture. Yet Williams and his fellow Christians, confident of the superior truths of Western religion and morality, were themselves deeply enmeshed in the racist mind set.[30]

Illusions of superiority on the part of the West were matched, in all but the power to give them effect, by the Chinese. Commissioner Ward faced a counterexample when, having separated his party from the allied military expedition, he reached Peking ahead of his Western rivals. There, instead of achieving the long-sought goal of reception at the imperial court, Ward found himself confronted with the demand that he conform to Chinese tradition and kowtow (kneel and touch his head to the floor) before the Emperor as barbarian suppliants were required to do. This symbol of subjection to imperial authority had long irked Western governments, which were hardly prepared, given their own firm convictions of superiority, to countenance those of the Chinese. Under considerable pressure to arrange a reception of the Americans before the British and French should fight their way into Peking, Chinese officials proposed elaborate and deceptive compromises to deal with the kowtow. The Emperor, resisting change to the last, insisted that some part of the American representative in addition to the soles of his feet must touch the ground. On this, the proposed interview foundered since Ward, with proper American dignity, announced that he was prepared to kneel "only to God and women!" How the Chinese courtiers reported this statement to their master, if at all, is not a matter of record—it was probably taken as another evidence of Western inscrutability. Ward returned to the coast and ratifications of the treaty were exchanged without an imperial audience. Only after fifteen years, most of which he spent in Peking as secretary of the American legation, did Williams finally achieve the honor of attending an imperial audience. By then, near the end of his career and with failing health and eyesight, the experience was marred by the fact that, since eyeglasses were not permitted in the Emperor's presence, he could hardly see; in addition, the presentation occurred on a Sunday, thus offending Williams's religious principles.[31]

Having completed his mission, Minister Ward returned to Hongkong with his party. While awaiting permission to return home, he and Williams faced another problem which was to vex Chinese-American relations for many years to come. A growing trade in Chinese coolie labor was being exploited by British and American shippers, who delivered the unfortunate workers along the Pacific coast of the Americas and in the Caribbean region. Ward managed to stop this disreputable enterprise in Canton for the time being, but it quickly shifted to Macao where he lacked authority. Williams, shocked by testimony concerning the treatment of the coolies, prepared a tract in Cantonese, "Words to Startle Those Who Are Selling Their Bodies Abroad," hoping by this means to warn the Chinese against Western exploitation. 32

The years of Williams's tenure as secretary of the American legation in Peking can be reviewed rapidly. The treaties of Tientsin and the controversies over their ratification had marked a turning point in China's relations with the West. Foreign diplomats had gained direct access to the court; by official action, China was now largely open to Western commercial, religious, and political penetration. Under such circumstances, American expansion into China might have proceeded at a rapid pace had not domestic circumstances intervened. Four years of the American Civil War were closely followed by the rapid development of the American West and the expanding opportunities offered by the Industrial Revolution. With political and economic interests centered closer to home, only the missionaries were in a position to exploit the new opportunities in China. The spread of Christianity from the coastal ports up the rivers and into the interior initiated a period of growth as missions, churches, schools, hospitals, and universities were opened during the later years of the nineteenth century. Within the imperial capital, American missionaries were called upon to advise and teach a new generation of Chinese leaders. The duties of America's representatives to the Chinese government grew also but consisted of much routine work: aiding and advising fellow nationals, exchanging courtesies and counsel with members of the Chinese bureaucracy, processing claims, visiting consular posts, and entertaining distinguished visitors. His responsibilities permitted Williams ample time for pursuing scholarly interests, for scouring the countryside in search of interesting botanical samples, and for exchanging pleasantries with Chinese villagers and townsfolk. 33

Of the American ministers under whom Williams served during his final years in China, Anson Burlingame was the most significant. Appointed by President Lincoln in 1861, Burlingame was a man of great personal charm who shared Williams's genuine interest in the Chinese people and their government. These qualities helped him win the confidence of the Emperor's brother, Prince Kung, a powerful advocate of steps toward modernization. Burlingame was also able to gain the respect of other foreign representatives in Peking despite, or perhaps in part because of, the fact that his government was obviously in no position to exert significant political power in Far Eastern affairs. All that Burlingame could hope to achieve at this time was the mitigation of pressures on China by the British and French, and since these governments had for the time being concluded that their interests, like those of the Americans, could be pursued adequately within the structure of concessions already won, Burlingame's task was not difficult. This coincidence, together with the confidence which he commanded in court circles, made Burlingame a logical and effective intermediary between the Western powers and the Chinese government. His "cooperative policy," aimed at shoring up the uncertain imperial government while restraining pressure from eager, self-serving mercantile interests (at this stage, chiefly British), won Burlingame the enthusiastic support of Williams. The extent to which Burlingame's policies may themselves have been influenced by Williams can only be conjectured; in any case, it is clear that they worked together harmoniously. [34]

Burlingame's benevolent and idealistic approach to the Chinese rested on the assumption that under Western guidance they would soon grasp the realities of their situation and begin to face their problems more effectively. It took only a few years to reveal the twofold nature of this misperception. Not only did the Peking government prove incapable of responding promptly to the challenges of modernization, but there were growing indications that Western benevolence, such as it was, was an inadequate counterweight to other, less worthy motives. Chinese conservatism and corruption were matched by Western impatience. The coolie trade, tariff and shipping regulations, claims for protection by missionaries and their converts, and demands for further trade concessions all provided opportunities for controversy and conflict while underscoring the inability of the Chinese government to manage its affairs firmly. Foreign aggressiveness, on the other hand, aroused Chinese fears of further Western incursions.

In 1867, with the time specified for treaty revisions drawing near, the Chinese approached Burlingame, who was about to retire as American minister, with a request that he visit the Western capitals as their official representative, urging the case for patience and restraint. This unprecedented proposal, that a foreigner act as China's ambassador to the treaty powers, was of course a tribute to Burlingame's success in winning respect and trust. It was also a device to buy time and relief from foreign pressures, and it offered an opportunity for Chinese officials, two of whom were included in the mission, to familiarize themselves with Western diplomacy. As the delegation was finally constituted, it included British and French representatives as well, with a view to presenting the broadest possible front for the effort at international persuasion.

In 1868 and 1869, the Burlingame Mission traveled across the United States and Europe. The eagerness of European business interests for unrestricted access to China and their impatience with Chinese recalcitrance and obstructionism were too great and their influence with their home governments too substantial, however, for a successful outcome. Burlingame's sympathy for the Chinese, together with his failure to understand the strength of the forces resisting change, caused him to exaggerate China's readiness for progress. Carried away by his own enthusiasm and eloquence, Burlingame aggravated the opposition, which would in all probability have defeated him in any event. The mission, begun as an apparent model of Chinese-American understanding and good faith, ended by exposing its superficiality and self-deception.[35]

In the United States, at the outset, Burlingame was received with enthusiastic curiosity. The unorthodoxy of an American democrat's appearing as the official representative of the ancient Chinese empire guaranteed a sympathetic hearing. America's preoccupation with the coming impeachment of President Johnson and other domestic concerns minimized criticism and opposition. Although it has been designated with Burlingame's name, the treaty he signed with Secretary of State William H. Seward in June 1868 seems to have been drafted largely by the latter after a brief exchange of views.

The Burlingame Treaty consisted of eight articles to be added to the Treaty of Tientsin to further define relations between the two nations. It acknowledged China's authority over its territory and people, including control over inland trade and navigation except as these had been relinquished in earlier treaties; it guaranteed freedom of religion and protection of cemeteries for foreigners in either country; it provided for freedom of voluntary migration between countries but banned the coolie trade; it recognized rights of travel and residence, but forbade naturalization by either party of the other's citizens; and it acknowledged the right of the Chinese emperor to make internal improvements without foreign intervention and in accordance with his own priorities. Burlingame argued that the treaty at last placed China on a footing of full equality with other nations, reasserting its right to regulate its own people and its own internal affairs. Since American business interests were occupied elsewhere, this reaffirmation of the authority of the Chinese government concerned them very little. It did, however, provoke an angry response from European business circles which resented any interference, however nominal, with their plans for penetration and profit. Had the treaty proved effective in this respect, it would have imposed some additional restraints on Western business expansion at a time when European, much more than American, interests were in a position to take advantage of China's weakness.

The treaty's formal approval of Chinese immigration into the United States was subsequently criticized, with some justice, for fostering the coolie trade despite its expressed intent and thus flooding the American West Coast with cheap, ignorant Chinese laborers. Seward's inclusion of this article made possible the recruitment of cheap labor for the construction of the transcontinental railroad system, and California's business community hailed the treaty. The formal ban on the coolie trade was hardly meaningful, since only an organized trade could possibly have brought the Chinese to America in sufficient numbers to meet the demand. Yet the treaty did place Chinese immigration on precisely the same legal footing as that from Europe, which Burlingame represented as a victory for equalitarian principles in the face of the racism which had long characterized American relations with China. That the "victory," which helped to enrich American businessmen and investors, was partial and short-lived need not entirely discredit it. In the face of the violent hostility which soon began to be vented upon Chinese immigrants by native American and other immigrant labor groups and continued to distort American immigration policy for a century, Burlingame's idealism stands out in sharp, if naïve, relief. [36]

For S. Wells Williams, who remained at the American legation at Peking, the Burlingame Mission appeared "perhaps the highest compliment ever paid by one nation to another." Burlingame's policy of defending and encouraging the forces of modernization in China was one which Williams had come to advocate, though with frequent lapses into discouragement and parochialism. China was "really a pagan, half-civilized land," he wrote, and "infinite allowance must be made for what we could never approve. She is trying to understand." Missionary and educational efforts, with which Williams identified himself, could help greatly. So, too, would the training and provision of a more knowledgeable American foreign service. As he grew older, Williams acquired something of Chinese patience and perspective. "One thing is certain," he conceded ruefully, "that the elevation, instruction, reformation, and strengthening of this empire, and fitting its people for the duties and privileges of a civilized nation, is a greater work than anyone can understand until he tries it." [37]

The Burlingame Mission marked the last major diplomatic involvement of Williams's career. His remaining years in Peking were largely devoted to routine official duties and unremitting pursuit of his scholarly interests. He resigned his post in 1876 and returned to the United States after a career of forty-three years in Asia. In the short time remaining to him, Williams continued his efforts to promote understanding of the Chinese and their civilization. Accepting a post as professor of Chinese language and literature at Yale, he devoted himself to revisions of his volume, _The Middle Kingdom_, and to public efforts to defend the Chinese in America against the rising tides of prejudice and hostility. At his death in 1882, Williams was the most experienced, the most knowledgeable, and perhaps the wisest of nineteenth-century Americans in the field of Asian affairs.[38]

Williams's knowledge and experience spanned the full range of factors which played upon and helped to shape the direction of Chinese-American relations during his lifetime. Having been closely associated with American merchants during his early days in China, he noted the aggressive insensitivity many of them displayed in their dealings with the Chinese. He became increasingly critical as he found commercial motives less and less restrained by Christian morality and charity. Toward his missionary colleagues Williams turned a more sympathetic face. Fully sharing their confidence that Divine Providence intended China to be brought into the orbit of Western Christian civilization, he could overlook much evidence of smug, overbearing behavior on the part of the zealous. Nor was he, under pressure, able to resist the justification of forceful measures to accelerate the process of change. Yet Williams recognized, as did few other Americans, that the Chinese people and their civilization were worthy of serious respect. He foresaw the day when China would attain equal status in the family of nations and he did what he felt he could to advance it.

In many respects, Williams's ideas paralleled and may well have influenced the policies worked out by the succession of American diplomats responsible for the representation of their nation's interests and image in Asia. As Dennett and Tong have argued, these men, acting with few instructions and equally slight support from Washington, laid the foundations for a century of American policy toward China. With little experience and no preparation for their responsibilities—and subject to strong pressures from missionary and commercial interests alike—they committed the United States to uphold the principle of China's territorial integrity and right of self-determination. Although far from unselfish, the policy might, under other circumstances, have bought time for China to refashion its society and its approach to the West—as, in fact, it did in the case of Japan.

In the face of Chinese weakness and Western pressure, the policy proved more symbolic than effective. Yet, given their own weakness and inexperience, the Americans could have done little more. That genuine idealism and concern for the Chinese people was a factor in the attitudes of a Burlingame or a Williams is undeniable. It was naïveté and lack of understanding of the problems of a society so different from their own which dogged and frustrated their good intentions. Such qualities led them to minimize unrealistically the problems of China's modernization. They were equally blinded to American economic and ideological aggressiveness, in which they themselves participated. Yet, if contemporary perspectives emphasize the culture-bound character of the Americans' actions and understanding, they also remind us that Williams's dedication to a serious study of Chinese history and society pointed in a different direction, one whose full value we are only beginning to appreciate.

The Open Door policy, which Secretary of State John Hay formally enunciated in 1900 and early American experiences and treaties in China so clearly foreshadowed, came at the end of more than a century of Western expansion and Chinese cultural deterioration. Throughout that century, American policy toward China was essentially consistent, and in its consistency it measured and reflected to a remarkable degree the interplay of economic, political, and social forces that bore upon it. It combined assumptions of American racial and cultural superiority with the desire to forestall the designs of European merchants and imperialists. It opened China to the ambitions of American economic and religious interest groups while holding political commitments to a minimum. And it glossed the transaction with the rhetoric of freedom and self-determination so dear to American sensibilities. A fuller expression of America's cultural predispositions in international affairs would be difficult to imagine.

NOTES

1. Tyler Dennett, *Americans in Eastern Asia* (New York: Macmillan, 1922), pp. 6-7, 62-63.

2. Dennett, *Americans in Eastern Asia*, pp. 555-559; Te-Kong Tong, *United States Diplomacy in China, 1844-60* (Seattle: University of Washington Press, 1964), pp. 24-25.

3. John K. Fairbank, *Trade and Diplomacy on the China Coast: The Opening of the Treaty Ports, 1842-1854* (Cambridge: Harvard University Press, 1953), p. 160; U.S. Department of Commerce, Bureau of the Census, *Historical Statistics of the United States, Colonial Times to 1957* (Washington, D.C.: U.S. Government Printing Office, 1960), p. 251.

4. Dennett, *Americans in Eastern Asia*, pp. 102-103, 115-127; Tong, *United States Diplomacy in China*, p. 15.

5. Dennett, *Americans in Eastern Asia*, pp. 247, 559; Paul A. Varg, *Missionaries, Chinese, and Diplomats: The American Protestant Missionary Movement in China, 1890-1952* (Princeton: Princeton University Press, 1958), p. 5; Frederick Wells Williams, *Life and Letters of Samuel Wells Williams, L.L.D.* (New York: Putnam, 1889), pp. 49, 61, 76-78, 80-93, 120.

6. Akira Iriye, *Across the Pacific: An Inner History of American-East Asian Relations* (New York: Harcourt Brace Harbinger Books, 1967), pp. 3-7.

7. Dennett, *Americans in Eastern Asia*, pp. 110-113.

8. Tong, *United States Diplomacy in China*, pp. 7-8; Claude M. Fuess, *The Life of Caleb Cushing*, 2 vols. (New York: Harcourt Brace, 1923), vol. 1, pp. 404, 416; Jessie G. Lutz, ed., *Christian Missions in China—Evangelists of What?* (Boston: D. C. Heath, 1965), pp. 56, 61, 96.

9. Fairbank, *Trade and Diplomacy on the China Coast*, pp. 23-28, 177; Tong, *United States Diplomacy in China*, p. 45; Earl Swisher, ed., *China's Management of the Foreign Barbarians* (New Haven: Yale University Press, 1953), pp. 43-54, 138, 177, 191.

10. Dennett, *Americans in Eastern Asia*, pp. 160-168, offers a more sympathetic interpretation of American support for China's territorial integrity.

11. Dennett, *Americans in Eastern Asia*, pp. 146, 161, 168-169, 180-181; Tong, *United States Diplomacy in China*, pp. 51-52. Dennett (p. 559) suggests that the Chinese granted permission for Christian churches out of gratitude for the Rev. Peter Parker's medical assistance.

12. Tong, *United States Diplomacy in China*, pp. 9, 12, 20, 24, 64, 69; Fuess, *Caleb Cushing*, vol. 1, p. 407.

13. Dennett, *Americans in Eastern Asia*, pp. 186-188.

14. Dennett, *Americans in Eastern Asia*, pp. 187, 191; Tong, *United States Diplomacy in China*, pp. 25, 70-81; Varg, *Missionaries, Chinese, and Diplomats*, pp. vii-ix, 5-6, 25-26.

15. Tong, *United States Diplomacy in China*, pp. 91-92; Varg, *Missionaries, Chinese, and Diplomats*, pp. 19-23; Dennett, *Americans in Eastern Asia*, p. 559; W.A.P. Martin, *A Cycle of Cathay; or, China, South and North* (New York: F. H. Revell Company, 1900).

16. Williams is quoted in Dennett, *Americans in Eastern Asia*, p. 558; Varg, *Missionaries, Chinese, and Diplomats*, pp. 106-107; see also Williams, *Life and Letters*, pp. 130, 146, 287; S. Wells Williams, *The Middle Kingdom: A Survey of Geography, Government, Literature, Social Life, Art, and History in the Chinese Empire and Its Inhabitants* (New York: Scribner, 1914).

17. Williams, *Life and Letters*, pp. 64, 91, 161, 282, 352-354, passim.

18. Tong, *United States Diplomacy in China*, pp. 113-115, passim; Charles P.

Fitzgerald, *Revolution in China* (New York: Praeger, 1952), quoted in Lutz, *Christian Missions*, p. 97; Eugene Bowers Boardman, *Christian Influence upon the Ideology of the Taiping Rebellion, 1851-64* (New York: Octagon Books, 1972).

19. Tong and Dennett offer the most complete treatment of American diplomacy during the 1840s and 1850s.

20. Dennett, *Americans in Eastern Asia*, pp. 260-277; Samuel Eliot Morison, *"Old Bruin," Commodore Matthew C. Perry, 1794-1858* (Boston: Little, Brown, 1967).

21. Morison, *"Old Bruin,"* pp. 297, 306, 406, 430; Williams, *Life and Letters*, pp. 197, 206-224.

22. Tong, *United States Diplomacy in China*, pp. 173-209; Swisher, *China's Management of Foreign Barbarians*, pp. 50, 311-316, 325.

23. Williams, *Life and Letters*, pp. 174, 180, passim.

24. Tong, *United States Diplomacy in China*, pp. 210-218.

25. Tong, *United States Diplomacy in China*, pp. 219-234; Dennett, *Americans in Eastern Asia*, pp. 306, 314; Martin, *Cycle of Cathay*, pp. 154, 180-181, passim.; Varg, *Missionaries, Chinese, and Diplomats*, pp. 11-12.

26. Swisher, *China's Management of Foreign Barbarians*, pp. 448, 455.

27. Williams, *Life and Letters*, pp. 251, 257-258, 266, 268; S. Wells Williams, "Journal of S. Wells Williams: The Reed and Ward Missions," *Journal of the North China Branch of the Royal Asiatic Society*, 42 (1911): 7-10, 21, 28.

28. Williams, "Journal," pp. 31-32, 37, 50, 64-65, passim.

29. Tong, *United States Diplomacy in China*, p. 263; Williams, "Journal," pp. 103, 111-145.

30. Williams, "Journal," pp. 130-145; Williams, *Life and Letters*, p. 280; Varg, *Missionaries, Chinese, and Diplomats*, p. 76.

31. Tong, *United States Diplomacy in China*, pp. 268-273; Williams "Journal," pp. 164-194, 200-212; Williams, *Life and Letters*, pp. 401-402.

32. Tong, *United States Diplomacy in China*, pp. 273-282; Williams, *Life and Letters*, pp. 325-327. Williams, however, intervened to prevent the Chinese from bestowing additional honors on Ward in the conviction that Confucian honors were "heathen" and thus inappropriate.

33. Ibid., pp. 352-362, passim.

34. Frederick Wells Williams, *Anson Burlingame and the First Chinese Mission to Foreign Powers* (New York, 1912), pp. 32-37, passim; Williams, *Life and Letters*, p. 358.

35. Williams, *Burlingame*, p. 126, passim.

36. Ibid., pp. 113-160; Dennett, *Americans in Eastern Asia*, pp. 378-386.

37. Williams, *Life and Letters*, pp. 371, 376-377, 382, 463.

38. Ibid., pp. 412-461.

CHAPTER SIX

Conscience and Consciousness in the Philippines: The Imperial Impulse, 1898-1903

The blazing guns of Commodore George Dewey's fleet, steaming past the feeble Spanish flotilla in Manila Bay early on May 2, 1898, signaled the end of an era for Spain and the beginning of one for the United States. As the last vestiges of Spanish glory collapsed, the foundations of a new American empire emerged. The defeat of Spain in Cuba, Puerto Rico, and the Philippines was no clearer than was the fact that the United States had achieved world power status. From time to time, the American people and—with greater difficulty—their leaders might ignore, resist, or resent the implications of this status, but they could not deny or elude them. The astonishing victory at Manila Bay sharpened controversy in the United States over America's role as an emerging world power and especially over the nation's stake in the Far Pacific. The debate, hardly new, now became both public and pointed. Yet, few Americans sensed even vaguely the intricacies of the strategic and cultural arena into which their new military hero had sailed. Despite Dewey's precursors on the rim of Asia, the region still remained a vague and distant mystery to most Americans.

This widespread ignorance of Asian conditions was by no means inconsistent, as recent scholarship has shown, with the long-standing, if intermittent, enthusiasm many Americans had displayed for expansionist goals there. The merchants and missionaries who had settled in Asia, well ahead of even their country's own transcontinental development, had been advance agents of a society that scarcely questioned its members' right to pursue their own purposes when and where they wished. Such an outlook had discouraged, when it had not totally crushed, whatever latent inclinations men such as S. Wells Williams might have had to consider Asia and its people in other than American terms.[1] Now, after several decades of domestic preoccupations, business and political circles were awakening to new interests in the Far East. America's own social and domestic dislocations, sharpened by the depression of the 1890s, encouraged the view that the nation's future depended increasingly upon the opening of foreign markets and investment opportunities. Steam navigation had made the acquisition of coaling stations along the Pacific routes to China attractive to businessmen and strategists. China itself, offering a seemingly vast potential market under a feeble, deteriorating imperial regime, was a tempting prize, but the prize was contested by Japan and European powers. As the U.S. fleet steamed toward Manila, the specter of exclusion from China as a consequence of intensified European incursions there was already haunting concerned Americans. The Philippines offered insurance against total exclusion from Asia markets as well as a base from which to strengthen America's competitive position in the gathering struggle for the Chinese mainland.

Probably more intriguing to most Americans than such hypothetical strategic and economic interests in the Far East was the heady prospect of victory over an ancient European rival and the opportunity to appear, in their own eyes and in those of the world, as the champions of international freedom and progress. The American concept of mission had long combined idealistic with materialistic elements. It was President William McKinley's achievement during the months between Dewey's triumph at Manila and the signing of the Treaty of Paris to find a formula for reconciling the divergent elements of the mission ideal with an unprecedented political commitment in Asia. McKinley's program eventually won convincing, if not overwhelming, public support in two successive national elections. If disillusionment set in later and if doubt was never entirely overcome, for a brief period at least a new era of American growth and democracy seemed in the making. Cultural, as well as economic and political, imperatives pointed to an enlarged role for the United States in Asia as well as the Caribbean.[2]

Neither past experience nor present enthusiasm suggested to most Americans that Asians might themselves have different or contrary purposes that would demand consideration. Unfamiliar with or insensitive to many aspects of the Asian scene, Americans were totally unprepared for the fact that in the Philippines they would encounter another offshot of Europe in the form of an incipient colonial independence movement in some ways comparable to their own Revolution. Spanish rule in the islands since the sixteenth century had brought Christianity to large numbers of Filipinos. The Spaniards, harsh though their regime had been, had introduced the sons of a small but growing middle class to the currents of recent Western thought. These *ilustrados*, while studying in Spain, had been struck by the contrast between the rights and freedoms enjoyed by Europeans, even in Spain itself, and the total domination of their homeland by the Spanish government and religious orders. By the 1880s a self-conscious movement for political and religious reform in the Philippines had taken shape. The *Liga Filipina*, whose most distinguished leader was the physician and writer José Rizal, pressed for recognition, within the framework of the Spanish empire, of the fundamental rights of free speech, religion, and property that were the hallmarks of Western liberalism.

Returning home, Rizal and his associates attempted to organize a general reform movement. Spanish repression frustrated their efforts, but at the cost of greatly popularizing the resistance. Under the leadership of a secret society, the *Katipunan*, open rebellion flared in August 1896 as Filipino peasants joined a movement rapidly becoming more radical and more insistent upon independence. The Spanish managed to contain the rebels without defeating them, but the conflict produced an indigenous military leader and hero in the person of Emilio Aguinaldo. In October, Aguinaldo issued a manifesto calling for "Liberty, Equality, and Fraternity" and a republican government "similar to that of the U.S.A." The following spring, a revolutionary convention proposed a constitutional republic with Aguinaldo as president and a bill of rights guaranteeing the fundamental liberties of the people. A combination of desperate Spanish efforts and internal divisions among the rebels led to a truce under which the Filipino leaders went into exile while the Spanish promised to institute reforms. Neither side, however, was prepared to abandon its objectives. [3]

Even before Dewey reached Hongkong on his way to Manila, the Filipino exiles there had made contact with American agents and received encouragement from them. In addition, the United States had maintained a consulate at Manila since 1877, although commercial relations there were insignificant. American officials thus were aware of the existence of discontent in the islands. It seemed reasonable to expect that an attack upon Manila would be welcomed by native leaders and its likelihood of success thereby increased. Beyond this, the McKinley administration knew and cared little about social and political conditions in the Philippines, and its unconcern accurately mirrored that of the American people. [4]

It seems doubtful that a fuller appreciation of Philippine conditions would have persuaded many Americans that an aspiring democracy that had received its tutelage from Spain deserved to be taken seriously. The Filipinos were Asian, colored, and in some respects primitive by Western standards. Their claims and prospects for independence were unlikely to impress those in the United States who were already regretting the few freedoms the Civil War had won for their own black citizens. Little wonder that Dewey, once he had maneuvered the Spanish surrender of Manila out of the hands of the Filipino rebels (or the McKinley administration, from the beginning), brushed aside Filipino claims for independence. Basking in victory and the promise of empire, Americans looked upon their new protégés with benevolence, disinterested or otherwise, but scarcely with respect. Attempting to bring their version of freedom to a colonial people, the Americans were to encounter bloody resistance and resentment. Their hopes for economic advantage were to prove equally illusory. And the Filipinos, who under other circumstances might have welcomed American aid and guidance, were to find their freedom warped and delayed. Out of the tangled motives, perceptions, and misperceptions accompanying the occupation of the Philippines emerged an experience in mutual frustration and bitterness, and disappointed or half-realized hopes. [5]

While the McKinley administration concentrated its attentions on the prosecution of the war in the Caribbean and Dewey awaited the arrival of American troops to secure the Spanish surrender, the Filipino rebels proceeded with their revolution. Aguinaldo had been brought back to the islands by Dewey and received with honor aboard the flagship *Olympia*. With Dewey's encouragement, he set about rallying insurgent forces and pushing the Spanish back into Manila. The peasants rose throughout central Luzon, and cautious liberals who had hesitated to join the earlier rebellion now threw in their lot with Aguinaldo. Filipino soldiers serving the Spaniards deserted to the insurgents. Dewey, impressed by the initial rebel successes, was soon informing Washington that they were more capable of self-government than were the Cubans.

Self-government was clearly the rebels' objective. On June 12 a declaration of independence modeled in part on that of the United States was publicly proclaimed and signed. Municipal and provincial governments, meanwhile, were seized and reorganized under a plan developed by Apollinaro Mabini, an *ilustrado* who was the revolution's leading theoretician. A central government was created with civil, diplomatic, and military branches and an advisory council with judicial powers. Aguinaldo, pressing hard for formal American recognition of his regime, proclaimed himself president of a newly constituted Philippine Republic on July 1. Although Dewey declined to acknowledge the new government, out of necessity he continued to cooperate with its leaders. To hopeful Filipinos it appeared that the first modern Asian revolution was on its way to fulfillment with the aid and encouragement of the American republic. [6]

Yet from the beginning the nature and extent of the United States commitment had been in doubt. Dewey's reluctance to recognize Aguinaldo's new status formally was only one of a number of signs that American policy was ambiguous. Aguinaldo, publicly attempting to associate Filipino aspirations with the American tradition of freedom, addressed a request for recognition of Philippine independence to President McKinley. No such commitment was forthcoming. On the contrary, Washington was already sending a military force to occupy and pacify the islands and had instructed Dewey to enter into no political arrangements with the rebel leader.

Although the case has been made that these actions committed the McKinley administration to a policy of annexation, the argument is not conclusive. Given the President's characteristic caution, the rapid pace of events, the absence of detailed information, and the unexpected collapse of the Spanish regime, McKinley's orders can equally well be understood as an effort to maintain the status quo as nearly as possible in a situation in which the extent of Spanish authority and the intentions and capacities of the Filipino insurgents were in question. Nothing in his orders to the American general, Wesley C. Merritt, precluded any eventual outcome; they did strongly emphasize the protection of Filipino rights and interests. In a situation muddied by uncertainties, McKinley was keeping his options open and awaiting further information.[7]

American public opinion, meanwhile, rode a wave of expansionist enthusiasm that all but drowned out the few voices urging caution and restraint. Ill-informed and disregarding the Spanish forces in Manila almost as cavalierly as they did the Filipinos, Americans seem virtually to have concluded that the islands had already fallen to Dewey. Few outside government circles had given even casual consideration to the Philippines before the outbreak of war, but the islands' strategic location on the highroad to Asia now captured the general fancy. Businessmen, journalists, clergy, and others visualized new opportunities for commerce and investment, converts and uplift. Few considered the awkward possibility that the Philippines might offer little of value to the American economy or that their inhabitants, having been converted to Catholicism several centuries earlier, might not welcome Protestant missions with open arms.

The example of other imperial powers, moreover, challenged Americans to outmatch Europe in power, profit, or service. Reports from European capitals noted a surge of interest in the future of the islands, based on the assumption that Spain could no longer hold them. The Kaiser, anxious to acquire imperial real estate wherever it could be found, had already sent a fleet to

Manila Bay where its commander challenged Dewey's smaller force with sailings and soundings along the coast. The British were interested, too, but preferred to encourage American annexation rather than confront Germany. Pride, profit, and racism, stimulated by popular Social Darwinian rhetoric, encouraged Americans to join the international race for markets and empire, much as they encouraged parallel efforts to restrict the freedoms and opportunities of Negroes and recent immigrant groups at home. Dewey's casual dismissal of the Filipinos as "little brown men" summed up in a few careless words an assumption that was prevalent even among the critics of American expansion. [8]

McKinley may have begun by seeing Manila as a mere way station for the more promising China market, but events rapidly widened his horisons. To support the thrust toward the East, the President pressed for passage of a long-dormant congressional resolution annexing Hawaii. Orders for the capture of Guam had already been issued to the forces streaming to the support of Dewey. A Philippine coaling station was now assured, to complete the chain, yet even this startling series of acquisitions seemed inadequate to the occasion. The rapid progress of the Filipino insurgents convinced the McKinley administration, not of the logic of independence, but of the likelihood of chaos if the United States were to withdraw. If Spain could not control the islands and America would not, then the specter of anarchy or probable European intervention loomed. The President was aware that the execution of his pacification orders might provoke resistance, but his informants had minimized the strength and competence of the revolutionary movement. What he failed to understand was that the introduction of American troops now posed the most immediate threat to peace and stability in the islands. [9]

The capture of Manila by the American army on August 13, 1898, encountered greater opposition from the Filipino than the Spanish forces. The following day, General Merritt issued a proclamation, based on McKinley's instructions, that promised friendship and protection but made it clear that the United States expected to define the terms of peace. Power and initiative now rested with the Americans; the future status of the Philippines would be decided in the United States. Aguinaldo might still influence the outcome, but he could do so only by winning concessions from McKinley. Diplomacy and outright warfare were his only alternatives. Meanwhile, Filipino frustrations and American ambitions were creating a power keg that might at any time blast through the forces of restraint. 10

With the fall of Manila, more imformation began to reach the United States; it largely served, however, to reinforce already existing preconceptions and prejudices. Military reports systematically downgraded Filipino strength and determination while stressing evidences of disunity which had begun to surface within the nationalist movement. Filipino conservatives in and around Manila, gaining the ear of American leaders, reported that the revolutionary movement was limited to Luzon and, within Luzon, to the Tagalog tribe. Fearing more radical elements within the independence movement, they emphasized that centuries of foreign domination had not equipped the masses for self-government. Despite the self-serving character of these charges, there was some truth to them. The Spaniards had allowed the Filipinos virtually no self-rule and had, indeed, fostered factional interests and rivalries that were already proving divisive. Under the most favorable circumstances, questions about their capacity to take charge of their own destiny might have arisen. Given the American intellectual climate and the state of international relations, such questions were not easily dismissed. 11

McKinley's critics, both then and since, have censured him for succumbing to annexationist pressures. Yet, in view of the information available to him, the interpretations of it current even in supposedly informed quarters, and the popular and special interests involved, it seems remarkable that he resisted as long as he did. Margaret Leech has shown that the President recognized the serious commitments involved in annexation. The Philippines were far beyond Hawaii, over whose acquisition Congress had been vacillating for several years. The economic potential of the islands was an unknown quantity, although assumed to be great. It was also becoming clear that substantial resistance to American rule would drastically increase the costs involved. Such considerations make it likely that the islands' proximity to the Chinese mainland, rather than their own inherent value, weighed most heavily with McKinley.

A cautious man, the President let his Cabinet and the country debate the nation's course during the summer and fall of 1898 without declaring himself. On a much-analyzed Midwest speaking tour, he suited his expansionist rhetoric to the mood of his audiences, but while this was indicative of the trend of his thinking, it was not necessarily commitment. His nomination in August of the commissioners to negotiate peace with Spain at Paris pointed to a further step toward annexation. Three of the five— Whitelaw Reid, and Senators Cushman K. Davis and William P. Frye—were expansionists, while Senator George Gray, the fourth, staunchly opposed annexation. The chairman, former Secretary of State William Day, held views that were probably closer to McKinley's. Day favored holding the port of Manila yet hesitated to expand America's claims beyond that. McKinley's instructions to the commissioners balanced professions of high moral purpose with references to commercial opportunities which, he noted, might be secured adequately through a guarantee of equal access to all nations. This suggestion of an open door for other nations in the Philippines paralleled America's traditional policy toward China, which was again facing challenge by the European powers and Japan. On one crucial point the President was explicit: the island of Luzon must be held by the United States. [12]

McKinley's terms, moderate in the context of American opinion, nonetheless struck directly at the basis of the Filipino independence movement. Nothing could have revealed more clearly the degree to which American policy was being shaped in the ignorance of Philippine conditions. Luzon was the center of revolution and its most powerful tribe, the Tagalogs, were the revolution's most advanced and determined supporters. McKinley's insistence on Luzon, therefore, placed him in full opposition to the hopes of the fledgling Philippine republic. Meanwhile, the less advanced peoples of the outlying islands, for whose welfare and freedom from Tagalog domination Americans were expressing deep concern, might under McKinley's proposal have been abandoned to whatever fate awaited them.

While the United States attempted to define its Philippine

policy, Aguinaldo and his associates worked to consolidate their position and win recognition as the legitimate Philippine government. On September 15, only one day before McKinley issued his instructions to the American peace negotiators, the first Filipino Congress convened at Malolos, northeast of Manila, Aguinaldo's temporary capital. Although called to function as a national legislature, the Malolos Congress devoted much of its attention to drafting a constitution for the new Philippine Republic.

The revolutionary regime was maintaining an army and extending its control throughout the archipelago in the face of widely varying degrees of national awareness and class or tribal loyalties. It was also attempting to maintain and define a delicate relationship with the Americans in a situation that threatened to degenerate at any moment into outright military, political, and racial conflict. Many Filipino liberals, of whom Apollinaro Mabini was the most influential, argued therefore that it was premature to launch a democratic, representative government. Only an authoritarian regime could act quickly and decisively; full-scale democracy must await the achievement of independence. On the other side, members of the wealthy and educated classes, whose support the republic also needed, were fearful of the principle of democracy itself and especially of the sweeping powers its advocates called for. They demanded a legislative assembly with substantial powers to serve as a check on executive authority. A classic struggle was being waged within the ranks of the Filipino leadership on the issue of separation of powers for the new national government. [13]

It was the task of the Malolos Congress to find a workable compromise between the contending factions. Its members included an impressive number of educated and professional men chosen by provincial councils, which had in turn been selected by an extremely limited electorate. More than half of the congressional delegates had been selected by Aguinaldo to represent districts not yet reorganized under the provisional government. Representative only in a very loose sense, the Congress proved to be a conservative body. The constitution it produced reflected the outlook of the Filipino elite. It provided for the election of municipal officers by male property holders over twenty-five years of age and for the choice of provincial officials and congressmen, in turn, by the municipal chiefs. At the national level, it created a parliamentary system of government, with the president and members of the Supreme Court chosen by the Congress. A controversial provision for the separation of church and state was adopted, together with a bill of rights guaranteeing freedom of speech, press, property, and religion. The large landholdings of the Catholic orders were to be confiscated.

So strongly did the Malolos constitution favor the wealthy landholders and middle classes that Mabini persuaded Aguinaldo to delay its promulgation for the sake of national unity. The tension between the left and right wings of the nationalist movement thus dragged on through the fall of 1898. As Aguinaldo continued to govern on a provisional basis with the Assembly acting in an advisory capacity, conservative elements increasingly questioned the desirability of independence. Already suspicious of Mabini and the liberals, some concluded that American annexation offered greater security for their interests. On January 21, 1899, in a final effort to maintain a united front, Aguinaldo formally accepted the Malolos constitution, but it was already too late to prevent defection. In the end, the constitution had no chance to function or evolve under normal peacetime conditions. Its significance is rather as a symbol of hope for national unity and self-government, an indigenous effort to adapt Western democratic forms to Philippine conditions. [14]

Despite the problems besetting it, Aguinaldo's government proved reasonably effective and popular at first. Whatever its limitations as an instrument of democracy, it offered a larger measure of local autonomy and representation than Spain had ever offered the Filipinos. Provisions were undertaken for a national system of public education, reform of the tax and currency systems, and the organization of the army, a small navy, and a diplomatic corps. Nationalist clubs and newspapers were launched to help rally popular support. American observers travelling through the provinces testified to the prevalence of orderly local government and unity behind Aguinaldo's leadership; the Filipinos could rightfully claim to have rapidly established the foundations for national independence under the most trying circumstances. [15] Meanwhile, Washington's attention had focused elsewhere, on the peace negotiations in Paris. Once again, American preconceptions and preoccupations were combining to deny the Filipinos a full and fair hearing.

In an effort to win foreign support for his cause, Aguinaldo authorized negotiations for recognition and military assistance. Representatives were sent to plead the Filipino case in Japan, France, and England. Aguinaldo's instructions to the overseas agents showed concern lest foreign powers intervene directly. Even association with the United States, possibly under a protectorate, seemed to him preferable to a division of the Philippines among the imperialist powers. Felipe Agoncillo, a member of the Hongkong junta, was dispatched to Washington in the hope of securing a direct hearing from the American government. Agoncillo wrote to McKinley, congratulating him on the conclusion of hostilities with Spain and requesting representation for the Philippine government at the peace conference. Meanwhile, he advised Aguinaldo to maintain friendly relations with the Americans pending conclusion of treaty negotiations. [16]

Agoncillo sailed from Hongkong to San Francisco on the same ship which carried Gen. Francis V. Greene. Greene, a businessman and an officer of the New York militia, had commanded one of the first American contingents to arrive in the islands. Returning to report on conditions there, he would be the first American who had visited Luzon since 1869 to be consulted by the President. Greene's views, however, were hardly favorable to the insurgents. He questioned their support in the islands other than Luzon and compared Aguinaldo's government with the South American dictatorships more familiar to Washington. An American protectorate, which some Filipinos were ready to consider, also seemed impractical to Greene. Impressed by possibilities for trade and economic development, he favored maintaining Philippine unity through American annexation. Nevertheless, Greene talked with Agoncillo several times as their ship crossed the Pacific and again as they continued by rail to Washington. Although he was unable to win Greene over to the Filipino cause, Agoncillo secured his assistance in arranging an interview with President McKinley. Received unofficially as a private citizen on October 1, 1898, Agoncillo had the opportunity to put the case for independence directly. Courteously but noncommittally,

McKinley invited Agoncillo to submit his statement in writing
and assured him it would be transmitted to the American commissioners. He was even encouraged to pursue his plan of going
to Paris to present his arguments to the commission—evidently
more as a way of ridding Washington of his presence than of be-
friending his cause. 17

The Filipinos had at last received a direct, if inconclusive,
hearing. Agoncillo told McKinley that his people had joined
gladly with Dewey's forces to recover their national integrity
and rights. Peace in the Philippines, he argued, depended upon
the creation of a government independent of both Spain and the
United States. Claiming the status of a government which rested
upon the consent and the votes of its citizens, the Philippines re-
quested representation and a "decisive vote" in the determination of their future. They were guided, Agoncillo asserted, by
"the same principles of liberty, justice, and human rights, which
are set forth in the . . . famous and holy 'Declaration of Independence!'" America's own historic principles of freedom should
ensure its support for Philippine independence.

It was a strong case which the ambassador put to the President. By the standards of a later generation it was very possibly
a convincing case, but there was no likelihood of its persuading
McKinley. The President had already heard from General
Greene—a man whose background he respected and whose preconceptions he shared—the arguments which ended his hesita-
tion and brought him down squarely on the side of annexation.
After all, other Filipinos in the United States, Hongkong, and
even Manila itself were disclaiming readiness for independence.
Under the circumstances, Agoncillo could do little but pursue his
course to Paris in the unlikely hope that there he might find a
sympathetic hearing. 18

Paris, however, proved even less receptive than had Washington. Of the five American peace commissioners, only Senator
Gray opposed the acquisition of territory in the Philippines.
McKinley's instructions specifying the retention of Luzon as the
minimum American demand had focussed discussions on how
much, if any, more than the minimum might be claimed. General
Merritt, on his way home from the islands, had already offered
his views, as had other military and civilian experts. Merritt had

never met Aguinaldo; his understanding of the Philippine situation was limited. He depicted the Filipinos as backward educationally, culturally, and politically, divided among warring tribes and religions, and incapable of resisting American power and firmness.

The State Department, anxious to avoid embarrassing hostilities between Filipino and American forces during negotiations with Spain, had forwarded Agoncillo's statement for the commissioners' consideration. The Commission agreed to see him upon written application and in an unofficial capacity only. Whitelaw Reid, its most influential and aggressively expansionist member, cursorily dismissed this "so-called representative of Aguinaldo" as a "half-Malay" and termed his presentation of the Filipino case "extraordinary." [19] On October 25, the commissioners cabled their views to President McKinley, asking for final instructions. The reply came swiftly; McKinley had concluded that the United States must insist upon cession of the entire archipelago. Agoncillo had been duped into addressing the wrong audience, although it is doubtful that he could have accomplished a different result if he had remained in Washington. Negotiations between Spain and the United States dragged on, but so far as the Filipinos were concerned the crucial American decision had been reached. Independence was to be denied. Little chance remained of avoiding an all-out conflict between Filipinos and Americans. With the signing of the Treaty of Paris on December 10, 1899, the locus of decision returned to Washington and the islands. [20]

Much has been written elsewhere about the U.S. Senate debate over ratification of the treaty. The deliberations were extensive and ranged broadly over the issues involved in the projection of American responsibility over a distant, alien, and unwilling people. They have sometimes been interpreted as a national dialogue on the policies of expansionism and imperialism at a turning point in the development of America's foreign relations. Yet the debate was neither so probing nor the lines of division between defenders and opponents of the treaty so clearly defined as this interpretation suggests. In any case, as Maximo Kalaw has pointed out, the debate centered on the significance of annexation for *American* policy, tradition, and interest, with only incidental attention to its meaning for the Philippine nation. On the matter of Filipino fitness for self-government, the administration held the initiative since it dominated the sources of information. The idea that the substantial, responsible majority of Filipinos desired American tutelage while the masses were ignorant and unprepared for self-rule had been widely disseminated for months. Even those opponents of the treaty who attacked its denial of self-determination emphasized the implications of that denial for American democratic values rather than for the Filipinos. Some critics of annexation did suggest that the capacity for self-government could be acquired only by actual practice not by inculcation, but this position was weakened, as David Healy and others have shown, by the extent to which the anti-imperialists shared the expansionists' assumptions regarding the racial inferiority of the backward peoples. Not even the most sympathetic annexationists believed them suitable for absorption into the American nation. Moreover, while opposing annexation of the Philippines, many so-called anti-imperialists actually favored economic expansion in other, more accessible or more promising regions.

Certain economic and political considerations buttressed the antiannexationist position. Prospects of competition with cheap Filipino labor, of deeper American involvement in Asian politics, of expanding military and naval costs all suggested the advisability of disengagement, but these arguments carried little weight at the time. Political considerations played a familiar role, with Republicans hoping to capitalize upon the new symbols of national glory while Democrats hesitated to oppose either a popular peace or the spoils of a seemingly glorious victory. But party divisions were not firm, since traditionalists such as Republican Senator Hoar of Massachusetts opposed the treaty while William Jennings Bryan supported it in the hope of separating the issue of annexation from that of ending the war with Spain. In the end, and for all the arguments, the Senate debate and vote on the treaty offered no clear-cut resolution of the issues underlying annexation. McKinley drew upon all his resources of patronage and persuasion as debate proceeded in the Senate during January 1899. Furthermore, the elections of the preceding November had defeated eight antiexpansionist senators, making it a certainty that the new Congress to assemble in March would ratify the treaty. McKinley, anxious to secure ratification before conflict erupted in the Philippines, pressed steadily for action. Resolutions looking toward ultimate independence for the Philippines were rejected. The most promising of these, the Bacon amendment, received a tie vote with the Vice-President casting the decisive negative ballot.[21]

As the debate proceeded, Agoncillo, who had returned from Paris in a final effort to stave off American acceptance of the treaty, approached both the administration and the Senate. He urged that the example of the United States had inspired Filipino desires for independence, expressing hope for recognition "of the first Republic of Asia by the greatest Republic of America." McKinley and Secretary of State John Hay would not see him. Instead, the President attempted to use Agoncillo to secure peace in the Philippines. A telegram was drafted urging the abandonment of resistance to American sovereignty, and General Greene proposed that Agoncillo send it to Aguinaldo over his name. Agoncillo refused, bargaining futilely for Philippine independence under an American protectorate; his rejection of McKinley's proposal concluded his contact with the administration. In a final statement on January 30, Agoncillo argued that the Philippine revolution had preceded American intervention and had been encouraged by American officials. He cited testimony of American observers as to Filipino support for Aguinaldo, but the American press had meanwhile opened an attack upon him. It was clear that his mission had failed. The only Filipino voices Americans chose to listen to were those which told them precisely what they wanted to hear.[22]

During the Paris negotiations and the Senate debates, McKinley was torn between the desire to secure American control of the islands and fear that hostilities between Filipinos and Americans would endanger the passage of the treaty and the political hopes of the Republican party. Believing that the majority of Filipinos favored annexation, he took every opportunity to assure them of America's concern for their interests and welfare, but he insisted upon acknowledgment of America's sovereignty. As pressure mounted from those, American and Filipino alike, who thought a show of strength and determination would discourage resistance, on December 21 McKinley ordered Gen. Elwell S. Otis to announce the cession of the Philippines by Spain and to extend military government throughout the archipelago. This order, coming even before the Senate had begun consideration of the Treaty of Paris, indicated the depth of the President's concern. Aguinaldo's government was winning acceptance throughout the islands while the American forces remained idle in Manila. Wishing to avoid a direct clash, McKinley halted an American mission to seize the port of Iloilo held by forces loyal to Aguinaldo. To further soothe popular feelings, he instructed the military to assure the Filipinos "that full measure of individual rights and liberties which is the heritage of free peoples, and . . . [to prove] to them that the mission of the United States is one of benevolent assimilation." Otis, recognizing the provocative character of such assertions in the context of the imposition of military rule, edited the announcement to emphasize conciliation rather than sovereignty, but the full text of McKinley's order leaked out, further aggravating its impact. [23]

To Philippine nationalists the President's instructions seemed a virtual declaration of war. Aguinaldo responded bitterly that Filipinos had "entertained absolute confidence in the history and traditions of a people which fought for its independence and for the abolition of slavery, and which posed as the champion and liberator of oppressed peoples. We felt ourselves under the safeguard of a free people." But it was no more in his interest than in McKinley's to resort to fighting at this stage. As the wavering conservatives within the Malolos government drifted toward the new American power center, Aguinaldo struggled to retain the widest possible backing. The avoidance of hostilities with the Americans was essential to any hope of achieving a compromise.

A proposal for meetings to explore a settlement was accepted by General Otis, who stipulated, however, that such meetings did not constitute formal negotiations. Several conferences were held during January 1899, but no progress was achieved. By this time the Philippine negotiators might have accepted an American protectorate with a promise of future independence. Otis insisted, however, that American sovereignty be acknowledged without qualification. His inflexibility convinced the Filipinos that Otis was encouraging the talks simply to buy time for the

Senate's action and for the arrival of more troops. On the night of February 4, tensions finally burst when American soldiers shot at a Filipino patrol and their fire was returned. Treating the outbreak as an accident, Aguinaldo attempted to resume negotiations, but Otis refused. Conflict could no longer be contained. In Washington, word of the clash rallied hesitant Senators to the support of the treaty, and the last votes needed to ensure ratification were found. Peace with Spain was achieved as American troops went into action against the Philippine nationalists.[24]

Much as Dewey's opening shots upon the Spanish fleet in Manila Bay had involved the United States more deeply in the Philippines than had been foreseen, so the outbreak of hostilities between Americans and Filipinos opened an unexpectedly long and bloody war. In each instance, the United States government badly underrated the strength of Philippine nationalism. On the first occasion, there had been no background of experience to prepare the United States for the enthusiasm with which the Filipinos rallied to Aguinaldo's standard. No such excuse covered the miscalculation concerning resistance to annexation. Thousands of Americans, including top army leaders, had spent months in the islands during 1898 without producing an accurate assessment of the situation. True, some journalists and field officers had learned to respect Filipino fighting qualities and determination. Their reports, however, had been censored by the army or neglected by the American people and their government. A smug confidence in American superiority prevailed while inconvenient facts were ignored or withheld from view. Consequently, the United States, whose citizens conceived of themselves as bearing Western democracy and progress to the East, now faced the awkward and costly task of attempting to suppress a popular national independence movement.

Caught in an embarrassing and unfamiliar posture in their own eyes and in those of the world, Americans responded with a mixture of bitterness and idealistic zeal that once again led them to misperceive Philippine realities. They were tempted to accept every argument, justifiable or otherwise, which discredited their new and ungrateful charges; at the same time, they could justify the cost and sacrifice of repressive war only by insisting upon the high ideals in whose name they professed to wage it. Having chosen annexation under circumstances that seemed to him to offer no satisfactory alternative, President McKinley now faced a dilemma. Committed to the principle of Filipino incapacity for self-rule, he could justify American intervention only as a mild and beneficent effort to uplift a backward people. Yet the toughness of Filipino resistance threatened to make a mockery of both the assumption of inferiority and of American beneficence.

In an effort to arrange a settlement, McKinley organized a commission to visit the Philippines, explain America's honorable intentions, and recommend a suitable form of government. He selected Jacob Gould Schurman, president of Cornell University, as chairman. The other civilian members were Dean C. Worcester, a University of Michigan zoologist who had visited some of the more backward areas of the islands, and Charles Denby, a democrat who had long served as American minister to China and worked for the expansion of business interests there. Neither Denby nor Worcester, who had greater experience in the Philippines than any of his colleagues, considered the Filipinos capable of self-government. Schurman, upon being asked to serve, told the President that he had opposed annexation, only to have McKinley respond mildly that he, too, had not wanted the islands but had concluded that there was no satisfactory alternative. Admiral Dewey and General Otis, representing the military, completed the commission's membership. Schurman and Worcester proceeded rapidly to Manila, reaching their destination early in March 1899. [25]

The experience of the Schurman Commission and, indeed, those of military and civilian authorities in the Philippines for many years to come, reflected the basic ambivalence of American policy and attitudes concerning the new island empire. The army, chafing under the restraints imposed by McKinley and provoked by repeated clashes with Filipino forces, pressed for an all-out campaign to wipe out Aguinaldo's army and lay the foundations for peace on the basis of military victory. Military leaders displayed an incongruous mixture of attitudes toward the Filipinos. General Otis continually minimized Filipino opposition, while the racist preconceptions of many military men of all ranks argued that the natives could be defeated readily. Yet a number of experienced field officers, among them Gen. Arthur

MacArthur, developed a marked respect for Filipino fighting qualities.[26]

At the outset, the civilian members of the Schurman Commission agreed in hoping for an early end to military government. They sought out leading citizens of Manila and attempted to reach beyond the capital through visits to the hinterland, although inevitably they listened chiefly to conservatives or others anxious to curry favor. Arguing that America's intentions had been misunderstood, they insisted that there was no real conflict between American sovereignty and Filipino freedom. On the contrary, American authority offered the surest safeguard for internal freedom and home rule. If the rebels would lay down their arms, an era of peace, progress, and freedom without precedent in Philippine history would be initiated. Limited in their understanding of Philippine conditions and restricted by cultural and racial blinders as well, the commissioners struggled to reconcile American preconceptions with Filipino realities and aspirations.

Having studied the Malolos Constitution and the statements of insurgent leaders, the commission issued its preliminary recommendations on April 4, 1899. Although persuaded that without American rule the islands would collapse into a chaos of warring tribes, it recommended provision for local self-government. In principle, the commissioners acknowledged the desirability of grounding government in the "needs, judgment, character, ideals, potential and self-image of the people,' but they were puzzled by the islanders' un-American preference for a strong central government and a parliamentary system. They recommended instead a large degree of local autonomy under a central government on the American model, headed by an American governor-general with an appointed cabinet, an independent judiciary, and an elected advisory council. Acknowledging a basic similarity in the views of Americans and Filipinos concerning the ends of government, they readily agreed to a bill of rights guaranteeing the basic individual freedoms to which both peoples subscribed.[27]

While the commission sought conciliation and accommodation, General Otis pushed his troops forward into the Luzon hinterland. Malolos and a number of other rebel centers had fallen to the Americans by the end of April 1899. Further American successes pressed Aguinaldo's dwindling forces into the mountains, but they could not be cornered. The onset of the rainy season found the American forces overextended and discouraged. Despite American gains, only a military and diplomatic stalemate had been achieved; victory was little closer. [28]

A Filipino request for negotiations on the basis of the Schurman Commission's proposals was blocked by Otis, but disagreement arose among the commissioners. Schurman favored efforts to broaden support for annexation through compromise with the insurgents, while the others upheld Otis's demand that resistance be put down by force before negotiations could begin. Unable to persuade his colleagues, Schurman returned to the United States, leaving Denby and Worcester to continue discussions with Filipino conservatives. Despite their differences, the commissioners had agreed on the key principles of American sovereignty and local self-rule based on limited suffrage. Their preliminary report strengthened popular expectations in the United States that the Philippine conflict could soon be brought under control. [29]

Indeed, despite its shortcomings, the Schurman Commission had come close to achieving a Philippine settlement. Its conciliatory efforts, coupled with General Otis's offensive, had aggravated differences within the insurgent ranks. Mabini, as head of Aguinaldo's cabinet, had been forced by the conservatives to seek a truce with the Americans, although he would not accept Otis's demand for surrender without some assurances as to eventual independence. On May 6, however, the Philippine Assembly voted to accept the Schurman Commission's proposal as a basis for peace. A "pacifist" Cabinet replaced Mabini's, but its efforts at negotiation were also rebuffed by Otis at the same time that they further embittered the divisions within the deteriorating nationalist ranks. Desperately, Aguinaldo continued to hold out in the hope that resistance would persuade the American people to defeat McKinley in the 1900 elections. In November 1899, however, he was forced to disband the remnants of the Filipino army and turn to scattered but still bitter guerrilla warfare. Meanwhile, the United States government was interpreting Aguinaldo's difficulties as evidence of the inability of his government to command popular support. [30]

As the fighting dragged on into 1900, the American people were also beginning to question its purpose. Having been led to expect an early settlement, they were discovering that falsely optimistic reports and the censorship of unfavorable news had deceived them. Equally shocking, reports of brutality on the part of both American and Filipino soldiers, suppressed by the authorities, had begun to leak out. These provoked demands for congressional investigation while suggesting that what had begun presumably as a brief, glorious venture in benevolence was grinding down into a grim and hateful bloodbath. Opponents of annexation now ironically compared American treatment of the Filipinos with the Spanish atrocities in Cuba that had only recently so horrified the public. Guerrilla warfare in the Philippines had become a continuing source of embarrassment to American officials. It frustrated and angered the generals who, having fostered expectations of easy victory, now found their forces harassed by a determined and elusive enemy. It annoyed the McKinley administration, eager to reduce its military establishment and present a record of peaceful and constructive government in the newly acquired dependencies. [31]

McKinley pressed for peace, hoping to establish an orderly civil administration in the islands before the national election scheduled for November 1900. A second Philippine commission was created to carry forward the task of framing a governmental system and putting it into actual operation. The experience of the Schurman Commission offered a basis upon which to build, while the appointment of Dean C. Worcester, who had served with the earlier commission, provided continuity of personnel. As chairman of the second commission McKinley appointed Judge William Howard Taft of Cincinnati, a conservative Republican and able lawyer who lacked administrative experience or familiarity with Asian affairs. Initially reluctant to accept the post, Taft soon threw himself into the work with great enthusiasm. He and his associates on the commission had the advantage of strong support from the new secretary of war, Elihu Root, with whose department responsibility for Philippine affairs rested. Neither Root nor Taft had favored annexation, but they devoted their efforts to the establishment of an orderly civil government for the islands with as much popular participation as, in their view, the circumstances warranted. Neither believed the

Filipinos fully capable of self-government and they therefore anticipated a long period of American supervision, but they agreed with the Schurman Commission that a workable, orderly government must build upon Philippine traditions and values. [32]

The Taft Commission's instructions, drawn up by Root and approved by McKinley, laid the foundations for American colonial administration in the islands. Root argued that the United States Constitution did not confer any rights directly upon subject peoples, but he believed nevertheless that it bound the United States to observe "the underlying principles of justice and freedom" and "the essential safeguards of every individual against the powers of government" which were at the core of its own system. The United States had an obligation, Root stated, to make "the interests of the people over whom we assert sovereignty the first and controlling consideration in all legislation and administration which concerns them, and to give them, to the fullest possible extent, individual freedom, self-government in accordance with their capacity, just and equal laws, an opportunity for education, for profitable industry, and for development in civilization."

The diversity of conditions prevailing in the Philippines, Root held, justified differing degrees of participation in government. Local municipal officers should be elected and natives should be appointed to higher level offices wherever possible. The Filipinos were to be accorded "the widest possible opportunity to manage their government, commensurate with their growing capabilities, within the framework of American rule." The commission was authorized to assume legislative responsibility for the islands, thus enabling it to reconstitute civil government when and where in its judgment conditions were suitable. The commissioners were reminded that, in so doing, they should be guided by the principle that "the government they are establishing is designed not for our satisfaction or for the expression of theoretical views, but for the happiness, peace, and prosperity of the people of the Philippine Islands, and the measures adopted should be made to conform to their customs, their habits, and even their prejudices, to the fullest extent consistent with the . . . requisites of just and effective government." All American officials appointed under the new regime were to be "impressed

[with] a sense of duty to observe not merely the material but the personal and social rights of the people of these islands and to treat them with the same courtesy and respect for their personal dignity which the people of the United States are accustomed to require for each other."

Root's instructions, which further specified the provision of a bill of rights and an independent judicial system, have been termed, by Filipino as well as American historians, "a model of constructive statesmanship." They were in keeping with McKinley's policy of benevolent assimilation in their extension of American rights and forms to the Filipinos, and their acknowledgement of native values and traditions appeared to move toward recognition of the integrity of Philippine culture. [33]

Root, Taft, and McKinley were understandably anxious to allay Filipino resistance and to win over those conservatives whom they considered responsible. Good will as well as shrewd tactics commended a conciliatory approach. They insisted, however, upon acknowledgment of American sovereignty. Deeply imbued with their own sense of the meaning of democracy and convinced of its universal applicability, they boggled nonetheless at the democratic professions of a socially and racially "backward" people who had not had the advantage of long tutelage under American supervision. Racism and paternalism were clearly expressed, too, in the harshly repressive measures employed by the American military and in the slurs and slights directed at the Filipinos by both American soldiers and civilians. Yet the trappings of benevolent statesmanship and the tight screen of military censorship concealed for the time being the conflict of cultures and purposes at the core of the annexation issue.

Although neither he nor Root believed the Filipinos ready for self-government, Taft moved swiftly upon his arrival in Manila to give substance to the promises of consideration for Filipino needs and wishes. The commission was besieged by wealthy and conservative Filipinos, eager to assure themselves of the protection and favor of the new authorities. The commissioners held open hearings and toured widely through the provinces to assure the people of America's interest in their welfare and to hear recommendations for the new governmental system. They were warmly received and readily persuaded that their reception showed the true feelings of the people. Taft was not entirely naïve as to the self-serving motives involved, but inevitably the commission relied heavily upon the views and services of those most willing to cooperate with it.

From the outset, Taft tried to counteract the racial hostility which had sprung up between Americans and Filipinos and which he recognized as destructive of true cooperation. He made an effort to learn and to speak Spanish and he insisted that there be no racial bars to social and political intercourse. In so doing, he openly challenged the prejudices and practices of Manila's European community, as well as of most white Americans. Struggling with his Puritan preconceptions, Taft forced himself to attend a cockfight, to show the Filipinos that the Americans had not come "to restrict their ordinary enjoyments." On another occasion, Puritanism won out when he banned saloons from the *Escolta*, Manila's central shopping plaza, which was frequented by American women. Taft enjoyed Filipino music, attended numerous banquets, and danced at festivals, attempting to demonstrate an interest in the people. Yet, he could not fully overcome the attitudes and preconceptions which had been bred into him. He has been credited with coining the dubious phrase, "our little brown brothers," to describe the Filipinos. To the modern ear, the phrase is clearly racist, but Mrs. Taft insisted that the key word was "brother" and stated that her husband's efforts at open and equal-handed friendliness aroused bitter resentment among those who considered him dangerously "soft" on the Filipinos. A popular song which circulated among the American forces underlined the point: "He may be a brother of William H. Taft, but he ain't no friend of mine." Significantly, however, genuine feelings of mutual sympathy and respect developed between black American soldiers and the Filipinos.[34]

Simultaneously with efforts to win Philippine friendship and trust, the Taft Commission began the task of governmental reorganization. Civil government had previously been initiated in a few provinces by General Otis, in keeping with McKinley's wish to hasten the return to normal peacetime conditions. Civil courts had also been appointed, as well as a Supreme Court composed of both Americans and Filipinos and presided over by a conservative lawyer, Cayetano Arellano. The commission established a Philippine civil service to assist in the recruitment of responsible Filipino and American public servants. A public works program was undertaken to provide better transportation and communication between Manila and the provinces. A system of municipal and provincial governments was established after public discussion in February 1901, once the outcome of the American presidential election had made it clear that there would be no early change in American sovereignty. Municipal officials were to be chosen by an electorate restricted to literate male property holders who had previously held office, a limitation less restrictive than those earlier provided in the Malolos constitution. Provincial governments were set up in regions which the commission found reasonably free of organized resistance. Americans were appointed as governors and treasurers, while Filipinos served in the positions of provincial secretary and prosecuting attorney.

As the creation of the new governmental structure progressed, Filipino resistance deteriorated. Mabini, the most determined advocate of independence, was captured in December 1899. In captivity, he served as a channel between Aguinaldo and the Americans. Pressing for conciliation through a promise of eventual independence, he relayed promises of good treatment for Aguinaldo if he would acknowledge American sovereignty. Meanwhile, moderate Filipinos were increasingly attracted to the American side by the belief that further resistance was futile, by the Taft Commission's demonstrations of goodwill, or by the prospect of orderly government and lucrative positions under the American regime. Aguinaldo still continued to hold out, with little hope but that of dragging out a costly and embarrassing war until the United States should tire of it. [35]

The rebels, nevertheless, had managed to provoke considerable controversy between American leaders over the proper strategy for bringing resistance to an end. The military and civilian members of the Schurman Commission had differed in their approach to Aguinaldo; now Taft and General MacArthur, Otis's successor as commander-in-chief, found themselves at odds over the relative merits of conciliation and military pressure as a strategy for overcoming Filipino resistance. From the very beginning, MacArthur had opposed and resented the presence of the Taft Commission as an infringement on his authority and a deterrent to his campaign to defeat the scattered but still formidable Philippine guerrillas. At every step MacArthur opposed the process of civilianization. As resistance dragged on, many Americans began to lose enthusiasm for the Philippine venture. Even Theodore Roosevelt, who succeeded McKinley as president in September 1901, had second thoughts. Still, there seemed no alternative but to press ahead and complete the pacification process, hoping that the results of American involvement and tutelage would eventually justify the costs. The ambivalent American policy was aptly described by an English lady resident in Manila as one which attempted "to have lots of American school teachers at once set to work to teach the Filipino English and at the same time keep plenty of American soldiers around to knock him on the head should he get a notion that he is ready for self-government before the Americans think he is." The capture of Aguinaldo in March 1901 and his declaration of allegiance to American authority a month later ended the last hope of Philippine independence, yet in remote regions of the archipelago guerrillas held out until 1907.[36]

In the month of Aguinaldo's capture and McKinley's second inaugural, Congress granted the President broad peacetime powers to govern the Philippines, removing dependence upon his war powers. Taft had argued that this shift in the source of authority would broaden Filipino support for the new government. On this basis, the Taft Commission had proceeded with its organization of local and provincial governments. The judiciary was developed along American lines, with local and district courts beneath the Supreme Court. Filipino justices were appointed to many local courts, but Americans were usually assigned to the more important centers. A law providing for a voluntary elementary school system was passed, while nearly one thousand American teachers, the "Thomasites"—often seen as predecessors of the Peace Corps—were recruited to train native teachers in English and American educational methods. In July 1901 Taft took the oath of office as the first American governor-general of the Philippines. In September the commission, its five American members having been supplemented with three Filipinos, assumed full powers as the Philippine legislature. Since the Filipino commissioners had been carefully selected and were in the minority, they posed no obstacle to American rule. Still, they could act in an advisory capacity, and their status, symbolically at least, represented still another step in the direction of ultimate self-rule.[37]

Taft, whom his wife considered "the most active anti-imperialist of them all," by now had secured a sufficiently solid foundation for the new government to make long-range planning possible. During the winter of 1901-1902, he returned to the United States to consult with Root, Roosevelt, and others on the creation of a permanent Philippine government. A central feature of this final structure should be, Taft argued, early provision for an elected assembly. With administration support, Taft spoke vigorously before congressional committees on behalf of the proposal, urging its value in creating a forum for the expression of responsible Filipino views and persuading those who still doubted American intentions that "we desire to educate them in self-government and give them a measure of self-government." In July 1902 Congress passed the Philippine Organic Act, which provided for such an assembly two years after peace was fully achieved and a census of the islands taken. The act included provision for two Filipino resident commissioners in Washington, with the right to sit and speak, but not to vote, in the U.S. House of Representatives.[38]

Taft was less successful in persuading Congress to lower tariffs on Philippine products to promote American investment in the islands. Although he held that such measures could contribute "to the material, and therefore the spiritual, uplifting of the Filipino people," he found congressmen and senators at least temporarily skeptical of such missionary appeals, and perhaps even more so of possible competition with domestic economic interests. American economic penetration of the islands, indeed, was destined to be considerably less sizable than enthusiasts such as Taft and Denby anticipated. In the end, the attraction of Philippine investment opportunities was to be outweighed by the competition that Filipino raw materials, especially sugar, offered to domestic American producers. Although the American stake in Philippine economic development never realized the hopes of its more ardent promoters, it nevertheless became sufficient to dominate the economy of the islands. [39]

Another achievement which helped win acceptance for the American regime concerned the disposition of the lands held under the Spanish by the various Catholic orders. The Taft Commission had discovered the unpopularity of the Spanish friars and the strong desire of both middle-class and peasant Filipinos to recapture this rich resource. The Treaty of Paris, however, had guaranteed the rights and property of the religious orders. Recognizing a legitimate complaint as well as a popular issue, Taft tried to arrange for purchase of the lands and their redistribution. He returned from Washington to the Philippines by way of Rome where he opened negotiations to that end with the papal court. Again, his sensitivity to an ancient grievance helped to win support for American sovereignty.

The proclamation, on July 4, 1902, of the new Philippine government based upon the Organic Act formally settled the status of the island as an American dependency. A pro-American conservative political party, the Federalists, had come into existence with Taft's encouragement while nationalist groups favoring independence were proscribed. Yet the extension of political freedoms led to the gradual reemergence of an independence movement. In 1907, an elected Philippine assembly came into being, the first such body to be established in any colony of the Western powers. Although American sovereignty had denied the Filipinos the right to determine their own national destiny, it had still "dowered" them, in Jacob Gould Schurman's words, "with the freest government in Asia." [40]

Controversy over the American annexation of the Philippines has continued since many of the issues and circumstances surrounding the action were neither simple nor clear. That the Filipinos could have maintained their independence in the face of internal divisions and inexperience, as well as of external pressures, seems doubtful. That it was the obligation of the United States to protect them from the likely unfortunate consequences of the experiment may also seem dubious, although it should be added that popular pressures and prejudices at the turn of the century gave President McKinley little support for an opposite conclusion. There can be no doubt that economic and strategic considerations, real or presumed, played a major role in McKinley's decision to preserve the fullest possible latitude for American interests in the islands. Even before the status of the Philippines was fully settled, the United States found itself more deeply engaged in the deteriorating Chinese situation that culminated in the Open Door notes of 1899 and 1900. The acquisition of the Philippines unquestionably contributed to whatever credibility the Open Door policy achieved, even more perhaps with the American people themselves than with the European powers. The close relationship between the Philippines and China in the thinking of American policy makers was underlined by McKinley's commitment to the Open Door principle in both instances. The fact that real commercial interests and opportunities in the region failed to fulfill the expectations of economic expansionists does not negate their importance as influences upon the thinking of American business and political leadership. Circumstances required different approaches in the islands and on the mainland, but the basic objectives were similar.

The necessity of reconciling the movement into the Philippines with America's historic libertarian principles further distorted perceptions of both the cultural and strategic issues involved. The application of America's concept of its mission for democracy to the Philippines, as well as to the Caribbean, carried it well beyond the continental limits and the practical possibility of future incorporation into the nation itself, as Frederick Merk has pointed out. [41] At the same time, the rhetoric of mission in all likelihood did help to quiet the fears of Americans who might otherwise have resisted expansion overseas more strongly. And the mission idea helped to shape the nature of American commitments in the Philippines. It required that freedom and self-government be institutionalized, translating professions of democracy into form and substance. In the end, however, the idea of mission distorted understanding of the full dimensions of the problem. It veiled the actual impact of American economic and cultural intervention upon Philippine society behind a facade of Western political forms and freedoms. Thus, a highly visible record of political and educational advances obscured the further disruption and corruption of the already shaky Philippine economic and social order.

America's benevolent and democratic impulses were given concrete form partly as a consequence of the actions of the Filipinos themselves. Acknowledging and welcoming the liberal principles invoked by the United States, they nevertheless bitterly criticized and resisted American performance. In so doing, they probably hastened American willingness to permit them a significant share in their own self-government. Thus, the Filipinos themselves must be credited with a contributory role in the development of American policy. This policy, for all its shortcomings, was relatively mild and enlightened by the standards of its day. It attempted to balance, in an awkward and often inconsistent way, the basic American cultural imperatives of democracy and opportunity; neither could be wholly denied but neither could gain uncontested primacy. If it failed to break free of the paternalism and racism upon which colonialism fed, it at least erected institutions and guarantees capable of limiting some of the worst abuses of imperialism.[42] If the freedoms granted to the Filipinos were themselves distorted by the predominance of American power and culture, American conscience, too, left its mark in a record which foreshadowed continuing patterns in our ambivalent cultural confrontation with Asia.

NOTES

1. See Chapter 5.

2. Foster Rhea Dulles, *America in the Pacific: A Century of Expansion* (Boston and New York: Houghton, Mifflin Company, 1938), pp. 51-52, 63-67, 74-79; Walter LaFeber, *The New Empire: An Interpretation of American Expansion, 1860-1898* (Ithaca: Cornell University Press, 1963); Julius W. Pratt, *America's Colonial Experiment* (New York: Prentice-Hall, 1950), pp. 3, 60-61; Marilyn Blatt Young, ed., *American Expansionism: The Critical Issues* (Boston: Little, Brown and Co., Inc., 1973).

3. Caesar Adib Majul, "The Political and Constitutional Ideas of the Philippine Revolution," *Philippine Social Science and Humanities Review* 22, nos. 1-2, (1957), ix, 1-6, 13-21, 24-31, passim; Leandro H. Fernandez, "The Philippine Republic," *Columbia University Studies in History, Economics and Public Law*, 122, no. 1 (1926): 9-50; Bonifacio S. Salamanca, *The Filipino Reaction to*

American Rule, 1901-1913 (Hamden, Conn.: The Shoe String Press, 1961), pp. 14-17; George Taylor, *The Philippines and the United States: Problems of Partnership* (New York and London: F. A. Praeger, 1964), pp. 32-40, 43-46; Apollinaro Mabini, *The Philippine Revolution* (Manila: Republic of Philippines, National Historical Commission, 1969); Peter W. Stanley, *A Nation in the Making: The Philippines and the United States, 1899-1921* (Cambridge: Harvard University Press, 1974), pp. 19-28, 52.

4. Dulles, *America in the Pacific*, pp. 199-203; Teodoro A. Agoncillo, "Malolos: The Crisis of the Republic," *Philippine Social Science and Humanities Review* 25, nos. 1-4 (1960): 73-75, 133-136; Taylor, *The Philippines and the United States*, p. 41; Honesto A. Villenueva, "A Chapter from Filipino Democracy," *Philippine Social Science and Humanities Review* 17, no. 2 (June 1952): 138-144; James H. Blount, *The American Occupation of the Philippines, 1898-1912* (New York and London: Putnam, 1913), pp. 20-23; James A. Leroy, *The Americans in the Philippines*, 2 vols. (Boston, 1914), vol. 1, p. 185.

5. David Healy, *U.S. Expansionism: The Imperialist Urge in the 1890's* (Madison: University of Wisconsin Press, 1970), pp. 57-59; Margaret Leech, *In the Days of McKinley* (New York: Harper, 1959), pp. 209-210; LaFeber, *The New Empire*, pp. 360-362; H. Wayne Morgan, *America's Road to Empire: The War with Spain and Overseas Expansion* (New York: John Wiley, 1965), pp. 71-73; Dulles, *America in the Pacific*, pp. 199, 203-207.

6. Fernandez, "The Philippine Republic," pp. 64-79; Villanueva, "Chapter from Filipino Democracy," pp. 103-104; Leroy, *Americans in the Philippines*, vol. 1, pp. 203-204, 207-208; Blount, *American Occupation of the Philippines*, pp. 32, 58; Mabini, *The Philippine Revolution*, pp. 52-53; Dulles, *America in the Pacific*, p. 210.

7. Leroy, *Americans in the Philippines*, vol. 1, p. 147; Blount, *American Occupation of the Philippines*, pp. 27-28; Dulles, *America in the Pacific*, pp. 209-210, 216-217; Leech, *In the Days of McKinley*, pp. 210-212; Healy, *U.S. Expansionism*, pp. 59-62; Leon Wolff, *Little Brown Brother: How the United States Purchased and Pacified the Philippine Islands at the Century's Turn* (Garden City: Doubleday, 1961), pp. 60-62; Agoncillo, "Malolos," p. 147.

8. Pratt, *America's Colonial Experiment*, pp. 60-61; Richard H. Miller, ed., *American Imperialism in 1898: The Quest for National Fulfillment* (New York: John Wiley, 1970), pp. 128-130; Healy, *U.S. Expansionism*, pp. 11-15, 41, 53-57, passim; E. Berkeley Tompkins, *Anti-Imperialism in the United States: The Great Debate, 1890-1920* (Philadelphia: University of Pennsylvania Press, 1970), pp. 4-16; LaFeber, *The New Empire*, pp. 371-374, 383, 408-410; Jacob Gould Schurman, *Philippine Affairs*, 2nd ed. (New York: Scribner's, 1902), pp. 82-83; Dulles, *America in the Pacific*, pp. 203, 209; Maximo M. Kalaw, *The Case for the Filipinos* (New York: Century, 1916), p. 24; Agoncillo, "Malolos," pp. 149-152. Dewey's statement is from Leroy, *Americans in the Philippines*, vol. 1, p. 179; Villanueva, "Chapter from Filipino Democracy," pp. 151-156; Salamanca, *Filipino Reaction to American Rule*, p. 208n.

9. Thomas J. McCormick, "Insular Imperialism and the Open Door: The China Market and the Spanish American War," *Pacific Historical Review*, 32: 155-169, reprinted in Miller, *American Imperialism in 1898*, pp. 131-137; Leech,

In the Days of McKinley, pp. 209, 212-214, 284-285, 324; Agoncillo, "Malolos," pp. 138, 147, 158-161; Pratt, *America's Colonial Experiment*, pp. 61-70.

10. Leroy, *Americans in the Philippines*, vol. 1, pp. 253-254; Agoncillo, "Malolos," pp. 186-188, 631; Blount, *American Occupation of the Philippines*, pp. 50-53.

11. Agoncillo, "Malolos," pp. 113-114, 140-143; Leroy, *Americans in the Philippines*, vol. 1, pp. 142-143; Majul, "Political and Constitutional Ideas," pp. 13-15.

12. Leech, *In the Days of McKinley*, pp. 285, 323-332; William Appleman Williams, ed., *From Colony to Empire* (New York: John Wiley, 1972), pp. 197-198.

13. Leroy, *Americans in the Philippines*, vol. 1, pp. 284-290; Agoncillo, "Malolos," p. 240; Fernandez, "The Philippine Republic," pp. 81-86, 95-106, 185-188; Salamanca, *Filipino Reaction to American Rule*, p. 18; Villanueva, "Chapter from Filipino Democracy," p. 108.

14. Majul, "Political and Constitutional Ideas," pp. 65-68, 159-177, 185-192; Agoncillo, "Malolos," p. 563; Fernandez, "The Philippine Republic," pp. 95-108; Salamanca, *Filipino Reaction to American Rule*, pp. 18-24; Leroy, *Americans in the Philippines*, vol. 1, pp. 290-306, 378-382.

15. Majul, "Political and Constitutional Ideas," p. 9; Blount, *American Occupation of the Philippines*, pp. 75, 107; Agoncillo, "Malolos," pp. 424-430; Wolff, *Little Brown Brother*, p. 147ff.; Fernandez, "The Philippine Republic," pp. 109-115, 141.

16. Agoncillo, "Malolos," p. 316; Villanueva, "Chapter from Filipino Democracy," pp. 110-112.

17. Agoncillo, "Malolos," pp. 321-324; Leech, *In the Days of McKinley*, pp. 334-346; Fernandez, "The Philippine Republic," p. 117; Villanueva, "Chapter from Filipino Democracy," pp. 110-115; Morgan, *America's Road to Empire*, p. 82.

18. Villanueva, "Chapter from Filipino Democracy," pp. 116-117.

19. Agoncillo, "Malolos," pp. 326, 329-334; H. Wayne Morgan, ed., *Making Peace with Spain: The Diary of Whitelaw Reid, September-December, 1898* (Austin: University of Texas Press, 1965), pp. 82-86; Villanueva, "Chapter from Filipino Democracy," pp. 117-119.

20. Leroy, *Americans in the Philippines*, vol. 1, pp. 362-373.

21. Healy, *U.S. Expansionism*, pp. 55-57, 213-218, 238-246; Kalaw, *Case for the Filipinos*, pp. 44-45; Miller, *American Imperialism in 1898*, pp. 11-12; Pratt, *America's Colonial Experiment*, pp. 70-73; Leech, *In the Days of McKinley*, pp. 350-357.

22. Agoncillo, "Malolos," pp. 357-364; Villanueva, "Chapter from Filipino Democracy," pp. 120-125.

23. Kalaw, "Case for the Filipinos," pp. 82-86; Leech, *In the Days of McKinley*, pp. 350-352; Dulles, *America in the Pacific*, pp. 251-253; Blount, *American Occupation of the Philippines*, pp. 139, 164; Leroy, *Americans in the Philippines*, vol. 1, pp. 398-404; Salamanca, *Filipino Reaction to American Rule*, pp. 27-28.

24. Blount, *American Occupation of the Philippines*, pp. 170, 180; Fernandez, "The Philippine Republic," pp. 107-108, 143-151; Leroy, *Americans in the Philippines*, vol. 1, pp. 378-382; Agoncillo, "Malolos," pp. 372-377, 434-450, 563; Leech, *In the Days of McKinley*, pp. 357-359.

25. Schurman, *Philippine Affairs*, pp. 2-6; Leech, *In the Days of McKinley*, pp. 351-352, 363.

26. Blount, *American Occupation of the Philippines*, pp. 300-306, 310, 376.

27. Kenneth S. Hendrickson, "Reluctant Expansionist—Jacob Gould Schurman and the Philippine Question," *Pacific Historical Review*, 36 (November 1967): 408-410; Schurman, *Philippine Affairs*, pp. 6-9, 15-18, 31-32, 39-41; Agoncillo, "Malolos," p. 504; Healy, *U.S. Expansionism*, pp. 188-189.

28. Leech, *In the Days of McKinley*, pp. 363-365.

29. Hendrickson, "Reluctant Expansionist," pp. 411-416; Majul, "Political and Constitutional Ideas," pp. 174-177; Leech, *In the Days of McKinley*, pp. 364, 422; Schurman, *Philippine Affairs*, pp. 31-35, 59; Healy, *U.S. Expansionism*, pp. 188-189, 199; Taylor, *Philippines and the United States*, pp. 60ff.

30. Agoncillo, "Malolos," pp. 397-402, 516-517, 540; Fernandez, "The Philippine Republic," pp. 154-159; Majul, "Political and Constitutional Ideas," pp. 12-13; Philip C. Jessup, *Elihu Root*, 2 vols. (New York: Dodd, Mead and Company, 1938), vol. 1, p. 353; Mabini, *The Philippine Revolution*, pp. 59-63.

31. Blount, *American Occupation of the Philippines*, pp. 251-252, 273-274, 278-281, 285-306, 326, 331-332, passim; Jessup, *Elihu Root*, vol. 1, pp. 336-343; Tompkins, *Anti-Imperialism in the United States*, pp. 246-253, 275.

32. Blount, *American Occupation of the Philippines*, pp. 219-222, 281-286; Henry F. Pringle, *William Howard Taft*, 2 vols. (New York: Farrar and Rinehart, 1939), vol. 1, pp. 166, 171-174; Leech, *In the Days of McKinley*, pp. 483-485, 552; Leroy, *Americans in the Philippines*, vol. 1, p. 14; Helen H. Taft, *Recollections of Full Years*, (New York: Dodd, Mead and Company, 1917), pp. 32-35, 41.

33. Jessup, *Elihu Root*, vol. 1, pp. 329-332, 353-357; Salamanca, *Filipino Reaction to American Rule*, pp. 30, 36-38; Pratt, *America's Colonial Experiment*, p. 196; Wolff, *Little Brown Brother*, p. 308; Kalaw, *Case for the Filipinos*, pp. 92-94.

34. Salamanca, *Filipino Reaction to American Rule*, pp. 30-32; Pringle, *William Howard Taft*, pp. 174-177, 180; H. H. Taft, *Recollections of Full Years*, pp. 84-85, 99-100, 114-115, 123-127, 148; William H. Taft, *Civil Government in the Philippines* (New York: The Outlook Company, 1902), pp. 69-74; Kalaw, *Case for the Filipinos*, p. 130; Willard D. Gatewood, *"Smoked Yankees" and the Struggle for Empire* (Champaign-Urbana: University of Illinois Press, 1971).

35. Majul, "Political and Constitutional Ideas," pp. 73-74; Agoncillo, "Malolos," pp. 576-580; Mabini, *The Philippine Revolution*, pp. 3-4; Fernandez, "The Philippine Republic," p. 174.

36. Blount, *American Occupation of the Philippines*, p. 340; Agoncillo, "Malolos," pp. 600ff.; H. H. Taft, *Recollections of Full Years*, p. 149.

37. Leech, *In the Days of McKinley*, pp. 568-573; Pratt, *America's Colonial Experiment*, p. 197.

38. Salamanca, *Filipino Reaction to American Rule*, pp. 39-43; Kalaw, *Case for the Filipinos*, pp. 131-132, 145-146; Jessup, *Elihu Root*, vol. 1, pp. 359-363; W. H. Taft, *Civil Government in the Philippines*, pp. 86-95; Blount, *American Occupation of the Philippines*, pp. 370-376, passim.

39. W. H. Taft, *Civil Government in the Philippines*, pp. 101-103, 208ff.; Kalaw, *Case for the Filipinos*, p. 230.

40. Salamanca, *Filipino Reaction to American Rule*, pp. 35, 46-48, 55-62, 157-158; Pratt, *America's Colonial Experiment*, pp. 195-197; Majul, "Political and Constitutional Ideas," p. 87; W. H. Taft, *Civil Government in the Philippines*, pp. 31-39, 50-53ff.; H. H. Taft, *Recollections of Full Years*, pp. 150-151.

41. Frederick Merk, *Manifest Destiny and Mission in American History: A Reinterpretation* (New York: Alfred Knopf, 1973), pp. 256-265. Merk distinguishes American expansionism in the Caribbean and the Philippines from both Manifest Destiny, which he sees as limited to the North American continent, and the idea of mission, which he associates with an idealistic, pro-democratic stance contrary to the spirit of aggressive political expansion. The fact remains, however, that the missionary idea was relied upon heavily and with considerable success by those who urged American annexation of the Philippines.

42. Robin W. Winks, "American and European Imperialism Compared," in Miller, *American Imperialism in 1898*, pp. 174ff.; Schurman, *Philippine Affairs*, p. 53; Kalaw, *Case for the Filipinos*, pp. 177, 236, 267; Dulles, *America in the Pacific*, pp. 3, 256; Pringle, *William Howard Taft*, pp. 176-177, 194, 205-206.

CHAPTER SEVEN

The United States and the Soviet Union: The Problem of Recognition, 1917–1933

If the twentieth century was the coming of age of the United States as a great power, it was also the century in which the isolationist traditions of the past remained firm enough until World War II to inhibit acceptance of leadership, both in the establishment of international organization and in the management of binational relations. Ironically, it was in the twentieth century that the United States deviated from the apparently realistic diplomacy of the nineteenth century, when recognition of foreign powers was made irrespective of the regimes in power providing that those governments controlled their societies and discharged appropriate international obligations. This practice prevailed partly because foreign relations were not major matters of public concern and partly because recognition was not attached to morality as long as one foreign country was as good or bad as another. For example, the president or the Congress might deplore the repressive policies of czarist Russia, which sent millions into flight at the turn of the twentieth century, but this state of affairs was to be expected in the evil old world and was not an aberration to be corrected by breaking relations.

This laissez-faire sentiment seemed to change with greater American involvement on the world stage. The moralism which had always been present in America's self-image of superiority was to be displayed repeatedly in the first half of the twentieth century — by Wilson in 1913 in his loathing of Huerta's Mexico, and by Truman in 1949 when the America of the Cold War refused to accept the legitimacy of Communist China. The act of nonrecognition was accompanied, in the case of Secretary of State Stimson's expectations in Manchuria in 1932, by the assumption that American power was in a position to change the offending policies of Japan by the weight of its disapproval. Although Stimson himself may have expected this step to be a prelude to economic or military pressures against the aggressor, American opinion, along with President Hoover, accepted nonrecognition both as a proper expression of moral aversion and as a signal for the eventual dissolution of the offending government. The latter anticipation was realized in Mexico, after a fashion, and even in Japan if the disaster of 1945 is considered a consequence of earlier misdeeds. The People's Republic of China stands today as a reproach to this pattern, but then many other assumptions about international affairs have faded or been exploded in the latter half of the twentieth century.

Is the conception of recognition as a moral problem really an aberration from the course of American diplomatic history? In turning to the precedent of 1793, historians generally agree that Secretary of State Jefferson established that the alliance with republican France was just as valid as the alliance with monarchical France had been and that the former's minister should be as acceptable as the latter's had been. From one angle of observation Jefferson's behavior was a species of realpolitik. From another, it was an emotional response. His passionate belief in the goodness of the new French republican government led him to the position of recognition. Conceivably, Jefferson might have adopted a Hamiltonian stance if the situation had been reversed and a monarchical, Anglophile France had asked for recognition after deposing a republican regime by violence. Speculative though the answer may be, the question is worth posing in light of twentieth-century behavior.

The Russian Revolution of 1917 invites an examination of this question more than any other issue in the twentieth century. For one thing, its similarity to the French Revolution is striking. Both represented dynamic challenges to the existing world

order, and both evoked strong emotional reactions from the
United States. Although America's position in the world had
changed radically over two centuries, many of its moral postures
have persisted unchanged. From their enemies the French and
Russian revolutions both brought forth charges of anarchy and
atheism, with attending dangerous implications for the United
States. In both cases the chances of revolutionary triumph in
America were remote. Yet hysteria was induced by the fierce
advocacy of American partisans—"Jacobins" and "Bolsheviks"—who saw in the French and Russian revolutions the
realization of American principles. A larger number of Americans saw in them threats to the American system. Both debates
lasted a generation. The one major difference was that the
United States had formal relations with the governments of
France, except during an interlude of naval warfare. The Soviet
Union, on the other hand, went unrecognized by the United
States.

For over fifteen years the question of recognition hung over
American-Russian relations. The terms of the internal debate
frequently took on economic forms: recognition would or would
not bring trade profits to America, or it would or would not prop
up a failing Russian economy. But behind the language of commerce lay the vital fact of the Soviet Union as a new experiment
that America must embrace or destroy. An image of Communist
Russia as the destroyer of the capitalist world order more than as
a country which failed to pay its debts underlay the objections of
the enemies of the Soviet Union. With equal passion, defenders
of the Soviet experiment insisted, with Lincoln Steffens, that it
was a vision of the future and that it worked. Whatever its blemishes, it elaborated upon the promise that was originally
America's, to make a better society for the oppressed peoples of
the world. In its educational programs, social services, and equitable distribution of resources, it promised what the Progressives in America had failed to achieve in the 1920s. Such was the
view of the radicals, the devotees of a cause, which affected even
those less susceptible to the blandishments of communism.
Trade advantages for American manufacturers, investment
potential for American capital, and the Americanizing effect of

formal relations were far more frequently advanced as reasons for recognition. But underlying the logical arguments ran a deep vein of emotion.

Russia was either a dream or a nightmare, not simply a nation changing its form of government. The French Revolution held some of this quality, but, unlike the Americans of 1793, twentieth-century Americans felt their power must be exercised for or against the new system. The recoil of isolationism in the 1920s was against the old balance of power, the familiar evils of Europe. Communism was something new, but the weapon of recognition was deemed compatible both with abstention from the affairs of the Old World by keeping the communist virus away from American shores and with the active promotion of the downfall of an unnatural politico-economic system. By abstaining from a formal connection with this evil, America could combat the threat without departing from the spirit of isolationism.

The rejection of Europe following the painful experiences at Versailles may have been an inevitable consequence of the unrealistic expectations aroused by Wilsonian rhetoric. It is questionable, though, whether rejection of revolution was equally inevitable. After all, the United States had always looked upon its foreign relations as a species apart from Europe's. The Bolshevik opposition to the traditional power structure and to national wars might have reinforced an American position toward a disordered world and could have yielded a Russo-American entente on international affairs. While the angle of observation was quite different, a common aversion to European imperialism might have offered a genuine link. The Soviet vision of a new world order might have held attractions for a broad spectrum of American liberals.

But from the beginning, no such harmony was achieved amid the confusion of events, although the Fourteen Points represented an American offering toward understanding. Part of the problem was the timing of the entry of Bolshevism into American consciousness. It came on the heels and in place of an earlier moderate revolution which had replaced the autocracy of the Czar early in 1917 with what appeared to be a republican regime similar in values to the American republic. Moreover, the Kerensky government, in contrast to the Bolsheviks, was committed to a vigorous prosecution of the war with Germany. Their Bolshevik leaders, Lenin and Trotsky, seemed to be puppets of the Kaiser, sponsored by Germany for the express purpose of undermining Russia's will to fight. Their withdrawal of Russia from the war confirmed these suspicions. Thus, the Bolshevik revolution emerged just as the passions of war had swept America. Whatever goodwill or indifference might have been extended to any new government under ordinary circumstances was lost in the mood of an America mobilized for war. In this context alone Bolshevism appears as an ally of the enemy.

Wilson's apprehension over the course of Russian events was first expressed in the mission of Elihu Root to Russia in the spring of 1917 to strengthen Russian determination to pursue a war that had no imperialist objectives in view. The regime was in trouble, struggling to maintain itself amid the revolutionary waves made when the Czar was removed. Yet the commission's report was optimistic, to the surprise of Secretary of State Lansing. Its members saw the Bolsheviks in action and dismissed them. Even Charles Edward Russell, a prowar Socialist, drew the wrong conclusions about Bolshevik prospects. Unlike Root and Charles Crane, his fellow members, he did not want a separate peace with the Germans. A sound thrashing from German forces would wake them up fully to the menace of the Kaiser.

Having emphasized the essential steadfastness of the Kerensky government in pursuing the war and containing the Bolsheviks, the Root Commission returned home in the summer of 1917 only to find the Bolsheviks in power and the war coming to an inglorious end for Russia in the fall. An explanation of this turn of events was seemingly provided when Edgar Sisson, a former editor of *Cosmopolitan* and representative in Russia of the Committee on Public Information, uncovered the "Sisson Documents" in the winter of 1918, which seemed to prove that Lenin and Trotsky were German agents. According to the contents of these papers, which were circulated widely by Sisson's propaganda agency, the Bolshevist leaders were paid by Germany expressly to remove Russia from the war. Although these documents were quickly exposed as forgeries, their story was too satisfactory an explanation for Soviet behavior to lose currency.

The man who identified the forgeries was another informal agent in Russia, Col. Raymond Robins of the American Red Cross, a friend of Theodore Roosevelt and a leader of the Progressive party. Robins had arrived in Russia in August 1917 with much the same objective as Sisson was to have a few months later, namely, to revive the flagging war spirit of the Russians. A social worker as well as politician, Robins quickly immersed himself in Russian politics, supporting Kerensky. When the latter fell, Robins was prepared to work with the Bolsheviks, not out of sympathy for their program but out of recognition that "revolutions never go backward." Unlike Sisson, he operated on the assumption that the new men in power would remain active in the war with Germany if the United States provided some support or at least a strong earnest of intentions to provide aid. In late 1917 and through the winter of 1918 Robins was the conduit between Lenin and Trotsky and the American government.

Throughout this confused period there was an American ambassador in Petrograd in the person of David Francis, a former governor of Missouri, who never quite understood what was going on around him. He had been no more acute than the Root Commission in anticipating the demise of the Kerensky government, and he had less excuse. While Foster Rhea Dulles has characterized him as "well-meaning, visionary, and kindly," he was also insensitive and inept.[1] After dismissing the Bolsheviks as some species of anarchist nuisance, he clung to the notion that even if they took power, they could not hold it. His recommendation to do nothing, to ignore the Soviets until they disappeared, was accepted by the State Department. The immediate result was the immobilization of American diplomacy, with Francis remaining in Petrograd doing nothing and understanding nothing. The Soviets accepted this self-isolation lest his expulsion serve as an excuse for active American collaboration with anti-Bolsheviks. To his credit, Francis initially made no overtures to White forces or czarist groups in the remote hope that, temporary as the Bolshevik phenomenon was, it still could be enlisted in support of the war. Eventually, he came to the conclusion that only Allied intervention in Russia would make a difference and, incidentally, make an end to Bolshevik rule.

In the face of Francis's inaction, the energetic Robins could operate without restraints. Indeed, the Ambassador was willing for a time to employ Robins's putative influence with the Soviet leaders to win their acceptance for American troops to be landed on Russian soil. Robins's air of confidence melted such hard-headed men as Gen. William Judson of the American military mission and Col. William Boyce Thompson, a mining engineer and Robins's predecessor as head of the Red Cross in Russia. For a time, Robins believed that he would have Lenin's approval to circulate Wilson's Fourteen Points, and he cultivated his Soviet acquaintances, leading them to believe that they would have American assistance if only they would follow his advice.

The Bolshevik vision of a new order would have been sufficient to deter massive American aid even if the ability to deliver it had existed. The continuing tales of property expropriation, bloody suppression of opposition, and the destruction of religious institutions all fastened upon the American mind to inhibit Wilson and Lansing from supportive action even if they had wished to provide it. Their answer to Russian developments in the spring of 1918 was simply the removal of the Bolsheviks. The final signing of the Treaty of Brest-Litovsk was apparent confirmation of their judgment. As surrender was being made, Trotsky made one final appeal before ratification, using Robins again as his intermediary, in which he asked what America would do if the Russians renewed the war. Wilson had answered this question even before he received it by the nature of his message to the All-Russian Congress of Soviets on March 11. His answer was negative, presumably because the United States was not in a position to provide the help needed at the critical moment. But it would have been all the more negative had he responded to Trotsky's provision that "the internal and foreign policies of the Soviet Government will continue to be directed in accord with the principles of international socialism." The elliptical qualities of the above were explicitly articulated in the reply of the Russian Congress, which looked to the day "when the laboring masses of all countries will throw off the yoke of capitalism and will establish a socialist state of society, which alone is capable of securing just and lasting peace."[2] The break seemed complete.

The course of events in the spring of 1918 destroyed the lively campaign that Robins, who had converted so many American doubters in Russia, had been mounting in Washington. Writing off Soviet participation in the war, Robins then urged recognition of the Bolshevik government "to use existing Russian opinion and governmental activity to undermine the morale of the German army." Let Bolshevik propaganda work against the Germans. As Colonel Thompson, en route to Washington, told Lloyd George in London, "Let's make these Bolsheviks our Bolsheviks; don't let the Germans make them their Bolsheviks."[3]

Thompson's credentials were impressive. A millionaire mining engineer, he had donated a million dollars out of his own pocket to the Kerensky Provisional Government of Russia to help prop up the war effort. When Kerensky failed, he spread the word that the new government could serve as well as the old. Robins and Thompson found auditors of some importance, ranging from Colonel House and George Creel to Russian expert Samuel R. Harper of the University of Chicago and the muckraking journalist Lincoln Steffens. It was through the latter that Walter Lippmann approached Colonel House to send the brilliant young William Bullitt to Russia to explore possibilities for a detente. But Robins remained the most important member of this circle, his authority bolstered by his close ties with his secretary and translator, the Russian-born Alexander Gumberg, a New York Jew with family links to the Communist leadership in the Soviet Union.

Why President Wilson refused to meet Thompson is a matter of speculation. One explanation may be personal pique with the man himself. Robins's service with Theodore Roosevelt and the support of the former President were not factors that would help their case with Wilson. But Wilson may have listened to the advice of the State Department, which had accepted Francis's immobilism as the only practical policy for the moment. Or he may have been influenced by Sisson's harsh judgment of Robins as both gullible and malleable.[4] Still, Wilson's silence was not necessarily hostile to Russia in early 1918. The Fourteen Points, as Thompson noted, accomplished nine-tenths of what he had urged on the President, and Colonel House's reactions were in favor of a rational exploitation of the Bolsheviks.[5]

On the surface, Wilson reacted in concert with the Allies, providing troops for occupation of strategic parts of Russia, from Murmansk to Vladivostok. Later, these actions would be justified as necessary to destroy the Communist virus that was spreading so widely with the help of radicals everywhere. Certainly, the end of the Bolshevik regime was expected to follow Allied liberation of the land. The anticipations of a journal such as *Iron Age*, welcoming the Allied Expeditionary Force for the Russian markets it would open up to Americans, suggest another familiar reason for intervention. Influential businessmen with experience in Russia, such as Frederick Corse, former manager of the Russian division of the New York Insurance Company, and R. D. McCarter, former president of the Westinghouse factory in Moscow, applauded intervention for its impact upon the Bolshevik position as an enemy of capitalism.[6]

But did Wilson move for these reasons? Military explanations are more fitting, even though his major military advisers — Secretary of War Newton Baker and Generals Peyton C. March and John J. Pershing — opposed the expedition to Russia on the grounds that the cost would be too great for the results. The hope was to keep Allied supplies out of German hands in the West and to keep Germans released from prisoner-of-war camps from threatening Russia sovereignty in the East. But the avowed intention was to station troops in such a way as to help Czech former prisoners of war, who, in the summer of 1918, controlled stretches of the Trans-Siberian Railway which they used to find their way back to fighting against the Germans. In retrospect, Wilson's protestations of helping the Russians or of helping the Czechs were disingenuous. He wanted the obnoxious Bolshevik government to disappear once the Allies arrived, but he did not want the United States to appear either as a fellow imperialist alongside the other intervening powers or as an open accomplice of reactionary White forces in Russia. Thus, the plight of the Czechs offered a convenient way to circumvent the major problem.

Pressures for withdrawal became intense once the war with Germany had ended. The plight of the Czechs was a thing of the past, while the Soviet position had not crumpled as expected. Demands for the evacuation of troops were not simply cries by friends of Communism; they were the voices of an America disillusioned with the entire outside world. Unless the purpose of the American presence in Russia was the assurance of a White victory over the Reds, almost all excuses for staying had disappeared. The only other remaining reason was a fear that Japan would annex parts of Siberia unless the United States and its 90,000 troops dissuaded it. Such an assumption would reflect a realpolitik that did not seem to characterize America policy generally in this period. Yet it fitted the fitful outbursts of suspicion over Japan's ambitions in Asia, and it fitted also the American need to present an altruistic face to its activities. American troops remained in Siberia until April 1920.

The Soviet leaders themselves had sensed American discomfort with their ambiguous position in Russia and looked to Wilson for assistance at the Paris Peace Conference. From Stockholm, Maxim Litvinov appealed to the President for Soviet participation in any discussion of Russian problems on the grounds of the similarity of Soviet and American war aims. To soften the Allies, the Russians spoke of recognizing czarist war debts and granting concessions for foreign exploitation of natural resources as well as of abstaining from interference in domestic affairs of other nations. Such was the information gained by W. H. Buckler, an American attaché at the London Embassy, whom the United States had sent to Stockholm to learn more about Soviet attitudes. Wilson, at this junction, appeared to be influenced more by House's realism than by Lansing's rigidity. Although he was unable to win the Allies over to accepting a Soviet delegation in Paris, he did succeed in a plan to have all the Russian factions meet at Prinkipo Island in the Sea of Marmora. Anti-Bolshevik obstinacy, nourished by some of the Allies, frustrated all accommodation; the Whites refused to meet with the Reds.

But American hopes had not expired. Wilson's new flexibility sparked a new mission, led by youthful William C. Bullitt, a newspaperman and former Washington bureaucrat well connected with the State Department. Along with the veteran Lincoln Steffens, Bullitt made a fact-finding tour of the Soviet Union to see for himself what terms the Russians would accept for a détente with the United States. That this mission had the blessings of Colonel House was obvious. That it had the full understanding of the President was another matter. Wilson knew of Bullitt's proposals and endorsed them implicitly, at least in regarding informal meetings useful to create conditions for ultimate settlement of differences between the two countries. Bullitt jumped to the conclusion that he had the mission to conclude a definite program of rapprochement, and he took it upon himself to make an agreement with Lenin whereby the debt problem would be solved and hostilities cease in exchange for removal of Allied troops and the end of Allied support to any faction. The impressionable Bullitt returned to Paris convinced of Soviet honesty and goodwill, only to find himself first ignored and then rejected by the President. Angry and disgusted, he resigned and returned home to embarrass Wilson subsequently by revealing details of his visit at a hostile Senate Foreign Relations Committee hearing.

Whatever solution the President might have taken alone, he was inhibited in the longer run by his nation's mood. Rejected as he was to be over his plans for Western Europe, he would have been much more vulnerable had his plans for Eastern Europe included recognition of the Soviet state. American disillusionment with involvement in the World War was rapidly degenerating into the Red Scare in 1919 with its focus on subversive Russian agents.

Advocates of recognition themselves damaged their cause by the passions they inspired in others. In this respect, Bullitt was of a different breed from that of Thompson or Robins. The latter were realists who, during the war, wanted to harness the energies of Bolshevism to America's purposes. Romantics—poets, journalists, social workers—who visited Russia in large numbers from the time of John Reed in the midst of the Revolution down to Franklin Roosevelt's accession to the presidency were moved not only to voice their loud praise of the Soviet Union but also to use that praise to damn American institutions. By urging America to learn from and emulate the Soviet model of the good society, they frightened and angered potential friends of recognition among the industrial and political communities.

The liberals' eloquence and sincerity impressed Soviet leaders, who made themselves remarkably accessible to many of the devoted American tourists. Not that Lenin or Trotsky or Chicherin, the foreign minister, genuinely anticipated immediate revolution in America with their visitors as the instigators. But they hoped to exploit such enthusiasm to influence American policy in ways which could serve the Soviet Union, from formal recognition to acknowledgment of Russia's usefulness as a buffer in Asia against Japan. The Russians were occasionally misled into believing that their American informants had more power than was the case, but they did not stop their attempts at reaching the larger society through special constituencies. Trotsky's failure with Robins did not prevent Lenin from trying to work through Bullitt.

They counted also on the cupidity of American businessmen and financiers to influence American policy. On the strength of such expectations, Foreign Minister Chicherin had his informal agent in New York, Ludwig C.A.K. Martens, seek recognition as the Soviet ambassador to the United States in 1919. Martens, a New York resident since 1916, was at first ignored and then, after dealings with American business firms, was arrested and ultimately deported as an undesirable alien. Later in the same year, Russian eagerness to woo American capitalists led Lenin to confuse Washington Vanderlip, a fast-talking California mining engineer, with the distinguished Frank A. Vanderlip of the National City Bank of New York. In a spectacular deal with the Soviets, Vanderlip represented twenty leading financiers in winning from Lenin a sixty-year lease of vast areas in Kamchatka which were apparently ripe for developing coal and fisheries. This bonanza of some three billions of dollars in the future never materialized, although it was never clear who was taken by whom. Lenin's purpose was to use "American kulaks" of the Vanderlip stripe to involve the United States in the Soviet-Japanese conflict in Kamchatka, since Japan controlled much of the territory at the time. [7]

With all the rebuffs following the war, Russian leaders could not resist the temptation of using their connections, despite the limitations. The romantic intellectual was more attractive to deal with than the business shark, if only because the former flattered their egos, much as the French intelligentsia had done for Jefferson during his service in France. Those followers who had lived through the revolution, as Lafayette had in America, were the purest of this genre. They were converts. Perhaps John Reed, who wrote *Ten Days That Shook the World*, was the most notable. The young, brash, and intolerant Reed and his wife Louise Bryant revealed in full their distaste for the society of their own country as they expounded the virtues of the new Russian paradise. Reed may have been the "foolish and rebellious child" of George Kennan's judgment, but his account of the Revolution is honest, evocative, and memorable.[8] The Soviet leaders were fully appreciative of his potential service, as they revealed in appointing him the Soviet consul-general in New York.

In the 1920s this kind of romanticism would be refueled by the cries of appreciative pilgrims from the social sciences as well as the rats. Lewis Feuer claimed that social workers found the Soviet Union a kind of Hull House on a national scale.[9] Indeed, Jane Addams's flat verdict was that the Russian Revolution was "the greatest social experiment in history."[10] Educators were equally ecstatic for a time. John Dewey wrote in 1928, "I have never seen anywhere in the world such a large proportion of intelligent, happy, and intelligently occupied children." His colleague at Columbia, George Counts, who spent almost a year in Russia in the late 1920s, felt that the Soviet experiment in education was "so bold in its ideals and in its program that few can contemplate it without emotion."[11]

Emotional responses also marked the approval of American minority groups observing the Soviet promise of equality for citizens and respect for the cultural diversity of the many races and nationalities in Russia. Jews, in particular, looked with some surprise and much pleasure upon the transformation of a society that had expelled them. The new Russia seemed to have eliminated anti-Semitism, an achievement symbolized by the prominence of Jews among the Soviet leaders, and at the same time publicly cultivated Yiddish culture. Jewish philosopher Horace Kallen and Negro historian W.E.B. DuBois saw in Russia, for a time, solutions to the problems of cultural pluralism.

The very fervor of the friends of the revolution helped to solidify anti-Bolshevik feeling in the United States in the early postwar years. The intimacy of some enthusiasts with Russian officials rendered them suspect as propagandists and agents of radical dogma, preaching the destruction of American values. In their anger over a war in which America felt betrayed, the public lashed out at the new menace bred by that war. The fundamental challenge to American institutions made Bolsheviks a more usable scapegoat than the defeated Huns or the sons of perfidious Albion. Revolutionary calls for the destruction of capitalism, echoed by such men as John Reed as a worthy goal, helped to arouse a hysteria which remained alive if not always virulent for fifteen years after the war. In 1919 it permitted the attorney-general to arrest almost 5,000 and deport 249 Russian aliens accused of being Communists. Congress did its part in sounding the alarm over Soviet subversion through a series of hearings on Bolshevik propaganda before a subcommittee of the Senate Committee on the Judiciary in 1919, with a sequel before a subcommittee of the Senate Committee on Foreign Relations in the following year. The possibility of recognition of the Soviet Union was not even in question in these circumstances.

This theme of subversion was developed more consistently by organized labor, particularly by Samuel Gompers of the American Federation of Labor, than by any other interest group in the country. A flickering sympathy for a proletarian heaven was tentatively put forth by a few leaders, such as Sidney Hillman of the Amalgamated Clothing Workers of America, and there was a more anxious concern for Russian trade during the postwar depression on the part of such leaders as Timothy Healy, president of the International Brotherhood of Stationary Firemen and Oilers. These feelings were vague and minor notes in the response of labor to the idea of recognition.

Gompers's position was both articulate and widely heard. During the war Gompers had cheered the revolution in April 1917 for purging the czarist taint from the crusade against the Kaiser. Once he became aware of Bolshevik power as an enemy of the war, he also identified it as an enemy of American labor. The Soviet government's disregard for human life and its autocratic dictatorship of the proletariat were all the more dangerous for its concurrent claims to being spokesman of the laboring classes. Gompers pointed to the system of forced labor, with the worker chained to his job as if he were a medieval serf. More resolutely than capitalist agencies, the AFL attacked the Soviet Union condemning any signs of trade relations and opposing recognition. Indeed, Gompers attacked businessmen for their faltering resolve: "If the Soviets are given a certain permanence and success as 'moderates' by the aid of certain governments and financiers, they will certainly continue to represent this success to the labor of the world as having come from their own efforts as 'ultra-revolutionists.'"[12] In the end, labor would pay more dearly than capital if communism should survive and spread. The AFL Convention of 1920 passed a resolution rejecting any action "which could be construed as assistance to or approval of, the Soviet government of Russia. . . ." The union maintained this position throughout the next ten years with a vigor not found in other sectors of society.

The contrast is striking between this stern stance and the softer position of financiers and industrialists, who were frequently tempted by Soviet economic inducements. Capitalists, however strong their distaste for Bolsheviks, could rationalize commercial or diplomatic relations with the Soviet Union out of an awareness of a great market to be tapped. Yet they usually retreated before reproaches from colleagues who saw a threat to American civilization in the Russian challenge. Even more pointedly, the majority of American businessmen were aware of the instability of the communist system implicit in the imprisonment or banishment of technicians and the decline in production of goods. A leading journal, *Iron Age*, quoted figures provided by a special mission sent to Russia by the International Labor Office to find out the effects of Bolshevism upon industry. They found the metallurgical industry in complete collapse and locomotive labor suffering increased costs of 1300 percent.[13] Still other industrialists were alarmed by Soviet economic practices which undercut American competition, as in the manganese industry. It is not surprising that a spokesman for that industry before a congressional committee in 1931 should have equated the communist world plan to destroy America with a Russian attempt to monopolize the world's manganese market.[14]

But fear of Soviet economic power was a minor note, at least
until the depression of the 1930s. The basic capitalist assumptions repeated throughout the 1920s were that Bolshevism could
not survive without a return to capitalistic methods and that the
New Economic Policy in the early 1920s was a confession of
failure. The absurdity of Soviet pretensions were well expressed
when Julian Barnes, president of the Chamber of Commerce,
asked incredulously in 1925 how a nation, "living just above the
verge of utter barbarism," dared to tell "orderly America, busy
with its expanded economic life and social opportunities, typified
by its eighteen million automobiles and its towering skyscrap-
ers," how to run an economy. [15] Most businessmen were prepared to accept the verdict of Secretary of Commerce Herbert
Hoover, that economic rehabilitation of Russia was impossible
as long as the Bolsheviks remained in power. But confidence in
American superiority led a minority of businessmen to favor a
closer relationship with Russia on the assumption that Americans would profit. American capitalists were not the most solid
component of the national front against recognition of the Soviet
Union.

There was some ambivalence among religious leaders. Charges
of atheism and lurid examples of godlessness in action fastened
upon the American mind. In 1923 the widely publicized execution of Monsignor Buchkavitch, vicar general of the Roman
Catholic Church in Russia, on grounds of counterrevolutionary
activity invigorated the atheist issue and impressed many
Americans with the brutality and antireligious fundament of
communism. From the Vatican point of view, the death of Buchkavitch was all the harsher because it dashed hopes for the
Romanization of Russia in the wake of revulsion against Russian
Orthodoxy.

Despite setbacks, Soviet leaders hoped that a new administration would look more favorably upon their interests. Recognizing
the frailties of their most enthusiastic supporters, after 1920
they looked to the influence of moderates and realists who seemingly felt that business on every level should and could be done
with Communists. Although most of these interests were in-
herently hostile to the Soviet system, the Russian leaders anti-

cipated a favorable American response to Soviet resistance to Japanese expansion in Asia, to Soviet purchase of American manufactures, or to the Soviet's honoring of czarist war debts. Such responses could be found coming from many diverse sources in the United States, including industrialists with second thoughts about ideological opposition to anti-communism to liberal journals such as the *Nation* and *New Republic*, and even to less liberal newspapers of the order of the *New York Times*. Most significant was the cooperation of a group of well-connected political men, public and private, who tried to use their influence to promote recognition of the Soviet Union.

The key figures in this group were the aforementioned Colonel Robins and his confidant, Alexander Gumberg. Despite his sharp disappointment with Wilson, Robins was not discouraged for long. He allied himself quickly with powerful senators, such as William E. Borah of Idaho, a foe of Wilsonianism who viewed the President's Russian policy as another example of an absurd world outlook, and Hiram Johnson of California, another devout isolationist. Borah succeeded Lodge to the chairmanship of the Senate Foreign Relations Committee in 1924. This alliance was to be joined in the 1920s by a host of business interests, including ultimately the Fords and the Morgans.

The election of Harding initially raised the hopes of proponents of a new Russian policy, only to have them dashed against the obstinacy of Secretary of State Charles Evans Hughes. The Republican secretary underscored his predecessor's refusal to deal with the Soviets until problems of stability, debts, and propaganda had been solved. Indeed, the Republican opposition to recognition was apparently all the firmer because it emphasized the economic crimes of Russia, a matter of considerable weight in Harding's America. Hughes had the backing of Secretary of Commerce Herbert Hoover, who was convinced there could be no successful dealings with Russians until the Soviet system was abandoned. Litvinov's suggestion that recognition must precede trade was summarily rejected, subject to reconsideration only "if fundamental changes are contemplated, involving due regard for the protection of persons and property and establishment of conditions essential to the maintenance of commerce."[16]

Borah and Robins contested these decisions, but with little effect. Not that Harding was not open to their views. Against Hughes's better judgment, the President was persuaded to send Robins to Russia to explore possibilities of a new policy. Even more influential was the report of Albert Fall, the secretary of the interior, who not only visited Russia but returned full of enthusiasm over economic opportunities in that country. By 1923 he in turn had interested Attorney-General Harry Daugherty and oil executive Harry Sinclair in a syndicate to develop oil properties in Baku and Sakhalin. Oil was a powerful force in the Harding administration. But Harding's death and the subsequent Teapot Dome scandal ended this scheme abruptly, since the principals in that affair involved oil, Fall, and Sinclair.

One of the ironies in the problem of recognition was that the motives of the most powerful proponents were commercial (in a nation dedicated to the advancement of business), while the major defenders of the status quo rested their claims primarily on morality. Moralists Hughes and Hoover easily overcame opportunists of the stripe of Fall and Sinclair. Robins and his associates, with all their claims to realism, were forced to make their case on the same moral grounds as their opponents, and they lost. While Robins mocked Hughes in asserting that the Secretary of State "would like to have all Bolsheviks join the Baptist Church," his own demands for recognition were based less on commercial profit or strategic interests than on the ability of the Soviets to create order, redeem claims, and permit freedom of worship.[17] Robins had to contend further with the fact that Hoover's and Hughes's moral posture on recognition was underpinned by the conventional wisdom of the day that the communist system was doomed to failure in any event. The New Economic Policy, with its indulgence of private enterprise, was seen as a sign of the impending demise of Bolshevism.

For a time in the mid-1920s it seemed that Coolidge might be the bridge to recognition, if only because of his desire to woo the liberal wing of the Republican party. In 1925, when Borah replaced Lodge as chairman of the Foreign Relations Committee and Hughes left office, new hearings on recognition were held by the Senate. Borah failed that year, and again in successive years, to effect change. And, with repeated failure, the élan of Borah and Robins collapsed. In fact, Coolidge's conciliatory gestures toward the Soviet Union in his annual message of 1923, wherein he spoke of concessions in the interest of closer relations, underlined their failure. The Russians immediately seized upon the message as if it were a proposal of recognition, thereby producing a public reaction so negative that Hughes, in the closing days of his service, managed to issue a rejection to the Russians in offensive terms. Coolidge wilted under this pressure, and the spirits of the liberal reformers who would bring Russia back into traditional relations with the United States wilted with him.

The opposition to recognition was too strong in the 1920s. But even had the circumstances been different, it was not clear just what the Robins-Borah group wanted of Soviet-American relations. Was it an embrace of Russia to help reconstruct the world, as the outlawry-of-war propagandists desired? Was it an understanding that the Soviet system was really no threat to the American system and that anti-Bolshevism was simply a mask for repression of American liberties? Or was it the promotion of trade, penetrating and recasting the Russian economy by means of America's industrial power, thereby refashioning Russia in the American image while winning profits from the transaction? Their objectives were never clarified, while the hostility based on revulsion against the economic, political, and religious heresies of communism had the advantage of clarity and simplicity.

If liberal senators, from Burton Wheeler and Robert LaFollette, who visited the Soviet Union in 1923, to William Borah and Hiram Johnson, were ineffectual on the issue of Soviet recognition, the failure mirrored their general ineffectuality. The scores of journalists, social workers, educators, and economists who visited the Soviet Union throughout this period were even less successful in imprinting their mark on Americans. A delegation of trade unionists, guided by innovative young economists Rexford Tugwell of Columbia and Paul Douglas of Chicago, came away from interviews with Stalin in 1927 impressed that "the big fact, the spiritual fact behind all this material evidence, is that there is a real community of belief, a national idea and moral unity, which is the solid basis of the new Russia." As for dictatorship, "the real rights, that is their economic rights, are much better protected than in any other country." [18] But a fellow dele-

gate, Silas Axtell, a lawyer and member of the International
Seamen's Union of North America, was far closer to the national
reaction to these encomia in claiming that the ecstatic guests
saw only what their hosts wanted them to see. They were manipulated, Axtell asserted, by men who "seem to have acquired
the modern American method of salesmanship so far as selling
the idea that communism or state socialism, whichever it is, is a
success."[19]

While it is likely that neither recommendations nor dissent
had much impact on American opinion, there were two forces in
the 1920s which did carry weight. One of them, the spirit of altruism which tapped an American sense of mission, was temporary
if impressive. Famine in Russia in 1921 moved Hoover to his
familiar role of provider as America poured millions of dollars'
worth of food into the stricken country without caveats about its
government. This gesture represented no national change of
heart about communism; it was an American reflex in the face of
a tactical and quantifiable problem of service. In winning twenty
million dollars out of the unspent profits of the United States
Grain Corporation to expand the Russian relief mission, Hoover
was proving to himself and to his countrymen the superiority of
the American system over communism. An unshakable confidence was demonstrated here.

If any other force could have demanded and won change in this
period, it should have been the words and actions of business and
industrial leaders and engineers in building Soviet Russia in the
middle and late 1920s. As has been noted, from the beginnings of
the Russian Revolution, interest in Russia as an outlet for investment and development had softened business attitudes toward
communism. Even as businessmen anticipated the fall of the
Bolsheviks, they listened to the blandishments of Soviet leaders
seeking connections with American capitalists. Their complaints
forced revocation of the trade embargo in 1920 and opened the
way for adventurers to seek their fortunes in Russia. Fall and
Sinclair were not isolated figures. Yet their unsavory reputa-
tions, along with the failures of most of the enterprises, stiffened
the hands of Hoover and Hughes in refusing the extension of
credits to Soviet-American projects and in refusing Soviet gold
in payment for American services. The gold was represented as

stolen property of the czarist regime expropriated by the Bolsheviks, and credits were inconceivable for a regime without morality. This position remained firm until the middle of the decade.

There was a change in the atmosphere of economic relations after 1924, induced in part by the willingness of such large American firms as Standard Oil, General Electric, and International Harvester to grant their own commercial credits to Russia on relatively favorable terms. While the American official position had not budged, the Soviet Union was receiving more materials from the United States in the 1920s than czarist Russia had before the war. In fact, the United States led the world in 1924-1925 among nations exporting to the Soviet Union. In the latter part of the decade, the giants of American industry accelerated their Russian operations so that the 1,000 American engineers in Russia in 1921 had grown to 10,000 ten years later. American industry exploited the Russian appetite for technical skills to such an extent that the Russian automobile industry was essentially an American creation. Henry Ford was as much the symbol of the Russian as of the American automobile age. The intimacy between Ford and the Soviet Union inevitably affected at least one powerful element in the American capitalist establishment in its attitude toward communism. The affair began in 1926 when Ford was invited to send a delegation to train staffs to service 20,000 or more tractors and to investigate the feasibility of building a tractor factory in the Soviet Union. Ford's involvement expanded rapidly over the next few years.

The observations of the Ford observers and planners were not uniformly flattering to the Russians; they recognized the paucity of managerial talent, the inefficiency of labor, the primitive state of technology, and the constant interference of political commissars. Their perceptions were shared by most of the men who went to work in Russia, and many commented at length upon these conditions. Engineer George Burrell, under contract with the Soviet petroleum industry, spent eighteen months in the Caucasus mountain country where he experienced firsthand the drabness of Russian life with its bad housing, poor quality of food, and harassment from Soviet officials. Another engineer, Walter Rukeyser, working in an asbestos mining community in the Urals in 1929, witnessed similar conditions and placed special emphasis upon the activities of the GPU, the secret police, who "are police, judge, and jury. They are the dictatorship."[20]

Despite this knowledge, American engineers and entrepreneurs, from Ford to Hugh Cooper, builder of the great dam on the Dnieper, looked upon Soviet shortcomings as challenges to overcome rather than symbols of ideological malaise. If they thought about it, they expected capitalism to replace communism eventually, but they dealt with the here and now. It seemed to them that the Russians were offering Americans a chance to rebuild a country on American terms. Ford would not build a single factory which would be subject to mismanagement, but he would and did construct an entire industry with a four-year plan of his own in 1929. Having created a kind of *imperium in imperio* in Russia, Ford professed satisfaction, as he told *Nation's Business*, in the wisdom of the Communists' coming to America for industrial guidance. The United States thereby became an instrument for world peace: "I have long been convinced that we shall never be able to build a balanced economic order in the world until every people has become as self-supporting as possible."[21]

Similarly, Thomas Campbell of Montana, one of America's greatest mechanized-farm operators who dreamed of a farm corporation larger than United States Steel, accepted Stalin's offer to develop a million acres of land. He regarded the Communist leader as a fellow technician whose grand vision rendered political persecution or brutality toward peasants resisting collectivization unimportant. Although he saw that "Communism in its present state is the most absolutist form of Government in all the world," it made little difference to him. He was not afraid of communism. On the contrary, American superiority to the Russians was so overwhelming in every area that trade channels should be fully opened between the two countries rather than allow European competitors to enjoy their present advantages. Campbell's major message was to press America's interests in the "greatest market in the world today for America's goods."[22]

The voices of powerful industrialists, along with the large number of personal accounts of businessmen and engineers resident in the Soviet Union, should have comprised a powerful pressure group of recognition—and did, up to a point. Even Hughes had relented before his departure from government. The ban on trade with the Soviet Union ended in 1923. The following year, the Russians were allowed to organize Amtorg, a Soviet-owned trading corporation with its headquarters in New York, to facilitate economic relations. Also, the State Department finally sanctioned short-term credits to Russian state organizations to finance American exports. Pressures for further concessions developed at the onset of the Depression, which made the prospect for increased trade all the more attractive at a time when the Soviet Five-Year Plan appeared in a new light to an unregulated capitalist society in agony.

What is noteworthy about the industrial connection with Russia in the 1920s is not that American recognition was its ultimate consequence, but that recognition took so long to accomplish, that resistance remained so strong even during the Depression, and that, when the change was made, the great entrepreneurs had relatively small roles in the action. Part of the reason for their ineffectiveness lies in the debit side of the experience of engineers, financiers, and industrialists dealing with Communists. Most, including Ford, made no money out of their investments. The Five-Year Plan was a failure for them. Moreover, many of them were more impressed by the continuing industrial inefficiency and the glaring errors of the Soviet bureaucracy than they were by the potential of profits in trade. The information reported by such influential journals as *Barrons*, the *Commercial Financial Chronicle*, or *Iron Age* was weighted on the side of failure. America's Depression notwithstanding, the Soviet system had failed. Where they did show appreciation of Soviet abilities or the Soviet market, they frequently linked their optimism to an assumption that Russia was returning to capitalism. Hugh Cooper was convinced that the Soviets would alter their opposition to capitalism, while Campbell suspected that the rising educational levels in the Soviet Union would doom communism in a dozen years.

These views tended to counteract support for recognition and instead reinforced the stereotyped views of the Soviets. Although the Depression made the dream of a great Russian market all the more appealing, it also brought the reality of

Soviet dumping, their selling of competing products at low prices, which further exacerbated the international economic crisis. A new version of the Red Menace had appeared in the early 1930s to sustain Hoover's old hostility to recognition. Business interests may have been interested in using recognition as a weapon for trade expansion, but their voices held too many reservations to be effective against the adamancy of President Hoover.

Ultimately, the Depression's pall dampened all but the most violent opponents of recognition. Even with Franklin D. Roosevelt in the White House, the path proved to be tortuous. Perhaps the most striking sign of enervation among anti-communists in the face of the Depression was the language of the established press. As Ray Long, editor of Hearst's *International and Cosmopolitan Magazine*, observed in 1931: "What wouldn't a lot of Americans submit to today if they might exchange their unemployment for Hope?"[23] Equally portentous were the recommendations of former World Court Justice John Bassett Moore and H. Stanwood Menken, chairman of the board of the National Security League, on behalf of recognition of the Soviet Union. Al Smith added his blessings in February 1933.

Such was the foundation on which Roosevelt could construct a new policy. The ideological and emotional constraints which had affected the personal views of his predecessor were no problem for him. The President's close adviser, Harry Hopkins, communicated the advice of his colleagues in social work who had visited and stayed to admire the work of the Soviets. According to Dr. Frankwood E. Williams, a mentor of Hopkins and editor of the *Journal of Mental Hygiene*, he felt that while in Russia in 1932, he had escaped "the atmosphere of competition and rivalry that vitiates everything from the start and at every step." The Russians provided him with almost a mystical experience of social change. Dr. John A. Kingsbury, another influential social work leader, found the Soviet system of free medical care "a portent to the rest of the world."[24] He was a friend of Roosevelt during his New York governorship. It is worth noting that Hopkins made Kingsbury his assistant in the Works Progress Administration a few years later.

Stuart Chase, a popular economist and popularizer of the expression *New Deal*, was another figure to whom Roosevelt listened. Chase admired the Soviet manager who was not pushed by "hungry stockholders, importunate for dividends." As for the future of communism, he claimed he did not know. "All I can report is that after ten lean years it still scorches the face of the curious onlooker. So must the flaming sword of Allah have come over the plains of Mecca." His book, *A New Deal*, not only provided a theme for Roosevelt but contained a rhetorical question very much in the Rooseveltian temper: "Why should Russians have all the fun of remaking the world?" [25]

Despite such influences upon Roosevelt, there is slight evidence that the recognition of the Soviet Union in 1933 proceeded from ideological considerations. What predominated were considerations of practical advantages to be gained from the action and of practical politics in achieving it. The President moved only after the crises of the Hundred Days had passed, and only after all the political components of a disparate coalition behind recognition had been fully mobilized. In a fashion familiar to students of Franklin Roosevelt in action, the President set a number of people to work individually on the problem, each unaware of the others' involvement. The Farm Credit Administration examined the prospects of credits for the Soviet Union; Secretary of State Cordell Hull began a study of the effects of a rapprochement with Russia upon Japanese relations; and Raymond Robins and William Bullitt came to life again as they went to Moscow, filled with new enthusiasm over a mission that would end in success. Roosevelt himself set the stage by including President Kalinin in his message to heads of state on peace and disarmament in May 1933.

With all the portents working so favorably, the Roosevelt administration still hesitated to make a final step until the State Department's concern over Soviet propaganda and Soviet debt repayment had been allayed. It was almost as if the President insisted on being pushed by public opinion. And he was. His own State Department proved to be the bastion of opposition when all others fell. Robert F. Kelley, chief of the Division of Eastern European Affairs, never overcame his skepticism about the chances of Russian-American accord.

But most other segments of society did not share his skepticism. A survey in 1933 reported that 63 percent of the country felt that the Soviet Union had proved its stability, that its philosophy was none of our concern, and that trade expansion was worth what little risk recognition might entail. The major religious communities remained calm, particularly after Father Edmund Walsh of Georgetown University met with the President in October and announced his approval of the new policy so long as the Soviets observed their promises to enlarge religious freedom in Russia and to release those imprisoned for having exercised that freedom. Finally, the *Literary Digest* and *Business Week* undertook to assay the mind of Wall Street and found that the United States could only benefit from recognition and that Russia was too backward to provide serious competition to the American economy. In appreciation of the Stimson alarums, the *Literary Digest* spoke of the "potential check to Japanese expansion in the Pacific." The United States, it asserted, should extend a Good Neighbor policy toward the Soviet Union, since it and Russia were the only "two first-class powers between whom there is no direct collision of interest: the colossus of Eurasia and the colossus of the Western Hemisphere."[26]

Against this background negotiations went smoothly. The Russians were more than ready, as they had been since 1917, to meet the Americans halfway. Boris Skvirsky, director of the Soviet Information Bureau in Washington and unofficial ambassador since 1922, made every effort to present a conciliatory front for the Soviet Union. Whatever the future might hold for America in the Communist world view, the Russians saw the United States in the short run as a buffer in their troubles with Germany and Japan. It was not simply new trade or industrial expertise they wanted from Americans; it was a greater sense of security in a hostile world. Thus, Roosevelt's wooing of Litvinov, the Soviet foreign minister, was essentially a pantomime. The Russians had already succumbed. They promised to end all subversive activities, to waive claims on damages done by American military forces in Siberia, and to surrender all Soviet claims to assets in the United States of Russian companies whose properties had been confiscated after the revolution. Russian war debts were scaled down, but then so were those of other Allies. Unlike the latter, the Soviets were not repudiating their share. These agreements were made conditional upon America's opening the way for future loans and credits to the Soviet Union, a condition that was to create difficulties later. For the moment, however, Roosevelt and Litvinov, bypassing the hostile State Department in their negotiations, made rapprochement look like a mutual victory. A sixteen-year-old chapter in Russian-American relations seemed to have ended.

But had it? While Roosevelt was never personally infected by the anti-communist passions of Woodrow Wilson, let alone those of Herbert Hoover or Hamilton Fish, he had never clearly repudiated the Wilsonian principle of recognition. The prerequisites of religious freedom, the cessation of subversive propaganda, and repayment of debts remained paramount in the American mind, veritable preconditions for future good relations with the Soviet Union. At any event, the President managed to recognize the USSR, as Joan Hoff Wilson pointed out, *"without changing the ideological orientation of the original nonrecognition policy"* (Wilson's italics). [27] For Roosevelt, such issues may have been serious or mere lip service to the electorate. What became clear was that the Soviets interpreted American recognition to reflect both America's need for new trade channels to move out of the Depression and its willingness to assume responsibility for peace in a world jeopardized by Nazi and Japanese aggression. The Russians were mistaken. Germany and Japan may have been disturbing specters to many Americans, but in 1933 this was not enough to jar the United States from its political abstention from European problems. While the economic plight of the country awakened many Americans to the anomalies in the old nonrecognition policy, it did not obliterate the emotions raised by Bolshevism. Communism posed a vital challenge to American society and its values. The Depression may have made recognition necessary, but it also made Bolshevism the more dangerous because America's faith in its own system faltered as a consequence of the Depression.

Roosevelt instinctively recognized the special qualities in a relationship with the Soviet Union through his own careful attempt to gain a consensus before acting. To his countrymen, and perhaps to himself as well, recognition was not granted simply because the Soviet Union was a major force in the world

whether Americans liked it or not. It had to confer special benefits and it had to observe special American standards of behavior. The future of Russian-American relations was to be over-
shadowed by the way in which recognition was finally granted.
Russia, more than England or even Germany or Japan, was a
threat to America; as Peter Filene expressed it, Communist
rivalry "became phobia because many Americans lacked confidence in the strength of their own ideals."28 When the Soviets
began to behave as many Americans felt they always would, the
result in the 1930s was to retreat from the world in which Communism was powerful in order to keep the United States out of
foreign involvements which would spread the Communist
infection.

NOTES

1. Foster Rhea Dulles, *The Road to Teheran: The Story of Russia and America, 1783-1943* (Princeton, N.J.: Princeton University Press, 1945), p. 101.

2. Ibid., pp. 124-125.

3. Quoted in Christopher Lasch, *The American Liberals and the Russian Revolution* (New York: Columbia University Press, 1962), pp. 70-71.

4. Edgar Sisson, *One Hundred Days: A Personal Chronicle of the Bolshevik Revolution* (New Haven, Conn.: Yale University Press, 1931), p. 213.

5. Lasch, p. 72.

6. See William A. Williams, *American-Russian Relations, 1781-1947* (New York: Rinehart Press, 1952), pp. 148-150.

7. See Albert Parry, "Washington B. Vanderlip, the 'Khan of Kamchatka,'" *Pacific Historical Review* 17 (1948): 315-328.

8. George F. Kennan, *Russia Leaves the War* (New York: Atheneum Press, 1967), p. 69.

9. Lewis Feuer, "American Travelers to the Soviet Union 1917-1932: The Formation of a Component of New Deal Ideology," *American Quarterly* 14 (1962): 128.

10. Ibid., p. 126.

11. Ibid., pp. 122-123.

12. Samuel Gompers, *Out of Their Mouths: A Revelation and an Indictment of Sovietism* (New York: E. P. Dutton & Co., 1921), p. vi.

13. Meno Lovenstein, *American Opinion of Soviet Russia* (Washington, D.C.: American Council on World Affairs, 1941), p. 18.

14. Testimony of J. Carson Adkerson, President of the American Manganese Producers' Association, Hearings Before Committee on Ways and Means, HR, "Embargo on Soviet Products," H.R. 16035, February 19, 20, 21, 1931, p. 114.

15. Quoted in Peter G. Filene, ed., *American Views of Soviet Russia* (Homewood, Ill.: The Dorsey Press, 1968), p. 61.

16. Quoted in Edward M. Bennett, *Recognition of Russia: An American Foreign Policy Dilemma* (Waltham, Mass.: Blaisdell Publishing Co., 1970), p. 54.

17. Quoted in Peter G. Filene, *Americans and the Soviet Experiment, 1917-1933* (Cambridge: Harvard University Press, 1967), p. 90.

18. Feuer, "American Travelers," pp. 123-124.

19. Silas Axtell, "Russia, and Her Foreign Relations," *The Annals of the American Academy of Political and Social Science* 138 (1928): 86.

20. Walter A. Rukeyser, *Working for the Soviets: An American Engineer in Russia* (New York: Covici-Friede Press, 1932), p. 33.

21. Allan Nevins and F. E. Hill, *Ford: Expansion and Challenge, 1915-1933* (New York: Charles Scribner's Sons, 1957), p. 679.

22. Thomas D. Campbell, *Russia: Market or Menace?* (New York, Longmans, Green and Co., 1932), p. 146.

23. Filene, *Americans and the Soviet Experiment*, p. 259.

24. Feuer, "American Travelers," p. 127.

25. Stuart Chase, *A New Deal* (New York: Macmillan Co., 1932), pp. 244, 252.

26. *Literary Digest*, October 28, 1933.

27. Joan Hoff Wilson, *Ideology and Economics: U.S. Relations with the Soviet Union, 1918-1933* (Columbia: University of Missouri Press, 1974), p. 131.

28. Filene, *Americans and the Soviet Experiment*, p. 284.

CHAPTER EIGHT

A Moment in Yenan: American Correspondents and Chinese Communists, 1944

Events surrounding World War II left little room for doubt concerning the substantial nature of America's national interest in Asia, whatever questions might have remained concerning the precise scope of that interest. For the United States, the war itself had both begun and ended in the Far East, despite the fact that wartime strategy gave priority to the European theatre of operations. Postwar American diplomacy also focused heavily on reconstruction in Europe and confrontation with the Soviet Union, but it was in the Asian arena ultimately that the United States was to encounter its most difficult and costly frustrations. The defeat of Japan and its subsequent conversion into a thriving, if uneasy, ally was one measure of the degree to which American interests in the region—as well as consciousness of those interests—had experienced an upheaval. Equally important was the changing character of Chinese-American relations. From the formally and sentimentally friendly—although, in the last analysis, superficial—ties which had bound the Chinese and American people over nearly a century and stiffened American opposition to Japanese expansion during the 1930s, there evolved, in the wake of China's postwar Communist revolution, a relationship of mutual hostility and suspicion which has continued to dominate American policy making. This rupture of old ties and assumptions laid the basis for the commitment of

American military forces to the Asian continent in Korea and Vietnam with political and cultural consequences we cannot yet fully measure. Clearly, the American response to the emergence of the Communist regime in China constitutes one of the central chapters in the history of our recent thought and diplomacy.

The seeds of hostility and misunderstanding in Sino-American relations had, of course, been planted much earlier; they have been referred to before in this volume. The American economic and religious impact on China may have been relatively slight, but interested business and missionary groups exercised an influence on American attitudes and politics far out of proportion to their numbers. Through their contributions to education, furthermore, American missionaries had played a substantial role in China's modernization movement. Meanwhile, the popular myth of the "open door," crediting the United States with disinterestedly and almost singlehandedly preserving Chinese freedom and territorial integrity—long discounted by historians but dear nonetheless to a credulous public—considerably inflated American views of the benevolence and goodwill characterizing their relations with the Chinese. To such diverse factors, the rise of nationalism and Communism in China, together with American resentment in the face of it, added merely the latest in a long series of sources of mutual mistrust.

Fundamentally, most Americans knew little of events and conditions in China and probably cared even less. Their chief informants, missionaries and businessmen, had little reason themselves to probe deeply into the nature and sources of Chinese civilization. Sectarian or material preoccupations encouraged foreigners to emphasize those qualities and characteristics of China best exploited for Western purposes, while minimizing sensitivity to Chinese cultural values or traditions. There were, of course, exceptions among the "Old China Hands," in particular missionary educators and diplomats who, as a result of years or perhaps generations of service, had developed warm appreciation for a rich and complex, if sadly deteriorating civilization. That China needed modernizing was an idea widely accepted by Americans as well as by many Chinese themselves; that China's path toward modernization might move along lines significantly different from those which the United States had followed was a notion scarcely conceivable to the most sympathetic and under-standing of Americans.

Western education and economic penetration had hastened the erosion of China's traditional social and political structure, preparing the way for the nation's thrust toward modernization in the twentieth century. As a people, however, the Chinese could hardly have been expected to welcome this assistance. It had been carried out often at gunpoint, with brutality, at consider-able profit to Western capitalists, and under the cover of the ex-emption from Chinese supervision and control secured by extra-territoriality. If the profits and the responsibility had initially accrued chiefly to the Europeans, particularly the British, Americans could not evade their share of the resentment. The limits of their power and self-interest had at first denied them leadership in the political and economic exploitation of China, but their missionary enthusiasm for the winning both of profits and of souls had spurred them to press hard on the heels of the pack. If, in the scale of intangible values and attitudes, it may be argued that Americans were less harsh and unsympathetic than Europeans toward the plight of the Chinese, American self-righteousness probably was at least equally galling.

When, at the end of World War II, it was clear that the day of European imperialism in Asia was ending, the United States and the Soviet Union, as the remaining great powers, inevitably suc-ceeded to the legacy of Chinese resentment against outside en-croachment. The issue now was which of the two powers would most accurately assess and sensitively respond to the reservoir of frustration, resentment, and nationalistic resolution which was postwar China. The difficulties experienced by the Soviet Union in this regard need not concern us here. For the United States, it must be said that a century-old pattern of cultural mis-perception, insensitivity, and smug superiority boded ill for the future.

Akira Iriye and others have pointed out the degree to which the American image of China during the war years was a product of the way in which Americans saw their own role. As resisters of Japanese aggression and totalitarianism, longtime friends of China and her people, and leaders of a world coalition of demo-cratic peoples, Americans felt a strong need to define their chief

Asian ally, China, as a valiant, if not necessarily thriving, democracy. The long, lonely resistance of China to Japanese aggression during the 1930s heightened the sentimental respect felt in the United States for the heroic Chinese. [1]

The image of an embattled, democratic China, however suited it might be to American preconceptions, represented a considerable distortion of reality. As growing numbers of American military personnel, journalists, and others new to Chinese traditions or circumstances filtered into the Chinese theater, disillusionment came swiftly. Chinese corruption in the face of national crisis horrified naïve Americans, who understood neither its historic roots nor its role in a society mired in poverty, factionalism, and disorder. Even worse, it soon appeared that the Chinese government was reluctant to commit its armies to combat against the Japanese invader, preferring—perhaps understandably after years of carrying the burden of defense alone—to let the United States now take the lead in the drive to defeat the common enemy. The slowly increasing assistance which Chiang Kai-shek's regime was receiving from the United States brought nothing like the strengthening of Chinese resistance for which the Americans hoped. Instead, much was siphoned off for the benefit of the generals, warlords, and political cliques composing the ruling Kuomintang party, over which Chiang Kai-shek maintained an uneasy authority. There were even reports of profitable trade between Chinese officials and the Japanese occupation forces, not to mention dark rumors of periodic secret negotiations between governmental agents and the Japanese.

Seen in the light of American expectations, Chinese military operations had many of the aspects of a "phony" war, and it is hardly surprising that observers, including Gen. Joseph C. Stilwell, the commander of American forces in China, were soon convinced that Chiang's government would prove an ineffectual ally. Unlike many, Stilwell based his assessment of the Chinese upon years of experience and familiarity acquired as an American military attaché and observer in Peking. There, he had developed a high regard for the fighting capacities of the individual Chinese soldier. He believed that, properly led, the Chinese armies could be forged into an effective weapon of war. This conviction embittered him even further against what he perceived as the incompetence and lack of dedication of Chiang's forces. Stilwell's ill-disguised contempt for the Chinese leadership undoubtedly influenced the outlook of other Americans, who could hardly have failed to learn of it.[2]

Among the more intriguing and mysterious areas of wartime China was the Communist-dominated region of the northwest, with its capital at Yenan. After a decade of bitter infighting between the Communist and Kuomintang forces, the former had reached Yenan in 1936 at the end of their "long march" from the south. Taking over a poor, isolated area, they had begun to build their new society on the basis of close association and identification with the rural peasantry. Soon thereafter, they had been visited by an American reporter, Edgar Snow, whose *Red Star Over China*, published in 1938, presented the first full and generally favorable account of the Communist program and its adaptation to the Chinese countryside. Snow's book had aroused a flurry of interest, but in 1937 agreement between Chiang Kai-shek, Communist leader Mao Tse-tung, and other regional warlords on a common front against the Japanese had soon pushed the Kuomintang-Communist controversy deep into the background of American awareness.[3]

As the United States became more involved with China after 1941, however, the status of the Communists became a matter of growing interest. The frail ties established between the Nationalist government and the Communists had not long survived in the face of Japanese pressure. The temptation was strong for each Chinese faction to seize every chance to improve its own position and strength at the expense of the other. American soldiers and journalists were dismayed to find the Nationalists attempting to seal off the Communist region with 500,000 of their best troops, who might otherwise have been turned against the Japanese. At the same time, there were reports of successful Communist penetration behind the Japanese lines and establishment of de facto regional governments in areas theoretically occupied by the invaders. Reports of Communist military successes contrasted vividly with the lackluster resistance which seemed all the Nationalist forces could mount. American curiosity and desire for firsthand information were blocked by Nationalist officials, who denied the claims of Communist achievements on the one hand while on the other they accused their rivals of using China's distress to advance their own political objectives.[4]

Of these internal conflicts, charges, and countercharges, the American public heard little. Wartime attention was focused on Europe, the Pacific islands, or, on the Asian mainland, Burma, where British-Indian and Chinese forces under General Stilwell were first defeated and driven back, then returned in early 1944 to open the Ledo and Burma roads. Eager for good news in the months before the Normandy invasion, American news media felt little incentive to explore tales of increasing demoralization and disruption in China. Nor was the Roosevelt administration prepared to release information certain to be regarded as critical and counter to the interests of an ally so long and so highly touted as the valiant defender of democracy in Asia. American reporters in China, however eager they might be to break a story, operated under severe restrictions. Few understood the Chinese language and most were, therefore, largely dependent upon official government sources for their news. The supervision and censorship exercised by the Nationalist officials made it difficult, if not impossible, to send out information considered unfriendly. In addition, the American War Department also censored news reports. Consequently, although official military and foreign service reports to Washington made it quite clear that all was far from well in China, the American people received little but thoroughly misleading information. Strategic and political considerations, reinforced by an underlying desire for "positive thinking" in respect to what was popularly understood as a global struggle in the defense of freedom, denied a realistic evaluation of the Chinese situation to the American people. In Barbara Tuchman's words, "Probably never before had the people of one country viewed the government of another under misapprehension so complete." The situation was conducive neither to the intelligent making nor the effective criticism of policy.[5]

Under the circumstances, American reporters in Chungking resorted to bitterness, cynicism, and occasional harassment of Nationalist officials. Yet events were working toward a partial break in the curtain of silence surrounding China's difficulties. In the spring of 1944, a new Japanese offensive was threatening

American air bases in the south, while the opposing Chinese Nationalist armies gave way with hardly a struggle. The Nationalist government could no longer contain criticism of its corrupt and dictatorial policies by its own newspapers, student groups, and dissenting liberal factions. General Stilwell, called from Burma in June to review personally the state of Chinese defenses, openly reiterated his criticisms of Chiang's political and military leadership.

Even before the news broke publicly, knowledge of the disarray in Nationalist China had spread widely through the community of American foreign correspondents circling the globe, a notoriously peripatetic and talkative group. As early as the summer of 1943, Eric Sevareid had flown into China seeking to clarify the situation there for the sake of friends in the American government as well as for the public. What he saw confirmed what he had heard. Sevareid, who had observed fascism in Europe, noted many of its trappings in Chungking, but here they were a mask for weakness rather than for strength. Chiang, he believed, was more a symbol than an outright dictator. Inaction and the preservation of the hollow forms of unity were the order of the day.[6] By early 1944, articles critical of the Nationalist regime had begun to creep more frequently into the American press. Most noteworthy, perhaps, was one in *Life* by Theodore H. White, ripping the Kuomintang as "a corrupt clique that combines the worst features of Tammany Hall and the Spanish Inquisition." Since *Life* and *Time*, controlled by Henry Luce, were among the most widely read and vociferous supporters of Chiang Kai-shek, such outspokenness was significant and unexpected. Even earlier, a few journalists, such as Edgar Snow, Leland Stowe, and Michael Straight, had noted the shortcomings of the Chinese Nationalists, but in the general euphoria over Chinese heroism and democracy their warnings had received little notice. In some instances, they had even been suppressed—just as Sevareid found his own report denied publication when he returned home.[7]

Disgust with the deterioration of Nationalist China whetted the appetites of both American military and newspaper men for closer contact with the Communists in the north. Continuing reports of their guerrilla tactics and successful infiltrations be-

hind the Japanese lines contrasted sharply with Nationalist ineffectiveness. The Communists' ability to mobilize popular support offered a glimpse of possible progress amid the encircling
disorder. Both for political and military reasons, Stilwell was
anxious to meet with the Communist leaders; among American
reporters, a combination of curiosity and professional pride
sparked repeated requests for permission to visit Yenan. In the
face of rising pressures, Nationalist officials yielded. In November 1943 foreign journalists were promised permission to visit
the Communist zone, while President Roosevelt's request to
send military observers was approved in principle the following
February. Six months of evasion, delay, and preparing of the
ground, however, preceded the actual departure of the journalists from Chungking. In May 1944 a party of five correspondents
was sent northward and two more reporters were permitted to go
in September. Only after a visit from Vice-President Henry
Wallace did Chiang Kai-shek agree to let an American military
mission go forward.

The experience and reports of the military mission have been
discussed elsewhere. It is to the findings of the American journalists that we now turn. The reporters were Harrison Forman of
the New York *Herald-Tribune*, United Press, and London
Times; Gunther Stein, a German-born British citizen, representing the *Christian Science Monitor*, Associated Press, and
London *News-Chronicle*; Israel Epstein, a Polish-born correspondent for the New York *Times*, *Time-Life*, *Allied Labor
News*, and Sydney *Morning-Chronicle*; Father Cormac Shanahan, representing American Catholic publications; and Maurice
Votaw, an American employee of the Chinese Ministry of Information, assigned to the Baltimore *Sun* and Toronto *Daily Star*—
all in the May delegation. The September group consisted of
Brooks Atkinson of the New York *Times* and Theodore White for
Time-Life. Of the seven, four—Forman, Stein, Epstein, and
White—subsequently wrote books based upon their observa-
tions, while Brooks Atkinson wrote a series of articles for the
Times in October 1944, at the time of the recall of General Stil-
well.[8]

The first party of correspondents left Chungking on May 17,
1944, for Sian, a city held by the Nationalists close to Communist

territory. Here an elaborate "orientation" had been prepared for them, complete with testimony by witnesses and supposed former Communists, designed to plant an unfavorable impression and to offset what they would soon be seeing. The obviously staged Nationalist effort failed to impress the Westerners, who were by now, in any case, too distrustful of Kuomintang propaganda to have been swayed even by more subtle efforts. [9]

Crossing into Communist territory, the correspondents were immediately struck by the relaxed, informal, yet serious mood which prevailed. The Communists had settled in a backward, impoverished and entirely agricultural region, remote from the centers of Chinese political and intellectual life. The peasants knew little of Communism, nor, under the pressure of the struggle merely to survive, did they show much interest in ideology or dogma. With remarkable sensitivity, Mao Tse-tung and his followers seemed to have adapted their ideas and programs to the circumstances at hand and made a point of drawing close to the people. Making a virtue of necessity, they lived simply, shared in the tasks as well as the recreations of the community, and made themselves readily accessible. All of this had, of course, been observed and reported by Edgar Snow earlier. What was the more remarkable to the newsmen who now visited Yenan was the fact that the war against Japan seemed, if anything, to have strengthened the acceptance of Communist leadership by the peasants. Unlike the Nationalist regime to the south, Communists and non-Communists working together in the border regions close to the Japanese invaders and even behind the enemy lines had forged a military and social system capable of offering effective resistance to the Japanese.

More impressive, perhaps, to the Chinese peasantry than the democratic manners of the Communists had been their introduction of desperately needed rent and tax reductions. Abandoning their earlier program of collectivization of land, the Communists had appealed to the small farmers as well as to the landless by reducing the high charges levied on their extremely limited incomes. After 1941, when the Nationalist blockade cut off trade with the outside, an all-out drive was launched to increase production for self-sufficiency. Abandoned, worn-out land was reclaimed; systematic and cooperative farming methods had increased food production significantly, while more equitable distribution, both of land and food, had been achieved. Better diet contributed to better health and a more satisfied outlook on life. Such progress, accomplished without help from the outside and under steady pressure both from the Japanese and the Nationalists, contrasted sharply with the steady deterioration of conditions under Chiang's regime and commanded the immediate respect of the American visitors. [10]

Before the war, industry had been unknown in this section of China. Its development under the Communists had been dictated by the sheer necessity for survival. Spinning had been organized on a household basis, while some primitive weaving mills had been built to meet the essential clothing needs of the people and the Communist army. Arms production, also, had originally been on a small-unit basis, but larger factories had begun to develop. Much military equipment had been captured from the Japanese or the Nationalists. Although handicraft production still predominated, Gunther Stein was told that the number of industrial workers in the region had risen from less than 300 in 1937 to 12,000 by 1944, and trade unions were playing an important role in fostering increases in production. Stein reported that the larger factories were overwhelmingly (78 percent) government owned, while 20 percent were held by cooperatives and only 2 percent by private owners. This distribution, however, reflected the reality of limited capital resources rather than Communist policy. Indeed, the Red leaders insisted upon their desire to encourage private capital at this stage in China's development. A mixed, rather than a socialist, economy was their immediate objective, and merchants, prospering as the economy flourished, seemed confident that the Communists represented no threat to their security. Chambers of commerce, of all things, existed in a number of towns and were fully cooperating with the government's economic program! [11]

Since reports of Communist military successes stood in sharp contrast to Nationalist feebleness, the journalists were particularly anxious to visit the Communist forces and their leaders. American interest in wartime China was preeminently military: the development of a Chinese capability to resist Japan and tie down its armies on the Asian mainland. General Stilwell, in the recent Burma campaign, had demonstrated that the Chinese, with proper training and leadership, were a match for the Japanese. Now he was eager to apply this experience to the remainder of the Nationalist forces, but Chiang refused to surrender the control necessary to put Stilwell's program into effect. Meanwhile, the Nationalist armies resisted half-heartedly; warlordism and factionalism increased; and the soldiers preyed upon the civilian population while generals and politicians seized opportunities for personal profit based upon the increasing amounts of American war materials now beginning to reach China. The military observers' mission to Yenan, following shortly after the visit of the correspondents, would test the viability of American-Chinese Communist cooperation. [12]

What the journalists found, meanwhile, was startling. Far from being a burden on the civilian economy, Communist soldiers were used to increase production. They engaged in large-scale reclamation programs and were held directly responsible for the production of their own food. Officers as well as men were working in the fields. The advantages of such measures for a backward economy were obvious; they had the additional effect of minimizing antagonism between the army and the peasantry on whom it depended for recruits and basic security. As an expression of the grass-roots approach of the Communist leadership, its insistence upon building from the ground up and staying close to the people and their interests, the program was dramatic. In the guerrilla areas behind the enemy lines, where resistance could flourish only with the support of the countryside, it had direct tactical value. Whatever the motives underlying Communist military policies, the results offered a sharp contrast with everything the visitors had seen and heard in Nationalist China. Indicative of the success of the Communists in bridging the wide gap between military and civilian elements were the Min Ping guerrillas, civilians armed by the Communists and used as adjuncts to the regular military forces. As Theodore White later pointed out, no other Chinese government had ever dared to distribute arms so freely to the populace; the Communists' willingness to do so was indicative of confidence in their popular support. [13]

The Communist military successes, even if partially discounted, were impressive. They had been achieved, moreover, entirely independently of foreign assistance. Indeed, although few noted its significance at the time, the absence of foreign aid and intervention had probably assisted the development of the Communist program of self-reliance and cooperative initiative. In stark contrast to Nationalist corruption, the Communists' closeness to the people, their direct involvement in measures for the common welfare, and the zealous conviction that they were building a new order for China's future combined to submerge motives of private advantage. Even now, when contacts with the United States at last seemed on the verge of opening, the requests of the top Communist general, Chu Teh, for military assistance were quite limited. Large and expensive items were of little interest; a short list of immediately useful weapons was all he asked for. The Communists' calm confidence that, with little assistance, they could hold their own was enormously refreshing. For political reasons, they were obviously interested in establishing contact with the American government and army. But neither their words nor their record suggested that they in any way felt or desired to be dependent upon American assistance. [14]

Because of what they had seen or heard of the authoritarian Communist regime in the Soviet Union, the correspondents were much interested in what they could learn of Communist political and governmental arrangements. Here, too, what they found was so different from the theory and practice of Communism as they understood it that some were inclined to question the designation itself. In contrast to the one-party dictatorship of the Kuomintang, where minor liberal parties struggled with difficulty to survive, the Communist region presented a picture of widespread and apparently open participation in the processes of government. Since 1941 a "one-to-three" system had been in operation, limiting the Communists to one-third of the elective offices. The deliberate effort to involve other elements in the responsibilities of government was in accord with the Communist effort to build a united front. A grass-roots democracy seemed to be functioning at both the local and regional levels, with open discussion of issues and criticism of government policies. If it was true that the Communists, as the largest and best organized political group, were able to dominate policy making, it was equally true that popular participation had been achieved to a degree never before known in China. Free elections were an accepted and regular feature of the system, and there was widespread acceptance of the sincerity of Communist democratic professions.

Government officials, like the army, were expected to contribute their share to the production of needed commodities. A goal of two-thirds of all their necessities had been set for government officials in 1944, and they were struggling to meet it. It was not unusual for the visitors to find even high Communist officials working in the fields, and Mao Tse-tung, a heavy smoker, was reputed to be growing and cultivating his own tobacco. The mayor of Yenan told Gunther Stein that he and his fellow officials followed a schedule whose pattern shifted with changes in the growing season, providing two hours of study each day in addition to office and field work. Tax reductions, combined with more equitable and honest tax collection, increases in production, the restriction of bureaucracy, and careful scrutiny of all expenditures had brought the budget of the Communist government into balance, he told Stein. If true, the balance, of course, represented a low level of economic development. Still, given the pressures of war and the limitations of resources and trade, it was no mean achievement, and one never even attempted by Chiang's government. Most impressive of all, the Americans agreed, was the virtual absence of any evidence of the corruption so widespread in Nationalist China.[15]

Inevitably, the question arose: was this down-to-earth, popular, progressive regime really Communist? Certainly, it seemed a far cry from the authoritarian, closed society of the Soviet Union, where the twistings of ideological theory often spelled the difference between life and death for party factions and where agriculture had been ruthlessly squeezed to extend the foundations of an industrial economy. By contrast, the Chinese Communists seemed almost Jeffersonian in their closeness to the soil, their reliance upon popular participation at the local level, and their equalitarianism in practice as well as principle. Their simplicity, pragmatism, and approachability contrasted not only with the distant, suspicious atmosphere of Soviet Russia, but, equally significantly, with that of Chungking as well.

The friendly approach of the Yenan leaders was, of course, in part a calculated effort to win friends and influence with the American government, but it was also more than that. It reflected a sense of self-confidence, based on demonstrated successes. When the astonished Americans put the question of the reality of Chinese Communism directly to its leaders, they received forthright, but calculated, replies. Talking with Harrison Forman, Mao insisted that his followers were "no longer Communists in the Soviet Russian sense of the word." They preferred to think of their efforts, he said, "as something Lincoln fought for in your Civil War: the liberation of slaves." Yet, urging a distinction too fine for inexperienced Americans to grasp clearly, both Mao and Chou En-lai openly stated that they were indeed Communists and that their ultimate objective was a socialist economy for China. Present conditions, however, dictated a long interim stage of development during which private capitalism was not only a necessary, but a welcome, agent in assisting the overthrow of Chinese feudalism. Such arguments, emphasized no doubt for the benefit of Western ears, made the Chinese version of Marxism appear benign and friendly. Forman concluded, ". . . today the Chinese Communists are no more Communistic than we Americans are," and Gunther Stein wrote that he could find "very little in Yenan that reminded me of Moscow."[16]

Not all of the correspondents were so favorably impressed. Father Cormac Shanahan, who was perhaps more interested in reestablishing Catholic missions in the border region than in objective analysis, was fundamentally hostile to communism. But he was correct in arguing that the forms of popular participation in government which the Communists encouraged bore little relation to Western democracy. Yet even he was impressed by the spirit and achievements of the Communists in military and economic affairs.[17] Both Stein and White expressed reservations as to the future direction Communism might take in China. Progress to date in education, agriculture, industry, and popular government had far outstripped that of the Nationalists. Yet the Communist sector had long been isolated from the outside world and the clash of contrary views and forces. What would happen, Stein wondered, when Communism spread from the isolated countryside into the cities and ports where outside influences were no longer negligible? The Communists exuded confidence, but Theodore White, reflecting upon what he had seen and heard in Yenan, was much less certain. He conceded that the Reds had given China "the most democratic system of government the villagers had ever known," but he noted that no serious challenge to the system had yet been posed. When that happened, as it inevitably would, White felt that the Communists would not hesitate to turn to sterner, less democratic methods to defend the regime they had struggled so long to create. [18]

The description of life under Chinese Communism and the analysis of its meaning for the future of both China and the United States which the reporters brought back from Yenan was echoed by the observations of others even more experienced in Chinese affairs. Their findings extended those which Edgar Snow had made seven years earlier, when he had written *Red Star Over China*, as well as on subsequent visits. They were also strikingly similar to the evaluations provided to the United States government by the Military Observers Mission, whose stay of over a year with the Communists overlapped the reporters' visit. The mission, commanded by Col. David D. Barrett, included a State Department China expert, John S. Service; its members were deeply impressed with the effectiveness of the Communists and reported favorably on the prospects for collaboration in the defeat of the Japanese. [19]

The counterpart of the Americans' impressions of the Chinese Communists was, of course, the attitude expressed by the Chinese toward the United States. Here, too, the correspondents tended toward optimism. Communist leaders had long cultivated friendly visitors from outside; now they wanted American military cooperation against the Japanese. Even more, sensing the growing American disillusionment with Chiang Kai-shek, they were eager to detach or diminish American support for their Nationalist rivals. Their suspicions of American capitalism were, for the moment at least, subordinated to a pragmatic recognition of the fact of American power in Asia both during and after the war. In the absence of political or military assistance from the Soviet Union, the United States seemed the likeliest source of outside assistance for the immediate future. The obvious respect of the American journalists and of the Military Observers Mission for what they found in Yenan may have played its part also in minimizing Communist hesitancies and increasing their hopes of finding an ally in the United States government.

Later critics of the American visitors to Yenan would accuse them of having been duped into describing the Red regime as democratic, led not by dangerous revolutionaries but by mere "agrarian reformers." There was some truth to the charge, since the obviously improved conditions of the peasantry made a deep impression on the outsiders and perhaps encouraged them to be less critical than they might otherwise have been of the show-case forms of Communist democracy. After dismal months of exposure to Nationalist Chinese ineptitude and corruption, it was perhaps too easy to be impressed by the Communist alternative at Yenan, particularly for Americans whose knowledge of Chinese history and culture was slight and who, in any case, had a vested interest in discovering whatever evidence they could of progress and democracy in forms with which they and their Western readers could identify. Yet the correspondents were neither simple dupes nor pollyannas. They could see for themselves the ways in which Mao and his followers were adapting Communist theory to the Chinese landscape and consciously departing from Russian precedents. The picture of China's future implied by the journalists' reports was, indeed, both more revolutionary and more realistic than their critics acknowledged. They frankly saw it as belonging to a new, unified people's movement, of which the Communists were constituting themselves the leaders, rather than to the ramshackle Kuomintang dictatorship. In their conviction that they had seen the strongest, surest basis for the development of postwar China in the Communist region, they were basically sound. Their conclusion, that the problem of American relations with the Chinese Communists was of vital importance to both peoples, followed logically, however much they might have underestimated the difficulties of that relationship. Their analysis was in any case sounder than that of their critics who, in the face of every evidence to the contrary, persisted in upholding Chiang's regime as an agent of Chinese democracy and progress. [20]

Most of the journalists left Yenan persuaded that they had found the Communists willing and able to work along lines consistent with American interests in China. In this, they may have misjudged Communist as greatly as they did American intentions. Yet, their conclusion that an opportunity existed for Chinese Communists and the United States to reach mutual understanding cannot be dismissed lightly. Theodore White, less enthusiastic than his colleagues, nevertheless argued that a basis for American-Communist cooperation could be found in the bedrock of mutual self-interest. Stressing the shrewd and tough nature of the Communist leaders, "grim, hardheaded pragmatists," rather than their goodwill, he believed them sincere in professing friendship for the United States. If their friendship was reciprocated, "it can become a lasting thing," he wrote; but he warned that they would expect acceptance as equals and would demand respect, not patronage or charity. A movement whose growing acceptance by the Chinese people stemmed largely from its effectiveness in organizing resistance to incursions by Japan was hardly likely in the future to prove more amenable to American, or for that matter Russian, domination.[21]

The problem of communicating what they had seen in the border region proved even more difficult for the American reporters than securing permission for their trip had been. Returning to Chungking, they found their efforts to report their observations hampered at every turn. The Nationalist government, embarrassed by evidence contradicting its denial of Communist achievements, imposed heavy censorship on outgoing news. Both Gunther Stein and Brooks Atkinson publicly protested drastic deletions from their stories at a government news conference. Stein claimed that over 5,000 words had been cut from the seventeen reports he had filed during his four-and-a-half month sojourn with the Communists. Atkinson's reports to the New York *Times* were slashed into almost meaningless fragments. Harold R. Isaacs of *Newsweek*, whose reports from Chungking had been outspokenly critical, was denied permission to visit Yenan. Both Nationalist officials and the new American ambassador, Gen. Patrick J. Hurley, ignored the journalists' complaints and did their best to discredit their objectivity and reliability.[22]

The recall of General Stilwell in October, at Chiang's insistence, gave reporters a partial opportunity to break open the story as they knew it. Brooks Atkinson flew back to the United States with Stilwell and was able, despite American censors, to file a story describing the deteriorating Nationalist regime and the failure of the Chinese under its leadership to organize themselves effectively either for war or peace: "China is falling apart." General Stilwell himself was silenced by the army, while President Roosevelt, on the eve of the 1944 election, dismissed the recall as the outcome of a mere personality conflict. The Stilwell episode enabled other papers and reporters to lift the curtain on some of China's difficulties, but "crisis" news could not in any case greatly enlighten the American public, long accustomed to garbled and uncritical reports. There were too many distractions. News of the dramatic Allied sweep across France dominated the press. The 1944 presidential election campaign was approaching its climax, with Chinese Nationalist agents supplying the Republican party with materials favorable to Chiang's position. Democrats had little incentive to challenge the Roosevelt administration's support for the Nationalist government. Publishers and editors were unable or unwilling to undertake a major reorientation of their presentation of events in the shadowy Asian theatre. Most journalists, like government officials, feared open criticism of a long-standing ally.

Among the most influential American publishers was Henry Luce, the owner of the popular news magazines *Time* and *Life*. Luce, the son of missionaries, had been born in China and retained a deep emotional and intellectual commitment to the old order there. An ardent supporter of Chiang, he did not hesitate to use the columns of his journals to present an unrealistically hopeful picture of Nationalist China or to discredit its critics. During the fall of 1944, Luce's editorial staff was severely editing or rewriting Theodore White's material. Not until more than a month after the election did *Life* print its first and only substantial summary of the observations of its reporter, paternalistically credited with a by-line as "Teddy" White, under the title "Inside Red China." [23]

As the war in Europe ground toward a conclusion during early 1945, the attention of Americans remained fixed across the Atlantic, with the result that the Chinese Nationalists and their American friends still dominated the images of Asia filtering through the news media. Barbara Tuchman has held that the recall of Stilwell marked the end of President Roosevelt's illusions that China would play a major role in the defeat of Japan; instead, at Yalta the President made concessions at China's expense to win Russian entry into the war. Stilwell and Ambassador Clarence Gauss, critics of Chiang, were replaced by Generals Hurley and Wedemyer, who became his staunch supporters even though they, too, occasionally and futilely urged reforms in the Nationalist government. The change in American representation gave the Chinese Communists the first clear signs that American policy was too deeply committed to Chiang to follow an independent course. Whatever the shifts in the thinking of the American president or of the Chinese Communist leaders about America's future role and stake in China, the American public had little inkling of change. With further reports from Yenan foreclosed, the scattered criticisms of Chiang which filtered through failed to dislodge the image of China as an embattled democracy. Meanwhile, Ambassador Hurley forced the replacement of the Foreign Service staff which challenged his assessment of the Chinese situation and secured the assignment to Chungking of reporters more favorable to Chiang, but of this the public knew little. At the same time, the Nationalists denied reentry permits to Harold Isaacs and other reporters who had criticized their regime.[24]

Against the background of the war's end and the search for a basis for peace in Asia, the reporters who had visited Yenan made a second effort to pierce the screen of public indifference and misunderstanding. Between 1945 and 1947 four books appeared, each devoted to a report on the Chinese situation and written by one of the 1944 visitors to Yenan. The first, in 1945, were Harrison Forman's *Report from Red China* and Gunther Stein's *The Challenge of Red China*. The following year saw the publication of *Thunder Out of China*, by Theodore H. White and Annalee Jacoby, another *Time* correspondent in China. In 1947, Israel Epstein's *The Unfinished Revolution in China* appeared. The substance of their reports has already been presented. Now for the first time the American people had the opportunity to read detailed reports of wartime conditions in the Communist region.

The books were widely reviewed, but only White and Jacoby managed to attract more than passing notice. Against the hardening of attitudes toward international Communism accompanying the early stages of the Cold War, the reporters' efforts proved to be largely "blowing in the wind." Ironically, the outbreak of civil war in China, and the rapid collapse of the Nationalist government in the face of Communist pressure — the very conditions which these volumes might have helped Americans to assess more realistically — acted in fact to divert attention from them. Communist successes in China, coming hard on the heels of Russian-American conflicts and confrontations elsewhere, fitted too easily into a picture of global strife, polarized around competing power and ideology centers: democracy vs. communism, the United States vs. a Russian-Chinese alliance. In such a climate of opinion, books which appeared sympathetic to the Chinese Communists received short shrift.

A partial exception was White and Jacoby's *Thunder Out of China*, whose more careful and critical judgments won it the Pulitzer Prize. Yet the authors' final evaluation of the Nationalists was every bit as unfavorable as the others' had been. The war in Asia, they wrote, must be understood as a mere episode in "the greatest revolution in the history of mankind, the revolution of Asia." This revolution, the century-old struggle of the Asian masses to free themselves from the restraints of tradition, antedated World War II and would extend far beyond it. Japan's invasion of China and subsequent defeat and even the struggle between Chinese Nationalists and Communists itself were merely chapters in the epic. The American desire for immediate order and stability in China was hopeless, White and Jacoby concluded. "China must change or die." Skeptical though they were of Communist professions of democracy, they recognized that the Communists spoke for many of the changes China needed and wanted. The United States could not stem the tide of change in Asia, but it might yet manage to influence change in democratic and friendly directions by acknowledging rather than opposing China's needs. [25]

That China was experiencing the throes of revolution had been asserted by the other American reporters as well, although in less measured terms. A year after the publication of White and

Jacoby's book, Harold R. Isaacs, who instead of visiting Yenan had traveled through much of South and East Asia, repeated the theme and broadened it by examining postwar developments not only in China but throughout the region in a book entitled *No Peace for Asia*. Everywhere, Isaacs found, Asian nationalism was pressing toward freedom and self-determination in the wake of Allied victory. Everywhere also, unfortunately, he found American policy and practice ranging themselves on the side of the old colonial powers or their conservative Asian comprador allies against the drive of the masses for independence and the right to determine their own national objectives. By 1947, the outlines of the emerging struggle in Asia between Russia and the United States were becoming clear. The contest was already molding American responses and subordinating awareness of the long-range interests of the United States in Asian independence to immediate Cold-War power considerations. Whatever the limitations of his analysis of country-by-country developments, Isaacs discerned with frightening accuracy the implications of American failure to see Asia on its own terms. [26]

Among the most revealing elements of Isaacs's book was his analysis of the attitudes which Americans, especially the thousands of GIs who had served in the China-Burma-India theatre, had developed toward Asia and the Asians. The gap between the standards and styles of life of the two continents had simply been too great for the ill-informed and unprepared Americans to grasp or bridge. Asian traditionalism, fatalism, poverty, filth, inefficiency, and corruption were too different from their American counterparts to be recognizable, while the conditions which Americans associated with democracy and progress in the light of their own experience bore little immediate resemblance to any that they observed in Asia. When these elements were further combined with Western racism and Asian suspicions of colonialist-imperialist motives, the result was virtually inevitable. The outcome of the largest American exposure to Asia in history was more than misunderstanding; it was contempt on the one hand and disillusionment on the other. [27] For many of the Americans involved, indifference and a desire to have as little to do as possible with Asia and the Asians was a logical, understandable—if tragically inappropriate—response to this experience. China seemed a hopeless, helpless tangle deserving to be left to its fate. The only consideration able to arouse concern for Asia among such Americans was fear of Russian competition and power, a consideration that discouraged understanding of distinctively Asian conditions and concerns. In this view, Asia's role was a diminished one, largely that of a pawn in the greater power and ideological contest.

In the face of such massive disinterest, it was relatively easy for special interest groups to dominate American public opinion and policy making. And there was, in fact, a number of such groups that, for differing reasons, shared a common desire to preserve the Chinese Nationalist government. A number of influential public figures, among them Henry Luce, Congressman Walter Judd, and columnist Joseph Alsop, had religious, sentimental, or ideological ties with prewar China. Many had lived there for considerable periods of time and had fond recollections of an era that no longer existed in reality, when American missionaries, educators, and businessmen had enjoyed extraordinary privileges, status, and respect. For them, democracy and modernization in China were only conceivable under Western, and particularly under American, sponsorship. They had worked closely during the war to increase American support for Chiang through both government military and financial aid and private contributions for relief of the suffering Chinese people. In this effort, they had been joined by other American humanitarians as well as shrewd businessmen such as New York importer Alfred Kohlberg. As the end of the war approached and American government aid was threatened with curtailment, these Americans were encouraged and assisted by Chinese Nationalist agents and lobbyists in intensified efforts to win both official and unofficial support. Their mobilization of a highly effective propaganda and political pressure campaign was, ironically, helped by the inadequacies of the Nationalist regime itself. Rampant opportunities for corruption and private gain mobilized powerful Chinese and American interests on their behalf. At the same time, the successes of the Chinese Communists fed the fears of concerned Americans, who were already being aroused to a feverish anti-Communism by prominent leaders, including Francis Cardinal Spellman of New York and ambitious young politicians such as

Joseph V. McCarthy of Wisconsin and Richard M. Nixon of California. [28]

In the face of this combination of emotional, ideological, and political pressures, the Truman administration would probably have been unable to organize a reassessment of American policy in China, even had it chosen to do so. The new president and his chief advisors were staunchly anti-communist themselves and had little experience or understanding of Asia. Deeply committed to efforts to strengthen democratic, or merely anti-communist, governments in other quarters, they would have been mostly unlikely to consider a seemingly contradictory approach to the Chinese situation. In 1946 Truman sent Gen. George C. Marshall on a mission of conciliation to China, hoping that the skill and prestige of the recently retired American chief of staff would persuade Chiang and Mao to come to terms. Marshall's mission was a failure, despite the General's own recognition of Chiang's inadequacies as a national leader. Since no serious consideration had been given to abandoning the commitment to Chiang, American pressure for a settlement was unavailing in any case; compromise was by then unrealistic. Meanwhile, at home, President Truman faced a new Republican Congress and a desperate struggle for survival on the domestic political front. Fighting to preserve and extend the New Deal, confronting the Soviet Union in Iran, Greece, Turkey, Berlin, and elsewhere, and facing charges of softness on Communism from frustrated and office-hungry Republicans, Truman had little time or inclination for further approaches to Asia. He could reduce American commitments to the Nationalist regime, whose cause he knew to be hopeless; he could, or would, not do more. By the time the hotly contested presidential election of 1948 had been won, it was too late. Communist forces drove Chiang's regime from the Chinese mainland the following year, and before the American people or government had had time to absorb the implications of this upheaval, the outbreak of war in Korea in 1950 destroyed the last remote possibility of accommodation with the Chinese Communist government. [29]

In the face of this seeming landslide of pressures and events, what possibility, if any, was there that opinions, arguments, and policy proposals favorable to accommodation with the Chinese

Communists might have gained a serious hearing in the United States? That there were such arguments and opinions is clear from the writings of the Yenan correspondents, among others. But their reports, finally published, were virtually ignored. The combination of factors already referred to focused both official and public attention elsewhere and made it relatively easy for them to be discredited by the pro-Nationalist forces as naïve, ignorant, or dangerously radical and pro-Communist. The fact that Asia still remained secondary to Europe in public and official attention encouraged such neglect and distortion, which were further increased by anti-Communist emotionalism. More revealing still is the treatment accorded American Foreign Service officials, many of them China experts of many years' standing, whose analyses and recommendations paralleled those of the journalists. John Paton Davies, John S. Service, John Carter Vincent, Edmund Clubb, and others had bluntly criticized the Chinese Nationalist government, favoring withdrawal of American support and steps toward recognition of the Communists. Davies feared that American policy was perpetuating the Open Door tradition of sentimental assumption of responsibilities in China based on an unrealistic assessment of national interest and power. Their recommendations were not only ignored but, as anti-Communist hysteria peaked in the wake of the collapse of Chiang's mainland government, they found themselves publicly attacked as Communist dupes or sympathizers. Driven from office and even from the country as betrayers of America's Asian interests and role, these men had to wait nearly twenty years for a public vindication that came too late to repair the damage either to their own lives and careers or to their country's foreign policy. [30]

It may well be true, as Harold Isaacs suggested, that Americans of all persuasions were ill-equipped to understand China in terms suited to the circumstances and traditions of that ancient culture. Yet, for such misunderstanding, the only possible remedy was open access to information and as many interpretations of it as possible. The experience of the American journalists in Yenan is a case in point. Private and unofficial contacts, reports and interpretations might under other circumstances have provided valuable supplementary and corrective information to the American people and their government. In the light of subsequent experience, the value of such information can hardly be underestimated. If there was indeed a moment near the war's end when the possibility of a realistic understanding between the United States and Chinese Communists might have been attainable, it passed too quickly to be recognized — let alone seriously explored — by the Americans. The potential usefulness of the full range of American contacts and experiences with the Chinese was casually or angrily dismissed. The price of that failure, in distortion, illusion, and bitterness, has been paid ever since, and the accounts still remain unsettled.

NOTES

1. Eric Sevareid, *Not So Wild a Dream* (New York: Alfred A. Knopf, 1946), p. 226; Akira Iriye, *Across the Pacific: An Inner History of American-East Asian Relations* (New York: Harbinger Books, 1967), pp. 232-243; Barbara W. Tuchman, *Stilwell and the American Experience in China, 1911-45* (New York: Macmillan, 1971), p. 251; A. T. Steele, *The American People in China* (New York: McGraw-Hill, 1966), p. 23.

2. Tuchman, *Stilwell and the American Experience*, pp. 321-322; Sevareid, *Not So Wild a Dream*, p. 316.

3. Edgar Snow, *Red Star Over China*, revised ed. (New York: Grove Press, Inc., 1968).

4. Israel Epstein, *The Unfinished Revolution in China* (Boston: Little-Brown, 1947), pp. 95-106, 129-136, 216-242; Theodore H. White and Annalee Jacoby, *Thunder Out of China* (New York: William Sloane Associates, Inc., 1961), pp. 129-144.

5. Tuchman, *Stilwell and the American Experience*, pp. 353-355, 409ff., 455-457; Oliver J. Caldwell, *A Secret War: Americans in China, 1944-45* (Carbondale: University of Southern Illinois Press, 1972), p. 91; Sevareid, *Not So Wild a Dream*, pp. 226-229, 310-320.

6. Tuchman, *Stilwell and the American Experience*, pp. 459-461; Iriye, *Across the Pacific*, p. 245; cf. Hollington K. Tong, *Dateline China* (New York: Rockport, 1950), pp. 56, 143-144. Kenneth E. Shewmaker, *Americans and Chinese Communists, 1927-45* (Ithaca: Cornell University Press, 1971), discusses the few Americans who visited the Communist region and reported their findings during these years.

7. Edgar Snow, *Journey to the Beginning* (New York: Random House, 1958), pp. 223-224; Charles Wertenbaker, "The China Lobby," *The Reporter* (15

April 1952); 6; Sevareid, *Not So Wild a Dream*, pp. 351-352; Iriye, *Across the Pacific*, p. 245.

8. Tuchman, *Stilwell and the American Experience*, pp. 460-464; Shewmaker, *Americans and Chinese Communists*, pp. 158-179.

9. Gunther Stein, *The Challenge of Red China* (New York: McGraw-Hill, 1945), pp. 33-44; Harrison Forman, *Report from Red China* (New York: Holt, 1945), pp. 4-9.

10. Stein, *Challenge of Red China*, pp. 110-112, 162-163, 269; Epstein, *The Unfinished Revolution*, pp. 264-272; White and Jacoby, *Thunder Out of China*, pp. 234-235; Forman, *Report from Red China*, p. 67; New York *Times*, 1 July 1944.

11. Stein, *Challenge of Red China*, pp. 113, 171-181; Forman, *Report from Red China*, p. 78.

12. Tuchman, *Stilwell and the American Experience*, pp. 466-476; Epstein, *The Unfinished Revolution*, pp. 336-340, 343-345; Stein, *Challenge of Red China*, pp. 312-322; White and Jacoby, *Thunder Out of China*, pp. 132-159.

13. Stein, *Challenge of Red China*, pp. 66-71, 333-346; Forman, *Report from Red China*, pp. 88-89, 204; White and Jacoby, *Thunder Out of China*, pp. 205-213.

14. Epstein, *The Unfinished Revolution*, pp. 346-348.

15. Forman, *Report from Red China*, pp. 56, 98-103; Stein, *Challenge of Red China*, pp. 97ff., 133-142, 203-209; Epstein, *The Unfinished Revolution*, pp. 250-265; New York *Times*, 6 August 1944.

16. White and Jacoby, *Thunder Out of China*, pp. xix, 231-236, 313-314, 320; Stein, *Challenge of Red China*, pp. 106-109, 135, 143-144; Forman, *Report from Red China*, pp. 61, 79, 97, 176-180; Epstein, *The Unfinished Revolution*, pp. 296-297.

17. Shewmaker, *Americans and Chinese Communists*, pp. 169-171.

18. Stein, *Challenge of Red China*, p. 363; White and Jacoby, *Thunder Out of China*, pp. vii, xii, 229, 237-239; Theodore H. White, "Inside Red China," *Life* (18 December 1944): 39ff.

19. Edgar Snow, *Journey to the Beginning*, pp. 226-227, 230-234; Jack Belden, *China Shakes the World* (New York: Monthly Review Press, 1949); Tuchman, *Stilwell and the American Experience*, pp. 476-478, 485-487. See Bruce Douglass and Ross Terrill, eds., *China and Ourselves* (Boston: Beacon Press, 1969), for the experience of John Carter Vincent, pp. 122-154. For John S. Service, see *The New Yorker* 40 (8 April 1972): 43-44; Stein, *Challenge of Red China*, pp. 347-365; Epstein, *The Unfinished Revolution*, pp. 347-348; Caldwell, *A Secret War*, pp. 108-111.

20. Iriye, *Across the Pacific*, pp. 246-248; Tang Tsou, *America's Failure in China, 1941-50* (Chicago: University of Chicago Press, 1963), pp. 219-236, passim; Shewmaker, *Americans and Chinese Communists*, pp. 216-217, 260-262, 294-296, 345.

21. Theodore H. White, "Inside Red China"; U.S. Department of State, Far Eastern Series 30, *United States Relations with China, 1944-49* (Washington, D.C.: Government Printing Office, 1949), pp. 87-88; Iriye, *Across the Pacific*, p. 246; Steele, *American People in China*, p. 26; White and Jacoby, *Thunder Out of*

China, p. 240; New York *Times*, 1 July 1944; Stein, *Challenge of Red China*, pp. 446, 478.

22. Stein, *Challenge of Red China*, pp. 461-462; New York *Times*, 6 October 1944, 12 October 1944; *Newsweek* (23 October 1944): 85, (6 November 1944): 34; W. A. Swanberg, *Luce and His Empire* (New York: Scribner's, 1972), pp. 226-227; Shewmaker, *Americans and Chinese Communists*, pp. 173-178.

23. New York *Times*, 14 August 1944; Stein, *Challenge of Red China*, pp. 75-76; Epstein, *The Unfinished Revolution*, pp. 302, 352; Tuchman, *Stilwell and the American Experience*, pp. 505-506; Swanberg, *Luce and His Empire*, pp. 226-229; Theodore H. White, "Inside Red China."

24. Tuchman, *Stilwell and the American Experience*, pp. 508, 510-516; Tong, *Dateline China*, pp. 255-256; Caldwell, *A Secret War*, pp. 119-120; Herbert Feis, *The China Tangle: The American Effort in China from Pearl Harbor to the Marshall Mission* (Princeton, N.J.: Princeton University Press, 1953), p. 274; Harold Isaacs, *No Peace for Asia* (New York: Macmillan, 1947), p. 73; Shewmaker, *Americans and Chinese Communists*, p. 174; Snow, *Journey to the Beginning*, pp. 348-349.

25. White and Jacoby, *Thunder Out of China*, pp. xix-xx, 298, 309-310, 320-321; Stein, *Challenge of Red China*, p. 478.

26. Isaacs, *No Peace for Asia*, passim.

27. Isaacs, *No Peace for Asia*, pp. 7-34; Caldwell, *A Secret War*, p. 32. See Sevareid, *Not So Wild a Dream*, pp. 230ff., for a more favorable view of American attitudes.

28. Ross Y. Koen, *The China Lobby in American Politics* (New York: Octagon Books, 1974), is the fullest treatment of the many-faceted China Lobby. The book itself was suppressed after its initial publication in 1960. See also Wertenbaker, "The China Lobby," *The Reporter* (15 April 1952); Philip A. Horton et al., "The China Lobby," *The Reporter* (29 April 1952); Belden, *China Shakes the World*, pp. 367-370; Richard E. Lauterbach, *Danger from the East* (New York: Harper, 1947), pp. 369-372; Swanberg, *Luce and His Empire*, pp. 259-267, passim; Snow, *Journey to the Beginning*, pp. 332, 348; Steele, *American People in China*, pp. 112-118; Sevareid, *Not So Wild a Dream*, p. 351.

29. U.S. Department of State, *U.S. Relations in China* (Washington, D.C.: Government Printing Office, 1949); Dean G. Acheson, *Present at the Creation: My Years in the State Department* (New York: Norton, 1969); Lloyd C. Gardner, *Architects of Illusion: Men and Ideas in American Foreign Policy, 1941-45* (Chicago: Quadrangle Books, 1970), pp. 148-162.

30. Caldwell, *A Secret War*, pp. xi-xii; John Leighton Stuart, *My Fifty Years in China* (New York: Random House, 1954), pp. 195-197, 203-207, 242-243; Douglass and Terrill, *China and Ourselves*, pp. 122ff.; Tuchman, *Stilwell and the American Experience*, pp. 409ff., 455-456, 512-515, 526; John Paton Davies, Jr., *Dragon by the Tail: American, British, Japanese and Russian Encounters with China and One Another* (New York: W. W. Norton, 1972), pp. 417-427.

CHAPTER NINE

Isolationism, the United Nations, and the Cold War

Experience in World War II taught Americans that the price the nation had paid for its isolationism in the 1930s was too high. They learned that war might have been avoided had the United States been able to accept the principles of collective security. But even as this knowledge impressed itself upon policy makers, the Roosevelt and Truman administrations recognized the difficulty of uprooting an entrenched idea. Political abstention from the Old World meant American freedom from the evils of spheres of influence, alliances, and balance-of-power struggles. The fate of Woodrow Wilson's attempt to bring the United States into the League of Nations was instructive to the makers of foreign policy during the war and postwar years. If America should break with the traditions of Washington or Monroe, the break would have to be in consonance with the spirit of the past, so that identification with Europe would not be identical with the immoral European system of international relations.

It was for this reason that the United Nations became such an important part of American policy in the 1940s. It would be America's chance to redeem the error of 1919 and to do so on its own terms. That is, the United Nations, under American auspices, would not only make another world war impossible but would guarantee security by means of America's traditional practices, or at least what it liked to consider to be its true approach to international affairs—conciliation, mediation, and use of international law. It was not important that the new league was in fact less powerful than the old on paper. It was important simply that America had embraced the world without embracing the destructive power politics of the past. To President Roosevelt and his advisers, the successful making of a world organization was second in priority only to the winning of the war.

Their plans succeeded magnificently. Senate Republicans as well as Democrats were intimately involved in the deliberations over American membership in the new organization, which was to have its headquarters in New York, and the United States would be one of the "Four Policemen" on the Security Council guaranteeing peace for all nations. While lively suspicions of the Allies persisted—of the British as well as the Russians—they were submerged in the expectation that the operations of the United Nations would undermine British and Russian spheres of influence in Asia and Eastern Europe, respectively.

In a way the United Nations was "oversold," as a Senate Foreign Relations subcommittee noted a few years later.[1] Acceptable as it was to all but a small band of isolationists, it produced an excessive sense of self-congratulation among a majority of Americans. They could regard it as a surrogate State Department that would permit them a return to more pressing domestic concerns. The Security Council would minimize need for an extensive national foreign policy. Under its umbrella, massive demobilization of a wartime economy could take place along lines similar to those following the Civil War and World War I, but with an assurance to the American public that the world leadership of the United States would remain intact. What the administration did not anticipate was the flourishing of a variation of the old isolationism that was fed by the hope that the new collective security organization would keep America as free of alliances and power politics as the Monroe Doctrine had done in the last century. When, two years after the end of the war, the National Opinion Research Council polled the public about a need to rearm unilaterally and to make defense arrangements outside the supervision of the United Nations, 82 percent in 1947, and 72 percent in 1948, responded that the United States should not try to work "outside the United Nations" despite the inability of the organization's machinery to function under the threat of a Soviet veto.[2] Ignoring the United Nations carried the pejorative connotations which the idea of entangling alliances once had; unilateral rearmament and bilateral agreements evoked memories of the nineteenth-century European system of balance of power. This reaction did not signify American conversion to world government; rather, it confirmed the identification of the United Nations with the traditional American revulsion against militarism and alliances.

Initially, statesmen of the distinction of Dean Acheson underestimated the meaning the United Nations had acquired for many Americans. Acheson never had illusions about the practicality of the United Nations Charter. The men in his circle shared this sentiment, for the most part, and wrote off the public acclaim for the charter as a romantic by-product of America's changing position in the world. This is not to say that Kennan or Acheson felt that the United Nations was useless; it was simply a very limited instrument of American policy. Belatedly, they were compelled to respect the fact that newly educated elites sympathetic with the abandonment of the older isolationism during World War II required appeasement of their devotion to the United Nations before they would follow the seminal changes implicit in the containment policy of the late 1940s.

There is some irony in the administration's predicament during the Cold War. Much of the opposition to its assumption of world leadership under the Truman Doctrine, the Marshall Plan, and the North Atlantic Treaty came from partisans of an organization which the administration itself had touted as the only appropriate expression of international responsibility. But when the conflict between the United States and the Soviet Union could not be resolved within the framework of the charter of the United Nations, the charter became an obstacle to the implementation of a new program suggested by the ideas of George Kennan. In order to win American support for a strong independent position against Soviet policies in the postwar world, the Truman policy makers had to cope with the shock Americans would feel if they had to recognize the failure of the United Nations.

It was not the extremists or the ideologues of the left or right who created the most problems for the administration's plan to contain Soviet power. Ultimately, the trouble was with those members of the articulate majority in the coalition behind the acceptance of military aid, massive economic assistance, and a military alliance. The great labor organizations and business associations—the American Federation of Labor and the Congress of Industrial Organizations, the Chamber of Commerce and the Committee for Economic Development—as well as most of the major religious denominations supported the American position on the Cold War. At the same time, they made known their concerns repeatedly over the apparent inconsistencies between American policy and the United Nations Charter, between pledges of loyalty to the world organization and actions taking place outside its confines. So disturbing were these considerations that the Truman administration felt itself constrained to append to all of its propositions an assertion of collaboration with the United Nations whether or not the professions of loyalty were appropriate or accurate. To win American allegiance to its policies, the administration had to do more than wave the banner of anti-communism; it had to assure the nation that those policies fitted the image of the world that had replaced the older isolationism—a universal collective security implicit in the existence of the United Nations. The Marshall and Acheson State Department of 1947 to 1949 had a difficult semantic task before it.

However wide the differences in interpretations of the origin of the Cold War may be, most historians would observe that until the end of 1946 the United States had offered no coherent rationalization of its foreign policy. The Soviet Union was dealt with piecemeal, with the expectation that a thrust in Germany or a parry in Iran would restore the working relationship of the war period under the benevolent eye of the United Nations. This expectation ended officially when George Kennan's observations, widely disseminated in 1946 by Secretary of the Navy James V. Forrestal, became the basis for policy. As chargé d'affaires in Moscow and as a scholarly and perceptive student of communism, Kennan had propounded the thesis that only patient but firm containment would manage the dynamic ideology of the

Soviet system. Conventional diplomacy was irrelevant to the relationship between the two nations. So was the United Nations. Hostility was inherent in the nature of the two systems of society. Only American leadership, by damming the force of the opposition, would save the world and the United States itself.

The first implication of the Kennan hypothesis was the fact of a divided world that could not be bridged by the United Nations. Such was the sense of the men who made policy in the Truman administration of 1947. Because the nation at large did not share their perceptions of international reality, the economic plight of Great Britain and the military problems of Greece provided a dramatic setting for policy makers to force America to come to grips with reality. Britain's inability to afford continuous support of the Greek government against Communist opposition became the occasion for the United States to assume the British burden in the eastern Mediterranean. As Kennan put it, "we had no choice but to accept the challenge and extend the requisite aid."[3]

But it was also the occasion to awaken Americans to a wider peril. There was a choice to be made in the trumpeting of a crusade against communism, "in terms," as Kennan put it, more ruefully this time, "more grandiose and more sweeping than anything that I, at least, had envisaged."[4] In the minds of Acheson, Forrestal, and Robert Patterson, nothing short of a morality drama would jar Americans from the complacency reflected in congressional unwillingness to provide aid for suffering Europe. Acheson warned that Greece, engulfed in civil war, opened the way for Soviet penetration of three continents. "Like apples in a barrel infected by one rotten one, the corruption of Greece would infect Iran and all to the East. It would also carry the infection to Africa through Asia Minor and Egypt, and to Europe through Italy and France."[5]

Thus, the British received more than they had bargained for in the Manichean response of President Truman, wherein he observed in his address to Congress that "the free peoples of the world look to us for support in maintaining their freedoms. If we falter in our leadership we may endanger the peace of the world — and shall surely endanger the welfare of our own Nation."[6] The gauntlet was thrown down in the winter of 1947 for Americans as well as Russians to pick up. The risk of failure with Congress was considerable. Republican leadership in the 80th Congress, sensitive to the high cost of foreign policy and the exaggeration of executive power that would follow, was not educated to the Soviet menace. Even under the 79th Congress the British loan barely passed in the summer of 1946. The victorious Republicans of 1947 were looking forward to cutting 50 percent from the military budget. As liberal Republican Henry Cabot Lodge, Jr., expressed it, Congress appeared to him "like a man wielding a meat ax in a dark room" who "might cut off his own head." [7]

Given this mood, senatorial reaction at a White House meeting on February 27, 1947, over the prospect of emergency help to the Greeks and Turks devolved on questions of British chestnuts, wasteful expenses, and the dangers of war. The administration had anticipated objections and countered them skillfully by reminding senators of the cost of appeasement and the enormity of the present threat. Senator Arthur H. Vandenberg of Michigan, chairman of the Senate Foreign Relations Committee, was impressed both by Acheson's eloquence and the absence of reasonable alternatives. Even isolationists were touched by memories of appeasement and contented themselves with grudging acquiescence in actions they described as politically inspired.

Effective though the administration was in winning over congressional leaders in informal discussions, it failed to confront the problem of the charter's role in American planning. Not that the United Nations was omitted from the President's message on the Truman Doctrine in March. But the language and tone concerning the United Nations were pessimistic about its future. Truman was blunt: "We have considered how the United Nations might assist in this crisis. But the situation is an urgent one requiring immediate action, and the United Nations and its related organizations are not in a position to extend help of the kind that is required." [8] Whatever hopes policy makers may have had of the United Nations a few years earlier were banished long before the President addressed Congress. The reality of world politics, as seen by the men around the President, was reflected, as Joseph Jones has pointed out, in the complete absence of the United Nations from the agenda for the drafting of the message. [9] No one raised an objection that the proposed aid to Greece and Turkey would bypass the United Nations. Vandenberg wrote on March 5 that "I am frank to say I think Greece would collapse fifty times before the United Nations itself could even hope to handle a situation of this nature." [10] Even the passing — and slighting — references to the United Nations in Truman's text were the work of lesser members of the State Department who prevailed over Acheson's advice. To the Undersecretary, time was short, and the Soviet veto should have made the futility of the United Nations obvious to all. [11]

Acheson was correct in his perceptions of the United Nations in this crisis. What he and his colleagues had neglected were the lessons they had helped to inculcate in Americans since the beginning of World War II, namely, that there would be no salvation outside the new collective security organization. The alternatives were a return to the suicidal power politics which had devastated the world in the twentieth century or a return to the isolationism which had stilled America's voice in the past. Neither alternative was now acceptable. The answer for most Americans aware of the larger world was only the United Nations, and yet the same men who had helped create it appeared suddenly ready to scuttle it without warning.

The storm that broke over the United Nations in the wake of the President's message to the Congress took the administration by surprise. The diversity as well as intensity of comment on the bypassing of the United Nations, the revival of power politics, and the destruction of the charter embraced more than just extremists. Public opinion polls revealed that, up until the Greek and Turkish crisis, the public had believed that the United States had been doing everything it could to make the organization effective. If there had been difficulties, they were all the fault of the Soviet Union. Now the public was less sure of guilt; the dismissal of the United Nations under the Truman Doctrine was disturbing. In the spring of 1947 a majority of 56 percent, compared with 25 percent in opposition, favored a greater role for the United Nations over an American unilateral action in aid to Greece and Turkey. [12]

Understandably, the most vigorous opponents of the administration took up the cry. For many, the United Nations was one among many sticks useful for beating the government. The left of Henry Wallace, representing internationalists who felt American obstructionism had pushed the Russians into active hostility, found in the President's message not only another attack upon the Soviet Union but also a sacrifice of the United Nations to a new "ruthless imperialism."[13] Isolationists on the right, always suspicious of Truman's fiscal policies, feared that the Truman Doctrine would be the opening wedge for a vast program of assistance that would destroy the American economy before it could damage the Russians.

For many congressmen, the United Nations was more than a partisan propaganda issue. While Truman's opponents were concerned with the waste of America's resources, as they claimed, they were also worried about the dangers of military aid leading to alliance and war. Senator Robert A. Taft, leader of the Republicans in the 80th Congress, was genuinely troubled over the military implications of the program and wondered why the United Nations had not been made the vehicle to serve the purpose. Peace was at stake. "If we assume a special position in Greece and Turkey, we can hardly . . . object to the Russians continuing their domination in Poland, Yugoslavia, Rumania, and Bulgaria."[14] Internationalists and isolationists, Republicans and Democrats could stand together on this ground.

Such sentiments forced the administration to reconsider the links between its aid proposals and the United Nations. More important, they moved Senator Vandenberg, chairman of the Senate Foreign Affairs Committee, to action. Vigorous and sincere, Vandenberg was also vain and shallow. As Robert Allen and William Shannon saw him from their peephole view of Washington, he was "a man who can strut sitting down."[15] He was susceptible to the flattery Acheson and Lovett were to apply to him over the next two years of his power. The Michigan Senator called the omission of the United Nations a "colossal blunder" that must be rectified. Since the influential columnist Walter Lippmann, who also wanted aid for Greece and Turkey, shared this view, the omission was all the more serious a blunder.[16]

Vandenberg, who had believed a month before that Greece

would fall "fifty times" before the United Nations would act, paid obeisance on April 8, 1947, to that organ by addressing it as "our first reliance and our prime concern." The Senator then urged Ambassador Warren Austin at the United Nations to notify that body of the "emergency and temporary character" of the program and to assure it that "the United States believes that the United Nations and its related agencies should assume the principle responsibility, within their capabilities, for the long-range tasks of assistance required for the reconstruction of Greece." [17] Carrying this point to Congress, Vandenberg tacked on a preamble to the aid bill, explicitly linking the program to the charter and explaining that the United States was acting only because the United Nations was not in a position to help. Moreover, Vandenberg, in conjunction with Tom Connally of Texas, his Democratic counterpart on the Foreign Relations Committee, wrote a provision into the bill authorizing the Security Council or the General Assembly to terminate American assistance whenever "action taken or assistance furnished by the United Nations makes the continuance of such assistance unnecessary or undesirable." In this way, the problem of compatibility was solved to the satisfaction of Senator Vandenberg and, presumably, to that of most of his countrymen.

The men who had framed the Truman Doctrine considered the Vandenberg addendum a charade to appease public opinion. Joseph M. Jones, a staff officer in the State Department, admitted that he and his colleagues had missed the issue, but, given the weakness of the United Nations and the urgency of the problem in the eastern Mediterranean, he was not prepared to admit their mistake. [18] Dean Acheson could never take the issue seriously. In his customary sardonic vein, he looked back years later to the act of "political transubstantiation" by which Vandenberg had embraced the Truman Doctrine with more ardor than before. Acheson observed that Vandenberg, joined by Lippmann, "that ambivalent Jeremiah of the Press," had discovered the dreadful crime of "bypassing the United Nations" and had rectified it by giving the international organization a specific role in the legislative program of the United States. Acheson speculated that the "fortunate" sin of omission had produced the opportunity for the Vandenberg blessing to be laid upon the Truman Doctrine, thus guaranteeing its success with Congress and the country. [19]

In its experience with the Marshall Plan, leading to the establishment of the Economic Cooperation Administration, the Truman policy makers were able to manage the issue with greater sophistication than they displayed in the enunciation of the Truman Doctrine. They were assisted by the fact that the assistance asked for was exclusively economic and that theoretically the Soviet Union could be a beneficiary. Title I of the ECA bill proclaimed that "Congress finds that the existing situation in Europe endangers the establishment of the objectives of the United Nations." Beyond this general statement, the administration consciously connected the new bill with other agencies in the United Nations that served economic purposes, such as the Food and Agricultural Organization and the Economic Commission for Europe. This harmony was specifically underscored by spokesmen for such prestigious public-spirited groups as the General Federation of Womens Clubs, the League of Women Voters, and the Ad Hoc Commission for the Marshall Plan. The powerful Committee for Economic Development, a group of liberal businessmen from which the leadership of the ECA would be drawn, identified the program as "an affirmation of our own civilization" and hence obviously as vital to American interests as "participation in the United Nations, in the International Monetary Fund, and the International Trade Organization." [20]

Not that voices against the Marshall Plan on the ground of incompatibility with the United Nations were wholly mute. The Progressive party and the American Labor party of New York offered the same objections to the new program they had expressed against military aid to Greece and Turkey; namely, it represented an American imperialist challenge to the United Nations and the Soviet Union. In some ways it was even more insidious. British and French assets would be assumed by Wall Street before the new program would go into effect. If the United States was serious in its professions of concern for distraught Europe, it would adopt the seven-point program of Henry

Wallace, which would place under full control of the United Nations the aid intended under ECA. So advised Arthur Schutzer, state executive secretary of the American Labor party. Far less stridently, but with more effect, the Society of Friends asked for a European program that "should be carried out in the closest possible cooperation with the United Nations." Clearly, the present plan did not meet this request. [21]

Consistent with their position on the Truman Doctrine, conservative nationalists struck at the Marshall Plan because of its identification with the United Nations. The latter was the menace drawing American resources out of the nation and into an octopus of collectivism. Merwin Hart, president of the National Economic Council, claimed in a radio address on February 23, 1948, that "while we are lulled into imagining the UN is all mouth, a harmless debating society, the Planners are busy attaching tentacles to its body.... These tentacles are the agencies of the UN." A few weeks earlier, Hart had testified in congressional hearings against the aforementioned preamble which "speaks highly of the attainment of the objectives of the United Nations." This was precisely the trouble with the program. [22]

But the opponents of European economic aid lost some of their natural constituencies. The administration's care to entangle the Marshall Plan with the United Nations from the outset and claim that it was another species of that organization's ongoing agencies, mollified some who had been turned away from the Truman Doctrine. Although the *Christian Century* found duplication of the Economic Commission for Europe, it contented itself with a warning, not a repudiation. Its suspiciousness manifested itself in a Freudian slip of the type when it quoted Acheson as saying that American economic aid would be concentrated "in areas where it will be most effective in strengthening the authority of the United States." In the next issue the editor apologized for its error in printing *United States* instead of *United Nations*. The Marshall Plan was a gamble in the eyes of the *Christian Century*. It was also "a great venture in statesmanship." [23] Even the acerbic *Nation*, a vigorous critic of the Truman Doctrine, agreed that the Marshall Plan "offers a new hope," although it assumed at first that the program would be under the aegis of the Economic Commission for Europe. Lippmann's clear distinction between "the Truman line" and "the Marshall line"—one unilateral, the other in harmony with the United Nations—made a difference for many friends of collective security.[24]

If there were lingering doubts about the conjunction of the Marshall Plan with the United Nations, the endorsement of leaders of the American Association for the United Nations should have resolved them. Clark M. Eichelberger, its national director, offered a blessing by association: "The Marshall Plan must not be considered disassociated from the United Nations. Its success means stability for the nations of Europe, and the United Nations must derive its strength from stable members." Although the majority of the Philadelphia branch of the United Nations Council would have preferred the plan be administered by the United Nations, its letter to the Senate Committee on Foreign Affairs observed that "it is important to point out that there was a very significant minority in favor of having the United States administer aid alone."[25] The majority's objection represented a minor caveat; the American friends of the United Nations put their imprimatur on the Marshall Plan.

The above success was a tribute to the new sensitivity of the administration's managers. Acheson had made appropriate gestures, as the report of the *Christian Century* suggested. The tactics of congressional approval were well planned and equally well executed. To soothe the endemic fiscal conservatism of Congress, the European aid program was divided into parts, with only a modest interim bill presented in the fall of 1947 and the remainder in the winter of 1948, after the nation was educated to the importance of ECA.

Europe had already done its part by organizing itself in the summer of 1947 into a conference, under the chairmanship of Sir Oliver Franks, that promised cooperation and self-help on the one hand and estrangement from Communist Eastern Europe on the other. The Soviet Union and its allies had never been formally excluded, and some of the Eastern European countries would have remained in the European meeting on the Marshall Plan if the Soviet Union had not summarily removed itself and its dependent friends from consideration. Whether a Communist belief in the plan as a dying gasp of capitalism or as an imperialist trick to dominate Europe moved the Russians is immaterial. Soviet hostility to ECA and its subsequent involvement in the coup d'etat in Czechoslovakia in February 1948 helped tip the balance in Congress in behalf of the Marshall program. As the New York *Times* claimed on January 18, 1948, "Kremlin, as Usual, Comes to the Rescue of ERP." The Communist menace eased the labors of the Herter Committee, a select committee of House members studying the feasibility of the Marshall proposal.

Even without the Soviet Union's inadvertent collaboration, the efforts at alerting the American public to the importance of European aid had been enormous, and the results were impressive. At the apex was the aforementioned Committee for the Marshall Plan, with former Secretary of War Henry L. Stimson as national chairman. Robert Patterson was chairman of an executive committee that included Mrs. Wendell L. Willkie, Dean Acheson (then in retirement), labor leaders David Dubinsky and James B. Carey, conservative Republican banker Winthrop Aldrich, and liberal Democratic Senator Herbert H. Lehman of New York.

Given the weight of the foregoing names, the particular economic expectations of the National Association of Manufacturers, the American Federation of Labor, and the American Farm Bureau Association, and the favorable views of groups as diverse as Americans for Democratic Action and the American Legion, the administration had reason for optimism. A Gallup poll released on December 7, 1947, showed that in a four-and-a-half-month period the segment of the public which had not "heard or read" about the plan dropped from 51 to 36 percent. Toward the end of the period, those with no opinion declined from 38 to 27 percent. Favorable opinion rose from 47 to 56 percent, leaving only 17 percent opposed to economic aid to Europe. The results were not merely passage of both aid programs by a substantial majority but the silencing of opposition, particularly from the fiscal conservatives and nationalists concerned with Asia more than Europe.[26] In other words, the men who had pressed isolationism before the war were unable to move in 1948.

A final factor in their immobility was an addendum to ECA that included Chiang's China among the beneficiaries in the final version of the legislation.

As of the winter of 1948 the administration could ignore dissenters on the Cold War. The nation had accepted the commitment to use America's enormous economic resources and potential military power to defend beleaguered peoples from Communist military threats and to rehabilitate a continent sufficiently to immunize it from the blandishments of communism. The Truman administration had succeeded in these objectives without unleashing the forces of isolationism in America. But if isolationism was held at bay, it was partly because the United Nations had been held aloft as the organization whose survival precluded the revival of balance-of-power politics and the alliance system. The efforts in behalf of the defense of Greece and Turkey and the economic revival of France and Great Britain under the Marshall Plan had been presented effectively as within the spirit, and even the letter, of the United Nations Charter.

The pose of compatibility could not survive the next phase of the Cold War, the joining of an entangling alliance in NATO. The step was taken reluctantly, but inevitably, given the commitment to the survival of Europe. Military assistance piecemeal and long-term financial support were not enough to secure the desperate nations of Europe. To fulfill the irrevocable political obligations they demanded meant reopening the question of the United Nations Charter. There was no avoidance of a direct conflict between a treaty of military alliance and a charter of collective security. To accept one meant to deny the other. The administration tried to keep the facade. It failed, but by 1949, when the alliance was made, the country had been sufficiently prepared to pay a price it might not have in 1947 or 1948.

At any event, the Truman administration policy makers could not enjoy the respite passage of the Economic Cooperation Act should have given them. Even before it was signed on April 3, 1948, five nations of western Europe, all future beneficiaries of the Marshall Plan, banded together to form the Western Union under the Treaty of Brussels. The ostensible occasion for this military pact was the Communist coup d'etat in Prague in February 1948, which ended the last vestige of western influence in Czechoslovakia. The twin shocks over the death of Jan Masaryk and Czech democracy reminded Europeans that economic recovery would be worthless, even if it was possible, without the accompaniment of physical security. Could a nation's economy be rehabilitated if its energies were absorbed in fears of invasion or internal subversion? If not, then cooperation in the military sphere was as vital as it had been in the economic. The Brussels pact, with its emphasis on self-help and interdependence in a common defense, was, as John Spanier noted, "a military counterpart to the OEEC."[27]

An American connection with the Brussels pact was necessary to advance such progress in security as had been made through the Truman Doctrine and Marshall Plan. There were few alternatives open. Whatever the merits of the argument that Soviet activity in 1948 — from the Czech coup in February to the Berlin blockade in June — was the product of American decisions tying the occupation zones in Germany to the West and successfully launching the Marshall Plan, the Truman administration could see only aggression, not response, in Russian behavior. A military link with the Western Union was a logical extension of policies of the past year.

What was distressing in the challenge of the Brussels pact was not the question of an American commitment. Rather, it was the clarification of the isolationist problem which had been successfully blurred before. Because the United Nations was to have been the new means of voiding the alliance system, the Charter of the United Nations became the forum for the confrontation. The initial hope of Secretary of State Marshall was association, not membership. When British Foreign Minister Ernest Bevin first broached the subject of a mutual defense treaty with France and the Benelux countries in January 1948, Truman and Marshall offered their general blessing. That the transatlantic connection should be construed as an American signature to an alliance was another matter. Alliance would mean that the United States would lock itself into a fifty-year entanglement in which it would be obliged, according to Article 4, to offer the member attacked in Europe "all military and other aid and assistance in their power." The last time the United States had made an entangling commitment to a European power was in 1778, and this had been terminated with relief in 1800. Would Americans in 1948 agree to an arrangement so blatantly at odds with the world view equated with the United Nations?

A temporary way out of the dilemma emerged from an important meeting at Blair House on April 17, 1948, at which Marshall, Lovett, Vandenberg, and Dulles spoke in private what they felt they could not speak in public: the prospect of a transatlantic pact widening the Western Union and built on the regional pattern of the Rio. They all agreed on its necessity, if it could be accomplished under the aegis of Articles 51 and 53 of the Charter of the United Nations, which concerned the legitimacy respectively of collective self-defense and regional activity. They admitted to themselves, however, that the question of compatability with the charter made the latter an insecure basis for such an alliance. [28]

In light of their irresolution, understandable on the part of an administration fearful of resurgent isolationism in a hostile Congress and of a President unsure of his nomination in an election year, Vandenberg's resolution for Senate approval of the Western Union appeared as a satisfactory, if temporary, compromise. Senate Resolution 234 of June 11, 1948, announced to the world affirmation of "the association of the United States, by constitutional process, with such regional and other collective arrangements as are based on continuous and effective self-help and mutual aid, and as affect national security." Here was an identification with the European organization in terms reminiscent of the Marshall Plan. More striking was the frame of reference for the United Nations. Of the six paragraphs in the resolution, five spoke of the United Nations and American pursuit of its goals "in accordance with the purposes, principles, and provisions of the Charter." A year later, Vandenberg made a point of noting that three of the six paragraphs in his Senate Resolution were specifically intended to make the charter more workable. [29] By virtue of the resolution, the United States resolved the dilemma of the Blair House meeting. The resolution announced its "association" with the alliance, not membership, and announced also its full devotion to the United Nations without having to prove it. The Senate vote of 64 to 4 permitted more to be done when the time was right.

Of itself, the Vandenberg resolution was never sufficient to give Europeans the sense of security they required. All parties knew this. While covert conversations proceeded among military staff of the prospective allies, no overt movement toward an alliance was initiated until the election campaign had ended. Alliance became the public issue in the President's triumphant State of the Union message of 1949, when the nation was told of negotiations for "a joint agreement designed to strengthen the security of the North Atlantic area." The five Brussels countries became the twelve members of the North Atlantic Treaty, ranging from Canada and the United States through Iceland to Portugal, Italy, and the Scandinavian countries of Denmark and Norway. Part of the reasoning behind the wider scope of the alliance was the greater protection enlarged membership would bring; a larger part of the reasoning, from the American standpoint, was its use in warding off attacks of isolationists against an alliance with exclusively European powers. President Truman observed in Point Three of his State of the Union message in 1949 that "such an arrangement would take the form of a collective defense arrangement under the terms of the United Nations Charter."[30]

Unlike Senate Resolution 234, the North Atlantic Treaty's attempt to exploit a connection with the United Nations evoked protests. The nature of the treaty made it difficult for even the most eloquent defenders to evade charges of American desertion not only of the traditions of the nineteenth century but also the idea of collective security which the nation had embraced during World War II. The treaty put the United States into a military alliance with the very countries Washington's Farewell Address and Monroe's Doctrine had warned against. It was an explicit acceptance of the reality of balance of power as the dominant force in international affairs, no matter how liberally the language of the treaty spoke of Article 51 or hinted at its likeness to Articles 52 and 53 of the charter. Exposure of the conflict between treaty and charter was unavoidable.

Not that the administration put aside its mask of compatibility. Acheson prepared the country for the Atlantic Pact in a major radio address on March 18, 1949, in which he made a point of observing that "the pact is carefully and consciously designed to conform in every particular with the Charter of the United Nations."[31] True, he also recognized the embarrassment such a statement could create for the government. He blamed the press for challenging the claim, suggesting in his memoirs that "they were inclined to bring to the reporting of foreign affairs the same nose for controversial spot news that they had learned to look for in City Hall and police-court beats. This did the country and their readers a disservice."[32] James Reston of the New York *Times* presented a different view. He felt that if the treaty planners had not emphasized the harmony between treaty and charter, opponents of one or the other would have had more difficulty in locating their targets.[33]

Acheson had as much difficulty with senators as he had with journalists. While his close collaboration with Vandenberg and Connally, chairmen of the Senate Foreign Relations Committee of the 80th and 81st congresses, respectively, repeatedly advanced the administration's position, including the professed reliance of the treaty on Article 51 of the charter, he could not control the mavericks in the Senate. Forrest Donnell of Missouri, in particular, "set off a land mine in our discussions." Donnell's reading of an inaccurate report in the Kansas City *Times* on a secret meeting between Acheson and Halvard Lange, Norway's Foreign Minister, angered the Secretary of State. Acheson was supposed to have promised Lange that a moral commitment in the treaty would guarantee American involvement in the event of an attack, no matter what caveats on constitutional processes might have been included in the test. To Acheson, Donnell and his stripe were irresponsible, prejudiced, and hopelessly isolationist. "Senator Donnell was not my favorite senator," is Acheson's sardonic understatement. "He combined the courtliness of Mr. Pickwick with the suavity of an experienced waiter with the manner of a prosecuting attorney in the movies — the gimlet eye, the piercing question. In administering the *coup de grace* he would do it with a napkin over his arm and his ears sticking out perpendicularly like an alert elephant's."[34]

For all the secretary's hauteur and sarcasm, he was dealing

with issues which were both emotional and newsworthy. The United States, by means of a military alliance, was abandoning a tradition of nonentanglement in the politics of Europe. It was hardly surprising that critics, despite the administration's disclaimers, should recognize this fact and react accordingly. The issue of the charter was nonsense to Acheson; he may have wanted to soothe the country with it, but he expected leaders to understand and to ignore.

Vandenberg, with a greater capacity for self-delusion, convinced himself that the pact could stay "strictly within the Constitution of the United States and within the Charter of the United Nations."[35] Warren Austin's position as ambassador to the United Nations was more painful and required even more elaborate rationalization. He was equal to the assignment. Committed to the ideals of the charter, he refused to find any incompatibility between the two instruments. He assured himself that the North Atlantic Treaty had nothing to do with older alliances or with the balance-of-power system. "The old veteran, balance of power," he revealed at the hearings of the Foreign Relations Committee, "was given a blue discharge when the United Nations was formed."[36] The treaty, meeting the principles of the charter, obviously would not permit reenlistment of the old system. What made the treaty necessary was its legal way, as Vandenberg informed one of his constituents, for "peaceful nations to defend international justice and security scrupulously within the Charter but outside the veto."[37]

All of the above images had been marshalled earlier in the Truman Doctrine and the Marshall Plan debates. Conformity of intention with the charter smoothed ambiguities. But unlike the other measures, the treaty demanded an explication of its text. It was not enough to sprinkle so many references to the United Nations in the text that the unwary reader might believe that the Security Council had drafted the treaty. A treaty whose title suggested a regional arrangement and whose language emphasized the common culture of a region invited challenge of its harmony with Articles 53 and 54 of Chapter VIII of the charter. Article 53 states that "no enforcement action shall be taken under regional arrangements or by regional agencies without the authorization of the Security Council." Article 54 provides that "the Security

Council shall at all times be kept fully informed of activities undertaken or in contemplation under regional arrangements or by regional agencies." The North Atlantic Treaty could meet neither requirement. The nation whose abuse of the veto made NATO necessary was a permanent member of the Security Council.

Nevertheless, the vagueness of the charter's definition of regionalism tempted policy makers to exploit a connection. Austin asserted that "in certain of its aspects, the Treaty is also a regional arrangement. . . . The point I am making is that if in the operation of the Treaty the signatories go into the exercise of duties that fall within the chapter, then the chapter applies."[38] It is worth noting, however, that the administration took no chances; no articles of Chapter VIII appear in the text.

The United Nations Charter, Article 51, on the other hand, with its emphasis on the right of individual or collective defense, was specifically identified in Article 5 of the treaty. Here was a major rampart of legality around which the defenders of the pact intended to rally. Unlike the articles in Chapter VIII, its implementation required no Security Council authorization. It involved an issue anterior to the establishment of the United Nations, the inherent right of self-defense. Ambassador Austin claimed: "In my mind Article 51 does not grant a power. It merely prohibits anything contained in the Charter cutting across existing power."[39] But whether a nation or group of nations could organize for this purpose before an attack was made remained a major question. It raised other questions as well. If the treaty really conformed to Article 51, was it a wise provision? Would a careless use of this vital article permit any nation to call another an aggressor and then go on to fight a war as if the United Nations did not exist? Senators Donnell and Claude Pepper of Florida pressed the administration for answers to all these questions. If the administration accepted these risks, they would also have to admit that behind the murky language of the treaty lurked "the old veteran, balance of power," whom Austin was so determined to bury.

The interest groups which had made themselves heard over the Truman Doctrine and Marshall Plan quickly found the trail opened by congressional critics of the Atlantic Pact. Liberals and pacifists who had reluctantly accepted the Marshall Plan now claimed to find in NATO confirmation of the fears first raised in the Greek aid bill. Quaker spokesmen were particularly eloquent in their concerns over the fate of the United Nations. In a widely publicized American Friends Service report, *The United States and the Soviet Union: Some Quaker Proposals for Peace*, a challenge was laid down: "Mere statements of loyalty to the United Nations are not sufficient. But statements of loyalty, followed by actions which contribute to the strengthening of the United Nations, and to an extension of its authority could help initiate a new era in which some of the present inadequacies could be overcome." [40] Specifically offensive, in the words of Reverend A. Stauffer Curry of the Church of the Brethren, was the power of the Atlantic Council "to determine when joint action should be taken by signatory nations against an alleged aggressor." [41] In this event, he claimed, "the Council created by the North Atlantic Treaty would in effect sit in judgment upon the United Nations." Familiar unhappy memories were raised by Reverend J. Paul Cotton of Cleveland, who was convinced that exploitive European powers would "undermine the prestige of the United Nations by the promotion of military alliances, which have always led to war, just as the League of Nations was undermined." [42]

The orthodox left, particularly the survivors of the Progressive presidential campaign, predictably spoke of doom for the United Nations, of war provoked by this measure. Henry Wallace saw the treaty not only as a violation of the charter but of Franklin D. Roosevelt's dream of the world's future. Accusing Acheson of "being less than frank with the American people," he said that "the pact substitutes for the one world of the United Nations the two hostile worlds of a 'divided nation.'" His own solutions would be "agreement by both nations to give up all military bases in other United Nations countries and to halt the export of weapons to other nations." [43]

Conservative critics were more muted than they had been about the Truman Doctrine and Marshall Plan. Outside Congress—and inside too—the rhetoric of anti-communism and the attractiveness of affirmative action on the part of the administration won adherents. Hamilton Fish, a former congressman from New York distinguished for his isolationism in the 1930s, felt "compelled, because of the rotten mess we made of it in Europe, to urge our joining the North Atlantic Pact as a peace measure in defense of the remaining free nations of Europe against Soviet aggression."[44] Although snares remained in the treaty, as in the United Nations, as long as Britain and France were present, many of the older isolationists joined reluctantly with liberal internationalists in accepting what they felt was inevitable. Consequently, testimony against the treaty from the right was confined to extremists who found NATO part of a Jewish conspiracy for world conquest or who found it, as Mervin K. Hart's National Economic Council did, a foolish waste of funds. Russia would occupy Europe anyway.[45] In such commentary the United Nations was irrelevant as an issue. The treaty simply substituted for the charter another insidious threat to American security.

What is impressive about much of the criticism of the pact in 1949 was not that the vulnerability of the administration's position went undiscovered or unexploited. Rather it was that the constituencies which cared were remarkably small. Pacifists and Progressives on the left were articulate but predictable. They lacked an audience. Even smaller and more eccentric was the radical right opposition, which appeared the captive of the lunatic fringes of politics; ten years earlier, some of its leaders had been part of the mainstream of public opinion.

A striking measure of Truman's success was the ingathering of former liberal critics who had chafed over the Truman Doctrine or the Marshall Plan but now saw no alternative to the treaty. Charles M. LaFollette, a member of Americans for Democratic Action, bowed to the administration's logic in light of the Communist peril. Borrowing from the record of Roosevelt, as Wallace had done for other purposes, LaFollette saw the treaty as a new version of quarantining aggressors, begun with Roosevelt's "famous speech of October 5, 1937." The ADA paid its respects to the conformity of the pact "with both the spirit and letter of the United Nations Charter." With more enthusiasm, LaFollette accepted the administration's point that the United Nation's "limitations must be faced" and that the troubles stemming from them must be blamed on the Russians.[46]

Acceptance was not without anguish. Unless the liberals ruled out the possibility of the redemption of Communists, they remained uneasy over Cold War measures. Gilbert Harrison, of the liberal American Veterans Committee, justified the pact only because it "buys time — time that can be used to renew our efforts to strengthen the United Nations and to work through that organization toward the ultimate security of some form of world government with limited but adequate power to prevent aggression."[47]

The administration's victory was dimmed only by the encouragement it continued to give to liberals and conservatives alike who wished to reshape the United Nations to American purposes. Some wanted revision of the charter to remove the veto power from the permanent members of the Security Council. Others wanted to expel the Soviet Union from the United Nations and create a smaller, more manageable organization. While reform of the charter was not of itself objectionable to the administration, the form it might take could undo the security of Europe and the international commitments of the United States.

The new Atlantic Union Committee was a particularly unwelcome ally of the partisans of the pact. An outgrowth of Clarence Streit's original vision of Anglo-American federation, the Atlantic Union Committee saw in the treaty a halfway house to a new Atlantic federation along the lines of the American Union. Its leaders had been makers of policy in 1947, former Secretary of War Robert P. Patterson and former Undersecretary of State William L. Clayton. Strongly anti-Communist, they believed, in the words of Clayton, that the treaty was "a step that is necessary in order to convince Soviet Russia that the members of the Atlantic Pact will stand together for the preservation of their independence and integrity."[48] They equated the Atlantic federation with a little United Nations that would fulfill the promise of peace.

The vigor of the committee and the fame of its directors were embarrassing to the administration. The Atlantic Union Committee's chairman, Justin Blackwelder, wanted credit for stimulating a "NATO mood" in 1949. He claimed that "people inside the Department of State have told us we were very helpful in getting the Atlantic Pact ratified. The extreme Right was so busy attacking us that it made the Department's job easier." [49] Be this as it may, pursuit of a transformed United Nations invited new attacks from right and left: from the right, because of the intimacy with Western Europe that it promised; from the left, because it would sacrifice the original United Nations.

Yet, the administration and its congressional allies were themselves responsible for holding out hopes of reforming the charter. The platform of both Republicans and Democrats in the election of 1948 had referred respectively to the removal "of any veto in the peaceful settlement of international disputes" and to leading "the way toward curtailment of the use of the veto." Senator Taft reminded his colleagues, in his denunciation of the treaty on the floor of the Senate, that the Vandenberg resolution opened with a recommendation for "a voluntary agreement to remove the veto from all questions involving specific settlements of international disputes, and situations, and from the admission of new members." He pointed out that this clause had been conspicuously ignored. [50] He was correct. The administration had no genuine interest in pursuing the removal of the veto to its logical conclusion. To do so would have resulted in the departure of the Soviet Union from the world organization and a worsening of Cold War tensions. Such a consequence might have ended the life of the United Nations or formally converted it into an American protectorate. Neither alternative was desired.

Senator Taft's battle against the North Atlantic Treaty failed. He could not even win the vote of Senator Guy Gillette of Iowa, who had asked rhetorically if the treaty "is a step within the framework of the United Nations Charter or is it independent action which might be subversive of the success of world cooperation?" [51] Gillette suspected the latter to be true but joined 81 other senators in voting in favor of the treaty on July 21, 1949.

The administration won an impressive victory. It had been won by marshalling a wide variety of public opinion willing to suspend reservations for the sake of realizing a common objective of peace and security. Without the association with the United Nations, the respectability of the enterprise would have been in jeopardy. NATO would then have been an alliance outside the law, open to attack from every side. Harmonizing Cold War policies with the United Nations was the path the administration followed doggedly from 1947 to 1949 as it hoped to pluck the fruits of collective security while avoiding the thistles of isolationism.

Deviousness and self-delusion were part of the process of decision making. But given the pressures from Europe in the late 1940s and also the lack of knowledge of Soviet intention, the administration achieved the stability it sought through a series of tradition-shaking changes in American foreign policy. Whatever one's estimation of the wisdom of the public or congressional mind, both the public and the Congress are involved in the making of policy in the American democracy. The administration succeeded in fashioning an executive-legislative consensus, undergirded by the support of the articulate public, that permitted passage and implementation of its program.

The process was cumbersome as well as devious. But a frank and detailed presentation of the military and economic assistance programs or an elaboration of the implications of an alliance would have constituted a full repudiation of the isolationist past and the United Nations present. Rightly or wrongly, Truman's advisors believed such acts would doom their cause.

NOTES

1. Quoted in Roland Stromberg, *Collective Security and American Foreign Policy: From the League of Nations to NATO* (New York: Frederick A. Praeger, Inc., 1963), p. 180.

2. W. A. Scott and S. B. Withey, *The United States and the United Nations: The Public View* (New York: Manhattan Publishing Co., 1958), pp. 24-25.

3. George F. Kennan, *Memoirs 1925-1950* (New York: Bantam Books, Inc., 1969), pp. 330-331.

4. Ibid., p. 332.

5. Dean Acheson, *Present at the Creation: My Years in the State Department* (New York: W. W. Norton & Co., 1969), p. 219.

6. 12 March 1947, Speech to the Congress on Greece and Turkey: Truman Doctrine, in *Public Papers of the Presidents of the United States: Harry S. Truman, 1947* (Washington, D.C.: Government Printing Office, 1963), p. 180.

7. Quoted in Joseph M. Jones, *The Fifteen Weeks* (New York: Harcourt, Brace and World, 1955), p. 91.

8. Truman Doctrine, in *Public Papers of the Presidents*, p. 177.

9. Jones, *The Fifteen Weeks*, p. 160.

10. 5 March 1947, Vandenberg to John B. Bennett, in Arthur H. Vandenberg, Jr., ed., *The Private Papers of Senator Vandenberg* (Boston: Houghton Mifflin and Co., 1952), pp. 340-341.

11. Acheson, *Present at the Creation*, p. 223.

12. Scott and Withey, *The United States*, p. 74.

13. Quoted in Jones, *The Fifteen Weeks*, pp. 178-179.

14. Quoted in Henry W. Berger, "Senator Robert A. Taft Dissents from Military Escalation," in T. G. Paterson, ed., *Cold War Critics* (Chicago: Quadrangle Books, 1971), p. 177.

15. Robert S. Allen and William V. Shannon, *The Truman Merry-go-Round* (New York: Vanguard Press, 1950), p. 253.

16. Jones, *The Fifteen Weeks*, pp. 180-182.

17. Vandenberg, *The Private Papers*, pp. 340-341, 345.

18. Jones, *The Fifteen Weeks*, p. 180.

19. Acheson, *Present at the Creation*, p. 223.

20. Research and Policy Committee of the CED, *The American Program of European Economic Cooperation* (New York: CED, 1947), pp. 28, 10.

21. U.S. Senate, Hearings, Committee on Foreign Relations, European Recovery Program, 80th Cong., 2d sess., pp. 934, 1145.

22. Quoted in Gabriel A. Almond, *The American People and Foreign Policy* (New York: Frederick A. Praeger, Inc., 1960), p. 204; Senate Hearings on ERP, p. 872.

23. *Christian Century*, July 2, July 7, July 20, 1947.

24. *The Nation*, June 21, 1947; Walter Lippmann, *The Cold War: A Study in U.S. Foreign Policy* (New York: Harpers, 1947), p. 52.

25. Senate Hearings on ERP, pp. 936, 1429.

26. Quoted in Harry B. Price, *The Marshall Plan and Its Meaning* (Ithaca: Cornell University Press, 1955), p. 60.

27. John Spanier, *American Foreign Policy Since World War II* (New York: Frederick A. Praeger, Inc., 1960), p. 46.

28. John Foster Dulles Memorandum on Conference at Blair House, in Dulles Papers, Princeton University. See also Vandenberg, *The Private Papers*, p. 406.

29. U.S. Senate, Hearings, Committee on Foreign Relations, North Atlantic Treaty, 81st Cong. 1st sess., pt. 1, p. 242.

30. Truman's State of the Union message, in *Public Papers of the Presidents*, p. 114.

31. U.S. Department of State, Bulletin 20 (March 27, 1949), p. 386.

32. Dean Acheson, *Present at the Creation*, p. 276.

33. New York *Times*, April 22, 1949.

34. Acheson, *Present at the Creation*, p. 281.

35. Vandenberg letter, February 22, 1949 in Vandenberg, *The Private Papers*, p. 478.

36. Senate Hearings on North Atlantic Treaty, pt. 1, p. 97.

37. Vandenberg letter of February 21, 1949, in Vandenberg, *The Private Papers*, p. 480.

38. Senate Hearings on North Atlantic Treaty, pt. 1, p. 96.

39. Ibid., pt. 1, p. 117.

40. American Friends Service Committee, *The United States and the Soviet Union: Some Quaker Proposals for Peace* (New Haven: Yale University Press, 1949), pp. 30-31.

41. Senate Hearings on North Atlantic Treaty, pt. 3, p. 836.

42. Ibid., pt. 3, p. 1128.

43. Ibid., pt. 2, p. 419.

44. Ibid., pt. 3, p. 950.

45. Ibid., pt. 3, pp. 853-854, 1144-1145.

46. Ibid., pt. 3, pp. 941-942.

47. Ibid., pt. 3, p. 920.

48. Ibid., pt. 2, p. 399.

49. Quoted in Emmett Panzella, "The Atlantic Union Committee: A Study of a Pressure Group in Foreign Policy" (Ph.D. dissertation, Kent State University, 1969), pp. 33-34.

50. U.S. Senate, Congressional Record, 81st Congress, 1st sess., July 11, 1949, p. 9198.

51. Ibid., p. 9205.

CHAPTER TEN

Ethnic Politics, the Palestine Question, and the Cold War

America's involvement with the creation of Israel in 1948 was something of an anomaly in postwar foreign policy. There is a natural tendency for students of diplomatic history to ascribe all behavior and policies in the postwar world to the most powerful perceptible force of the time, namely, the challenge of communism to the newly assumed world responsibilities of the United States. But at the very time the Truman Doctrine and the Marshall Plan were changing the shape of that policy in the service of anti-communism, the Palestine problem, which undermined the unity of the West and invited Soviet intervention, occupied almost equal attention of the American public. Ethnic and religious politics, so familiar in the nineteenth century, intruded into the midst of the Cold War.

It was no longer the Irish vote that fueled Anglophobia and created Anglo-American tensions, as it had in the nineteenth and early twentieth centuries. Nor was it Slavic-Americans, aroused over concessions at Yalta and Potsdam which putatively pushed their ancestral homes in Eastern Europe into the arms of the Soviet Union. The latter's discontent, while important in the elections of 1948 and 1952, conformed with the anti-Soviet stance taken by the administration independently of an East European vote. The most vocal group between 1945 and 1948 was the

American Jewish community, seeking support for a homeland in Palestine for survivors of Hitler's Europe. In effect, the Zionists' demand was to have the United States embrace their cause as its own. So articulate was the voice of this segment of the American public that the British Labour government, responsible for the mandate in Palestine and for order in all of the Middle East, was able repeatedly to blame all of its problems on the Truman administration's appetite for the Jewish vote or Jewish campaign funds. When Britain ungraciously unloaded the mandate on the United Nations, it was with a postscript noting that Truman's intervention made Britain's position untenable.

That domestic problems made the "tousled diplomatic bed," as Herbert Feis has called Palestine's effect on American diplomacy, is undeniable.[1] The forces unloosed by Zionism were impressive and seemingly overwhelming, particularly when they meshed with the mood of American public opinion. Within the Jewish community itself, there were many widely publicized differences. The American Jewish Committee, a small group of influential leaders, regarded itself as non-Zionist. Despite professions of neutrality, it desired actions from the United States which were hard to distinguish from the aspirations of Zionists. But the American Council for Judaism was a vociferous opponent of a Jewish state even as it supported a more flexible immigration policy in Palestine. The latter feared that Palestinian statehood would raise the question of dual nationality, cast doubts on loyalties of American Jews, and hence stimulate anti-Semitism in America. Beyond these concerns, the council accepted Judaism as a religion rather than an ethnic or racial group. But it spoke for only a small fraction of Jewry. The celebrated differences between the Republican Rabbi Abba Hillel Silver, always distrustful of Roosevelt's and Truman's promises, and the Democratic Rabbi Stephen S. Wise, always susceptible to Roosevelt's charm, made for spirited controversy in the American Zionist Emergency Council. They did not really provide much comfort, however, to those who wished to deflect Zionist pressures in the middle and late 1940s. American Jews were fixed on the goal of statehood for Palestine as the answer to both the immediate refugee problem in Europe and more vaguely as a fulfillment of a historic promise. The Roper poll of 1945 revealed consensus on this issue that placed only one Jew in ten in the anti-Zionist camp.

What is even more revealing is the extent of popular support for Zionism. At every turn, from the end of World War II to the establishment of Palestine, American public opinion was substantially in favor of increasing the number of refugees in Palestine, removing Great Britain from its mandate, dividing the land into Arab and Jewish states, and ultimately applauding if not sharing the defense of the new nation against invasion by its neighbors in collusion with Britain. An American Institute of Public Opinion poll of June 19, 1946, showed 78 percent of those polled in favor of the immediate admission of 100,000 Jews into Palestine. In the fall of 1947 AIPO recorded 65 percent in favor of a Jewish national home, 10 percent opposed, and 25 percent without an opinion.

Reasons for this outpouring of emotions are not hard to find; they bear resemblance to public empathy for suffering Ireland in the previous century. On one level, there was the familiar picture of Jewish pioneers carving a destiny for themselves out of a harsh frontier, with Arabs serving as Indians and the British occupying a familiar colonial role. On a more complicated level of interpretation, Americans were responding to the shock of Nazi genocide. Jews clamoring for entry into Palestine were more than Zionists wishing to fulfill a nationalist mission or a Biblical prophecy; they were survivors of an involuntary martyrdom. German bestiality under Hitler had only recently been revealed in full. Zionist activity was a form of expiation, particularly for American Jews who had witnessed the holocaust in impotence. And perhaps, as British and Arab critics have suggested, some of the demand for Jewish entry into Palestine was designed to evade a plea to change America's restrictive immigration laws. So, once again in American history, a foreign policy grew out of the pressure of interest groups that would profoundly affect another part of the world without a commensurate assumption of responsibility for the change or even a recognition of the consequences for the United States itself. The event took place at a time when American power in the world was never more dominant. In these circumstances, it is understandable if the state of

Israel was regarded as a product of American activity in an American-controlled United Nations. After 1945 a weak Britain could not withstand American power and had to bow to Zionist claims at the risk of losing loans vital to the British economy.

What is troublesome about the foregoing scenario is the contradiction between the assumptions of Zionist power over American politics and the realities of an administration announcing, without enforcing, its views on immigration, then edging its way hesitantly toward acceptance of partition of Palestine, and then waffling over the fact of an independent Israel. Given the stridency of Zionist propaganda and the apparent susceptibility of the Truman administration to its importunities, the tortuous path of the United States seems incongruous. It would be logical to accept the firm presidential recognition of Israel hours after its birth as indicative of American behavior throughout the period of gestation. The facts suggest otherwise. The remarkable feature in American behavior is how relatively unresponsive the government was to Zionist pressures; Truman's impulsive act of May 14, 1948, was an aberration. The record reveals no Pavlovian pattern of policy makers' following votes or money but rather a confused course from 1945 to 1948. American indecisiveness in turn stimulated the Arab world and, by indirection, the British government to challenge the United Nations' decision and to lead other members of that body to doubt the existence of a meaningful American policy toward the Middle East.

The end of World War II brought frustration rather than fruition to Zionist hopes as Palestine unwittingly became enmeshed in the Cold War. All plans for Jewish immigration or statehood were susceptible to interpretations dictated by the American conflict with the Soviet Union. Immigration from Eastern Europe meant an opportunity for Communists to send agents to Palestine in the guise of refugees. An end to the British mandate could mean its replacement by a Soviet presence. Zionism thereby became part of the Communist pattern of aggression and had to be contended with as such. These matters transcended any particular proprietary issue of the oil lobby or the military establishment. It affected all agencies. Nothing leveled obstructions in Anglo-American relations in this period more

quickly than the Russian menace. As Loy Henderson, director of
the Office of Near Eastern and African Affairs, informed Bartley
Crum, an American pro-Zionist member of the Anglo-American
Committee of Inquiry on Palestine in 1946: "There is one fact
facing both the United States and Great Britain, Mr. Crum. That
is the Soviet Union. It would be wise to bear that in mind when
you consider the Palestine problem."[2]

Kermit Roosevelt, widely traveled in the Middle East, wrote a
major article in 1948 that embodied both the positions of the
friends of Arab Palestine in America and, sotto voce, of the
Middle Eastern specialists in Washington. He appealed to anti-
communist sentiment, then widespread, as he identified the partition of Palestine with Soviet objectives. It was through a
Jewish Palestine rather than through the weak Communist
parties of the Arab states that the propagandizing and penetration of Soviet communism would triumph in the Middle East,
according to Roosevelt. This instrument should not occasion
surprise since "Communism, intellectually, is a European product and will appeal more easily to people brought up in Vienna,
Frankfurt, or Warsaw than to those who have lived in Nazareth
or Nablus all their lives." The kibbutz in Palestine, though rural
rather than urban, was modeled on the Soviet collective farm.
His main point, however, was to underscore the disruptive purposes of communism, equating partition with denying Middle
East oil to the Marshall Plan countries. It must be assumed, he
continued, that Soviet agents will be slipped in among genuine
refugees; after all: "The bulk of refugee traffic . . . has been from
Soviet occupation zones to British or American zones and thence
via France or Italy to Palestine. Only a very dull-headed intelligence service would let slip such a perfect occasion for planting
its agents."[3]

A variation on the Soviet dimension of Zionism had appeared
earlier in a desperate Arab attempt to counter the supposed Zionist control of American policy. If Arabs are estranged from
Britain and the United States, they will play on Soviet ambitions
in the area, predicted Walter L. Wright, a Turkish specialist
formerly on the faculty of the American University at Beirut:
"There is no reason to think that the Kremlin will be loath to

seize an opportunity to increase British embarrassment or our own."[4]

The Soviet Union loomed at every turn. On the one hand, the Arabs were presented as religious opponents of communism while the Jews were depicted as susceptible to the disease, making Zionism a vehicle for its dissemination. On the other hand, Arab anger with the West might force them into the Russian camp where they would be welcomed by the Communists. The latter's only goal was penetration of the area. In this light, Zionism, with the tensions immigration and statehood raised in Palestine, appeared as the obstacle to harmony and peace in the Middle East. More than that, without the complications of Zionism there would be no Communist problem among the Arabs.

Arab diplomatic representatives elaborated on this theme repeatedly with considerable effect. Given the increasing polarization of the world in 1946 and 1947, Zionism imposed a challenge to the ideas of containment of the Soviet Union drawn from the thesis of George Kennan. The newly established Policy Planning Staff, which Kennan chaired, and the National Security Council shared the belief that Zionism had become a Soviet wedge against the free world. Hence, the political power of Zionism had become a far more pressing issue in Truman's time than it had been in Roosevelt's. In the latter's last years, Palestine was on the periphery of his main concerns, and Zionist cries had been muted in deference to military priorities.

The diplomatic correspondence of American officials in the Middle East reinforced these fears. As early as August 1945, the American minister to Iraq had pointed out Russia's potential benefits from the popular anger over Palestine.[5] To some experts, the Soviet backing of partition in 1947 could be explained by their expectation of profit from ensuing violence. To others, rumors of Communist agents on every immigrant vessel were a powerful stimulant to opposition to immigration. As late as February 1948, British sources claimed that 1,000 Russian-speaking immigrants from Rumanian and Bulgarian ports contained agents, many of them non-Jews, designed to push the future state toward communism. Stories of this sort were incentive enough for Moshe Shertok, a leader of the Jewish Agency, to complain to the State Department.[6] Even though Henderson denied that credence was given them, they fitted the pattern seen everywhere. From Moscow, Ambassador Bedell Smith had no doubts; the Soviet purpose in the Middle East was to use any means to gain access to the area. Palestine was "considerably 'softer' for Soviet exploitation than the 'harder' Arab East, unshaken politically or economically by war and enemy occupation, shielded by firm US stand in Greece, Turkey and Iran. . . ."[7]

There were few among the advisers of Truman or in the foreign policy establishment who could look upon Zionism as anything but an embarrassment to American interests. Herchel V. Johnson, chief of the United States delegation to the United Nations, and Maj. Gen. John H. Hilldring, assistant secretary of state for occupied areas, were exceptions: they were among the few American officials whom Zionists found appreciative of their arguments. As for the President, Under Secretary of State Dean Acheson felt he was sincere in his support of the Jewish case for Palestine, but mistaken. While Acheson could understand the "mystical emotion" of a Jewish return to the Holy Land as expressed to him by his friend and mentor Felix Frankfurter, he could not share it.[8] For Secretary of the Navy James V. Forrestal and Secretary of State James F. Byrnes, as well as for Prime Minister Clement Attlee and Foreign Minister Ernest Bevin, political opportunism explained Truman's Zionist proclivities. Acheson disagreed. The President's identification with Zionism, like his dislike for Franco's Spain, was a deep conviction, in large part implanted by his close friend and former partner Eddie Jacobson, a passionate Zionist.[9]

Whether or not Truman's position on Palestine was opportunist, the Zionist position itself, according to Acheson, tended to "obscure the totality of American interests."[10] He did not say, however, that it ran contrary to American interests. Other men of influence, such as Forrestal, went much further in expressing their distress over Zionist importunities. His information came from "oil people in whom I have confidence," but his informants ranged far beyond that circle and he saw more serious challenges. His nightmares ranged from the solidifying of all Mohammedans to an alliance of colored peoples against America. More specifically, in his own area of responsibility, he was convinced that the partition of Palestine would require force to make it operative and that the United States lacked the spare manpower to undertake the mission. And should force be applied, it would be, in the eyes of Forrestal and his colleagues, on the wrong side. The United States would estrange forever those countries upon whom it would have to depend in the future.[11]

Forrestal believed that he had fought a losing battle against the interference of politics in American foreign policy. He tried his best to keep the Middle East out of elections and failed. Bitterly, he observed that "I thought it was a most disastrous and regrettable fact that the foreign policy of this country was determined by the contributions a particular bloc of special interests might make to the party funds." Zionist tactics of coercion of other nations in the General Assembly on the question of partition "bordered closely onto scandal."[12] In all this activity lay the implication of unpatriotic behavior on the part of the American Zionists. Kermit Roosevelt put it bluntly: "A Palestine Zionist, indeed, may dismiss the Russian threat to the United States from his consideration, but an American may not, even if he is a Zionist."[13]

These reflections point to an interpretation of events widely held about Truman's Palestine policy. Essentially, it was that the enormous grip of Zionists on the political arena, managed shrewdly by such agents as David Niles and Judge Samuel Rosenman, or even Eddie Jacobson, prevailed over the collective wisdom of the executive branch. Against the advice of almost all his advisers, the President pressed for admission of 100,000 immigrants into Palestine without regard for the ability of that country to absorb them and without regard for the effect of such immigration upon the Arab majority or British authority. Having failed to effect this goal, he used America's authority to strip the British of their mandate, dictate partition of Palestine into Arab and Jewish states, and ultimately provide de facto recognition of Israel within an hour of its official existence. The United States thereby stimulated permanent chaos in the Middle East, a condition useful only to the Communists. All of these actions took place at a time when the Cold War required close solidarity between Britain and the United States.

In retrospect, this interpretation is only partly accurate. It fails to take into account a number of elements, each of which subtly affects the conventional picture. For example, the grip of Zionist ideology on Jews outside the United States and Britain was either overlooked or discounted by American policy makers. The survivors of Nazi concentration camps were not mere dupes of Zionist propaganda. Palestine was the one place that could make sense out of their lives and their history. Even if American policy had remained strictly aloof from the refugee question, this fact would have plagued Britain. As it was, British reaction to immigration was only one of many signs that convinced Palestinian Jews that continued British control had to be resisted. Britain's stake in its dwindling empire dictated that the voice of the Arab states would predominate. For Jews, therefore, the choice for the future rested with a militant effort for statehood or resignation to being driven out of Palestine by Arab nationalism, whether or not 100,000 or more refugees would find their way into the country. The conception of binationalism, which the more tolerant supporters of the Arab cause in and out of the State Department raised as an alternative, was dead in 1945. Jewish Palestine prepared for a struggle to survive, and much of the outside world, except the British commander in Palestine, underestimated their ability to manage it. Repeated American references to the dispatch of troops to the Middle East to save Jews from Arab attack after independence suggest the predominant pessimistic American view of the problem.

British and Arab perceptions of American policy on the Middle East resembled those of Forrestal or Kermit Roosevelt. Bevin's open assaults on Truman's or Congress's demands for admission of refugees were built on an assumption that the President and Congress were hostages to ethnic politics. It was the rare American minister in Arab countries who did not predict dire consequences from continued American disregard for Arab Palestine.

But in light of the enormous weight America swung in international affairs in this period and the deepening British dependence on American beneficence, the Labour government operated with remarkable freedom both in its violent hostility toward American Zionists, frequently with crude anti-Semitic undertones, and its criticism of Congress and the President. The

British had a scapegoat for what might have been an inevitable bankruptcy of their mandate in Palestine. Arab opposition to Jewish immigration and later to the partition of Palestine moved quickly from verbal to military action, partly because they anticipated an easy victory over outnumbered Jews, but also because of tacit encouragement from American sources. British and Arabs picked up regular signals from policy makers, diplomats, oil representatives, and churchmen, encouraging them to ignore the statements of the President and the resolutions of Congress.

Even without civil servants' undercutting the politicians, there would be the question of the extent to which Truman was a captive of the Zionists. His sympathies and frequently his behavior were those of a Zionist when Zionism was a matter of the plight of refugees or the injustice of the White Paper of 1939 or the redemption of human and physical resources in Palestine. That the President was impatient at critical moments with the obstructionism of "the striped-pants boys" in the State Department is as obvious as his actions as a politician in wooing Jewish votes in 1946 by demanding immediate action from Britain on the immigration problem.[14] Moreover, he was genuinely moved by sympathy for the Zionist cause.

But it is not obvious that these considerations outweighed countervailing pressures. The President listened to his advisers more closely than he did to Zionist friends or connections. When Zionist spokesmen pressed him too hard, he expressed his annoyance loudly and clearly. Some of this appears, somewhat defensively, in his memoirs, when he complained to Chaim Weizmann at the time partition was recommended by the United Nations in 1947: "I do not think I ever had as much pressure and propaganda aimed at the White House as I had in this instance. The persistence of a few of the extreme Zionist leaders—actuated by political motives and engaging in political threats—disturbed and annoyed me."[15] Truman claimed that he had always recognized that there were limits to the identification of American foreign policy with the Zionist state. There is no reason to doubt his agreement with the words of Secretary of State Stettinius on Palestine six days after he assumed office: "As we have interests in that area which are vital to the United States, we feel that

this whole subject is one that should be handled with the greatest care and with a view to the long-range interests of the
economy."[16]

The result of clashing advice was an air of improvisation and
uncertainty in Middle Eastern policy from 1945 to 1948 which
contrasted sharply with the growing clarity of European policy
in this period. Such form as it had lay in the initiatives of the
State Department, which advised continuation of Roosevelt's
practice: namely, expressions of sympathy for Zionist aspirations without concomitant commitment and elliptically phrased
promises on the refugee problems which would neither open
America's doors nor assume responsibility for their resettlement
in Palestine or elsewhere. This would be the public posture.
Beneath the surface there would be continued assurances to the
Arabs that no changes would be made without their concurrence
and to the British that their recovery from the traumas of war
would always enjoy first priority.

Where the Secretary of State and his department differed from
the President in 1945 was in their relative insensitivity to the
plight of displaced Jews in Europe. The same insensitivity could
be found with better reason among the beleaguered British,
worried as they were in that year over Moslem unrest in India
and Arab restiveness in Palestine. The special mission of Dean
Earl Harrison, of the University of Pennsylvania Law School, to
the festering camps of Europe at the end of the war highlighted
the differences. The angry British seethed at the interference of
an unofficial American making charges that the displaced
persons were treated by British custodians much as the Nazis
had treated their victims. Harrison's report focused on immediate removal of 100,000 refugees to Palestine, a recommendation
much to the liking of the President but upsetting to the British.
It also distressed diplomats. All the information they had
received from ministers abroad pointed to serious damage to the
American position in the Middle East if the Harrison report was
implemented. Some talked of immediate Communist gains,
others of the need for hundreds of thousands of American troops
to maintain order, and still others pondered over the unfairness
to the hard-pressed British, who would have to suffer the consequences of the report. While probably few in the State Depart-

ment would subscribe to the crude accusations of Bevin that Jewish refugees were improperly trying to "get too much at the head of the queue," they would sympathize with the exasperation of the Foreign Minister which inspired those words.

Truman ignored these objections. To him, Harrison's story was a "moving document." [17] His respect for the public reaction to the report was equally strong. Yet he never considered the issue of Jewish statehood above or equal to that of immigration. The two remained separate in his mind as far as immediate American action was concerned. Nor did he accept an American role in acting on the movement of Jews from Europe to Palestine. That was a British problem.

It was the matter of recommendation without responsibility that infuriated the British and induced Prime Minister Clement Attlee first to postpone official response to the Harrison report in the summer of 1945 and then to initiate an Anglo-American committee of investigation which would entangle the United States in its implementation. The plan worked up to a point. The Foreign Office would have a nine-month respite from American harassment. If the committee did reach agreement, the Americans would have to bear a part of the product.

As events developed, the committee created further division between the allies. The American delegation has usually been described as pro-Zionist. The combination of Jewish suffering in European camps, Arab unwillingness to yield any point, and general British hostility toward change in Palestine inclined the Americans toward this position. They had an ally in Richard Crossman of the British delegation. Crossman and Bartley Crum, a San Francisco lawyer, subsequently wrote stirring accounts of British prejudice against the Zionists.

Yet the committee was no Zionist pawn. The British delegation, with the exception of Crossman, followed the Foreign Office's guidance. The American members included former Ambassador William Phillips and Dr. Frank Aydelotte, secretary of the American Rhodes Trust, both sympathetic to British difficulties. Phillips, depicted by Crum as "so perfectly the diplomat he could have worked on any Hollywood set type-cast for the part," recognized the dominance of radical Zionists over American Jewish opinion. [18] He felt that "the more moderate American

Jews who feared the effects of statehood did not present their case strongly."[19] The Arab conception of the Jew as an intrusive alien impressed him, as did the American politician's harmful pandering to the Jewish vote. Here was no kept man of Zionism. Aydelotte had reservations about the American role in Palestine. He was uncomfortable about involvement without responsibility. The Americans advised, the British had to act.[20]

Behind the committee stood specialists in Middle Eastern affairs, prepared to help the inexperienced commissioners with their expertise. These, too, inclined toward the Arab side. The chief British adviser, Harold Beeley, was the leading figure in Britain's Arab policy. Evan Wilson of the State Department's Near East Desk, Beeley's American counterpart, was respectful of British knowledge and experience. In a conversation with Wilson aboard the *Queen Elizabeth*, Crum caught the note of deference to British views when the American diplomat harped on the "aroused Arab world."[21] The principal American specialist with the commission was Professor William F. S. Stinespring, an archaeologist and Old Testament scholar at Duke, whose preparatory work for the mission produced a speech on the "misguided efforts of the Zionist movement to secure political control of the country for the Jews."[22]

The committee did emerge with a unanimous report to the surprise even of the members themselves. The price of unanimity was compromise along broad lines. The White Paper of 1939, with its strict limits on Jewish immigration, would no longer guide future settlement. The recommendation was for a development of a Jewish national home, with protection for Moslems and Christians through a binational agreement under United Nations sanction. The most immediate action concerned 100,000 certificates to be authorized for admission of European Jews. While much of this report, submitted in April 1946, displeased Zionists, they were gratified with the attitude on immigration. It was this aspect of the report that Truman seized on in announcing American support. As for the British, Bevin's promise to act on a unanimous recommendation was immediately subject to circumvention. Clement Attlee wanted assurance of American responsibility for its execution, militarily and financially. Furthermore, admission of large numbers of Jews would have to wait until the illegal Jewish military organizations had been disbanded.

The result of such conflicting interpretations of the report led not to a clash between the two countries or to the bending of the British position. Rather, it was the American stand that changed. The State Department continued to talk of inaction until full consultation with all parties had been made on the committee reports. One month after the President had spoken of immediate implementation of the immigration proposal, a State Department memorandum, with copies to all Arab states and the Institute of Arab American Affairs as well as to American Jewish bodies, noted that the report was advisory. It is not surprising that the United States acquiesced in the establishment of a new joint committee to modify the findings of the original group, which was to be distinguished by its technical experts.

The British point of view was far better expressed in the Grady-Morrison Plan in the summer of 1946, which pushed immigration onto a new federal government that would preside over separate Arab and Jewish provinces under British control. This modified the original recommendations to the point of unrecognizability. The admission of 100,000 immigrants would turn on the success of the federal plan.

American hostility to this new proposal was sparked by the reaction of the American members of the Anglo-American Committee. It was subsequently fanned by the congressional elections of 1946, in which the parties vied with each other in raising the quota of immigrants. In October the administration suggested a plan of the Jewish Agency which would resolve the problem through a partition of Palestine. The Palestine question was thus in greater turmoil at the end of 1946 than it had been in the beginning.

When Bevin threw Palestine to the United Nations, he had American politics as a serviceable scapegoat. British public opinion was solidly behind him. Bevin could play on anti-Semitism rising from the events in Palestine. He could make a conspicuous distinction between humanitarian concerns and the crimes of fanatic nationalists whose illegal operations were encouraged by American supporters. For the popular British press, such American notables as Walter Winchell, the gossip columnist, and Ben

Hecht, the Broadway playwright, were villains in the service of right-wing Zionists killing British Tommies. The hanging of British troopers in retaliation for the execution of guerrilla leaders stoked acts of vandalism against Jewish properties in England.

The passions of the British against the United States and Zionists are easy to exaggerate. British friends of Zionism continued to be embarrassed by the blatant pro-Arab policy of the Labour government. The final scene in British Palestine was set by Churchill himself, a friend of the Jewish cause, who initiated the transfer of the problem to the United Nations out of recognition of Britain's false position. Yet even Churchill made his proposition on the assumption that the United States was unwilling to accept an appropriate share of the burden. And Richard Crossman, a staunch opponent of Bevin's anti-Zionism, was no source of comfort to Zionists at this time. He saw the Irgun Zvai Leumi as a semifascist group whose acts of terrorism against Britian deserved reprobation.[23] The high feelings against Zionists and their supporters in 1947 were essentially byproducts of what the British public felt were unfair attacks against a nation that had done so much for Jews in Palestine and elsewhere. They certainly did not show themselves to be in the mood for a pogrom, even a pogrom British-style.

Understandable as many British grievances were, there was guile in Bevin's stance. The charge of betrayal at the hands of America is hard to justify. The British government was very well aware of the strong sympathies its Palestine policy evoked from the Secretary of State, the bureaus of the State Department, and the religious establishments with Middle Eastern connections. British leaders also knew that the President and the Congress were not quite the enemies of the empire or tools of the Zionists that they made them out to be. Despite his various political announcements, Truman had been willing to use the existence of the Anglo-American Committee to tamp down Anglophobic sentiments in Congress in December 1945. He failed to defer the Senate resolution on a Jewish commonwealth proposed by Senator Wagner of New York, but Senator Tom Connally's vote against it on the Senate Foreign Relations Committee, the single negative, represented the voice of the President. The British knew how little effect such resolutions had on policy making, particularly when the President was not inclined to support them.

The real test of congressional strength was its response to a British request for a massive loan in June 1946. By this time, the Anglo-American Committee had submitted its report and it had been summarily dismissed in Britain. In that very month, Bevin asserted that the United States wanted the Jews in Palestine because they were not wanted in New York. Predictably, this gratuitous insult brought forth a mass protest at Madison Square Garden which urged punishment of Britain not only by stripping away its mandate, but, more immediately, by denying the loan. Yet the loan survived the popular uproar. It had already been approved by the Senate, and the more volatile House, presumably more susceptible to Zionist pressures, passed the measure in July. While Sol Bloom, chairman of the House Foreign Affairs Committee and a Jewish congressman from New York, condemned Bevin's slurs, he did not help to block the loan. The life of Great Britain itself was at stake, and in this crisis British errors in Palestine were converted into a minor blemish.

If America's stake in Britain impressed Congress as vital in 1946, it became even more so over the next two years as the Communist challenge became stronger. Seven days after Palestine was turned over to the United Nations, the British confessed their inability to maintain their traditional obligations in Greece and Turkey. To bolster a faltering Britain in the face of a surging Soviet tide, the Truman Doctrine and the Marshall Plan were created over the next few months, centering on the need to restore Britain and Europe as bulwarks against Communist expansion. In this context, there was, paradoxically, special freedom for Bevin to speak out, even spitefully, against American policy, which derived its strength from weakness and dependency; the Soviet menace was far too important to allow British petulance over Palestine to disturb relations between the two countries. Hence, the Foreign Office had an opportunity to blame American politics without fear of retribution for spoiling what Bevin claimed was agreement among the contending parties in Palestine rather than accept the fact of impotence before the obduracy of Arab and Jewish nationalism. 1947 was also the year that Britain evacuated India in the face of similarly competing nationalisms.

But, unlike its reaction in India, the Foreign Office had not surrendered hopes of remaining in the Middle East, even if a British presence had to assume new forms; there were too many interests in the area which could not be surrendered. These help to explain the continuing obstructiveness of the British position on Palestine after the question of the mandate was raised in the United Nations. Indeed, the British never announced they were officially giving up the mandate; on April 2, 1947, they simply asked to have the question placed on the agenda of the General Assembly. If the independence of Palestine or the partition of the country should follow, their expectation was a quick Arab victory that would ensure maintenance of a British presence in the area. The fact that King Abdullah of Transjordan could claim openly in March 1947 that he would occupy Palestine in the event of a British evacuation is in keeping with British behavior at the time.[24] If they could not hold Palestine, surrogates might hold it for them. Here was an assumption of the superiority of the forces of an Arab Palestine abetted by neighboring states, all tied into the British-sponsored Arab League.

Over the next nine months, the future of Palestine seemed to rest with the decision of the United Nations on partition. For the Arabs it posed no problem; they unanimously denounced any arrangement which would permit either autonomy or immigration of more Jews. They would accept only termination of the mandate and the independence of Arab Palestine. For Zionists, there was considerable agonizing over the retreat involved in the argument for partition. The Jewish commonwealth embraced all of Palestine, according to the Zionist interpretation of the Balfour Declaration. But the opportunities inherent in partition were in the end irresistible. They offered Jews at least some territory of their own to which immigration might be directed. Thus, a united American Zionism exerted intense pressures in American politics and elsewhere. Republicans Joseph Martin and Thomas E. Dewey joined Democrats Senator Robert Wagner and Eleanor Roosevelt to promote the cause of partition. Zionist lobbying before the United Nations was unremitting. Every means of persuasion from telegrams to letters to political and economic threats were used to suggest that the United States would settle for nothing less than the two-thirds vote in the General Assembly. Haiti, Liberia, the Philippines, China, Ethiopia, and Greece were major targets. Congressmen, Supreme Court justices, governors, and prominent figures connected with the White House worked to convert the hesitant. Liberia was reportedly impressed by an economist hinting at retaliation if the vote was wrong. An ex-governor with entrée to the White House personally telephoned the Haiti government to ask for a change in its voting plans. Behind all this activity was the mobilization of the American Jewish community to a degree never experienced before.

That the Zionists agitated vigorously was openly admitted. That they presumed to speak for the United States is equally a matter of record; Congressman Sol Bloom boasted of his approaches to representatives of several countries. But the opposition of the State Department to these activities and its coolness toward partition were also visible. Its position was that the United States would not use its influence to swing votes for partition. Leaders of the Jewish Agency, Moshe Shertok and Eliahu Epstein, expressed their concern to Loy Henderson a month before the United Nations action that the

> United States had not really meant what it had said in supporting the majority report. Would it not be possible for the United States Delegation to correct this impression with certain South American countries, and state that we would consider it a friendly act to follow our lead and vote for the majority report? I informed Mr. Shertok that we were extremely anxious that any solution of the Palestine problem be a United Nations solution, and that we not give the impression it was an "American solution."[25]

Henderson's response was not one to allay Zionist fears or to stop the flow of Arab rumors. Nor would it have any softening effect upon British hauteur. The attitudes of the State Department were well known to Arabs and British and were taken seriously. If the General Assembly ultimately delivered a two-thirds majority for the recommendation to partition Palestine, it was hardly the American position that moved it. Nor was it wholly a matter then of private threats and blandishments from Zionist friends who exploited the American name, or the Soviet bloc prepared to profit from the troubles between the allies. The recommendation for partition was made by the respected United Nations Special Committee on Palestine (UNSCOP) appointed in May 1947. It issued its report despite the opposition of Arabs and the snubs of the British. The British government would enforce no recommendation which lacked approval of Arabs and Jews; if no agreement could be reached, it would withdraw its forces, leaving chaos in its wake. Yet there was little alternative. The Arab Higher Committee for Palestine had rejected a minority recommendation for a federated Palestine put forth by Moslem members of UNSCOP.

There is probably a causal connection between American cautiousness in the State Department and Arab and British boldness in opposition; American hesitancy invited harder positions which in turn fed fears of violence and Soviet profit in the Middle East. Jorge Garcia-Granados, a strongly pro-Zionist member of UNSCOP from Uruguay, was convinced that American appeasement of Arabs and British was the crux of the problem.[26] He was correct about the wish for appeasement. Such misgivings as American officials had over the viability of a divided state were magnified by the anger of the Arabs, the lack of cooperation from the British, and the hysteria of the oil interests.

Looming above every other consideration was the Cold War. Why, Kremlinologists asked, did the Soviet Union finally offer its support for partition after combining a traditional hostility to Zionism with a willingness to capitalize on Arab resentment against the West? The most convincing answer was a Soviet plan to join in a pacifying action once warfare began, alone or with the United States. Suspicions of Russian motives were scarcely surprising in the fall of 1947 when Congress passed an emergency bill providing economic aid to Europe, or in the winter and spring of 1948 when the United States had to cope with the Berlin blockade, the coup d'etat in Czechoslovakia, and the seemingly desperate attempt of Western Europe to defend itself through the

Brussels Pact. If Ambassador Herschel V. Johnson's statement to the General Assembly's Ad Hoc Committee on Palestine in favor of partition lacked conviction for many delegations, it was not just because Secretary of State Marshall had assured Arab statesmen less than a month earlier that the United States had an open mind. It was because their mind was on Soviet behavior.

These misgivings deepened among American diplomats between November 1947 and May 1948, when independence would take effect. Specifically, they had their roots in the recognition that partition was not workable. Arab resistance in the form of widespread riots in Palestine and widely publicized invasion plans of neighboring states confirmed this assumption. Whether or not Britain was fully in collusion with the Arab opponents of partition, its position stimulated increased anxieties for the success of the United Nations' recommendation. As Bevin expressed it in Parliament, "We have no intention of opposing that decision but we cannot ourselves undertake, either individually or collectively in association with others to impose the decision by force." [27] This meant that the British intended to withdraw their forces in May without regard for the state of public order in Palestine at the time of their departure. Should the Arab states enter the country as Britain left, one of the invaders would be the British-officered Arab Legion.

A way out of this dilemma was offered in a Policy Planning Staff paper to the State Department emphasizing that the United States was under no obligation to fulfill a plan that could be realized only through force. The country might be pushed into accepting unilateral responsibility for carrying out the decision, or, even worse, a Security Council intervention that would include the Soviet Union. This prospect particularly troubled Forrestal and Senator Arthur H. Vandenberg, both of whom agreed that the dangers would be exaggerated by Palestine's entanglement in American politics. The Defense Secretary went to both parties, asking to have the explosive Palestine issue removed from partisan politics. He received little encouragement. Events seemed to confirm the wisdom of the warnings diplomats had given the President before the vote was taken. These forebodings account for much of the latitude given to the stumbling blocks Britain was then placing before the United Nations in Palestine.

Henderson claimed that "it is extremely unfortunate that we should be criticizing the British for following the only kind of policy which, it seems to me, they can follow if they are to remain in the Middle East."[28] Had Britain welcomed partition, the wrath of the Arab world would have fallen on the empire to the detriment of American interests.

In flailing about for a change in the administration's position, officials were not wholly blinded to shortcomings in their own recommendations. The ideal of a Jewish state was understood; the suffering of the European refugees was distressing; and the anti-Semitism involved in some of the British actions in Palestine as well as British favoritism for Arabs were recorded with regret. The double standard was hard to conceal. As the United States Consul General at Jerusalem observed in December 1947, "There is probably some reason for the Jewish complaint that the British are favoring the Arabs."[29] But there was little choice; the world was larger than the Jewish problem.

The arguments confronting the President on every side had their effect. Truman bowed before their weight. He was no more prepared than any of his advisers to send troops — American or Russian — into Palestine. So, seizing on the legal distinction between a United Nations recommendation and a United Nations decision, Ambassador Austin attempted to minimize the movement toward partition and replace it with a temporary expedient, a United Nations trusteeship which would cushion the shock of Britain's abrupt departure. A binational state had always been his preference for Palestine.[30] Austin presented the new American position on March 19, less than two months before partition was to go into effect, and he did so with full presidential approval. If the President later blamed the diplomats for independent action, it was only in the matter of timing; just a day before, Truman had spoken with Weizmann, the future president of the Jewish state, without mentioning the reversal of policy. He was embarrassed by the prospect of Weizmann's thinking he was "a plain liar."[31]

It was not only Weizmann or Zionists who would feel betrayed. The General Assembly itself was confused over the direction American policy was taking. Trygve Lie, in a state of shock, regarded the shift as an underhanded blow against the United

Nations and impulsively suggested to Austin, who he believed shared his feelings, that they both resign. He wondered what had happened, with his speculations ranging from American apprehension over Arabs turning to the Russians to the protection of oil concessions in Arab territories. [32]

The motives Lie was probing for were probably less devious or sinister than his outcries suggest. Nor, in retrospect, was the reversal in policy quite as abrupt. The record shows a long-standing concern for the feared consequences of a Jewish Palestine. [33] While the President had misgivings about backtracking on partition, he was not led unwittingly into a gambit of the State Department. His faith in the advice of Secretary of State George C. Marshall was never greater. Truman's subsequent reflections played on the theme that the trusteeship plan was "not a rejection of partition, but rather an effort to postpone its effective date until proper conditons for the establishment of self-government in the two parts might be established." [34] It is ironic, however, that the decision to retreat from the United Nations position coincided with the most dramatic piece of evidence of Zionist influence over the President: the appeal of his old haberdashery partner, Eddie Jacobson, to Truman's sentimentality to win a presidential meeting for Chaim Weizmann. [35]

But what should have warned observers of the change were not the signals identified by Lie. Rather, they were to be found in the events of the Cold War. Two days before Austin's speech to the Security Council on March 19, the Brussels Treaty was drafted. On March 20, the day Secretary Marshall took responsibility for the new modified Palestine policy, the Soviet Union walked out of the Control Council in Germany. Troops were not available, as Marshall noted, to enforce peace in Palestine. Hence, trusteeship was an immediate, if temporary, solution.

If there had not already been so many twists and turns in American statements on the Middle East, the final reversal of May 14, the United States de facto recognition of Israel, would have upset the United Nations as much as it did the American delegation to the General Assembly. Instead, it merely bemused the delegates as they watched members of the American delegation admit their ignorance of their government's actions.

It would fit the pattern of American policy toward Palestine if the influence of domestic politics had once again asserted itself and the explanation for Truman's decision lay in the urgent warnings of New York City Democratic leaders that propitiating Zionist supporters was vital for success in the presidential election year. The voice of Edward J. Flynn, national committeeman for New York, was loud enough to be heard by Thomas J. Hamilton, the chief United Nations correspondent of the New York *Times* on May 16. [36] But if Truman's ear was cocked to a difficult election ahead, other factors were even more persuasive. The trusteeship plan had failed to conciliate the Arab states; invasion was already under way in Palestine. The British had refused to accept even a postponement in the date of departure from Palestine. While State Department officials scurried around for new proposals to accommodate Arab demands, the President cut off everything with his abrupt action. In essence, Truman and advisers such as Clark Clifford confronted a practical problem. Chaos had already overtaken Palestine; there was no point in accepting vague proposals which would not work. A state of Israel was in being whether or not the United States would recognize it. Whatever his personal inclination toward Zionism or appreciation of the political weight of American Zionists, they were peripheral influences in the decision of May 14. [37]

While the wisdom of hindsight usually seems overwhelming, it is not easy, even from the distance of a generation, to sort out all the pieces in this particular problem. From the knowledge available to them at the time and the fears that knowledge engendered, the powerful counterpressures within the administration against Zionism are fully comprehensible without resort to conspiracy or special interests to explain them. Similarly, the command of American public sympathy by Zionists in this period was not the product of propaganda and threats of political reprisal. Jews embracing the idea of a Jewish state rejected the charge of dual allegiance and pointed instead to the American tradition of service as a beacon to other peoples. As in the case of the Irish, Hungarian, and Greek national movements, an identification was made between American democracy and the new state. The nation by and large shared this sentiment.

The wisdom of hindsight becomes sharper in the matter of

American actions. Had a clear picture of American interests been offered at the end of the war, ethnic politics might have been minimized. The country had the strength to have made possible the survival of Arab and Jewish states in Palestine without necessarily being pro-Zionist or pro-Moslem. By failing to offer a consistent policy, the United States encouraged the British and Arabs in a militancy and obduracy that defeated concurrent American attempts at pacification. A resolute embrace of partition could have encouraged a more responsible British position in Palestine in the last months and might have discouraged the eager Arab invasion of Palestine. By surviving the Arab onslaught, Israel surprised the experts in the military and diplomatic services and in the oil industry. While the United States deserves recognition for the psychic and material nourishment it provided in the gestation of the Zionist state, Israel's survival at birth was not a consequence of that benevolence.

NOTES

1. Herbert Feis, *The Birth of Israel: The Tousled Diplomatic Bed* (New York: W. W. Norton & Co., Inc., 1969).

2. Bartley L. Crum, *Behind the Silken Curtain: A Personal Account of Anglo-American Diplomacy in Palestine and the Middle East* (New York: Simon & Schuster, Inc., 1947), p. 8.

3. Kermit Roosevelt, "Triple Play in the Middle East," *Harpers* 196 (April 1948): 363.

4. Walter L. Wright, "Contradictory Foreign Policies in the Middle East," *Virginia Quarterly Review* 23 (April 1947): 189.

5. *Foreign Relations of the United States, 1945*, vol. 8, *The Near East and Africa* (Washington: Government Printing Office, 1969), pp. 725-726.

6. Ibid., 1947, vol. 5, pp. 1197-1198.

7. Ibid., pp. 1263-1264.

8. Dean Acheson, *Present at the Creation: My Years in the State Department* (New York: W. W. Norton & Co., Inc., 1969), pp. 169.

9. Ibid.

10. Ibid.

11. Walter Millis, ed., *The Forrestal Diaries* (New York: The Viking Press, 1951), p. 81.

12. Ibid., pp. 347, 363.

13. Kermit Roosevelt, "The Partition of Palestine: A Lesson in Pressure Politics," *The Middle East Journal* 2 (January 1948): 16.

14. Harry S. Truman, *Memoirs*, 2 vols. (New York: Doubleday & Co., Inc., 1956), vol. 2, p. 186.

15. *Foreign Relations of the United States, 1945*, vol. 8, p. 705.

16. Quoted from Chaim Weitzmann, *Trial and Error* (New York: Harper & Bros., 1949), p. 440.

17. Truman, *Memoirs*, vol. 2, p. 164.

18. Crum, *Behind the Silken Curtain*, p. 6.

19. William Phillips, *Ventures in Diplomacy* (privately printed, 1952), p. 424.

20. New York *Times*, May 3, 1946.

21. Crum, *Behind the Silken Curtain*, p. 31.

22. Quoted in Crum, *Behind the Silken Curtain*, p. 34.

23. New York *Times*, February 1, 1947.

24. Ibid., March 24, 1947.

25. *Foreign Relations of the United States*, 1947, vol. 3, p. 1198.

26. See Jorge Garcia-Granados, *The Birth of Israel: The Drama As I Saw It* (New York: Alfred A. Knopf, Inc., 1948).

27. Quoted in Feis, *Birth of Israel*, p. 48.

28. *The Forrestal Diaries*, pp. 348, 359-360; *Foreign Relations of the United States*, 1947, vol. 5, p. 1282.

29. Ibid., 1947, p. 1325.

30. George T. Mazuzan, "United States Policy Toward Palestine at the United Nations, 1947-1948: An Essay," *Prologue* 7 (Fall 1975): 167, 174-175.

31. Quoted in Jonathan Daniels, *The Man From Independence* (Philadelphia: J. B. Lippincott Co., 1950), p. 318.

32. Trygve Lie, *In the Cause of Peace: Seven Years with the United Nations* (New York: The Macmillan Co., 1954), pp. 170-171.

33. Philip C. Jessup, *The Birth of Nations* (New York: Columbia University Press, 1974), pp. 268-269.

34. Truman, *Memoirs*, vol. 2, p. 192.

35. See Eddie Jacobson, "Two Presidents and a Haberdasher—1948," *American Jewish Archives* 20 (April 1968): 1-16.

36. New York *Times*, May 17, 1948.

37. John Snetsinger, *Truman, the Jewish Vote, and Israel*, (Stanford University Press, 1974), p. 140, sees recognition as a belated triumph of Clifford and other political figures in Truman's personal staff over the State and Defense departments, which hitherto had enjoyed Truman's ear.

CHAPTER ELEVEN

The Green Revolution: The United States and India in the Mid-Twentieth Century

Recent years have seen a growing awareness, aroused by scientists, publicists, and policy makers, of the threat posed by the world's rapidly increasing population to its limited agricultural resources. In the United States, where the productivity of agriculture has steadily increased for decades, response to such warnings has, until recently, taken the form chiefly of private activities on behalf of population control and family planning. Across much of the globe, however, and particularly in less industrialized regions where population growth is more difficult to restrain and agricultural productivity lags, measures to increase food production have appeared more likely to bring early results. Bridging the widely different socioeconomic circumstances and the many political issues which separate the industrialized from the still primarily agricultural nations, an international network has arisen which is dedicated to increasing the capacity of poverty-ridden nations to feed their swelling populations. The effort has ranged from the work of the United Nations World Food and Agriculture Organization to that of individual scientists in the laboratory or the field. It has included national, binational, and multinational programs and agencies; it has involved private universities, foundations, and research centers as well as public institutions. It has fostered, in effect, the emergence of a cooperative international undertaking, often functioning with little public recognition or understanding, to lay the foundations of a better, more hopeful life for the world's millions. In any assessment of the international relations of our era, this global venture in peaceful collaboration merits consideration along with that ordinarily commanded by the political tensions and conflicts that dominate public consciousness.

The announcement by the government of India in 1968 — subsequently recognized as premature — that it expected to achieve self-sufficiency in food grains by 1975, reversing the dangerous tendency of its population growth to outstrip increases in agricultural production, dramatized the advent of a "green revolution," made possible by this worldwide effort. So, too, did the award of the Nobel Peace Prize in 1970 to an American scientist, Norman E. Borlaug. Borlaug, heading the wheat program for the International Maize and Wheat Improvement Center in Mexico City, had developed the higher yielding varieties of wheat upon which India and other nations based their hopes. The center had been jointly supported since 1943 by the Mexican government and the Rockefeller Foundation, a private philanthropic foundation in the United States devoted to research in the fields of science and health. The dramatic shipment of the center's improved wheat seeds in the summer of 1965, through the riot-torn Watts section of Los Angeles and the hostile waters of India and Pakistan, locked in a recurring cycle of bitter war, symbolized the hopes of man for the triumph of reason and cooperation over the forces of prejudice and passion.[1]

The wheat which reached India in 1965 came to a land prepared to receive it as a result of more than fifteen years of planning and effort by the Indian government and people. They had been years both of hope and disappointment as a new nation struggled to build progress and better living standards for a people mired in poverty and hampered by the weight of tradition, ignorance, and exploitation. A significant part in the Indian struggle had been played, although they themselves were scarcely aware of it, by the American people through their diplomatic representatives, foreign assistance programs, and voluntary associations. If the Indians could take pride in their survival and achievement under difficult circumstances, the Americans could recognize that they, too, had been well served by the contributions of many who had represented them officially or unofficially. Although Indo-American political relations were often marked by mutual suspicion and misunderstanding, the record of accomplishment in economic and technical assistance, if far from perfect, indicated the possibility of achieving some mutually desired and beneficial results.

World War II had left the United States in a position of unparalleled power and prosperity. Alone of the great powers, it had suffered little damage to its power and resources. Indeed, the war had reversed the uncertainties of the Great Depression, restoring to America a sense of pride in its power and productivity while the other leading industrial nations were in virtual ruin. The American democracy and economic system—mobilized for purposes of war, to be sure, under a degree of government direction hitherto unknown—had triumphed. The energy, resources, and leadership required for the task of postwar global reconstruction only America seemed likely to supply. The inevitable needs and requests of less fortunate nations for assistance were met, therefore, with a high degree of self-confidence and the conviction that both American generosity and self-interest had combined to define a new, more ambitious role for the United States in the remaking of an orderly, democratic world.

At a time when neither American wealth nor generosity seemed subject to reasonable challenge and the American system of private enterprise appeared to have achieved a pinnacle of performance, the emergence of the Ford Foundation as a leader in world philanthropy was peculiarly appropriate. The disposition in 1950 of the estate of Henry Ford, long an international symbol of private entrepreneurship and industrial modernization, transformed the Ford Foundation into the largest private philanthropic agency of its kind. Such foundations, of course, were not new in the United States or elsewhere. Here, they had flourished since at least the turn of the century when industrial magnates such as Carnegie and Rockefeller turned to the disposition of the fortunes their shrewdness and ability had amassed. Confident that the system of private initiative that had fostered their business successes offered the best model for organizing philanthropy and social welfare, these men chartered their foundations and endowed them to support private undertakings on behalf of human betterment across a broad spectrum of social problems and concerns. The growth of organized private philanthropy had not, however, been such as to equal rapidly gathering social pressures for the assumption by government as well as greatly increased responsibilities in the field of social welfare.

Now, with new wealth amassed out of wartime and postwar profits, with a new sense of global needs and urgencies, and with confidence that modern science, technology, and organizational techniques could solve the most troublesome problems, philanthropic foundations — like other American institutions — entered a phase characterized by rapid growth and new challenges. Although a few, the Carnegie and Rockefeller foundations among them, had previously concerned themselves with such international problems as war or disease, they had done so for the most part in a climate that relegated foreign relations to the background of public interest. Now, in a world which war, revolution, science, atomic power, economic expansion, disease, and poverty were painfully making "one," private philanthropy took on a global scale never before conceivable. In 1950 the directors of the Ford Foundation asserted its involvement in international affairs by marking out, as two of the five foci of the foundation's future concern, "significant contributions to world peace and the establishment of a world order of law and justice" and "activities designed to advance the economic well-being of people everywhere and to improve economic institutions for the better realization of democratic goals." Dean Rusk, assuming the presidency of the Rockefeller Foundation two years later, reaffirmed the long-standing and ambitious commitment of that institution to the promotion of "the well-being of mankind throughout the world."[2]

The global consciousness expressed in the policies of these foundations reflected a similar awareness in American business and government circles. In the wake of the war, the floodgates of opportunity for overseas commercial and industrial expansion had opened. The stability, prosperity, and growth potential of other nations became matters of growing concern. The chief threats to America's postwar international security were economic dislocation and ideological rivalry. The spread of communism into nations disrupted and debilitated by the war, as well as the rapid rise of nationalist movements in the former colonial regions of Asia and Africa, seemed threatening to traditional relationships and interests. Still further, the Western liberal ideals of freedom and democracy, in whose name the recent war had been fought, now faced a dual challenge from the same sources. For most Americans, there was no doubt in principle as to the universal applicability of those ideals. There might be confusion and perplexity over their application in unfamiliar settings, but there remained a vague yet unshaken confidence that principles which had proved so beneficial in their own case might eventually be extended to others who could learn from the American experience and example. Confidence, wealth, self-interest, idealism, and parochialism all sustained the frame of mind with which the United States confronted the outside world, particularly the non-Western world. America proposed to offer itself as a model and its people and resources as aids to other nations anxious to share the benefits of economic development and rising living standards.

Within two years of the war's end, the United States government had moved to check what it perceived as threats to stability and freedom launched from the Soviet Union toward Iran, Greece, and Turkey. In 1947-1948, a broad commitment to support the economic stabilization and reconstruction of Western Europe was undertaken through the Marshall Plan. And, in the wake of his surprise reelection in 1949, President Harry S. Truman proposed a comparable plan, which came to be known as the Point Four program, to assist the economic growth of the less developed nations of Asia, Africa, and Latin America. With the major engines of American power involving themselves on a global scale in the political and economic development of foreign nations, the ideological climate that saw American leadership and democracy as the chief hope for a free and peaceful world inevitably affected the thinking of the trustees of such great foundations as the Ford and Rockefeller. Many had business or governmental backgrounds which exposed them to all of the influences we have noted. Had they wished to, they could scarcely have resisted the temptation to define their foundations' roles in equally sweeping terms. The American commitment to assist young and poverty-ridden nations toward prosperity, freedom, and order, it was natural for such men to conclude, should be private as well as public, philanthropic as well as commercial and political, idealistic as well as self-interested.

The combination of internal and external circumstances that motivated the Americans was naturally quite different from that leading a newly independent nation such as India to welcome assistance for its economic development and modernization programs. At once proud and insecure in its newfound freedom, India was the largest and one of the poorest of the non-communist third-world nations. Possessor of a rich historic culture, it had also produced two outstanding spokesmen of the twentieth century struggle for freedom from Western domination: the shrewd and saintly Mohandas K. Gandhi and Jawaharlal Nehru, its world-respected prime minister. Both in its leadership and its problems, India symbolized on a grand scale the status and the difficulties of many newly emerging nations: westernized but nationalistic leadership elites, and ambitions for modernization and a better life coupled with suspicious resistance to Western domination and Western forms. They were societies heavily burdened by traditional institutions and beliefs, mortgaged to poverty, illiteracy, and ill health, yet increasingly determined to share the benefits and opportunities that science and technology seemed to have bestowed on the more fortunate and powerful nations of the West.

In one sense the gap between India, with its ancient culture and new democracy, and the United States, the oldest and most dynamic of modern democracies, might seem too great to be bridged. This gap has, certainly, accounted for much in the way of recurrent misunderstanding between the two nations. Yet a number of influences on each side continually prodded their governments, despite differing perspectives and disagreements, toward cooperative relations. India's need for technical expertise and foreign capital was matched by America's surplus of resources and its growing, if still ambivalent, sense of international political and economic interdependence. Direct American economic interest in India was remarkably slight, a fact which may have both hampered and helped the development of effective collaborative efforts. India was large enough to retain an undeniable importance from the viewpoint of American policy, however strained relations might be at any particular time. At the same time, it was sufficiently removed from the prime centers of American international interest to escape at least some of the political involvement that complicated the relationships of the United States with Latin America or Southeast Asia.

Initial efforts to bring American resources to bear on Indian needs were nevertheless considerably stimulated by concerns in the United States aroused by the Cold War alignment of Western versus Communist-bloc nations, as had also been the case with the mobilization of support for the reconstruction of Western Europe through the Marshall Plan. The defeat of the Chinese Nationalist government and the emergence of a strong Communist regime there in 1949 were readily seen by Americans as major setbacks in the Asian ideological and power struggle. Much as the third-world nations for whom Nehru often spoke might wish to disengage themselves from the pressures and rivalries of the Cold War, they could hardly escape entanglement in what loomed as a worldwide competition. And in fact some were able to derive tangible assistance from their involvement. As a potential counterweight to Communist China, as a testing place for democracy in the non-Western world, and as a challenge to American technological know-how and humanitarian impulses, India was a logical focus for American intervention.

Many of these considerations were surely in the mind of Paul Hoffman, recently director of the Marshall Plan in Europe and new president of the Ford Foundation, who visited India in the summer of 1951 and discussed with Nehru the needs and opportunities with which the foundation might assist. Certainly, the same considerations were uppermost in the thinking of Chester Bowles when he reached New Delhi a few months later to take the post of United States ambassador. As an advisor to President Truman and United Nations Secretary Trygve Lie, Bowles had interested himself in problems of economic development and modernization. A committed liberal, he saw the struggle of the emerging nations to achieve independence and to carry out their domestic social revolutions as a new stage in the age-old effort of men everywhere to achieve the "universal values of personal liberty, racial equality, and the broad sharing of the benefits of development." Bowles openly interpreted his mission in this light as an opportunity to help save the Indians and, through them, Asia from the collapse of democracy which he believed China to have suffered. Yet, strongly opposed to communism as he was, Bowles believed it would be erroneous to consider communism rather than poverty the central problem for India. Convinced that the American experience and ideals had relevance for the Indian situation, Bowles lacked the arrogance and insensitivity to other values which so frequently has accompanied that conviction. Rather than present his country as the epitome of the ideal less favored nations should struggle to emulate, he took pains to emphasize to Indian audiences that the United States was itself still deeply engaged in an effort to realize the democratic ideals it professed.

Bowles's modesty and genuine concern soon won him the respect of many Indians; it was dramatized by such simple gestures as sending the Bowles children to Indian schools rather than to the elite missionary schools which were the expected places for diplomats' children. This startling break with a long-standing Western tradition attracted notice both in India and the United States; more significantly, it measured the spirit of mutuality in which Bowles approached his mission and India's problems. In two tours of duty and continuing involvement in Indian affairs extending over more than a decade, the ambassadorship of Chester Bowles was to prove one of the most successful in recent American diplomacy. The qualities which contributed to his effectiveness in the field made Bowles's experience and achievements less well understood at home than they deserved to be. His *Ambassador's Report*, on his first years of service, remains a valuable introduction to the pitfalls, as well as some of the possibilities for success, in American relations with the non-Western nations.[3]

It was fitting that both Chester Bowles and Paul Hoffman should have identified themselves with the launching of India's massive modernization program, then in its formative stage. The preceding year, a National Planning Commission had been established with Prime Minister Nehru as its chairman; after lengthy discussions among governmental officials and experts in many fields, the first Five-Year Plan was about to be presented to the nation. The plan was comprehensive, including provisions for irrigation, power, transportation and communication facilities, education, and health, as well as agricultural and industrial development. It called for an investment of some $4 billion by the Indian state and federal governments, and it aimed at increasing the national income by about 11 percent over the five-year period. To Hoffman, the proposals must have seemed at least as ambitious as the reconstruction of Europe's already developed economy. The image of India lifting itself by its bootstraps into the modern world seized the imagination of Bowles, for whom memories of the New Deal, TVA, and the miracles of American wartime production were still fresh. To assist and support such an undertaking seemed the truest and most logical extension of the American experience to the needs of a struggling new democracy.[4]

Economic development and social reform were the twin goals of the Indian government, eager to move its people from their traditional, village-oriented life toward a more open, industrial society. The Five-Year Plan aimed at fostering economic change through a process of widespread participation in democratic planning. The community development program which evolved drew from a number of sources, both Indian and American. It was based in part upon the Etawah Project, proposed by an American architect and planner, Albert Mayer, in 1948 and developed by the Indians to combine Gandhi's objective of revitalizing village life with an agricultural extension system modeled after that of the U.S. Department of Agriculture. Bowles and others who visited Etawah were impressed with the training given village workers and the involvement of the villagers in educational, public health, and related measures. The fact that food production had been increased by more than 50 percent was equally significant. Bowles, who had helped to develop the Truman administration's Point Four Program, was now in a position to negotiate the first capital grant agreement under its provisions. He had learned of the significant improvements in agricultural output achieved in Japan under Gen. Douglas MacArthur's land reform program and of similar results in Taiwan. He was enthusiastic about the possibilities for a peaceful democratic revolution in India's villages. It seemed to offer a striking alternative to the Chinese Communist land reform program, which Bowles saw as the chief alternative model for change available to the developing nations.[5]

Bowles proposed to Nehru that the community development program be extended to as many villages as possible, with American assistance chiefly for the procurement of the necessary equipment. Although he emphasized that there were no strings attached to the offer and India's decision as to how to proceed with its development plans would be respected, Bowles's enthusiasm probably encouraged Nehru to undertake the ambitious community development project. The Ford Foundation, meanwhile, had agreed to support a pilot village development program during the time in which the final version of the Five-Year Plan was in preparation. Nehru, apparently convinced of the sincerity of American interest, was himself eager to press ahead with efforts to interject new ideas and incentives into India's villages.[6] Although some Indians and Americans cautioned against premature overexpansion, there were strong political pressures to spread the benefits of the program as widely as possible.

The core of community development was the provision of a trained village worker for every three or four villages, encouragement of communities to undertake improvements in facilities and farming techniques, and involvement of villagers in actively determining their own future. Behind the village worker would be a staff of experts in agriculture, public health, and education to supply specialized knowledge and administrative support as needed. Fifty-four such community projects, each covering about five hundred square miles, three hundred villages, and 200,000 people, were designated for the first phase of the program to be initiated in October 1952. Bowles estimated that five-sixths of the cost of the program was provided by India, but Point Four assistance and Ford Foundation support for the pilot project played an important part. At the same time, an added dimension was provided for the overall national development effort by the Rockefeller Foundation, which was extending grants to Indian institutions for research on malaria and other tropical diseases. Chester Bowles was appointed a trustee and member of the foundation's executive committee in 1952, a step that undoubtedly encouraged closer coordination of such public and private American support programs. Assisted by the Rockefeller Foundation and the American government and in coordination with an international World Health Organization drive, India launched a massive and successful drive to eliminate malaria. The disease had long played a devastating role in reducing the productivity and life expectancy of its people. [7]

Initial reports on operations under the community development program were encouraging to those who hoped it might provide the key to a peaceful revolution for Asia's millions. While the effort to spark increases in production within a framework of national planning appealed to advocates of economic mobilization and reform, its emphasis upon village democracy and self-help was equally attractive to conservatives. Even so skeptical a critic of India's neutralist, socialist regime as U.S. Senator William Knowland was impressed, on a visit to villages under community development, by what he saw as "the real basis of democracy" in the rural extension program. Nehru, elated at the prospect of aroused and increasingly productive villages, stated: "All over India there are now centers of human activity that are like lamps spreading their light more and more into the surrounding darkness. This light must grow and grow until it covers the land." [8]

At the end of the first year's experience, enthusiasm continued high; in October 1953 the program was extended to over 400 blocks of some 100 villages each, covering a population of about 35 million people. Planning for the future contemplated complete coverage of all of India's villages by 1963. [9] Statistics of increased food production seemed equally promising. During the first Five-Year Plan, 1951-1952 to 1955-1956, the annual compound growth rate of food-grain production was more than 6 percent. Such successes encouraged the Planning Commission to place increased emphasis upon support for industrial development in its designs for the second plan period. Ironically, Chester Bowles, who had been the chief American advocate of the program, was replaced as ambassador after the inauguration of the Eisenhower administration in 1953, but he left India optimistic as to the future. Returning on a short visit the following year, he observed that many of the first plan goals had been exceeded, that India had achieved self-sufficiency in food grains in 1954, and that plans for increased irrigation held out hope that adequate food production levels could be maintained after 1956. [10]

Unfortunately, the enthusiasm of Bowles and others for what he termed "undoubtedly the greatest democratic rural revolution of our time" proved premature. After initial gains, due largely to the expansion of the area under cultivation, increases in output tapered off sharply. Although productivity continued to increase rather steadily, the gains were too slight to keep pace with the rapid population growth. Hopes for social reform, too, were disappointed. Village workers were too few and too poorly trained. Village democracy could not readily be imposed from above; bureaucratic tangles snarled the effort to make expert assistance available. Traditional practices did not yield easily to pressures for change. By the end of the second plan period, 1956-1957 to 1960-1961, India's food crisis was a cause for growing concern. The joint effort to launch a rural social revolution had come face to face with the first in a series of bitter frustrations and disappointments. [11]

Delays, disappointments, and detours as well as successes were realistically to be expected in so massive and momentous an undertaking as the effort to move India's agricultural millions toward modernization from a base characterized for centuries by scarcity, isolation, lack of education, exploitation, and traditional practices, relationships, and expectations. The inevitable shortcomings and failures of community development were discouraging to Indians and Americans alike. Unfortunately, they also aggravated differences in viewpoint and thus complicated the touchy but vital process of cooperation that demanded mutual respect and tolerance between unequal partners. External factors, notably the politics of the Cold War, made matters even more difficult. Bowles had warned from the beginning against mixing foreign aid with political considerations, but this had never been an entirely realistic position. Both the Marshall and Point Four programs had been partly inspired and presented to the American people and Congress as measures to strengthen the economic defense of freedom against international communism. Politics had thus been inherent in the American position from the start; with the outbreak of war in Korea in 1950 and the election of Eisenhower two years later, Cold War pressures rose steadily to endanger Indo-American relations. Congressional support for economic, as opposed to military, assistance programs sagged. Impatience with faltering, seemingly inadequate Indian development programs was openly expressed. The efforts of Secretary of State John Foster Dulles to build a military alliance through the Southeast Asia Treaty Organization, which Pakistan joined and India rejected, further widened the gap between Indians and Americans. Nehru's insistence upon maintaining a neutral stance toward Russian-American political rivalries aroused bitterness in the United States. In addition, India's official preference for socialism, although more rhetorical and pragmatic than outsiders recognized, only heightened American suspicions and resentment.

Indian doubts concerning the motives behind American assistance were likewise stirred by political pressures. Foreign criticism spurred national pride and resentment. Vested economic and political interests, still strong even within the Congress party of Gandhi and Nehru despite its official commitment to reform, found outside intervention in India's domestic affairs a useful argument for the defense of the status quo. Resentment of real or supposed American interference was a ready and comfortable alternative to self-criticism and reform.

Still other matters relating to the complicated and not yet fully understood process of development offered grounds for difference. Both technical and ideological arguments, for example, clouded the issue of the relative importance of social reform and production increases. Were land reform and the emergence of a vital new village leadership the necessary prerequisites of increased output, or vice versa? Did reform efforts divert needed resources from more pressing economic needs? What priority should be accorded agricultural as opposed to industrial development, foreign trade, public health, education, and a score of other claimants upon limited resources and capabilities? On none of these issues does there seem to have been a distinct split between Indian and American viewpoints. Still, the temptation for Americans to shrug off Indian failures and inadequacies was undoubtedly great. Indians, on the other hand, whose stake in the outcome was direct and inescapable, were often inclined to blame the United States for bad advice and insufficient understanding or patience. With this combination of unfavorable circumstances, it is remarkable, not that disagreements and misunderstandings could flourish, but that despite them all the American aid program in India "survived and haltingly broadened" in the 1950s, in the words of John Lewis, an American economist who undertook a study of India's problems in 1959 and 1960 and returned to New Delhi soon thereafter as head of the USAID (United States Agency for International Development) mission. [12]

In the midst of official discouragement and disagreement, the role of the private foundations took on added importance. As the American government shifted its order of priorities away from the Indian subcontinent, the private foundations, less swayed by political and strategic considerations, persisted in their support. Their broad commitments to the advancement of human welfare and their technical involvement in the search for solutions to fundamental problems demanded, if anything, an intensification of effort. Under the leadership of Douglas Ensminger, an agricultural economist, the Ford Foundation's India staff had developed close ties with the Indian government. The Foundation's interest in community development continued strong, while its staff worked with the National Planning Commission to modify and strengthen the program for agricultural development.

As early as 1957, official Indian study groups had reported most critically upon the operations of the community development program. In April 1959 a study team of Indian and American scientists—the latter recruited by the Ford Foundation— surveyed conditions and issued *Report of India's Food Crisis and Steps to Meet It*. Their recommendations, although signed by the Americans only, were designed for the attention of the Indian Planning Commission, then in the process of developing the Third Five-Year Plan. Recommending the retention and upgrading of the community development program, the report called for greater emphasis upon agricultural production and the concentration of scarce resources in selected regions upon public works, irrigation, fertilizer production, and similar measures tied directly to agriculture. Recommendations for guaranteed pricing and increased aid to cooperative financial and marketing facilities were aimed at strengthening economic incentives. The report's stress on production rather than reform made it politically unpopular in some quarters, yet the Indian government incorporated many of its proposals into the Third Plan. In particular, an Intensive Agricultural Districts Program involved a concentration of all available knowledge and resources on select pilot districts in each state, where farmers were to be supplied with adequate credit, fertilizers, seeds, and other related needs in order to achieve a breakthrough demonstration of modern farming techniques. The Ford Foundation, retaining the services of a number of experts who had contributed to the report, agreed to support the IADP with equipment and training programs over a five-year period. [13]

While this concentrated effort to stimulate agricultural production was being developed with help from both the Japanese and American governments, a number of related programs were evolving. To meet India's increasingly pressing food needs, the United States increased its shipment of surplus grains under Public Law 480; since India paid for the food in rupees, its limited foreign exchange resources were conserved. To further assist with the foreign exchange problem, the so-called Aid to India Club, composed of six industrial nations and the World Bank, was organized in 1961. Yet in a variety of ways the role of the private foundations remained crucial. As early as 1954, Chester Bowles had written of the Ford Foundation: "Wherever there was a gap, they filled it, whether it was agricultural, health education or administration. They took over, financed and administered the crucial village-level training schools. Their kind of straightforward service is in the finest traditions of our country." Several years later, John Lewis's somewhat more skeptical statement that Americans, including the foundations, church groups, and universities, as well as government officials, "have advised, kibitzed and assisted enough by now to have incurred some moral responsibility not to desert a grossly unfinished job," nevertheless acknowledged the importance of foundation contributions. Despite discouragement, Americans did not back off. In the field of family planning and population control, increasingly recognized by scientists and policy makers as crucial if gains in food production were not to be overwhelmed by India's high birthrate, action by the American government was politically impossible. In 1959 the Ford Foundation began contributions to research and training programs in this sensitive field, from which USAID assistance was barred until 1966. The Rockefeller Foundation extended its work beyond the public health field by signing an agreement in 1956 to contribute to the support of agricultural research, education, and extension work. [14]

In the field of economic development, however, there is no guarantee that any program of foreign assistance, however apolitical its source or humanitarian its motives, will automatically bring success, especially quick success. As the Third Plan years, 1961-1962 to 1965-1966, progressed, the evidence accumulated that the Intensive Agricultural Districts Program, for all its concentration upon bringing the best information on growing practices to the farmer, was still not producing the desired results. Only three of the fifteen program districts showed a significantly higher food-grain yield than in the preceding five years. The underlying assumption that backward Indian cultivators could be prodded toward increasing output by concentrating all of the resources of modern agricultural science upon them had proved overly simple. At the same time, the family planning program aimed at controlling the other factor in the population-food equation also faced serious difficulties. Despite India's commitment of substantial resources and the Ford Foundation's help, the program made little headway, outside the major urban centers, in the villages where the overwhelming majority of Indians still lived. To add to the discouragement, the failure of the monsoon rains in 1965-1966 and 1966-1967 brought famine and disaster to many regions. Only the accelerated shipment of food surpluses from the United States in all probability saved India from mass starvation. [15] In the recurring climate of frustration and failure, it was easy for both Americans and Indians to succumb to defeatism and recriminations again.

This time, however, there were important, if not immediately recognized, compensating factors. Throughout the 1950s India had been fortunate in the quality and sympathy of a succession of American ambassadors. In 1961, however, the appointment of the liberal economist, John Kenneth Galbraith, coincided with a period of reawakened interest in India on the part of the administration of President John F. Kennedy. Galbraith brought the further advantage of direct access to the President's inner circle. In 1963, Chester Bowles succeeded Galbraith as American ambassador, more convinced than ever of the need to support democratic change in Asia in view of America's experience in Vietnam. Bowles himself, however, had already lost favor in Washington, largely because of his continued and perceptive efforts to resist the Cold War psychology which the Kennedy-Johnson administration had failed to overcome. Although his influence in Washington was slight, he brought experience, patience, and dedication to the by-now far-flung American mission in India. Because of these qualities, he was also able to speak critically and emphatically to the Indians about shortcomings in their own performance in a way that perhaps no other foreigner could.[16]

As important as political and diplomatic rapport by this time, perhaps, was the determination to press ahead and the ability to learn from experience. Although the districts program had produced few immediate successes, valuable lessons were derived from it that pointed to new lines of development. One stressed closer attention to the factors influencing the individual cultivator's practices. It had become clear that, without reliable marketing and pricing conditions on the one hand and more emphasis upon cost-reducing technology on the other, the farmer had little incentive to increase his output no matter how much expert advice was offered him. The need for increased research, more attention to irrigation practices, and reliable access to adequate fertilizers had all been underlined by the districts program. In addition, attention had been drawn to the possibilities inherent in the use of new and higher yielding strains of the various food grains. Since the mid-1950s, Indian scientists, with the assistance of Rockefeller Foundation and American government funds, had undertaken an expanding program of agricultural research. Almost simultaneously, the Rockefeller and Ford foundations had jointly established an International Rice Research Institute in the Philippines in 1958, in an effort to duplicate for the most widely consumed Asian cereal the experience of the earlier Mexican wheat project. In less than a decade the institute was beginning to produce sturdier, higher yielding rice varieties, although a true breakthrough in rice development would be longer in coming. In 1964 the foundations' international connections encouraged Indian and American scientists to begin the experiments with the adaptation of Mexican wheat strains that led to the importation of large quantities of Mexican seed mentioned earlier. Two years of severe drought in 1965-1966 and 1966-1967 obscured the remarkable success of the high-yield wheat program, but at the same time scarcity brought price increases that encouraged Indian farmers to increase their output substantially. In 1968 the combination of favorable weather, higher prices, and new wheat varieties created the regional surpluses which provided the basis for confident pronouncements of the "green revolution." [17]

Although nearly two decades of effort, experimentation, failure, and rededication at last seemed on the verge of producing the desired result, it was important to be clear and careful in delineating what had and what had not been achieved. After the initial successes with wheat, it appeared that the rice program would lag considerably behind, although it too would eventually be brought into the modern development process. The high-yield wheat varieties programs achieved their results by concentrating upon scientifically developed seed, intensive use of fertilizers, and a two-crop-per-year pattern of production which required carefully regulated irrigation practices. The program had seemed at the outset to mark a step away from the reform emphasis of early community development days toward sharp concentration upon technical and economic considerations. Yet it soon became clear that high-yield grain programs, too, depended upon careful assessment and coordination of a number of agricultural, community, and marketing variables. Motivation, education, and cooperation on the part of villagers and cultivators were essential to its success. So, in a sense, the initial thrust of the community development program was vindicated in principle, while the experience in extension and community organization which that program had initiated had played a vital part in the outcome after all. [18]

Still more fundamentally, once the euphoria of long-awaited "victory" in the fight against mass starvation began to fade, it became clear that the benefits of initial increases in productivity were still limited. They were confined to those areas of wheat production where adequate and reliable irrigation could be assured. They depended, therefore, upon considerable capital investment, the use of expensive fertilizers, and other techniques of modern scientific agriculture and marketing. Such conditions inevitably favored the wealthier, better educated farmers and threatened further to depress the landless, already marginal agricultural laborers. If the green revolution should end by enriching the few while it pushed the poverty-stricken masses even more rapidly toward urban slums, unemployment, and starvation, it would prove a nightmare rather than a blessing. Thus, the issue of land reform was revived again in a new context; reform and productivity seemed likely to prove complementary rather than antithetical goals after all. But land reform was a domestic Indian political issue and one likely to prove particularly intransigent, since it required a redistribution of wealth and power that went deeply against the grain of Indian custom.

There were other difficult issues. Modern science and technology seemed to many Indians to threaten not only traditional power relationships but other cherished values as well. The fear that the price of modernization might be the alienation of the people from their deepest cultural and social values was real and understandable. It also lent itself to exploitation by those whose interests in the old order were more pragmatic. Even more crucial, the problem of population control remained the elusive key to any long-range progress for India. Such sensitive problems as these American diplomats and well-wishers would have to treat with great caution and circumspection.

The difficulties involved in maintaining a spirit of mutuality in the relations of two national parties to an aid-giving and receiving relationship were well illustrated in the American experience on the Indian subcontinent. Divergent national aims, ideologies, and cultural orientations plagued Indo-American relationships continually. Personal and political piques played over these inevitable differences and threatened time and again to fan them into outright hostility. Only the alertness of men such as Chester Bowles and Douglas Ensminger, some of whom fortunately could be found at many levels in both governmental and private agencies, managed to defuse a succession of major and minor misunderstandings. Unquestionably, their effectiveness stemmed from their capacity to establish the genuineness of their interest and concern in actions as well as words.

For the fact of the matter was that, despite the disagreements and unpleasantnesses, the failure and miscalculations which inevitably marred an enormously ambitious and complex undertaking, India did significantly improve its potential for a progressive, productive agriculture. The American contribution to the Indian achievement must in the end be judged an effective one. The irony was that the shifting focus of American power and influence in Asia toward the virtually all-consuming political-military intervention in Vietnam obscured the significance of the American role in India. Yet, when the conflict and confusion in Southeast Asia eventually subsided, the record of that Indian experience would remain as one of limited but constructive collaboration between the United States and the non-Western world.

Finally, it is clear that the involvement of the private foundations in the comprehensive American assistance program was of vital importance in sustaining the cooperative relationship over a broad front of related but diffuse projects and concerns. The combination of private and governmental programs enabled foreign assistance to go forward with a minimum of interruption or delay when political, economic, or ideological obstacles threatened it. The ability of the foundations to assist such controversial programs as community development and family planning, whose political implications made them difficult for a foreign government to support, provided a flexibility and responsiveness which public agencies could not always offer. Similarly, long-range programs of scientific or technical research, such as those which produced the high-yield food grains, were often unsuited to governmental support. In addition, the relative, although by no means total, divorce of foundation objectives from national political interests enabled the foundations to choose their staffs for technical competence alone and to retain or replace them on the basis of effective performance. Over the years, therefore, foundation staffs were able to build a relationship of mutual trust and understanding with their Indian counterparts that it was often difficult for government to match.

The result was that, while the scope and amount of foundation contributions to the Indian development program were small in relation to governmental aid, they were often disproportionately significant. It is impossible and probably unnecessary to assess the relative contributions of the public and private assistance efforts. What is important to recognize is that they reinforced and strengthened each other and that, in the process, they built a constructive contribution to Indo-American relations which political controversies may obscure but cannot obliterate.

NOTES

1. Carroll P. Streeter, *A Partnership to Improve Food Production in India* (New York: The Rockefeller Foundation, 1961), pp. iii, 10-14.

2. Ford Foundation, *Annual Report, 1952* (New York, 1952), p. 9; Rockefeller Foundation, *Annual Report, 1953* (New York, 1954), p. 18.

3. Chester Bowles, *Ambassador's Report* (New York: Harper, 1954), pp. 1-6; Chester Bowles, *The Making of a Just Society* (New Delhi: University of New Delhi, 1963), pp. 11, 13; Chester Bowles, *The Conscience of a Liberal* (New York: Harper, 1962), p. 7; Chester Bowles, *Ideas, People and Peace* (New York: Harper, 1958), pp. 132-138; Chester Bowles, *Promises to Keep: My Life in Public Office, 1941-69* (New York: Harper and Row, 1971), p. 248; Chester Bowles, *View from New Delhi* (Bombay: Allied Publishers, 1969), pp. 8-9, 16; Dwight Macdonald, *The Ford Foundation: The Men and the Millions* (New York: Reynal, 1956), pp. 50-51, 64-65.

4. Bowles, *Ambassador's Report*, pp. 157-172.

5. Carl C. Taylor, Douglas Ensminger, Helen W. Johnson and Jean Joyce, *India's Roots of Democracy* (Calcutta: Orient Longman's, 1965), pp. 10-18, passim; Bowles, *Ambassador's Report*, pp. 198-201; Bowles, *Promises*, pp. 384-386, 549.

6. Macdonald, *The Ford Foundation*, p. 64.

7. Bowles, *Ambassador's Report*, pp. 164, 201-207; Taylor et al., *India's Roots of Democracy*, p. 15.

8. Bowles, *Ambassador's Report*, pp. 208-214.

9. Taylor et al., *India's Roots of Democracy*, pp. 41-42, 69, 177-178, passim.

10. R. T. Shand, ed., *Agricultural Development in Asia* (Berkeley: University of California Press, 1969), pp. 64-66; Chester Bowles, *The New Dimensions of Peace* (New York: Harper, 1955), pp. 165-169; John P. Lewis, *Quiet Crisis in India* (Washington: Brookings Institution, 1962), p. 46; A. M. Khusro, ed., *Readings in Agricultural Development* (Calcutta: Allied Publishers, 1968), pp. 66-73; Taylor et al., *India's Roots of Democracy*, p. 245.

11. Lewis, *Quiet Crisis in India*, pp. 67-70, 80, 157ff.; Francine R. Frankel, *India's Green Revolution: Economic Gains and Political Costs* (Princeton, N.J.: Princeton University Press, 1971), p. 3; Taylor et al., *India's Roots of Democracy*, pp. 184-187ff., 238, passim; Dorris D. Brown, *Agricultural Development in India's Districts* (Cambridge, Mass.: Harvard University Press, 1971), pp. 4-6; Bowles, *Making of a Just Society*, pp. 57-59.

12. Lewis, *Quiet Crisis in India*, pp. 48-49, 115, 252-253; Bowles, *Ideas, People and Peace*, p. 3; Bowles, *Conscience of a Liberal*, pp. 95-96.

13. Taylor et al., *India's Roots of Democracy*, pp. 184-187, 238-252; Brown, *Agricultural Development in India's Districts*, pp. 1-27.

14. Lewis, *Quiet Crisis in India*, pp. 138-139; Leland Hazard, "Strong Medicine for India," *Atlantic* 216 (December 1965): 43-48; Bowles, *Ambassador's Report*, p. 340; Bowles, *Promises*, pp. 551, 554-556; Bowles, *View from New Delhi*, pp. 96-97; Streeter, *A Partnership*, p. iii; Ford Foundation, *Annual Report, 1962*, p. 59; ibid., 1963, p. 3.

15. Brown, *Agricultural Development in India's Districts*, pp. 28-60.

16. Bowles, *Promises*, pp. 457-471, 551-557.

17. Brown, *Agricultural Development in India's Districts*, pp. 92-101; Frankel, *India's Green Revolution*, pp. 25-33; Khusro, *Readings in Agricultural Development*, pp. 100-101, 118-121; Rockefeller Foundation, *Annual Report, 1971*, pp. 16-18, 20-26; Streeter, *A Partnership*, pp. 12-14; Bowles, *Promises*, p. 552; Bowles, *View from New Delhi*, pp. 77-79; Lewis, *Quiet Crisis in India*, p. 259.

18. Bowles, *Promises*, pp. 459, 523ff.; Bowles, *View from New Delhi*, pp. 81-84.

CHAPTER TWELVE

An American Business in Latin America: The Case of Sears, Roebuck and Company

From the early years of the nineteenth century, as we have seen, citizens and officials of the United States have taken a lively interest in the affairs of peoples and nations to the South — in Mexico, the Caribbean and Central American regions, and on the South American continent. The motives and interests of the North Americans have ranged widely, at different times and under differing circumstances, from enlightened idealism to sordid self-seeking. Religious, philanthropic, economic, and political purposes have all played their part in shaping the images with which members of the two broad families of Americans have approached and dealt with each other. One of the central principles of United States foreign relations, set forth in the Monroe Doctrine as early as 1823 and frequently reiterated thereafter, was the assertion of a special relationship and responsibility on the part of the United States in the affairs of its southern neighbors. In the twentieth century, Latin America has sent increasingly large numbers of its people to live and work in the United States; more recently, United States citizens of Latin origin or descent have been making their way into positions of leadership and influence in many areas of this nation's life. Yet, despite these historic and important ties of proximity and interest, relations between the two peoples have seldom been clearly and mutually defined, and even more seldom have they been mutually satisfactory. In contrast to Asia and Africa, more remote and more sharply differentiated regions, our visions of Latin America have been blurred and blocked, perhaps as much by the similarities its people have shared with ours as by the differences which distort our perspective. Latin America, after all, has developed its own distinctive blends of European, African, and American Indian cultural features and traditions and the combinations have been so different from our own as to seem utterly foreign and somehow, perhaps, peculiarly perverse.

In the face of this special set of circumstances and perceptions, only geographical proximity, with all of its implications for vital political and economic interests, could probably have kept relations between the northern and southern Americans as close — and as painful — as they have often been. In the United States, the processes of industrialization that, toward the end of the nineteenth century, were causing increasing numbers to look beyond their own borders for future resources and markets added substantial economic incentives to the political and ideological concerns that had earlier been uppermost in the minds of politicians and diplomats. As American business shifted its gaze and extended its reach for new opportunities across the Pacific in the 1880s and 1890s, it was only to be expected that its interests should also focus strongly on promising regions even closer to home. The Spanish-American War, liquidating the last vestiges of significant European political power in the Americas, opened the way for economic expansion and penetration to the South on a previously inconceivable scale. With the encouragement and assistance of successive administrations in Washington, United States investments in Central and South America rose rapidly during the first three decades of the twentieth century. A parallel and related development was that of military intervention by the United States government in the internal affairs of a number of the countries bordering the Caribbean. Twenty separate instances of such intervention occurred between 1898 and 1920. The most notable entailed responsibility for assisting the separation of Panama from Columbia as a preliminary to the creation of a United States-held Canal Zone and the construction of a major economic and strategic thoroughfare across the isthmus. Most of the other, less extended, interventions were undertaken for the purposes of assuring political stability, the protection of property, or the payment of foreign debts by governments of countries in which United States business interests were substantially involved.[1] The effect of such operations on Latin attitudes toward the United States, to say nothing of their consequences for the growth of self-reliance and self-confidence on the part of peoples anxious to find their own pathways toward modernization and higher living standards, is too complicated a problem for detailed analysis here, but it was hardly healthy.

In the late 1920s and 1930s the withdrawal of American troops, the announcement of the Good Neighbor policy and the acquiescence of the United States government in Mexico's expropriation of foreign oil holdings combined to set the stage for an era of somewhat warmer relations. World War II brought prosperity and growth to many Latin American economies, as the need of the Western allies for their resources increased sharply. Simultaneously, Latin nationalism was stimulated and encouraged by the political, ideological, and economic currents which the war released. The liquidation of most European investments in the course of the war left Latin America in a new relationship to the outside world: a new sense of national pride and potential direction had developed side by side with the emergence of the United States as the overwhelmingly dominant outside political and economic power. The stage was thus set for an almost inevitable confrontation of national systems and purposes.

The rapid transition from peace to Cold War further heightened the sources of tension and disagreement between North and South. United States exuberance and self-confidence as the leader of a worldwide victorious coalition for peace and freedom was quickly transformed into suspicion and hostility in the face of apparent new threats to the values in whose name the war had been waged. Readily equating its own political-economic system and interests with the needs and desires of other nations, the United States, in a burst of idealism and insensitivity, proclaimed its leadership of a worldwide anti-communist bloc pledged, in effect, to defend the status quo. In Latin America, meanwhile, those who hoped for continued progress toward modernization were finding little virtue in a status quo which seemingly consigned them to near-colonial status as suppliers and consumers for an expansive United States economy. Even conservative Latin nationalists were restive in a relationship which assigned them the role of second-class partners in profits, power, and pride.

Out of the congeries of experiences, attitudes, and interactions which made up the totality of United States-Latin American relations during these years, it is obviously impossible to select one, or even a few, that could adequately represent or symbolize the full range. The diversity of conditions across the South American continent, the variety of United States involvements, the conflicts of need and interest, and the shifts in ideology or approach as regimes succeeded one another and directions changed on both continents, all defy any simple, unitary analysis or representation. As already indicated, the most common assessments of the complex relationship—from the perspective of either partner—have been critical. To most citizens and certainly to many writers in the United States, their Latin neighbors seemed in many respects perverse and inscrutable. Demanding recognition, equal treatment, modernization, and rising living standards, they often seemed proud, lazy, corrupt, and unwilling to submit themselves to the disciplines on which modernization builds. To the Latin eye, on the other hand, the North Americans appeared domineering, profit-hungry, cold, and unsympathetic. United States pride and power, coupled with Latin resentment and ambivalence toward change that was inevitably associated with outside forces, provided an arena in which few realistic possibilities for constructive understanding and cooperation existed. Monolithic interpretations of United States-Latin American relations, whether based upon capitalist, Marxist, or other criteria, fail to do full justice to the diversity of actual experience—in part, no doubt, precisely because they attempt to subject the experience to too rigid and exclusive a definition. In a field beset with theoretical biases, it is particularly important to check theory against the raw data of experience: yet, because theories or systems are so strongly held, they have long tended to screen and dominate the data which should provide their bases.

During the 1950s, when the Cold War was in many respects at

its height, the Eisenhower administration looked with favor upon private business as an agent of freedom and democracy abroad as well as at home. To oppose communism wherever and in whatever form it appeared was often equated with the defense and promotion of a private enterprise economy, in whatever forms it assumed, as the necessary prerequisite of effective political democracy. Particularly in Latin America, relatively remote from the points of political conflict between Russian and United States interests, it seemed appropriate that private initiative and capital take the lead in contributing to the continued opening up of the region to economic development and progress. Unfortunately for United States preconceptions, the free enterprise approach to Latin American modernization achieved only limited successes in the 1950s. It did not go the heart of the economic and social problems of a region caught in the transition from preindustrial to modern conditions. Indeed, it often aggravated those problems by expanding foreign interests and influences while siphoning off the proceeds and incentives for further development in profits to outside investors.

Politically, too, the rapid growth of private foreign investment created difficulties. It was perpetually suspect for—and often guilty of—seeking and receiving special government favors and concessions. In turn, both the reality and the suspicion of such corrupting influences were used by Latin Americans wishing to rationalize shortcomings and failures on their own part, with widely discouraging and demoralizing effects. Meanwhile, United States business and political leaders found it easy to explain away Latin criticisms of their role as indications of procommunist, anti-American sentiment, as well as of the inability of the Latin Americans to understand and adhere to the gospel of free-enterprise capitalism as revealed north of the Rio Grande.

If the pace of economic development in Latin America in the 1950s was disappointing, so was the status of democratic government. Military and other authoritarian governments appeared to flourish. Toward the end of the decade, the overthrow of such a regime in Cuba and its replacement by the aggressively anti-United States, pro-Communist regime of Fidel Castro seemed to climax years of Latin American hostility and resentment while it simultaneously stiffened United States suspicions of radical, or even reformist, movements and governments. Against this background, the foreign policy of the Kennedy administration after 1961 moved in the direction of more public and publicly planned foreign assistance programs, together with an increased emphasis upon Latin America initiative and reform. It is beyond the scope of the present chapter, yet in the spirit of the subject we are considering, to note that the Kennedy policies as exemplified in the Alliance for Progress showed little, if any, greater success than those they followed. Both reformist and traditional approaches by U.S. public and private agencies evidently had failed to ground themselves in a realistic assessment of Latin social and cultural, as well as economic, conditions. The failure of United States initiatives in hemispheric economic relations cleared the way, at least in theory, for a reassessment of conditions and objectives on both sides, while the diversion of United States attention largely to Asia during the late 1960s added a perhaps rather healthy distance to the perspectives through which North and South Americans viewed each other across their geographical, national, and cultural barriers.

Since, as already indicated, it is impossible to treat fully the convergence of interacting and conflicting images, purposes, and actions characterizing United States-Latin American relations in a single chapter, no attempt is made here to do so. Rather, it has seemed wiser to examine a single, and obviously unrepresentative, episode for whatever clues it can offer as to the terms of understanding or misunderstanding between the two Americas. The instance chosen, the experience of Sears, Roebuck and Company in opening a series of department stores in several Latin American countries in the 1950s, offers evidence to illustrate the difficulty of easy generalizations. Sears's movement into Latin America in the 1950s can be seen as one measure of the outward thrust of United States capitalism in the postwar era, which saw our investment in that region swell from less than $3 billion in 1945 to more than $9 billion by 1961. Yet Sears's impact upon the Latin economies into which it moved seemed at times so substantial and progressive as almost to justify the term *revolutionary*, readily applied to it by both North and South Americans. Wholly United States-oriented by background and experience, Sears nevertheless accomplished a successful adaptation to, and of, Latin American culture under the guidance of motives which were primarily profit-oriented and rational, rather than philanthropic or idealistic. Finally, in the welter of failures, complaints, and disappointments which have marked inter-American relations and marred efforts at mutual understanding, little attention has been paid to an experience which can tell us something, although certainly not everything, about the possible conditions of success.

The factual story of Sears, Roebuck in Latin America can be briefly summarized. It began with an outlet opened in Havana, Cuba, in November 1942, evidently with the objective of testing Latin response to Sears products and methods. Not until the end of World War II, however, were conditions right for a serious "invasion" of Latin markets, and then the initial target was not Cuba, but Mexico. Personal ties of Sears executives with American real estate interests in Mexico, combined with an evaluation of the Mexican market as dynamic and expanding, led to the opening of a retail store in Mexico City in 1947. After a resounding initial success in Mexico, Sears entered Brazil in 1948, Venezuela in 1949, Columbia in 1952, and Peru in 1955. In 1953, after six years in Mexico, Sears was operating 7 stores with sales exceeding $15,000,000 and had already become one of the largest firms operating in Mexico. By 1959 Sears was operating 55 stores and 13 sales offices in nine Latin American countries, employing nearly 10,000 workers—nearly all of them Latin Americans—and carrying out sales valued at $100,000,000 annually. By 1970, with slightly more than twenty years' experience behind it, Sears was managing 72 stores throughout Latin America: 15 in Brazil, 9 in Columbia, 1 in Costa Rica, 22 in Mexico, 1 in Nicaragua, 3 in Panama, 2 in Peru, 6 in Puerto Rico, 1 in El Salvador and 12 in Venezuela. The record was one which seemed to call for superlatives, and the superlatives on an apparent success story south of the border were forthcoming.[2]

Yet the remarkable thing is not that the evident successes of United States businesses abroad were duly hailed, but rather that they received so little attention and thoughtful analysis. The fact that Sears flourished in a period when United States public policy toward Latin America, as well as the activities of United States companies generally in that region, were widely under attack probably diverted attention from the Sears experience. As a giant national corporation, marketing a full range of consumer products throughout the United States, both through its legendary mail-order catalogue business and its more recently developed chain of large department stores, the Sears enterprise was at once a symbol and an achievement of progressive, mass-consumption capitalism. Its reputation for selling products of solid quality at reasonable prices with full utilization of large-scale marketing and distribution techniques made Sears as appropriate a symbol of mature consumer capitalism as Henry Ford had been of an earlier mass-production phase. The encounter of such an enterprise with the supposedly backward, tradition-minded, and unenterprising Latin American economies had a dramatic, representative quality that would be difficult to match. The fact that the encounter has been so largely overlooked by scholars, businessman, and political leaders on both sides suggests that prejudices and preconceptions in inter-Americans relations still strongly discourage open-minded reassessment of mutual roles, needs, and interests.

Sears's movement into Latin America in the late 1940s and 1950s coincided with a period of self-conscious United States expansion. To most United States citizens this probably seemed a natural and even a desirable consequence of the obvious preeminence of their nation in political and economic affairs. Some, however, did recognize the perils associated with a sudden thrust of United States influence and interest into unfamiliar terrain. A self-conscious effort to focus attention on the arts of "overseasmanship" flourished in the 1950s, as government officials, foreign economic and military advisors, company executives, and others began to consider the need to prepare themselves and their associates for the experiences of "culture shock" and the need to adapt to foreign ways and expectations. Considerable stress was laid in the literature of this movement on the idealism of American purposes and the democratic and revolutionary potential of United States influences on traditional societies, in contrast to the evil consequences which these societies might anticipate from too close association with Communist forms of modernization. There was also a somewhat more realistic and down-to-earth concern expressed for the day-by-day problems of individual men and women, as well as of companies, who found themselves having to cope as best they could with unfamiliar situations and cultures. Harlan Cleveland's *The Overseas Americans*, published in 1960, distilled much of the best advice and experience of these years, while in 1956 W. F. Whyte and Allan R. Holmberg edited a special issue of *Human Organization*, the journal of the Society for Applied Anthropology, entitled "Human Problems of U.S. Enterprise in Latin America" and based in part upon a conference at which scholars and corporation executives discussed these issues.[3] Amid the sound counsel and solid analysis these forums supplied, considerably less attention was paid to the importance of self-understanding than to that of sensitivity to others' values.

Sears management undoubtedly shared both the ideals and the concerns that formed the common ground of public, private, business, and academic discourse at this time, but Sears made no effort to disguise the fact that the motives which impelled it were chiefly and unashamedly pecuniary. It was seeking and testing a market for its goods, and it found such a market, but it found much more. What distinguished Sears from other large companies then expanding their Latin American investments and commitments was the fact that its central purpose was neither the exploitation of natural resources nor the development of industrial facilities. Its interest, rather, was in selling a broad range of consumer products and thus in establishing mutually satisfactory relationships with the largest possible number of potential buyers. In its efforts to do so, Sears found that in some respects, at least, the presumed gap between the highly developed North American economy and that of the southern nations beginning to emerge into modernization was not so great as had been thought. In a number of Latin American countries, industrial development, capital formation, and the emergence of a modernizing middle class had been accelerated by the forced draft of wartime opportunities. Some of the resources, skills, and desires needed to provide a base for a mass production-mass consumption economy were ready at hand. What was needed was the mechanism and the managerial skill to bring these elements into fruitful combination. Sears's assessment that the time was ripe for the introduction of modern distribution techniques was rapidly vindicated.

The basis for Sears's initial success in Latin America lay in the quality of its commodities and its marketing techniques, yet, despite its characteristically careful calculation of market opportunities, the company entered upon its Mexican experiment with a number of preconceptions and expectations that soon proved unjustified. Sears had cautiously estimated that the Mexican market would be restricted, for the most part, to members of the upper middle class. They alone would be able to afford the United States goods which were expected to compose 70 percent of the store's stock. In addition to selling American-produced goods, the company proceeded to design a retail store very much along American lines, with open-stock displays, goods clearly marked with prices, and with the satisfaction-or-money-back guarantee which had become customary in the north-of-the-border, consumer-oriented economy. In so doing, Sears was flouting traditional Mexican market mores which, based upon European models, left prices delightfully vague and subject to haggling while quality—also unregulated—was subject to time-honored caveat-emptor standards. Sears dared to challenge the advice of Mexicans who flatly asserted that goods left open to public scrutiny would vanish from the shelves faster than they could be sold. Altogether, the Sears approach to the Mexican market represented an imposition of United States methods and standards on a sensitive foreign neighbor. It was evidently a case of arrant cultural imperialism, but, remarkably, it worked. [4]

On opening day in Mexico City, the new Sears store was jammed with customers and observers of all classes, workers as well as the elite. Within two hours, the stock was sold out and hurry-up orders for more were winging their way back to Chicago. In the eyes of United States free-enterprise enthusiasts, capitalism was justified and an American-style hemispheric "revolution" heralded on that day. What is clearer and more fundamental is that Sears had offered something that Mexicans and, as it later developed, other Latin Americans wanted, and nationalistic or ideological reservations took second place in the face of that. The rising middle-class market was potentially greater than either

Sears or its Latin advisors had recognized. For guaranteed quality and reasonable prices, Mexican consumers were prepared to forego the pleasures of genteel bargaining and the risks of uncertain value. Much the same experience was repeated over and over as Sears extended its Latin American operations in the ensuing years. Significantly, the implications of mutuality and equality inherent in the open-shelf, satisfaction-guaranteed policies registered a basic respect for the consumer which transcended nationality and ideology. (A parallel to this experience would be found, incidentally, when American and Indian politicians and agricultural experts discovered a few years later that India's peasants were willing to break sharply with traditional cropping practices as soon as it became unmistakably clear that it was to their economic advantage to do so.[5]) Although traditional merchants were hard-pressed to meet this new form of competition, the more foresighted and able soon were paying Sears the ultimate compliment of emulation.[6]

Scarcely had the initial successes in introducing North American marketing methods been recorded, however, when other unanticipated events created new problems — and ultimately forced new solutions — that carried Sears far beyond the limited objectives of its initial undertaking. An unfavorable foreign trade balance, augmented by swelling economic nationalism and the resentment of disgruntled merchant competitors, led the Mexican government to raise tariffs and other import restrictions to prohibitive levels. Faced with an encouraging market, Sears now confronted an unexpected obstacle to its plans for selling homemade products abroad. The only alternative to the abandonment of a promising start was the discovery of local producers to fill the threatened gap between supply and demand. But, although Mexico was among the more advanced of Latin American economies, the production of most consumer goods was still small scale and craft oriented. The resources, the capital, the skills, and the equipment necessary to undertake manufacturing on the scale required by Sears were largely lacking, and their provision and organization could be supplied by only one source, Sears itself. The second phase of Sears's entrance to the Latin American economy, therefore, began with the search for, identification of, and assistance to hundreds of small producers who, in the view of the Sears staff, seemed most likely to be able to develop the capacity for the scale and quality of production needed. The Latinization of Sears had begun.

Eventually, there were to be over 8,000 such local manufacturers throughout Latin America, some of which literally began as cottage industries. Advancing funds, supplying technical and managerial advice, stipulating and supervising standards of production and accounting, and providing a guaranteed market on a scale sufficient to justify steady production and low prices, Sears urged, coddled, and encouraged the development of a modern consumer-goods industry. Further than that, capital goods manufacturing was also stimulated as machinery for the manufacture of textiles, paint, plaster, glass, and similar items was required. In some instances, Sears acted not only as investment banker and technical consultant but as joint manager or owner as well. Thus, a major outcome of the intrusion of one North American business into Latin America was a significant stimulation of local industry. To carry its contribution in this respect further still, Sears arranged, after having enabled the new producers to stand on their own feet, to withdraw its capital and personnel when they were no longer needed. Local producers were even encouraged to seek other outlets for some of their goods. Such practices, which served Sears's desire to economize its financial commitments and costs, had the additional and crucial advantage of eliminating the danger that a foreign company might try, or might appear to try, to dominate a new sphere of Latin American economic achievement.

By 1960 a rough index of the progress of these ventures into the promotion of local industrial development could be seen in the fact that 99 percent of all Sears sales in Brazil were of products manufactured in that country, while the corresponding figure for Mexico and Columbia was 97 percent, for Venezuela 47 percent, and for Peru 50 percent. Meanwhile, the development of consumer credit along North American lines as a device for further extending the market was also under way. The entire Sears system of quality merchandise at moderate prices, with emphasis upon service and satisfaction for the customer, was being transported into Latin American economies with remarkable success. [7]

Paralleling the emergence of an integrated consumer goods industry was, of course, the development of the skilled, trained, and experienced personnel to operate it. This was achieved largely on the spot and under Sears's supervision. On occasion, technical and management specialists could be flown to the United States to observe operations there and to talk with North American counterparts, but for the most part managers and technicians as well as skilled laborers had to learn their skills and functions through on-the-job training programs sponsored by Sears. In addition to serving the needs of Latin America's industrial middle class, the Sears system thus was helping it grow and acquire new competencies. The result was that Sears operated its Latin American companies from an early date with a very small full-time complement of United States personnel. John F. Gallagher, Sears's vice-president for foreign administration, testifying before a congressional committee in 1960, stated that only 45 of the over 5,000 employees in South America were from the United States. Nineteen stores and all of the sales offices were staffed entirely by Latin Americans, while 90 percent of the buying, 95 percent of retail credit, 98 percent of retail merchandising, and 98 percent of the retail accounting were handled by local nationals. Obviously, Sears had followed a policy of training its personnel and promoting them to positions of responsibility without regard to national bias.[8]

In the field of labor relations, too, Sears combined Latin American and United States practices in interesting ways. Latin labor and welfare laws, reflecting patriarchal traditions and concern for the security of the worker, required the provision of fringe benefits often more comprehensive and costly than those Sears provided its employes at home. These were coupled, in addition, with Sears's customary provision of employee profit-sharing and stock ownership opportunities. The combination of benefits, of both northern and southern origin, made an attractive package and undoubtedly contributed both to worker and customer acceptance of the foreign corporation.[9] Still another instance of Sears's combination of traditions was its initiation at an early stage of the types of community-oriented activities long common to business organizations in the United States. Boy Scout troops, scholarship programs, 4-H-type activities, and

similar community betterment programs received company
support. The personnel development and community welfare
policies of large corporations in the United States have often
smacked of a basically undemocratic paternalism. In Latin
America, however, they suited the image of the powerful patron,
or benefactor, familiar in its history. There, they were tempered,
too, by the company's self-conscious deference to national sensi-
tivities and its obvious contributions toward building up local
self-reliance. 10

Any balanced assessment of Sears's role in Latin America
must take account of shortcomings and problems as well as of
successes, and it is possible in the scattered literature to find indications that there were, indeed, many difficulties. The training
of men and the fostering of new producing companies often have
entailed failures or, at any rate, less than fully satisfactory
results. After having initially underestimated the Mexican
market, Sears later became overly enthusiastic and expanded
beyond its consumer potential and then had to cut back a number of its smaller stores in 1959. In Brazil, runaway inflation in
the 1950s cut profit to the vanishing point and seriously retarded
potential growth. Undoubtedly, there were other problems although the limited information available is less than adequate.
Resentment on the part of small merchants, manufacturers, and
craftsmen, whose traditional ways faced Sears's modern organization and methods at a disadvantage, was heightened in some
quarters by nostalgia for a pattern of values now threatened by
growing exposure to modern mass culture. In a sense, the successes of a modern, consumer-oriented company were more
threatening to vested interests, both reactionary and radical,
than its failure would have been. In addition to ideological resistance, regret at the decay of a traditional craft-oriented society
and culture, undermined by modern mass-production techniques, stimulated a resentment that was probably stronger
among disaffected intellectuals than it appeared to be among the
rank and file. Nationalism and ethnocentrism compounded such
feelings even though Sears's policies did more to compensate for
them than did the policies of many foreign firms. 11

Sears did not, of course, single-handedly bring the "consumption revolution" to Latin America. Many of the prerequisites of a

mass consumption market were already there—in the postwar prosperity, the growing middle classes, and the eagerness of the people for "modern" products and ways. Sears functioned as a catalyst and mobilizer of these factors while focusing the necessary capital and business expertise on a hitherto underdeveloped sector. It should also be emphasized that large regions of Latin America and a substantial portion of its population remained virtually unaffected by mass-marketing techniques. A mass-consumption society is an urban-oriented society and a considerable segment of the Latin American peasantry remained isolated from urban centers. Nevertheless, a pattern for successful development into the stage of consumer-oriented economics was set. Continuing, even accelerating, political and social turmoil may well characterize Latin America for many years to come, but the elements of a modern mass-production and consumption economy have been well established for the future. 12

The pattern of Sears's imposition of its own techniques and systems on the Latin economies and of its adaptation and modification of procedures to suit the exigencies of a different culture is an intriguing and suggestive one. Sears seems to have been able to export virtually its entire system of operations—management, sales, accounting, inventory control, maintenance of standards and service, and even consumer credit. In what was essentially a vacuum, and with a locally felt need, there were few limits upon Latin willingness to accept methods, guidance, and even control from experienced outsiders.

In other fields, where norms were clear and legally established, such as welfare and import regulations, Sears readily complied and, incidentally, benefited by doing so. In the less explicit but equally sensitive area of local taste and customs, Sears found it both necessary and advisable to adapt to the realities and tastes of the market. A number of commodities that played a major role in the North American context were less suited to Latin America. Purchasers demonstrated a surprising acceptance of United States styles, particularly in household goods, while local tastes and preferences were marked in areas such as women's clothing styles, but do-it-yourself hardware items did not sell well in societies well supplied with machismo and household servants. In some instances, Sears encountered resistance on the part of local artisans, proud of their craft, to the speed and techniques required by mass production. Occasionally, it was possible to add such high-quality craft goods on top of the standard line as specialty items, but the mass-produced items clearly had to predominate. Thus, a process of mutual learning and adaptation had developed almost from the beginning. [13]

The experience of Sears in Latin America offers a number of insights concerning the conditions under which Americans operating overseas may be able to achieve more satisfactory relations and results, in terms both of their own objectives and of the purpose and values of the host country. Most striking, perhaps, is the evidence that goodwill and philanthropic motives need not be the only or even the prime influences underlying a successful foreign venture. Sears's motives in its Latin American undertakings were by no means unfriendly, but its fundamental objective was the presumably selfish one of profit. The profit motive provided, in fact, some incentives and perspectives that proved crucial to Sears's successes. Not least among these was an element of realism sometimes lacking in more idealistic projects. The fact that Sears was a private corporation organized for profit provided a basis for frank and honest assessment of mutual advantage at points where moralistic or ideological-political posturings could have proved disastrous. Sears's management certainly voiced its share of concern for the vindication of United States-style democracy and free enterprise, just as it showed a genuine interest in advancing the welfare of the peoples of Latin America. But it never attempted to disguise its primary purpose, nor could it have done so. Consequently, it had a relatively clear standard on which to base policies and by which, in turn, to be judged. That Sears applied this standard in an enlightened fashion in no way detracted from its value as an ultimate criterion of performance on both sides of the bargaining table. The fact that Sears was a private, rather than a public, institution may also have worked in its favor. As such, it was subject to the laws and political authorities of the nations which it entered. In a region where nationalism and anti-United States sentiments were endemic, Sears's acceptance of its subordinate status in relationship even to laws—such as import restrictions, taxes, and employee welfare legislation—whose effects were costly to its short-run profits indicated due regard and respect for the pride and authority of those with whom it wished to do business. Unfortunately, evidence is abundant that many United States companies have not been so careful to acknowledge the proper limits of their status and power in foreign countries. In Sears's case, respect for the sovereignty and essential dignity of the nations with which it dealt was repaid in kind and in profits as well.

It was to some extent a happy accident that Sears's profit objectives coincided with the interests of many Latin Americans in economic development and social change. Sears's management, in reaching its decision to move southward, had carefully taken into consideration the prospects for economic growth and expanding consumption. Still, in the wake of that basic decision came many other decisions whose consequences and implications had to be carefully and sensitively calculated. Decisions to expand by fostering the growth of local suppliers, to trust the basic honesty of shoppers and borrowers, to rely upon the ability of Latin Americans to master the techniques of modern production and management, to encourage suppliers to seek other, competitive outlets for their products, or to initiate virtually unknown profit-sharing and stock-ownership plans for employees, all registered a continued and growing confidence in the local capacity for self-reliance and responsibility. At each stage, the dangers of ethnocentrism and paternalism were minimized, while Sears's policies were simultaneously helping to enlarge and strengthen a modern middle class. Potential mutuality of interest was thereby made real.

In an excess of enthusiasm, observers of Sears's remarkable accomplishment were sometimes given to overgenerous praise. A *Harper's* article, for example, termed Sears "the most effective ambassador the United States has sent abroad in many a year." Others credited the company with being, virtually single-handedly, a revolutionary force in Latin America. Without denying the significance of Sears's achievement, such claims can clearly be seen as exaggerations, obscuring the true significance of the Sears experience. The image of the United States and of American business in Latin America was not made by Sears alone or even primarily. The history of foreign business investment in Latin America—from Europe as well as from the United States—is long, and its consequences have provided a fruitful source of scholarly and ideological controversy as well as international ill will and misunderstanding. There is a sense in which Americans, in particular, do enter other, more traditionally oriented societies as revolutionary agents of modern, equalitarian, mass culture, whether they do so consciously and intentionally or otherwise. When they pride themselves on their revolutionary dynamic, it would be highly unrealistic not to recognize that, to their hosts, they often represent the threat of unwanted change and disruption. In such countries, there is probably no way in which United States influence and interests can operate without provoking substantial hostility and resistance. But if such responses are indeed inevitable, given the distinctive combination of United States culture and power, they can at least be understood as such, their underlying sources recognized, and their nagging symptoms alleviated to whatever degree possible by heightened sensitivity to the conditions and preconceptions of both parties to the exchange.

As has often been pointed out, the United States image in Latin America, as elsewhere around the world, may well be influenced more by national policies and attitudes at home, including the treatment accorded Latin American immigrants, than by the behavior of United States citizens or companies abroad. [14] The significance of Sears's experience in Latin America, then, is less as an active influence on our foreign relations than as a case study suggesting some conditions apparently conducive to mutually satisfactory international undertakings. It is an instance whose key features are rational assessment of mutual needs and circumstances and a decent respect for each other's purposes. Such considerations point beyond the cultivation of cultural sympathies, idealisms, or indignations so familiar to liberal and neoradical thought. They challenge equally the naïve self-assurance that still views United States methods and purposes as inevitably appropriate to the conditions and goals of widely differing societies.

NOTES

1. Bryce Wood, *The Making of the Good Neighbor Policy* (New York: Columbia University Press, 1961), pp. 4-6; Scott Nearing and Joseph Freeman, *Dollar Diplomacy: A Study in American Imperialism* (New York: B. W. Huebsch, Inc., 1925; reprint. Monthly Labor Review Press, New York, 1966).

2. Daniel James, "Sears, Roebuck's Mexican Revolution," *Harpers* 218 (June 1959): 65-70; "How Sears Moved into Mexico," *Business Week* (9 May 1953), p. 168; David L. Cohn, "Private Point Four South of the Border," *Nation's Business* (May 1954), p. 68ff.; Stanley C. Hollander, *Multinational Retailing* (East Lansing: Michigan State University Press, 1970), pp. 4-5, 26, passim; Louis S. Bing, "Sears, Roebuck in South America," *Stores* (November 1970): 8-10; Richardson Wood and Virginia Keyser, *Sears, Roebuck de Mexico* (New York: National Planning Association, 1953, reprint ed., 1956; William R. Fritsch, *Progress and Profits: The Sears, Roebuck Story in Peru* (Washington D.C.: Action Committee for International Development, Inc., 1962).

3. Harlan Cleveland, Gerard Mangone, and John Clark Adams, *The Overseas Americans* (New York: McGraw-Hill, 1960); Harlan Cleveland and Gerard J. Mangone, *The Art of Overseasmanship* (Syracuse: Syracuse University Press, 1957); William F. Whyte and Allan R. Holmberg, "Human Problems of U.S. Enterprise in Latin America," *Human Organization* 15 (Fall 1956); Harold H. Martin, "Yankee Don't Go Home," *Saturday Evening Post* 233 (5 November 1960), p. 38ff.; Theodore V. Houser in *Sears World*, vol. 1, no. 3 (September 1958), p. 5; *Latin America: Opportunities and Responsibilities*, by John F. Gallagher, Vice-President International Operations, Sears, Roebuck and Co. (n.p., n.d.).

4. James, "Sears, Roebuck's Mexican Revolution," pp. 65-70; Cohn, "Private Point Four," pp. 68ff; "How Sears Moved into Mexico"; Gallagher, *Latin America*; Martin, "Yankee Don't Go Home."

5. See Chapter 12.

6. James, "Sears, Roebuck's Mexican Revolution," pp. 65-70; Charles K. Mann, "Sears, Roebuck de Mexico: A Cross-Cultural Analysis," *Social Science* 40 (June 1958): 149-157; Cohn, "Private Point Four," pp. 68ff.; John H. Fayerweather, *International Business Management: A Conceptual Framework* (New York: McGraw-Hill, 1969), p. 28.

7. Mann, "Sears Roebuck de Mexico," pp. 150-153; James, "Sears, Roebuck's Mexican Revolution," pp. 65-70; Martin, "Yankee Don't Go Home," pp. 38ff.

8. James, "Sears, Roebuck's Mexican Revolution," pp. 65-70; Mann, "Sears, Roebuck de Mexico," pp. 149-157; John F. Gallagher's testimony, *Hearings Before the Subcommittee on Inter-American Economic Relations of the Joint Economic Committee of the Congress of the United States, May 10-11, 1962*, in Marvin D. Bernstein, ed., *Foreign Investment in Latin America* (New York: Alfred A. Knopf, 1966), pp. 160-162; Gallagher, *Latin America*, pp. 14-15.

9. Wood and Keyser, *Sears, Roebuck de Mexico*, pp. 17-18; Fritsch, *Progress and Profits*, pp. 29-30.

10. Martin, "Yankee Don't Go Home," pp. 38ff; Mann, "Sears Roebuck de Mexico," pp. 153-154.

11. Martin, "Yankee Don't Go Home," pp. 38ff; Lincoln Clark, "Sears, Roebuck 'Subverting' Latin America," *The Nation* 176 (6 June 1953): 53; Flavia Derossi, *The Mexican Entrepreneur* (Paris: Development Centre of the Organization for Economic Cooperation and Development, 1971), pp. 75, 80.

12. James, "Sears, Roebuck's Mexican Revolution," pp. 65-70; John F. Gallagher, *The Sears International Story* (Sears, Roebuck and Co., nd.).

13. Bing, "Sears, Roebuck in South America," p. 8; Cohn, "Private Point Four," pp. 68ff; James, "Sears, Roebuck's Mexican Revolution," p. 68; Martin, "Yankee Don't Go Home," pp. 56ff.

14. Claude McMillan, Jr., and Richard F. Gonzalez, *International Enterprise in a Developing Country: A Study in U.S. Business in Brazil* (East Lansing: Michigan State University Business Studies, 1964), pp. 41-42, 50-51, 54, 122; Mann, "Sears, Roebuck de Mexico," p. 155; W. Jack Butler, "Public Relations for Industry in Underdeveloped Countries," *Harvard Business Review* (September-October 1952): 63ff.; Raymond Vernon, ed., *How Latin America Views the U.S. Investor* (New York: Frederick A. Praeger, 1966), pp. 13-16.

CHAPTER THIRTEEN

Toward Freedom and Beyond: Afro-Americans and the African Independence Movement

"The problem of the twentieth century is the problem of the color line, — the relation of the darker to the lighter races of men in Asia and Africa, in America and the islands of the sea."[1] This prophetic statement by W.E.B. DuBois, the Afro-American scholar and militant leader, introduced an eloquent volume of essays, *The Souls of Black Folk*, published in 1903, that explored the problems and posture of American Negroes in the face of encircling segregation. The words had first been uttered in another context: a 1900 London conference protesting white colonization in Africa and urging recognition of the rights of Africans in the face of aggressive European imperialism. The conference had attracted some thirty delegates from Great Britain, the West Indies, and North America. Despite failure to achieve its stated objectives, it gave international currency to the term *Pan-Africanism* and it launched DuBois's career as promoter, propagandist, and long-time leader in the movement for African freedom and unity.[2] DuBois was emerging simultaneously as a major figure in the movement to secure equal rights and opportunities for American blacks. His argument that the prospects of freedom and equality both for African and American blacks were interrelated was unique, if not in conception, then at least in the clarity, dedication, and eloquence with which it was pursued through a lifetime. Later, the leaders of free African nations would acknowledge that the ideal of Pan-Africanism—that Africa's descendants throughout the world share cultural and political-economic interests—had substantially originated in America and that efforts on behalf of freedom for Africa's peoples had been encouraged and supported by Afro-Americans.

That the sons and daughters of Black Africa living in the New World should have played a leading part in fostering the concept of a united and free Africa is hardly so surprising as it may seem at first glance. Long separated from their local and tribal origins, ignorant or uncertain of their African historical and cultural backgrounds, and confronted with a dominant white society whose treatment of them was justified on the basis of common color and racial characteristics, Afro-Americans were understandably more sensitive to the common than to the diverse elements of their African connection. "What is Africa to me?" queried the American poet Countee Cullen, but, in posing the question, he voiced the unconscious assumption of most of his fellow American blacks that Africa was unity, with meaning for its children and perhaps for the world. By the time Cullen wrote, in the 1920s, some Africans—but chiefly those who had studied or lived abroad in Europe or America—were beginning to think of a common African cause against European imperialism. Yet even these leaders of anticolonial freedom movements tended to think in terms of the conditions or interests of a particular colony or tribe. The notion of Africa as a unity came more naturally to those who saw it from a distance and without too much familiarity or involvement with local issues and loyalties.[3]

Countee Cullen's question revealed a second aspect of the Afro-American response to the mother continent, its perennial uncertainty and ambiguity. Both during and after slavery, American Negroes had displayed ambivalence about their relationship to their ancestral home. Forcibly torn from family and community, cruelly transported across the Atlantic, separated for the most part from their cultural roots, and immersed in a strange, unfriendly society, blacks had limited opportunity for conscious preservation of the traditions and customs of their homeland. Recent scholarship is bringing to light new evidence of surviving African patterns in speech, music, dance, and elsewhere, but such survivals, important as they now appear, were for the most part unconscious clingings to ways whose origins and meanings had faded into dim recollection. By the nineteenth century, when the possibility of a return to Africa began to win serious consideration in some quarters, only a small minority of those Afro-Americans free to consider the alternative chose to do so. For the rest, their homes, their families, their struggles, and their future seemed more closely identified with the United States.

Still, as the promises of the American Revolution, Abolitionism, and the Civil War proved a mirage to slave or free blacks and their descendants, it was natural that thoughts of Africa as a place of refuge and fulfillment should arise. Under white leadership, the American Colonization Society recruited a small group of Negroes in the 1820s to establish a colony in Liberia. Later, black leaders such as Martin R. Delaney, Bishop Henry M. Turner, and Rev. Alexander Crummel looked to Africa for the fulfillment of Afro-American identity long denied in the United States. Black churches, meanwhile, scraped their treasuries to support missions carrying the Christian gospel back across the sea. A dream of spiritual and cultural reunion among the sons and daughters of the dark continent hovered behind the American and West Indian blacks who gathered in London in 1900. Against this background, DuBois spoke on behalf of common resistance by blacks of all continents in the face of white exploitation.

Pioneer though he was in urging Pan-African unity against oppression, DuBois at this stage of his career shared with many Afro-Americans an assumption of superiority toward the African masses. This posture mirrored in part the preconceptions of the dominant white society. It also reflected the reports of black missionaries concerning the prevalence of ignorance and backwardness in Africa. In the face of such discouragements, the continuing urge to make common cause with their African brothers measured a sense of rejection by America as much or more than a sensitivity to remote traditions and ties. DuBois, in any case, took it for granted that he and others from the West should take the initiative in presenting the case for African freedom and unity. The primacy of America in his own thinking was even more convincingly demonstrated by the fact that between the

1900 conference and World War I he turned his full energies toward the drive for Negro rights in America through the Niagara Movement, the NAACP, and his editorship of the latter's publication, *Crisis*. Not until the war once again focused attention on the international scene did he resume active advocacy of the Pan-African relationship he had earlier espoused. [4]

A sense of common cause and purpose, more in resistance to white oppression than in exploration or celebration of racial and historic mutualities, thus brought blacks from Africa and America together briefly at the century's opening. Events on both sides of the Atlantic would expand the number, frequency, and intensity of such contacts. In times of special stress or opportunity, Africans and Afro-Americans increasingly would come to look to each other for sympathy, assistance, and support. Such expectations would be met in ways which showed both a growing sense of mutuality and a persistent gap in understanding between the two continents. In the political sphere, especially, efforts to organize programs of mutual assistance and support proved largely ineffective. Despite their dramatic drive for equality in the 1950s and 1960s, American blacks remained too weak and preoccupied to exercise significant influence on the African policies of their government. Africans, on the other hand, won political control of their own destinies in the wake of World War II only to find that the force and effectiveness of their new states were as yet too slight to bring meaningful pressure to bear on the domestic or international policies of the American superpower. Political cooperation between the two peoples was nullified by the cross purposes which closer contact revealed, yet the experience of growing mutual awareness and understanding laid the foundations for more effective political ties in the future.

For DuBois, World War I reemphasized the interdependence of race relations on the national and international scenes. On the home front, it brought new opportunities for blacks in northern cities and factories, while overseas service exposed them to alternative cultural patterns and social relationships. At the same time, the rivalry of the European powers pivoted, in part, on their conflicting colonial ambitions. The struggle that began the collapse of European imperialism in Africa thus helped to lay the foundations for a new effort to resist racial segregation and discrimination in the United States. Both of those concerns took DuBois to Paris early in 1919. He went on behalf of the NAACP to investigate charges of racism in the armed forces and to prepare a record of the participation of Negroes in the war, but he went also with a determination to secure a hearing for the colored peoples of the world at the forthcoming peace conference. Although the London conference of 1900 had aroused little response in Africa, the war years had given rise to scattered movements for independence and self-government there. With the help of an African, Blaise Diagne, who held a position in the French government and had recruited African troops on its behalf, DuBois managed to organize a Pan-African Congress. The delegates, recruited on short notice and under the disapproving eye of American and British officials, included 16 Americans, 20 West Indians, and 12 Africans.[5] DuBois had no great expectations for the 1919 congress, hoping chiefly to encourage contact and understanding among blacks of different regions. Yet the congress's call for a permanent League of Nations bureau to protect the rights of Africans and those of African descent around the world may have influenced the creation of the league's mandate system under which Britain and France assumed control of Germany's African colonies.[6]

Returning to their respective homes, both African and American delegates quickly became preoccupied with local concerns. In Africa, scattered movements to secure recognition and rights within the colonial system got under way, while in the United States Negro leadership turned its attention to the problems occasioned by the northward, cityward movement of the black population. During the 1920s, two leaders in particular struggled to arouse and focus the consciousness of their fellow blacks on Africa. Marcus Garvey, a West Indian whose United Negro Improvement Association exercised wide appeal among newly urbanized and disillusioned blacks, pressed the case for pride in and identity with black culture and black people everywhere. Doubting the possibility of a satisfactory accommodation in the United States, Garvey urged black separatism here while advocating closer physical, economic, and spiritual ties with Africa. Garvey's schemes for black unity were sometimes farfetched, but they awakened enthusiasm among those discouraged and disillusioned by white exploitation. His colorful parades and uniforms attracted attention while his ill-starred Black Star Line of ships attempted to promote travel and commerce between the two continents. His speeches and publications spread a positive image of African-Afro-American relations to a degree hitherto unknown. Garvey's ideas and activities were widely publicized in Africa, too; the king of Swaziland told Mrs. Garvey that her husband and Jack Johnson, the heavyweight champion, were the only two blacks in the western hemisphere he had heard of.[7]

One of Garvey's chief critics in America was W.E.B. DuBois, who, although deeply engaged in domestic issues, continued his efforts to extend the ties between American and African leaders initiated at the 1919 conference. In 1921 DuBois took the lead in arranging a second Pan-African congress in London, Brussels, and Paris, the capitals of the leading colonial powers. Advance planning made it possible to assemble a more representative group than before, including active workers for black rights and interests in a number of African colonies. Of the 113 delegates, 41 came from Africa, 35 from the United States, 7 from the West Indies, and 24 from Europe. In the face of strong colonialist opposition, the congress passed resolutions on behalf of racial equality, local self-government, and black rights to education, land, and religious and cultural freedom. Once again, effective supervision by the League of Nations was called for and the delegates met with sympathetic whites in the three capitals. DuBois and others visited Geneva to confer with league officials; they also attempted unsuccessfully to set up a permanent organization in Paris.

With difficulty, other Pan-African congresses were convened in London and Lisbon in 1923 and New York in 1927, and another was planned for Tunis in 1929. European resistance and the onset of the Great Depression in America, however, brought the effort to a sudden halt.[8] Although decay and a division among the colonial powers encouraged the growth of African economic and political organizations in the 1930s and 1940s, it took World War II, further sapping Europe's strength, to revive Pan-Africanism and African hopes for freedom. War enlarged the community of African intellectuals, political leaders, exiles, students, workers, and soldiers in Europe. Black delegates to a world trade union conference in London in 1944 joined African leaders to organize a fifth Pan-African congress in Manchester, England, in 1945. This time the Africans provided their own leadership. Two, Namdi Azikiwe of Nigeria and Kwame Nkrumah of the Gold Coast, had studied in the United States and been influenced by their experiences there. Nkrumah, in particular, spoke of the strong impact on his thinking of Marcus Garvey, whose ideas he had encountered in the course of his studies. Symbolically, W.E.B. DuBois was invited to serve as president of the congress.

Wartime experiences aroused a new self-consciousness and determination among Africans. Many had had the opportunity to travel abroad, observe the weakening position of the European powers, encounter socialist and communist critiques of Western capitalism, and meet with Africans of other regions as well as Asians and those of African descent in the Americas who shared a common desire for self-determination. The Pan-African Federation, which published its own journal, *International African Opinion*, pamphlets, and more extended studies of African problems, had already come into being before the Manchester congress. Leaders of the Manchester congress hoped that Great Britain's new Labour government would prove sympathetic to their desire for reforms and progress in the social-political conditions of the African colonies. When this hope proved ill founded, the congress issued a call for freedom and independence for black Africa, warned of the dangers of race warfare if white resistance should continue, endorsed the demands of France's African colonies for self-government, and asserted the need for reform and self-government in the British West Indies. Calling attention to the principles of the Atlantic Charter, the congress expressed the intention of Africans to press peacefully but determinedly for freedom and equal rights.[9]

To their fellow Africans, the congressional delegates stated the case for a united front against foreign imperialism. Pursuant to this call, a number of new regional and national organizations took shape. The 1945 congress was the first major step in the postwar African independence movement. By 1963 virtually all of Africa, with the exception of the Portuguese colonies, South Africa, and Rhodesia, had secured political freedom. The Pan-

African goal of self-government seemed on the verge of accomplishment.

The movement toward independence for Africa had won the support of a number of American black leaders during the war and immediate postwar years. In addition to DuBois, men of the stature of Paul Robeson and Rayford Logan, spokesmen for organizations such as the NAACP, the Urban League, the Pittsburgh *Courier*, and the Council on African Affairs, were urging fellow Afro-Americans and the American government as well to take a more active role in support of African freedom. [10]

As Africa moved toward independence, American leadership and policy responded in a number of ways. Wartime professions of commitment to the freedom and self-determination of colonial peoples proved remarkably fragile in the face of postwar power politics and the Cold War. The United States officially favored colonial accountability under an international trusteeship system built into the structure of the United Nations in 1945, but aside from some pressure on the Dutch and British with regard to the status of Indonesia and Palestine, little interest or effort was directed toward the encouragement of national independence movements elsewhere. Harold Isaacs had found the United States unconcerned with the efforts of the British and French to return Indo-China to the control of the latter after the defeat of Japan. [11] In Africa, DeGaulle had established authority over most of the French colonies in the course of the war itself; the position of Britain and the other colonial powers was never threatened. The most egregious case of all, the Union of South Africa, despite its somewhat ambivalent attitudes toward Hitler's regime, was deemed too important strategically and economically to be challenged officially or unofficially by the United States. For the rest, American idealism and sentiment weighed lightly in the balance against the commitment to support the shaken and embattled European allies against the perceived threat of Soviet power and Communist expansionism.

As their government rallied to the support of the European democracies, Americans found their influence in Africa being thrown almost inadvertantly on the side of colonialism. Some, at least, were troubled by this. Militant blacks concluded that American support for the European imperialists left the Soviet

Union as the chief hope for African independence. Even blacks who supported American foreign policy urged that efforts on behalf of liberation and economic reorganization in Europe be paralleled by a comparable concern for other regions and peoples. [12] Yet the Point Four program, initiated in 1949 by President Harry S. Truman in partial response to such arguments, failed largely to meet Africa's need. It and successive foreign aid programs were directed primarily to Asia and Latin America, where the threat of communism seemed more immediate.

Interestingly, American domestic problems did much to focus attention on relations with Africa. The Truman administration's civil rights policies were formulated in conscious recognition of the fact that the nation's treatment of its own minorities affected its standing in the eyes of the third world of colored, formerly colonized peoples. In its 1954 brief against segregated higher education, the Justice Department asserted that racial discrimination in America provided communism with a Cold War asset and raised doubts "even among friendly nations as to the intensity of our devotion to the democratic faith."[13] In 1957, Vice-President Richard M. Nixon returned from a tour of Africa that included participation in the ceremonies marking the independence of Ghana. Calling for closer relations with the new African governments together with political and economic assistance, he, too, noted that America's success in building ties with independent Africa would depend in no small part on the treatment accorded American blacks at home.[14]

The sweep of rising expectations both at home and abroad was underlining the interrelatedness of American domestic problems and foreign policy. Yet, ironically, it was the imperial powers themselves, hard pressed by the costs of empire, that took the initiative in responding to African demands for the right to participate in determining their own futures. Only as Great Britain and France undertook preparations leading to the independence of Tunisia, Morocco, the Sudan, the Gold Coast, and Guinea between 1956 and 1958 did laggard American diplomacy begin to move. In 1956 a separate Office of African Affairs was established in the State Department which in 1958 achieved bureau status and its own assistant secretary.[15] Negroes began to appear in the American delegation to the United Nations. The appointment of John H. Morrow in 1959 as the first black ambassador to a newly independent African nation, Guinea, was a landmark. Morrow later wrote, however, that his briefings in preparation for assuming the post still indicated that "prevailing Washington sentiment on Africa seemed to be that the United States should proceed with 'all deliberate speed.'"[16] A general consistency seemed to underlie the approach of the American government toward the sons of Africa, whether on the domestic or the international front.

Black independence movements on both continents inevitably attracted one another. Despite their preoccupations at home, Afro-Americans were naturally intrigued and encouraged by the evident successes of African nationalism. American journals increased their coverage of African events. African leaders were honored at civic ceremonies in the United States, interviewed in the press, and entertained at the White House. African delegates to the United Nations began to speak and vote as equals with the white powers; they felt free to criticize and take advantage of conflict among the great powers to press for new concessions. If white resistance could crumble or be exploited so readily by the Africans, the American freedom movement too might hope for eventual success. Africa might still seem remote to most American blacks, but many experienced a lift of spirit at the thought that their African brothers were at last coming into their own.[17]

The progress of the American struggle for minority rights was simultaneously being watched with sympathetic interest by Africans. African newspapers devoted more space to reporting racial tensions in the United States: racist speeches, violence, the activities of white and black civil rights leaders, and governmental responses to the race problem. Africans in the United States joined in demonstrations against segregation and discrimination. African leaders and journals praised Presidents Eisenhower and Kennedy for using federal power in support of equal education for blacks. Nkrumah of Ghana, in particular, publicly criticized American segregationists and expressed solidarity with "people of African descent everywhere who are striving for a richer and fuller life."[18]

On the surface, the mutual ties and interests of blacks in Africa and America might seem to have provided a sound basis for the revival of a self-conscious and effective Pan-African movement. Yet, despite gestures in this direction, the circumstances and problems of the two groups proved too different to be reconciled through any common organization or program. True, the "Black Power" movement of the late sixties did turn naturally, as disillusioned Afro-Americans had in the past, to Africa for moral—and now possibly even for political—support. There, freedom meant black control, not mere grudging acceptance into the white colonial system; there, blacks were demonstrating their capacity to stand and defy white power. Frantz Fanon's analysis of Africa's response to European colonialism, *The Wretched of the Earth*, became a handbook of black separatism in America and a message of solidarity with resistance to white oppression around the world. Africa, to whose freedom movement Americans had made an important contribution at the outset, now repaid the debt by providing inspiration and encouragement to the black nationalist drive for power and recognition in the United States.

Political Pan-Africanism, however, held little appeal for other American blacks—clearly a large number—who found some comfort and opportunity in the gains and concessions won from the system. Africa, whatever its sentimental attractions, offered little in the way of practical solutions to immediate American concerns and interests. As the gap between contending views widened, Pan-Africanism became a source of disagreement and disunity even within the Afro-American community itself. [19]

If Pan-African brotherhood failed to prove a cohesive principle for America, it proved in the course of the 1960s almost equally difficult to apply in Africa. At the outset, it seemed an important aid to the organization of a common front against European imperialism. To this end, Nkrumah called the Congress of Independent States and the subsequent All-African Peoples' Conference in Accra soon after Ghana had achieved its freedom. These, in addition to Nkrumah's outspoken advocacy of Pan-African unity and his appointment to office of men long identified with the unity movement, made Ghana a natural center for militant blacks from many nations. Here such Americans as Richard Wright, Julian Mayfield, Malcolm X, and DuBois himself, together with others from African or European nations, came to visit, to confer, and sometimes to live for considerable periods. But Nkrumah's abrasiveness and his espousal of an outspokenly socialist, pro-Soviet stance aroused suspicions in other African countries as well as in Europe and the United States. The radicalism not only of Nkrumah but also of other leaders, such as Touré of Guinea and Ben Bella of Algeria, soon split the African nations into two blocks, which were reunited only with great difficulty and for limited purposes in the Organization for African Unity created in Addis Ababa in 1963.[20]

The problems of nation building, as Asians as well as Africans were discovering, and as Europeans and Americans could have recognized had they closely considered their own histories, were overwhelming. Creating the machinery of state, of politics, of economic growth and stability, of education was an enormous task. Individual ambitions as well as tribal and party loyalties provided fertile ground for discord within the fledgling nations, many of whose boundaries, institutions, ambitions, and even languages were European imposed rather than indigenous. Local problems, jealousies, and interests demanded too much of many hard-pressed African nationalists to leave strong concern for the pursuit of Pan-Africanism. That, too, had been a foreign import, after all, although the realities of regional economic interdependence and continuing fear of foreign intervention did lend it a certain substance.[21]

Pan-Africanism, for all its sentimental appeal, remained, therefore, a somewhat exotic force both in Africa and the United States. Mutual contacts and awareness had increased over the years, but the images that Africans and Afro-Americans held of each other remained ambivalent. The model of America as a powerful, progressive democracy had appealed to the hopes and dreams of Africa, especially in the years before their own drive for independence achieved fruition. Yet even then African visitors to the United States were often dismayed to find poverty and discrimination their advance information had not prepared them for; most were appalled at the ignorance and unfamiliarity with Africa displayed by both black and white Americans. During the 1950s such criticisms, though they existed, were restrained by other considerations. Ndabaningi Sithole, the product of British mission schools in white-dominated Rhodesia, found his years in America among the happiest of his life and "the first time that I felt white people treated me like a real human being." The South had reminded him of home, but elsewhere he found little evidence of the "monster of racialism." Most Americans he found "very friendly, outgoing, largehearted, and tending to overreach themselves" under the influence of the ethic of achievement and success.[22] Students from West Africa, where white domination was less immediate and egregious, were often more troubled by the status of American blacks. Yet they, too, were impressed as much by the advantages and characteristics Afro-Americans shared with whites as by their inferior condition. Herbert Obiozo, for example, writing in the Lagos *Daily Times* in the early 1950s, argued that America's racial problem was not capable of being solved by legislation alone; he even criticized some efforts of organizations such as the NAACP as too militant, emotional, and possibly even Communist inspired.[23]

Such tolerance for American inequality might be understandable against the background of colonialism in Africa, but it was hardly likely to be popular among blacks in the United States. Other factors, too, blocked the achievement of full mutuality and understanding among the two peoples. For one thing, Africans often found Afro-Americans better off politically and economically than they expected or than the latter perceived themselves to be. The ignorance of Americans about Africa was another sore point. Also, it was not uncommon for Africans to be warmly received and favored by whites who ignored or discriminated against black Americans. Such preferential treatment sometimes misled the guests while it provoked bitterness among their American brothers, who felt them naïve and disloyal to the common cause. In Africa, too, misunderstanding was compounded by the images projected by American movies, the most popular source of information and misinformation about the United States.[24]

Sympathy for America's racial plight declined noticeably among Africans as the movement for black rights gathered momentum on both continents. Reactions varied, of course, with the expectations and ideology of the visitor. Leopold Senghor, a Senegalese statesman and protagonist of "Negritude," spoke to a group of Harlem youths in 1966 of his confidence that racial progress in America would continue slowly, perhaps, but surely. "What I admire about your great country," he said, "is not your material power, but rather it is your sense of dialogue, which is your salvation." Senghor's indifference to material power, however, did not prevent him from negotiating successfully for a grant of American grain in the course of his visit. Fred Kwesi Hayford, a young Ghanaian diplomat, on the other hand, came to the United States in 1968 as a Westernized African critical of American blacks and half convinced by the stories he had heard of their backwardness. A long succession of discriminatory incidents grating upon his sensitive ego thoroughly embittered him and convinced him of the painful situation of Afro-Americans, while reinforcing his awareness of a considerable gap separating African and American blacks. [25]

African socialists and neutralists found Afro-Americans, as a whole, too deeply committed to American Cold War ideology to respond favorably to alternative viewpoints. Even Black militants in the United States, sympathetic though they might be toward African anti-imperialism, neutralism, or socialism, were often too engaged in their own problems and perspectives to pay more than passing heed to those of Africa. The 1970 Congress of African Peoples, for example, brought together in Atlanta a wide spectrum of American black leadership under the banner of Pan-Africanism, with Imamu Amiri Baraka (LeRoi Jones) as program chairman. Following in the wake of three successive Black Power conferences in the years immediately preceding, the congress met in pursuance of the theme that "all Africans are part of the same racial, cultural, political, historical, emotional body," despite differences in circumstance and ideology. Yet it revealed a wide variety of approaches and philosophies among the American delegates, who composed the overwhelming majority of its members, from Stokely Carmichael's call to unite with Africans everywhere in a common struggle to Whitney Young's rejection of separatism or any back-to-Africa approach as a solution to the problems of American blacks. Against the rhetoric of unity, the actuality of diversity in the conditions, view, and approaches of those attending the conference was dramatically exposed. [26]

Kenya's Tom Mboya openly acknowledged differences between Africans and Afro-Americans. Remarking on the progress made by American blacks during the 1960s, Mboya warned that the new spirit of black pride, if carried to extremes, threatened to alienate potential allies. Noting with satisfaction that the example of African independence had helped to strengthen the Afro-American drive for equal rights, he warned against identifying too closely with Africa. Cooperation between peoples was admirable but, in Mboya's view, it was a mistake to build excessive hopes on concepts of racial and cultural unity. Failure to recognize that Americans and Africans belonged to different cultures and faced different problems could only undermine the ability of each to deal effectively with its own. Mboya's discouragement of any back-to-Africa movement grated upon those who recalled his earlier appeals for American aid for Kenya's independence. It dramatized the gap separating the two continents which the most enthusiastic Pan-African appeals could not obliterate. [27]

Mboya's Kenya, fearful that a flood of ardent Afro-Americans might pursue the ideal of Pan-Africanism back to permanent settlement in the home continent, had refused to grant automatic citizenship to blacks of other lands. The Kenyans need not have concerned themselves: the rhetoric of American black nationalism had far outrun reality. It was true, of course, that interest in Africa had never been higher among American blacks than it had become by the end of the 1960s. But dashikis, Afro hairdos, and Swahili classes do not make a movement: American youth culture, popular culture, and commercialism remained intriguing mysteries to most Africans. There was more, of course, to the new African orientation than mere faddism. Much of it, perhaps most, represented a valid and long-overdue search for cultural roots and identity, but it was in the United States and not in Africa that most Afro-Americans intended to put their new determination and self-confidence into operation. They were, as both they and the visiting Africans had been saying all along, Americans as much or even more than they were Africans.

A small number were able to visit Africa for more or less extended periods, although this influx represented, of course, a considerable increase over past patterns. Passports for African travel issued to Americans of all races increased from 5,000 per

year in 1950 to 8,000 in 1960: a greater increase occurred thereafter, with the annual figure reaching 20,000 in 1965 and hover-
ing at that level for the remainder of the decade. The exposure of
Afro-Americans to the realities of Africa inevitably produced
doubts and uncertainties, as well as joyful experiences. From the
African side, the influx of Western ideas, life styles, values, and
technology was threatening to those who, for the first time in
centuries, held the power to control their own destinies and resented the possibility of economic or cultural domination from
outside as strongly as they had resisted foreign political power.
The prospect that Westernization might come in black rather
than white wrappings made it scarcely more palatable to African
nationalists and traditionalists. [28]

For the Afro-American visitors, too, relationships with Africa
and Africans were far from automatic. Richard Wright, visiting
Africa in 1954, wrote at length of the "unsettled feelings" he experienced. Despite the deep interest which took him to the land of
his forefathers, Wright felt uneasy almost from the moment of
his landing, when the idea struck him that he was surrounded by
Africans whose ancestors might have sold his own into slavery.
Again and again Wright sensed suspicion and distrust of outsiders. He could understand why American Negroes "were eager
to disclaim any relationship with Africa", they had become too
assimilated to the ways of their second homeland. Yet, despite
these discomforts, Wright sympathized with African hopes and
plans. He decided that Africans were probably not suited for
Western-style freedom but would have to work out their own
needs — including, if need be, some more or less autocratic means
of hastening the modernization process. Wright ended by feeling
an "odd kind of at-homeness" in Africa, based less on ties of race
than on identification with the human struggle and sufferings of
the people. An outsider in the United States, too, Wright significantly chose to live out the remainder of his life not in Africa but
in the cosmopolitan intellectual community of Paris. [29]

Wright's responses were personal, but others experienced
their own difficulties. As soon as Ghana achieved its freedom, C.
B. Powell, editor of the Amsterdam *News*, urged blacks to immi-
grate to Africa, pointing to promising business opportunities
there. Yet Powell warned that "the African is as different from

the American Negro as chalk is from cheese," contrasting African pride and self-confidence with Afro-American deference to white values. In 1960 Louis Lomax reported on his two-month tour of Africa in a book significantly titled *The Reluctant African*. Lomax, an avowed integrationist and anti-Communist, had difficulty relating to much of what he found. He had been warned by African students: "The trouble with most American Negroes . . . is that when they go to Africa they go just like the white man: they think like him: they act like him: they react like he reacts. That is why they don't get to see too much: that is why they don't understand what little they see." African indifference to American anti-Communism and integration "unnerved" Lomax as did what he sensed as a feeling of African superiority. Lomax noted that Richard Wright had shared some of his suspicions of the "gospel of black brotherhood." Differences between African and Afro-American viewpoints became more apparent with increased exposure as attitudes and expectations became more sharply defined. [30]

Successful experiences in Africa were less frequent, or less well publicized, than their opposites. Many black participants in organized assistance programs, such as Crossroads Africa and the Peace Corps, managed to establish satisfying relationships and roles in working with Africans on useful projects, and the fact that, despite political differences between governments, a number of African states continued to request such assistance indicated that the satisfaction was to some degree mutual. African tours by student or adult groups, rapidly increasing in number, produced mixed responses. Many Afro-Americans, including some black nationalists, returned to the United States with a heightened sense of their own Americanness, yet such feelings did not necessarily preclude a more realistic appreciation of Africa and its meaning for them. Some, but by no means all, of those who went to Africa intent upon building new lives in their ancestral homeland found satisfaction and fulfillment previously denied them. Even then, however, the going was not easy. American living standards and preconceptions made for real difficulties in adapting to the African scene. Even the small group of political exiles and radicals clustered in such centers as Nkrumah's Accra or Ben Bella's Algiers found that a cordial welcome, and the deference offered them, did not necessarily extend to acceptance of their ideas or leadership as suitable for Africa's needs. Others, out of despair and disgust with America or in hopes of building a new and freer life in Africa, did remain more or less permanently, but the reports of their experiences suggest that they, too, found truth in Tom Mboya's warning that it would not be easy to become Africans. It was, of course, inevitable that such a complex and varied experience as the rediscovery of Africa by American blacks should produce mixed results. Despite surprises, disappointments, and misunderstandings, the overall outcome of the increased exposure was a marked increase in awareness and sympathy toward Africa among Afro-Americans.[31]

Africans and American blacks both hoped that their combined influence on American government policies might be mutually beneficial. Each group, recognizing its weakness, sought allies where they might logically and emotionally be found: among the members of another bound to it by race and common experience of white domination. Such ties, though real, were much attentuated. African leaders and students might speak on behalf of equal rights for American blacks, but they could scarcely exercise an influence comparable to that which blacks and whites together were already bringing to bear through the civil rights movement. Afro-Americans might urge their government to support Africa's development efforts more actively, but, with marginal political power and little international experience, their influence too was negligible. Cultural Pan-African awareness had been stimulated by a decade of growing contact, yet blacks on both continents still had to face the fact that neither separately nor together had they mobilized enough power to force a basic reorientation of the stance of the United States government or its people toward their interests.

Yet there were, in fact, ways in which each movement was already helping the other. The very presence of African diplomats in the United States, representatives of free governments whose goodwill and cooperation America sought to cultivate, did help to advance the pace of domestic desegregation. As the number of such diplomats increased, so also did the incidents in which they experienced discrimination. A rash of such incidents, early in the 1960s, caused the Kennedy administration to create a special State Department office to ease the problem. Refusals by restaurants, apartment houses, and real estate agencies to serve the Africans attracted notoriety in the world press, occasioning embarrassed apologies by American officials, compensatory invitations to dine at the White House, and intensive efforts to persuade local governments and private parties to modify traditional practices. As such barriers began to weaken, American blacks inevitably benefited. [32]

In other ways, too, the Kennedy administration seemed committed to new approaches in domestic race relations and African relations. Although President Kennedy himself had little experience in either field prior to assuming office, both domestic and international pressures were rising and he was sensitive to a need for new policies. As a senator in 1957, he had called for self-determination for Algeria in a controversial speech that aroused eager interest in Africa and suggested a more flexible posture toward Europe and its colonies. At home, Kennedy's narrow election victory in 1960 had depended heavily on black support. Thus, the stage seemed set for closer ties between the American government and the black communities at home and in Africa.

Accomplishment was to fall far short of promise in both instances, leading to subsequent criticisms that the commitment was more cosmetic than substantial. Yet the remoteness of Africa from the centers of international confrontation did perhaps offer the President greater freedom of action than he felt at home. For a brief period, it seemed that a real breakthrough might be achieved. Thinking back over the experience, Chester Bowles later concluded that, for all its shortcomings, the African policy of the Kennedy-Johnson administration was "probably more consistently liberal and enlightened than in any other continent." [33]

Bowles was a member of the community of liberal intellectuals which had followed African developments with restive interest during the 1950s. His sensitivity to Third World problems had been heightened by his experience as ambassador to India. Following a tour of Africa in 1956, Bowles had argued strongly the case for a more sympathetic stance toward African needs and aspirations. In addition to Bowles, whom Kennedy appointed under secretary of state, the appointment of Adlai Stevenson as ambassador to the United Nations and of G. Mennen Williams, an ardent liberal, as assistant secretary of state for African affairs augured well for a more tolerant, open-minded approach to relations with the world beyond Europe.

In a variety of ways, both symbolic and substantial, the Kennedy administration indicated its desire to align itself actively with the interests and expectations of both black Americans and Africans. An effort initiated under President Eisenhower, to bring more blacks into the foreign service and to assign them more responsible positions, was intensified. Black ambassadors were assigned not merely to Africa but to other posts as well. An able and dedicated group of nonprofessionals was recruited for the rapidly expanding African field. In addition to representational functions, the Kennedy administration addressed itself to other issues touching closely upon the interests of Africa and other Third World nations. At the outset, the President expressed understanding for the neutralism of new nations wishing to separate themselves from the Cold War confrontations of the great powers, distinguishing his position in this respect from the Dulles doctrine of earlier years. In the highly touted Peace Corps, Kennedy hoped to combine American idealism and dedication with a down-to-earth approach to the needs of underdeveloped societies. He argued that the United States, as the first anticolonial nation, should be the natural leader and ally, not the opponent, of the Third World peoples' drive for freedom and advancement. [34]

American efforts to cultivate the friendship of African leaders took tangible as well as symbolic form. Early in 1961, reversing its previous position, the United States voted in the United Nations in opposition to Portugal's Angola policies. A limited attempt was made to achieve a more pragmatic approach to foreign aid, emphasizing economic rather than ideological considerations. The administration supported Ghana's Volta Dam project despite suspiciously hostile words and actions on the part of Kwame Nkrumah. In the Congo, Kennedy continued Eisenhower's backing of United Nations efforts to preserve stability and unity. When G. Mennen Williams aroused an outcry among white colonialists with a statement asserting American approval of the concept of "Africa for the Africans," the President answered criticism by stating that he could not imagine who else Africa should be for.[35]

G. Mennen Williams summed up the Kennedy-Johnson administration's African policy as support for self-determination and nonalignment, encouragement of Africans in the solution of their own problems through their own institutions, assistance in raising African living standards through trade and aid, discouragement of an arms build-up on the African continent, and efforts to persuade European countries to assist in African development. Within limits, these policies were consistent with Africa's own self-interest and were therefore acceptable and popular with Africans. Yet American interests were presumably served, too, by programs that aimed at restraining Africa's susceptibility to communism, limiting Soviet opportunities to penetrate the continent and winning friends for American positions on controversial United Nations issues.[36]

Despite efforts at more cordial relations and modestly increased economic assistance programs, the improvements achieved in American relations with Africa proved ephemeral. Only briefly, as the locus of great power confrontation shifted from Europe in the 1950s to Asia in the 1960s, was Africa able to command a share of American attention. Its cultural ties to a rising American minority strengthened political and sentimental motives for involvement. But the ambiguity of those motives, coupled with Africa's remoteness from the major centers of international confrontation, left them incapable of withstanding more insistent political and ideological pressures. Even so, the brief period of African-American cordiality left a tantalizing suggestion of what might have been accomplished had resistance both at home and abroad been less powerful and had mutual interests and needs been stronger.

Kennedy's apparent reluctance to confront America's domestic racial conflict contrasted markedly with his attempts at flexibility in Africa. The President moved slowly, in part because he did not feel strong enough to do more. Black leaders found themselves quickly protesting the administration's noncommittal approach toward civil rights legislation, restrictive housing policies, and other needed changes. The civil rights movement pressed demands for equal access to the full range of American rights and opportunities. Faced with a Congress dominated by southern Democrats and southern state governments angrily resisting the escalating demands of blacks, Kennedy acted somewhat more forcefully than his predecessor in bringing federal power to bear on behalf of equality. Executive pressure was exercised for increased employment, the extension of voting opportunities, and accelerated school desegregation for blacks. Finally, in the summer of 1963 the administration committed itself to new civil rights legislation focusing on the elimination of discrimination in public accommodations and education.

Not until the assassination of Kennedy evoked a national mood of self-criticism, however, was the vigorous leadership of a southern president, Lyndon B. Johnson, able to secure a series of civil rights acts which at last seemed to place the Federal government forthrightly on the side of equal rights and opportunities for all. Ironically, the civil rights policies of the Kennedy-Johnson administration, like its African policies, soon came under fire as having failed to reach to the roots of racist parochialism and self-interest. Since those roots, however, lay deep within a structure of personal, social, and international motives and institutions which had nourished them for generations, it was hardly to be expected that a brief half-decade of effort would eliminate the powerful forces which had long nourished them.

The apparent contrast between American governmental responsiveness to African and to Afro-American circumstances in the early Kennedy years provoked both satisfaction and some bitterness on the part of American blacks. Comments such as, "Soon all of Africa will be free and we can't get a lousy cup of coffee," circulated widely and were used by the freedom movement to heighten pressure for further concessions. From the perspective of Africa, however, black gains in the United States sometimes appeared more impressive. When federal power was brought to bear on behalf of the right of James Meredith to study at the University of Mississippi, for example, President Keita of Mali was moved. "What country in the world could mobilize a whole army to get a negro student into college?" he wrote in a congratulatory telegram to Kennedy. Afro-Americans were understandably more conscious of the many blacks at all levels for whom such support was still lacking. [37]

While the civil rights movement in America appeared to be winning concessions, Pan-Africanism was encountering problems on the African continent. The Addis Ababa conference in May 1963 led to the creation of the Organization for African Unity, with a permanent headquarters and secretariat in that city. The new agency, faced with a continuing round of interstate crises and tensions and the persistent provocation of white colonialism in Rhodesia, South Africa, and the Portuguese colonies, was too preoccupied with continental problems to leave much scope for involvement in larger world issues. Yet Africans who believed that, by settling differences among themselves by themselves, they could minimize the danger of great-power intervention were undoubtedly correct. In the short run, the organization served as both a register of the actual facts of disunity and an agency of hope that, in time, means might be found for reconciling differences and meeting common needs. The limitations and problems it confronted at the outset served to illustrate simultaneously both the limits and the validity of the Pan-African concept.

A crucial illustration of the danger posed by African disunity and great-power conflicts of interest arose in the Congo in 1963. This nation, granted independence abruptly and without preparation by Belgium in 1960, had struggled with difficulty to maintain unity in the face of separatist tendencies fostered at different times by both European financial interests and the Soviet Union. American policy under both Eisenhower and Kennedy had favored the preservation of a unified Congo and had supported multilateral efforts through the United Nations to insure stability and to minimize direct Russian-American confrontation. In the view of G. Mennen Williams, American support of the United Nations in putting down the conservative Katanga secession movement in the Congo in 1962 in the face of pressure by European and American financial interests eager to protect investments in Katanga and nearby Rhodesia did more to establish African confidence in the United States than any other single event. At the time, the United States seemed to have ranged itself on the side of unity, stability, and self-determination in a crucial region of Africa, although later evidence indicated the possibility of clandestine American encouragement of, or involvement in the assassination of the Congolese leader Patrice Lumumba.[38]

In mid-1964, however, a new Congolese rebellion, with ties to the Soviet and Chinese Communist governments, again threatened the nation's precarious unity. Since United Nations forces had withdrawn, the central government now headed by the former rebel Tshombe appealed to other African nations for assistance. The Organization for African Unity, seriously split along ideological lines by the new alignment of forces within the Congo, failed to endorse such intervention. Meanwhile, Americans and other whites captured by the rebels were being killed or held hostage and subjected to rough treatment. American negotiations for their release, accompanied by similar efforts by the United Nations, Red Cross, and Organization for African Unity, met with no success. As tension rose and reports of atrocities multiplied, President Johnson ordered American planes to drop Belgian paratroops to effect the rescue of Westerners. Despite slaughter of many captives by the rebels, the Belgians rescued over 2,000 prisoners.[39]

American military intervention in the Congo occasioned bitter criticism by blacks, both in the United States and Africa, who saw it as clear evidence of a persistently racist and exploitative posture underlying America's entire African policy. Their cries of outrage overlooked, of course, the provocation offered by Congolese dissension and mistreatment of white prisoners as well as the inability of the Organization for African Unity to mediate the issue effectively. But the incident provided both African and other critics of American policy an easily exploited propaganda issue. They could hardly be blamed for suspecting that the United States might have proceeded more cautiously if the incident had occurred in a situation involving black prisoners in a white nation.

Regardless of the touchy issues surrounding an extremely difficult situation, American prestige and cordial relations in Africa might have survived the shock of the Congo incident had not other developments aggravated the latent suspicion and mistrust which the episode exposed. The assassination of President Kennedy in November 1963 was one blow to African hopes that American responsiveness to their needs and aspirations would prove substantial and lasting. That the Kennedy administration, with a modest expenditure of resources and courtesies, had expanded the reservoir of goodwill and respect which Africans had for the United States was clear from the outpouring of expressions of appreciation and respect by their leaders. Even Nkrumah, the most outspoken of America's critics, termed Kennedy "a great statesman and relentless fighter for equality and human dignity." Massemba-Debat of the Congo Republic asserted that the American President's "stern efforts for racial desegregation are not likely to be forgotten by the Congolese people," and President Dacho of the Central African Republic struck a Pan-African note by terming the assassination an "affliction which strikes the whole black race." Azikiwe of Nigeria, on the other hand, responded more bitterly, holding that the manner of Kennedy's death called into question all the confidence in the essential goodness of the American system which he had for years been expressing to his own people. President Johnson, of course, moved quickly to reassure America's friends and allies that the nation's policies would remain unchanged, but the sense of identification which thousands of people, particularly in the developing nations, had come to feel for Kennedy could not be revived easily. [40]

Other events and conditions contributed more fundamentally to the lessening of friendly relations between the United States and a number of the African nations. As American involvement in Viet Nam intensified, its interest and commitments understandably focused on Southeast Asia. Africa's isolation from the new centers of confrontation left that continent at a severe disadvantage in the heightened competition for American attention and assistance. As military expenditures in Viet Nam grew, congressional appropriations for other foreign assistance programs were cut sharply. Events in Africa itself further rationalized the reduction of American commitments there, as political instability and economic disappointments in a number of countries enabled critics to question the African capacity to utilize assistance effectively. Skepticism about African performance was, of course, reinforced for many Americans by the widespread assumptions of racial incapacity which had long rationalized racial discrimination. The failures and shortcomings of the new African nations affected negatively the domestic status and morale of Afro-Americans as well. Meanwhile Africans, who felt no lessening of the urgency and immediacy of their own problems, readily interpreted the lessening of American enthusiasm and support as evidence of insincerity, self-centered pursuit of interests, and racism. Despite agreement to economic sanctions against the white supremacist regime in Rhodesia, the continuing failure of leaders to challenge the apartheid system in South Africa was a bitter disappointment to blacks on both continents. For critics of American policy, it provided constant reinforcement for the argument that the United States was unable to place principle before interest and prejudice. [41]

More than a decade of interracial conflict on both the national and the international scenes had shown that American relations with the outside world could in no way be divorced from the state and structure of American society itself. W.E.B. DuBois and other black Americans who had recognized this fact early in the century and who attempted to build a Pan-African movement upon it were, in this respect at least, well ahead of the overwhelming majority of their fellow Americans. It had been a sense of mutuality in misery and oppression, as well as in racial origins, which aroused these men to an awareness of their interdependence with their African brothers. Now it was becoming clear to an increasing number of Americans, white as well as black, that progress toward racial equality at home was inextricably tied to the nation's posture in international relations.

Among the many ironies of American foreign relations in the twentieth century, none is more poignant than the fact that during the very years in which the United States was moving toward a position of power, wealth, and leadership which was to set it apart in many ways from other nations, it continued to bear within its own society a large minority group whose condition, carefully considered, might have shed light on the circumstances and attitudes of many of the emerging nations. The failure of the civil rights movement of the 1950s and 1960s to bring full equality, coupled with the nation's discouraging experience in Viet Nam, called attention to relationships with the backward and colonialized societies that had long been overlooked. Not only, as some had boasted, was America the first "new" nation to achieve freedom and development, but it, too, had a backward, exploited, racially discriminated-against sector. In truth, the United States had more in common with the emerging Third World than its most ardent propagandists knew.

It was hardly surprising, of course, that black Americans were more sensitive to this common experience than were whites. In their time, white ethnic minorities had also sympathized with and worked for the liberation of their homelands—in Ireland, Czechoslovakia, Poland, and elsewhere. What differed about the black American experience was not that the Americans in question both worked and hoped for the freedom of their brothers overseas, but that they also hoped, through advancing that cause, to enhance their own standing in the United States. Pan-Africanism in the United States was both an expression of, and an effort to remedy, conditions here even more perhaps than in Africa itself. If black Americans followed a pattern common to whites in projecting the values of American democracy back upon their homeland, they displayed an even more common and human reaction—the sense that strength stems from united effort—when they turned to African blacks for support and hope out of the depths of their despair with America. As gains, however limited, were made in response to the civil rights movement, political Pan-Africanism appealed chiefly to the bitterness and disappointment of those who found progress in the United States inadequate and illusory. For a much larger number of blacks, however, Pan-African sentiment represented a long-delayed and deeply felt awakening to the significance and value of their parental culture.

In Africa, Pan-Africanism also arose as an indication of, and a counter to, weakness rather than strength in relation to the dominant white powers. The achievement of independence diffused the thrust of the Pan-African movement by setting it in apparent conflict with pressing local needs and interests. In the longer run, institutions created in the name of continental cooperation and unity might emerge as a powerful force in African development. For the immediate future, they seemed likely to play a less ambitious, although by no means insignificant role. Ideas of freedom, democracy, and equality had not originated in the United States, but the American experience had given them a force and immediacy which carried them back into the larger world with a new dynamism and, sometimes, in a combination so peculiarly American that they proved ill-suited to other situations. Pan-Africanism, in some respects, proved similar to other expressions of this American idealism. Stimulated, strengthened, and projected by the experience of Afro-Americans, it helped for a period to arouse and encourage the drive for freedom on the part of blacks of both continents. Shortly, however, it proved inadequate as a weapon for, or an expression of, the aspirations and conditions of either people. What the future might hold was uncertain, but one clear and important residue of the movement was a growing recognition on the part of some Americans, both black and white, that Africa had a meaning for their own national experience which might be eclipsed or minimized from time to time but could no longer be denied.

NOTES

1. W.E.B. DuBois, *The Souls of Black Folk* (New York: Fawcett Publications, Inc., 1963), p. 23.

2. George Padmore, *Pan-Africanism or Communism? The Coming Struggle for Africa* (London: D. Dobson, 1956), pp. 117-118.

3. Harold R. Isaacs, *The New World of Negro Americans* (New York: John Day, 1963), p. 235; K. A. Busia, *The Challenge of Africa* (New York: Praeger, 1962), p. 143.

4. Vincent B. Thompson, *Africa and Unity* (New York: Humanities Press, 1969), pp. xi-xiii; Isaacs, *New World of Negro Americans*, pp. 114-133; George Shepperson, "Notes on Negro American Influence on the Emergence of African Nationalism," *Journal of African History* 1 (1960): 299-312, reprinted in William J. Hanna, ed., *Independent Black Africa: The Politics of Freedom* (Chicago: Rand McNally, 1964), p. 194; Robert W. July, *The Origins of Modern African Thought* (New York: Praeger, 1967), pp. 210-224.

5. W.E.B. DuBois, *Dusk of Dawn: An Essay Toward an Autobiography of*

a Race Concept (New York: Harcourt, Brace and Company, 1940), pp. 260-262, 274; Padmore, *Pan-Africanism or Communism?* pp. 119-125; W.E.B. DuBois, *The World and Africa* (New York: Viking Press, 1947), pp. 8-9.

6. DuBois, *The World and Africa*, pp. 10-12; DuBois, *Dusk of Dawn*, pp. 260-262; Padmore, *Pan-Africanism or Communism?* pp. 119-125.

7. E. David Cronon, *Black Moses: The Story of Marcus Garvey and the Universal Negro Improvement Association* (Madison: University of Wisconsin Press, 1955), p. 205.

8. Padmore, *Pan-Africanism or Communism?* pp. 127-135; DuBois *The World and Africa*, pp. 236, 240-243; DuBois, *Dusk of Dawn*, pp. 276-279.

9. Padmore, *Pan-Africanism or Communism?* pp. 171-185; Ndabangingi Sithole, *African Nationalism*, 2nd ed. (Oxford: Oxford University Press, 1968), p. 47.

10. Mark Solomon, "Black Critics of Colonialism and the Cold War," in Thomas G. Paterson, *Cold War Critics: Alternatives to American Foreign Policy in the Truman Years* (Chicago: Quadrangle Books, 1971), pp. 205-209.

11. See chapter 9.

12. Solomon, "Black Critics," pp. 205-239; William C. Berman, *The Politics of Civil Rights in the Truman Administration* (Buffalo: Black Academy Press, 1970), p. 13; Rupert Emerson and Martin Kilson, "The American Dilemma in a Changing World: The Rise of Africa and the Negro American," *Daedalus* 94 (Fall 1962): 1073; Victor C. Ferkiss, *Africa's Search for Identity* (Cleveland and New York: World Publishing Company, 1967), p. 312.

13. Quoted in Emerson and Kilson, "The American Dilemma," p. 1073; Ferkiss, *Africa's Search for Identity*, p. 312.

14. The Lagos (Nigeria) *Daily Times* reported on the Nixon tour and a preceding one by George V. Allen, assistant secretary of state in 1956, 28 May 1956 and 13 May 1957; Henry L. Bretton, "U.S. Foreign Policy Toward the Newly Independent States," in Peter Judd, ed., *African Independence* (New York: Dell Publishing Company, 1963), p. 444; The American Assembly, *The United States and Africa* (New York, 1958), p. 22.

15. Emerson and Kilson, "The American Dilemma," pp. 1055-1064; John Gunther, *Inside Africa* (New York: Harper, 1953), pp. 891-892; Rupert Emerson, *Africa and U.S. Policy* (Englewood Cliffs, N.J.: Prentice-Hall, 1967), pp. 21-29; Solomon, "Black Critics," pp. 205-231.

16. John H. Morrow, *First American Ambassador to Guinea* (New Brunswick: Rutgers University Press, 1968), pp. 20-37; William Attwood, *The Reds and the Blacks, a Personal Adventure* (New York: Harper, 1967), p. 16.

17. American Assembly, p. 86, passim; Richard B. Moore, "Africa-Conscious Harlem," *Freedomways* 3 (Summer 1963): 315-332.

18. Isaacs, *New World of Negro Americans*, pp. 9-12; Accra (Ghana) *Daily Graphic*, 24 February 1958; *Africa Diary* (New Delhi, India), 26 December 1964-1 January 1965, p. 2114.

19. Isaacs, *New World of Negro Americans*, pp. 182, 270, 289-292.

20. Henry L. Bretton, *The Rise and Fall of Kwame Nkrumah* (New York: Praeger, 1966), p. 23; John Dumoga, *Africa Between East and West* (London: Bodley Head, 1969), pp. 82-84; Leslie A. Lacy, *The Rise and Fall of a Proper*

Negro (New York: Macmillan, 1970), passim; Padmore, *Pan-Africanism or Communism?* pp. 128, 178-185; Ali A. Mazrui, *Towards a Pax Africana* (Chicago: University of Chicago Press, 1967), p. 48.

21. Rupert Emerson, "Pan-Africanism," *International Organization* 16 (Spring 1962): 275-290, reprinted in Marion E. Doro and Newell M. Stultz, eds., *Governing in Black Africa* (Englewood Cliffs, N.J.: Prentice-Hall, 1970), pp. 313-323.

22. Sithole, *African Nationalism*, pp. 24-30.

23. Herbert Obiozo, "The Problems of the Negro," Lagos *Daily Times*, 28 May 1956; Lagos *Daily Times*, 18 June 1956, 18 June 1958, 4 July 1958, 26 August 1958, 1 September 1958, 9 May 1959; Accra *Daily Graphic*, 28 August 1965, 4 July 1966, 26 July 1967; Accra *Sunday Mirror*, 6 August 1967; P. Mego Ogbang, "Reflections on 'Language Vision' in the Black Writer," *Black World* (December 1972): 40-46.

24. Elliott P. Skinner, "Africans, Afro-Americans, White Americans: A Case of Pride and Prejudice," *Freedomways* 5 (Summer 1965): 380-396; Victor A. Olorunsola, "Interaction Between Africans and Black Americans," *Pan-African Journal* 2 (Winter 1969): 64-68; Accra *Daily Graphic*, 26 March 1956, 21 February 1957, 22 February 1957.

25. For Senghor, see *Africa Diary*, 31 October-6 November 1966, p. 3116; Skinner, "Africans, Afro-Americans, White Americans," pp. 380-396; Fred Kwesi Hayford, *Inside America: A Black Diplomat Speaks Out* (Washington, D.C.: Acropolis Books, 1972).

26. Imamu Amiri Baraka, ed., *African Congress* (New York: Morrow, 1972), pp. 35-42, 57, 63, 73, 82, passim.

27. Tom Mboya, "African and Afro-American," in his *The Challenge of Nationhood* (New York: Praeger, 1970). For Mboya's earlier appeal for help for Kenya, see Lagos *Daily Times*, 13 May 1959.

28. *U.S. Statistical Abstract, 1972* (Washington, D.C.: Government Printing Office, 1972); Mboya, "African and Afro-American"; Lacy, *Rise and Fall of a Proper Negro*, passim; Hayford, *Inside America*, p. 222; *Africa Confidential*, 14 February 1969; Nathan Hare, "Algiers, 1969, a Report on the Pan-African Cultural Festival," *Black Scholar* 1 (November 1969): 3-10; Stokely Carmichael, "We Are All Africans," *Black Scholar* 1 (May 1970): 15-19.

29. Richard Wright, *Black Power: A Record of Reactions in a Land of Pathos* (New York: Harper, 1954), pp. 35-37, 66, 289, 342, passim; Joseph O. Okpaku, "Let's Dare to Be Different, African," *Africa Report* 13 (October 1965): 13ff.; Olorunsola, "Interaction Between Africans and Black Americans," pp. 64-68.

30. Accra *Daily Graphic*, 22 March 1957 and 30 March 1957; Louis E. Lomax, *The Reluctant African* (New York: Harper, 1960), pp. 2, 15-16, passim; Philip W. Quigg, "The Changing American View of Africa." *Pan-African Report* 14 (June 1969): 8-11.

31. Accra *Daily Graphic*, 11 August 1966. For Operation Crossroads, see Stanley Meisler, "Peace Corps Teaching in Africa," *Pan-African Report* 11 (December 1966): 16; Stanley Meisler, "New York's African Summer," *Pan-African Report* 12 (December 1968): 8-12; *The Autobiography of Malcolm X* (New York: Grove Press, 1964), pp. 350-360; Lacy, *Rise and Fall of a Proper*

Negro, passim; "U.S. Negroes Content as Israelites in Liberia," New York *Times*, 6 November 1968; "Africans Are Cool to Blacks of U.S.," New York *Times*, 4 September 1971.

32. Isaacs, *New World of Negro Americans*, pp. 16-17, passim; Emerson, *Africa and U.S. Policy*, p. 56; American Assembly, pp. 1, 160-162; *Africa Diary*, 21-27 October 1962, p. 203.

33. Chester Bowles, *Promises to Keep: My Years in Public Life, 1941-1969* (New York: Harper and Row, 1971), pp. 422-424; G. Mennen Williams, *Africa for Africans* (Grand Rapids: Eerdmans Publishing Company, 1969), George W. Shepard, Jr., *Nonaligned Black Africa* (New York: D. C. Heath, 1970), pp. 106-107.

34. Bretton, *Rise and Fall of Kwame Nkrumah*, pp. 459-462; Morrow, *First American Ambassador to Guinea*, pp. 280-283; Bowles, *Promises to Keep*, pp. 422-427; Attwood, *The Reds and the Blacks*, pp. 1-7, 295.

35. Theodore C. Sorenson, *Kennedy* (New York: Harper and Row, 1965), pp. 537-540.

36. G. Mennen Williams, *Africa for Africans*, p. 170.

37. Bretton, *Rise and Fall of Kwame Nkrumah*, p. 463; *Africa Diary*, 30 December 1961-5 January 1962, p. 322; 20-26 October 1962, p. 82; 17-23 July 1965, p. 2427; Skinner, "Africans, Afro-Americans, White Americans," p. 389.

38. G. Mennen Williams, *Africa for Africans*, pp. 86-97, passim.

39. Ibid., pp. 98-103; Ali A. Mazrui, *On Heroes and Uhuru Worship: Essays on Independent Africa* (London: Longmans, Green, 1967), pp. 48, 50-57.

40. *Africa Diary*, 14-20 December 1963, p. 1495; 21-27 December 1963, p. 1514; 13-19 June 1966, p. 1804.

41. Colin Legum and John Drysdale, eds., *African Contemporary Record, Annual Survey and Documents, 1968-1969* (London: Africa Research Limited, 1969), pp. 32-34; Legum and Drysdale, *1969-1970*, pp. 41-42 (for the Nixon administration); Ferkiss, *Africa's Search for Identity*, pp. 313-314; *Africa Diary* 17-23 July 1965, p. 2427; Shepard, *Nonaligned Black Africa*, p. 107.

CHAPTER FOURTEEN

Conclusion: Foreign Relations, American Style

America began, in the minds of the English and other Europeans who settled that portion of it later to become the United States, as a country distinctively different from Europe. The combination of religious and economic motives which led the early settlers to undertake the risks of transatlantic migration grafted a dynamism born of great expectations upon the resources of an undeveloped continent. America's foreign relations, as well as its domestic history, have borne the mark of this dynamism from the beginning.

High ideals, a determination to serve God according to His desires, and a freer society, offering opportunities unfettered by traditional institutions and proscriptions, were the hallmarks of a pervasive sense of American distinctiveness. Yet distinctive as these ideas and hopes for the new American society might be, their applicability was not considered limited to the colonies alone. On the contrary, under Christian and, later, Enlightenment universalism, American idealism and opportunity were acknowledged as valuable not only for themselves but also as models which men everywhere might emulate. America might be fortunately different from other lands, but its mission was not only to preserve and protect that difference but also to foster its achievement wherever men yearned to attain their full stature.

Mission and opportunity served as dynamic forces in American life and thought. If the latter arose from a belief in the innate capacity of the free individual to achieve not only his own but also society's best interests, it also implied an obligation to extend that freedom widely. Mission, on the other hand, suggested at least in part the submission of individual desires to a collective responsibility, but it too could at times justify individual adherence to principle against the grain of social traditions and restraints. Mission and opportunity combined to activate an expansive American society and mentality already, by the eighteenth century, restive under the restraints exercised by a remote and distracted British government.

In the process of breaking through the bonds of empire, the Americans acquired a third ideological commitment which seemed at the time to accord well with the other two. Resistance to British encroachments upon their freedoms popularized the concept of the limited state, as exemplified in Lockean political theory, Adam Smith's economics, and the writings of the French philosophes. As children of the Enlightenment and its first self-conscious exemplars, the leaders of the American Revolution leaned toward a liberalism which, in its exaltation of the individual, aimed to reduce the role of the state to a minimum. As expressed in the United States by men like Jefferson and Jackson, this doctrine has been thought of primarily in its domestic applications, where it offered the widest possible license to private individual and group initiatives. In so doing, it underlined the American sense of distinctiveness from Europe, whose monarchies were ponderous, corrupt, and tyrannical. The new American state, too, in its Jeffersonian form would serve as a model of democratic virtue for all to see.

Ideas exercise their influence in the affairs of men, not primarily as abstractions for mere intellectual speculation, but as lenses or filters through which men can focus or distill the meaning of their experience. If American freedom multiplied opportunities for men and groups to seize the initiative in arranging their affairs, it correspondingly reduced their need to depend on government. And the new social and political order which Americans were building correspondingly defined their mission to preserve, to further, and to extend it. This new society had come into being not only on a continent of untold dimension and wealth but on the fringes of the European metropolis which, in the early years of the nineteenth century, was mired in a cycle of wars and revolutions from which Americans were eager to remain aloof. The ideal of American isolation from the alliances and conflicts of Europe, as enunciated by Washington and Jefferson and exemplified in the foreign policy of John Quincy Adams, was an attempt to guarantee the preservation of the young nation and its ideals. So firmly was the isolationist impulse engrafted in the consciousness of Americans that its appeal and its influence continue to be felt nearly two centuries later. Isolation would assure the preservation of American opportunity and distinctiveness. It would offer the firmest guarantee for the fulfillment of America's mission in a troubled world. Isolationism, of course, was also consistent with the liberal concept of the state. In foreign as well as in domestic relations, it, prescribed a limited role for government, circumscribed, inactive, and concerned primarily with the maintenance of basic interests and freedoms.

In categorizing the foreign policy of the United States through most of the nineteenth century as isolationist, however, we have tended to overlook the fact that the limitations it implied were directed against the state almost exclusively. So far as individuals or private interest groups were concerned, Americans accepted few limits on their freedom to roam the entire world in pursuit of whatever objectives they chose. On the international level, the American doctrine of opportunity assumed that the freedoms ensured by social and political arrangements at home should be universalized. Indeed, in addition to defense, the chief role which many Americans assigned their government in the diplomatic field was that of underwriting freedom of movement and enterprise on an international scale by promoting a general acceptance of international law. In effect, this meant that while the American government was to be restricted to an essentially. defensive, isolationist posture, private citizens in pursuit of the distinctive (yet curiously universal) American doctrine of opportunity were free to extend their interests and activities wherever conditions permitted. American isolation was never conceived of as limiting the dynamism and expansiveness of the American people within their own boundaries. The common thread uniting

American concepts of the role of the state both at home and abroad was its commitment to the multiplication of the private opportunities in both spheres.

Throughout most of the nineteenth century, as several of these chapters have shown, state involvement in American foreign relations was marginal. Private interests nevertheless ranged freely, carrying American interests far beyond the Caribbean into Latin America and across the Pacific to Asia. The role of diplomacy in this connection was twofold: to foster and support the aims of private citizens, and to provide a frame of idealism within which Americans could reassure themselves—and presumably the world—that in international relations, too, private advantage and the general welfare were reconcilable. The two most famous doctrines of American diplomacy, whose development and application roughly rounded out a century of private expansionism coupled with the formalities of isolation—the Monroe Doctrine and the policy of the Open Door—exemplify perfectly the balancing of opposites so characteristic of the American approach to foreign relations.

The assertion of a moral imperative to promote the extension of freedom rationalized policies whose actual effect was to widen the circle of opportunities for private exploitation. At the same time, the illusion of active commitment on the part of the American government screened policies whose enforcement rested on the self-interests or rivalries of other powers. American foreign policy relied on the nation's ability to persuade others to forego the exercise of powers which the United States was itself unable to wield by virtue of its own ideological or material limitations. America's ability to present policies geared to its own weaknesses and its citizens' wide-ranging interests as expressions of a moral mission encouraged those citizens to see their own activities, whether in pursuit of profit or of religious or political converts, in the same light. Since private initiative and freedom had proven themselves at home, all that remained was to demonstrate by example or, sometimes, merely by assertion that they were moral overseas as well.

In the course of the nineteenth century, industrialism and technology, working in America, at least, largely under the aegis of private enterprise, accelerated the rate and range of American expansion so that after 1898 it became increasingly difficult for the government to cling to a limited role in foreign relations. In the wake of the Spanish-American War, President McKinley inaugurated the task of reconciling the nation to an increasingly active state involvement in foreign relations, a task which his successor undertook with even greater gusto. The shift did not come easily or quickly; indeed, it hardly won general acceptance until World War II. Yet it seems reasonable to assert that the twentieth century has witnessed a steady, side-by-side growth of both private and state activism in international affairs, and thus a slow relinquishment of the illusion of isolation. The emergence of an activist state in American foreign relations was aided by the fact that it coincided with a deepening of involvement with Asian and Latin American peoples.

Toward Europe, at least until the aftermath of World War I made it clear that a new relationship was called for, Americans had long demonstrated an ambivalent posture in which deference and suspicion combined with presumptions of superiority. Over the years, the stridency of American critiques of Europe and American sensitivity to real or imagined slurs upon the New World by visitors from the Old had given unmistakable evidence of feelings of inferiority lying barely beneath the surface. Such feelings challenged the prevailing faith that the United States excelled in ways European sophisticates were too cynical or corrupt to appreciate. Uncertain though they might be in the face of Europe's age-old traditions and culture, Americans still affirmed their country's present and future superiority. It was an awkward position to maintain, but one made necessary by the fact that they or their ancestors had rejected Europe in coming to America and had staked their lives, their families' fortunes, and their convictions on the choice.

By the middle of the twentieth century, events seemed indeed to have vindicated American assumptions. Sapped by two wars, Europe was forced to acknowledge the fact of American leadership, if not superiority. Meanwhile, Americans moved, with only temporary hesitancy, to assume the role of heirs and defenders of the common Western tradition in a global Cold War against Communism.

So far as the non-European world was concerned, Americans

had seldom been troubled by the doubts that colored their atti-tudes toward Europe. Asia, Africa, and even much of southern and eastern Europe were clearly less advanced, politically or eco-nomically. To the south, Latin Americans had struggled to create sister republics grounded in the same traditions of Euro-pean liberalism, but they were hybrid Europeans at best, whose Catholicism made them further suspect in the eyes of strait-laced North American Protestants. Religion had played a considerable role in the shaping of American attitudes toward other peoples from the beginning. If European and Latin Catholics were sus-pect, Greek and Russian Orthodox Christians were even more exotic and unfamiliar, though less threatening by virtue of their remoteness. Beyond the bounds of Christendom, Americans could face the world with confident assurance as bearers of the true faith. The Jews were perhaps a special case. Widely scat-tered, they presented no concrete problems for American diplo-macy until the late nineteenth century, when mass immigration laid the basis both for anti-Semitism and Zionism as dynamic forces in domestic and foreign relations.

It was when they confronted the peoples and religions of Asia and Africa that Americans encountered cultures so unfamiliar as to require new images and categories. Even here, past experience offered clues and tendencies for further development. The earli-est contacts with non-Western peoples had been with the Ameri-can Indians and African blacks. The attitudes and relationships arising from those encounters had matured in contempt, hos-tility, and violence. As heathens, or pagans, these strangers could claim little respect on the part of those who had come to do their own or the Lord's work in a new land. Backward, by Euro-pean standards, in the technologies of economic exploitation and accumulation, they could scarcely resist the onward drive of those who found ways to express their sense of mission in the opening of new regions for development as well as, or rather more than, the opening of new souls to the vision of God. For many blacks and a few Indians, conversion to Christianity offered a claim for more humane treatment, but it soon became clear that race outweighed religion on the scale of American values. Non-white Christians could at best hope for acceptance as second-class human beings within American society. Racism, strengthened and developed in the contest for continental domination, thereafter colored virtually every contact between citizens of the United States and the peoples of Asia and Africa.

Racism combined with the conviction of religious superiority and the self-confidently smug evaluation of Western technological virtuosity to unfetter both missionary and opportunistic motives when Americans confronted Asia and Africa. It denied any values or virtues worthy of consideration to peoples of non-European origin. It replaced the lingering sense of inferiority which checked American dealings with Europe by confident superiority, justifying beforehand ignorance and lack of concern for the traditions and preferences of the benighted. There were, of course, exceptions, men and women whose concern and sensitivity approached the non-Western world in terms of simple brotherhood or genuine equality. Unfortunately, they were too few in number and lacking in influence.

In the face of obviously inferior and backward peoples, it became easier for Americans to rationalize an augmented role for the state in the regulation of human affairs. If the presumably universal values of freedom and equality were to be applied to these peoples, it could only be after a long period of tutelage under the benevolent eyes of the American government. Governmental paternalism toward the Caribbean and Pacific dependencies, acquired in the course of the Spanish-American War, served to justify the unexpected acquisition in acceptably idealistic terms while diverting attention from less moral considerations of power and profit. At the same time, the opportunity for the United States to set an example for European imperialists through the establishment of colonial regimes dedicated to the democratization and uplift of subject peoples offered a strong temptation. Through a policy of service to others, America's dedication to the fulfillment of its historic mission could be demonstrated to the world. On this basis, a considerable expansion in the responsibilities of government could be justified. At the end of the Civil War, the effort of the Freedmen's Bureau to assist Negroes in preparing for full participation in American society had foundered on the lack of support American liberalism offered for a policy of governmental paternalism, among other reasons. Forty years later, however, American colonial policy could justify an elaborate program of educational, physical, political, and economic uplift on the outer fringes of the new empire. The initiatives and experience gained in these remote regions provided precedents for a more active governmental role at home when individual and institutional weaknesses there became apparent in the 1930s.

The twentieth century has seen a steady increase in involvement of the state in both domestic and international affairs. Isolationism, in the traditional sense of the negation of governmental activism in foreign relations, became increasingly untenable, as did the attempt to insulate the government from active responsibility for internal social and economic conditions. The decade of the 1930s was in many respects crucial. The years which saw the New Deal undertake unprecedented domestic measures demonstrated beyond the possibility of doubt the futility of efforts to dissociate the United States from the international arena behind a screen of neutrality.

From the beginning, Americans had considered it the responsibility of diplomacy to advance the interests, economic or otherwise, of private citizens. As those interests grew in scope, complexity, and scale of organization, foreign policy assumed an ever-larger role in public affairs. By the end of World War II, the American government had emerged as a major participant if not the dominant partner in an economic system characterized by public and private collaboration at virtually every level. Viewpoints differed as to whether private interests, more affluent and powerful than ever, could effectively be constrained by the modern state or whether in fact they controlled and manipulated it to their own ends. Whatever the balance of this subtle and complex relationship, there could be little disagreement concerning the central role played by government in what had come to be termed the military-industrial complex. At the very least, the government served as coordinator and clearinghouse for a combination of public and private agencies and interests: the corporations, foundations, communications networks, and policies which constituted the American economic system.

Modern industrial technology may, in the words of the American businessman E. A. Filene, "make the whole world one," but attitudes and traditions as deeply ingrained as those that clus-

tered around the concept of isolationism do not die easily, even in
the face of overwhelming change. The idea of minimal state involvement in international as well as domestic affairs is clearly
no longer viable, except in the imaginations of a dwindling
corporal's guard of ideologues.

Like racism, anti-communism in the twentieth century has
served to justify major departures from the American tradition
of governmental noninvolvement in foreign affairs. The Cold
War, coming on the heels of the Great Depression and World
War II, sanctioned an enormous enlargement of the role and
responsibilities of American statecraft—all in the name of protecting private freedoms. Although the United States had early
offered formal recognition of the Soviet Union, the emergence of
a superpower with missionary claims more exaggerated than our
own was too threatening to be ignored. The last vestiges of
liberal isolationism were abandoned as the United States moved
to mobilize a worldwide structure of multilateral alliances and
organizations. Once again, the concept of the American mission
for freedom helped to rationalize responses to new circumstances
while at the same time it obscured rational analysis of the now-
international basis upon which freedom ultimately rested.

Disillusionment in the wake of Vietnam has led to fears of a
revival of isolationism. The term has recently been used, or more
accurately misused, as an epithet attacking those who call for the
withdrawal, or at least the severe limiting, of American intervention—political, economic, and cultural—in the affairs of
other nations. Conversely, internationalism, which has now
come to have almost the same unquestioned acceptance that isolationism once enjoyed, has been widely taken to justify uncri-
tically almost any form of American intervention. But surely, if
we consider the intertwining of the concepts of mission, opportunity, and isolation as they arose in the early stages of the
nation's history, we must reverse the definitions of internationalism and isolationism which contemporary polemics employ.
From the beginning, the isolationist principle aimed to defend,
as a matter of national policy, and to spread, through private
initiatives, a concept of man and his relationship to society
thought to be both distinctively American and ultimately universal. It could justify withdrawal from the world, but it could

also rationalize the obliteration of those groups or nations which stood in the way of its fulfillment. Like the American Indians, Negroes, and others who had encountered the thrust of the American missionary movement and like the Latin Americans who had stood in the path of American commercial objectives, those who contended with American military incursions could attest to the parochialism of American culture. Such interventions, undertaken to sustain ideologies and institutions wholly in terms of their affinity with American preconceptions, express the very essence of modern isolationism.

Internationalism, on the other hand, entails acknowledging the legitimate rights and interests of other peoples. The fact that so many Americans have from the beginning found it difficult to accept a truly pluralistic world view is highly revealing of their sense of national mission. Yet international, cross-cultural forces and influences could never be wholly evaded by a people whose isolation, after all, proved so limited. Again, from the beginning there were statesmen, merchants, missionaries, artists, members of ethnic minorities, and others who saw the need to come to terms with differing cultural groups and values. Their ability to reconcile cultural and political diversity with a sense of human mutuality laid the foundations for a realistic contemporary internationalism. Such an internationalism, and not isolationism, after all, urges withdrawal from Southeast Asia, recognition of Communist China, and restraint in intervening in the internal affairs of others.

The pluralism implied by the ideal of equal opportunity, which the American Revolution attempted to secure and isolation once hoped to defend against a hostile world, now depends for its survival upon cultural comity and peaceful accommodation. The concept of an American mission, which formerly justified both state isolation and private expansionism, now makes sense as a shared responsibility for balancing public and private values around the world. The effort to separate public from private, and foreign from domestic matters, which has provided a central theme through the American experience, can no longer be sustained or justified effectively. In recognizing the need to harmonize these often-conflicting elements lies new understanding of our past and reasonable hope for the future.

Index

About the Authors

Morrell Heald, professor of American studies at Case Western Reserve University, Cleveland, specializes in American foreign relations. He has written articles for such journals as *Business History Review* and the *American Quarterly*. His previous books include *The Social Responsibilities of Business: Company and Community, 1900-1960*, and he is presently doing research for a book on American journalists in Europe from 1919 to 1940.

Lawrence S. Kaplan, professor of history at Kent State University, Kent, Ohio, specializes in American diplomatic history. He has written articles for such journals as *Review of Politics* and the *Journal of American History*. His previous books include *Jefferson and France* and *Colonies into Nation: American Diplomacy, 1763-1801*. He is currently working on a book about the military assistance program and NATO, 1948-1951.